ILLUSTRATIONS OF THE HISTORY OF MEDIEVAL THOUGHT AND LEARNING

First Published . 1880
New Edition, Revised . 1920
" *Reprinted* . 1932

ILLUSTRATIONS
OF THE HISTORY OF
MEDIEVAL THOUGHT AND LEARNING

BY
REGINALD LANE POOLE

LONDON
SOCIETY FOR PROMOTING
CHRISTIAN KNOWLEDGE
NEW YORK: THE MACMILLAN COMPANY

Printed in Great Britain by Phototype Limited, Barnet, Herts.

PREFACE.

To republish a book after a lapse of thirty-six years can only be excused by the fact that it has long been out of print and that it is still asked for. When a new edition was proposed to me, my first intention was to issue the book as it stood, with no more change than the correction of obvious mistakes. But further consideration showed me that a good deal more than this was necessary if it was to be republished at all. Such revision, however, as I have made has been designedly made with a sparing hand, and the book remains in substance and in most details a work not of 1920 but of 1884. Had I written it now, the point of view would not have been quite the same. A large literature on the subjects I dealt with has appeared in the interval, and a fresh examination of the materials would certainly have recommended a different selection of 'illustrations' from that which I made then. It was indeed fortunate that I gave the book the title of *Illustrations*, because it made no claim to be a coherent history, though it has sometimes been mistaken for one.

The long interval of time which separates the new edition from the original seems to justify some statement as to the manner in which the essays collected in the book came to be written. In 1881 I resigned a post which I held in the department of manuscripts in the British Museum in order to spend two years in study on the Continent. This plan was made feasible by my election to a travelling scholarship on the Hibbert foundation, and I cannot too heartily express my gratitude to the trustees for thus enabling me to begin a course of work which I have carried on ever since. I settled myself then at Leipzig in the autumn of 1881, entered the university, and was 'promoted' doctor of philosophy in the following January. I started my own work by reading John of Salisbury, but soon saw that he could not stand as a beginning. I had become acquainted with the venerable Gotthard Lechler, one of the professors in the theological faculty of the place and superintendent in the reformed church, a man well-known in England for his pioneer studies of Wycliffe. He recommended me to read Hermann Reuter's *Geschichte der religiösen Aufklärung im Mittelalter*, and I took his advice. It would not indeed be true to say that I learned much from Reuter's exaggerated and often distorted presentment of facts; but I found his references useful, and in planning the first half of my book I followed pretty closely the scheme of his. But it seemed to me that the field which Reuter surveyed needed an introduction, and in writing this I derived many suggestions from the essay on *The Schools of Charles the Great* by James Bass Mullinger, whom in after-years I had the pleasure of numbering among my friends.

Not much of this work was done at Leipzig. In the spring of 1882 I removed to Zurich, where I took quarters in a cottage at Riesbach about a mile out of the town. There I had the advantage of access to two libraries well-equipped for my special purposes. Both were established in disused churches; the town library in the Wasserkirche, close by what was then the uppermost bridge over the Limmat, and the university library in the quire of the Dominican church high up on the Hirschengraben. From these two libraries I enjoyed the privilege of borrowing as many as ten volumes at a time, and I made use of the privilege to the full. The limitations of these libraries were also to my benefit. For example, there was no set of Migne's *Patrologia* in them, and I had to seek my texts in the Benedictine editions of the fathers, in the Lyons *Maxima Biblictheca Patrum*, and in the collections of D'Achery, Mabillon, Baluze, Pez, and others; a process which taught me a great deal on the way.

By the time that, working forward from a much earlier period, I had again reached John of Salisbury, the field of my studies was altered by an extraneous cause. It so happened that in the winter which I spent at Leipzig a society was formed with the object of editing Wycliffe's Latin works, and I undertook the charge of the two treatises *On Dominion*. It was not that I was particularly interested in Wycliffe; but I had a young man's ambition to print an *editio princeps*, to bring to light matter hitherto known only from scanty citations; and the work had a greater attraction for me because it belonged to an early time in Wycliffe's career, before he had come into conflict with authority on questions of theological doctrine. The treatises which I proposed to edit followed in direct sequel the work of other political theorists; they did not belong to that part of Wycliffe's activity in which he stands forth as a pioneer in the discussion of problems which lay apart from those to which my attention had been directed.

Thus after I had completed what I had to say about John of Salisbury I limited myself to the consideration of political theory; and this restriction prevented me from attempting to include anything which I had contemplated relative to the great period of mature scholasticism. But it was necessary to construct a bridge to join the two parts of my book. A bull of Pope Gregory XI at once directed me to trace the political system of Wycliffe back to Marsiglio of Padua and to William Ockham; and an exposition of John of Salisbury's views, in the setting of the type of opinion which he represented, was introduced to form a counter-piece to my summary of the opposed doctrine. On my return to England in the summer of 1883 I applied myself to filling in the gaps in my essays, which needed a larger library than could be found at Zurich, and to completing the last chapters. In the following year I paid a long visit to Vienna in order to examine the Wycliffe manuscripts in the imperial library, and in the course of the autumn my book was published.

The title which I gave to it was *Illustrations of the History of Medieval Thought in the Departments of Theology and Ecclesiastical Politics*. I have now abbreviated it and at the same time expanded its scope. In revising the text I have specially to thank my friend the Rev. F. E. Brightman, D.D., for his great kindness in reading the sheets and suggesting a large number of improvements both in form and matter. In two chapters only, iv and v, have I made extensive alterations. These were required by the new evidence that has been brought to light concerning Bernard of Chartres, whom I have been compelled to distinguish from Bernard Silvestris,[1] and by the discovery of Abailard's early work *de Trinitate* in 1891.[2] But changes and corrections of less importance have been made

[1] See my paper on the Masters of the Schools at Paris and Chartres in John of Salisbury's time, printed in the English Historical Review, 35. 321–342, July 1920.

[2] See my paper on Abailard as a Theological Teacher, in the Church Quarterly Review, 41. 132–145, 1895.

throughout the book, and I have added occasional notes referring to works which have appeared since its first publication. These are distinguished by brackets. I have not, however, given a false appearance of novelty by altering references to suit recent editions, except in a few instances, such as the second edition of Prantl's *Geschichte der Logik im Abendlande*, and Mr. Webb's edition of the *Policraticus*. Nor have I changed the plan of naming the place of publication of books quoted, except when English, French, and German works were published at London, Paris, and Leipzig; and of specifying their size, when it was anything but octavo. References to Bouquet are to the *Recueil des Historiens des Gaules et de la France;* those to Pertz indicate the folio series of *Scriptores* in the *Monumenta Germaniae historica*, and those to Jaffé to the *Bibliotheca Rerum Germanicarum.* In citations of manuscripts *b* denotes the verso of the leaf; but when a manuscript is written in double colums A, B, and C, D denote respectively the two columns of recto and verso.

R. L. P.

Oxford,
24 *October*, 1920.

CONTENTS.

APPENDIX.

INTRODUCTION

THE history of medieval thought falls naturally into two broad divisions, each of which is brought to a close not by the creation of a new method or system from native resources, but by the introduction of fresh materials for study from without. The first period ended when the works of Aristotle, hitherto known only from partial and scanty versions, were translated into Latin; the second, when a knowledge of Greek letters in their own language made it impossible for men to remain satisfied with the views of ancient philosophy to which they had previously been confined and upon which their own philosophy had entirely depended. An age of eclecticism, too eager in its enjoyment of the new-found treasure to care to bind itself, as its predecessors had done, to any single authority, was then followed by an age in which the interests of theological controversy drove out every other interest, until at length in the comparative calm after the tempest of the Reformation, philosophy entered a new phase, and the medieval or traditional method was finally rejected in favour of one common in this respect to both modern and ancient speculation, that it rested upon independent thought, and regarded no authority as beyond appeal. INTRODUCTION.

In the two periods of the middle ages we find nothing absolutely original; advance is measured less by the power with which men used their intellects than by the skill with which they used their materials. Still there is a difference between the periods which makes the earlier the more interesting to the student of human thought considered as apart from any specific production of it: for while the works of Aristotle were almost totally

INTRODUCTION.

unknown to the Latin world there was a wider sphere for the exercise of ingenuity, for something approaching originality, than there could be when an authoritative text-book lay ready to hand. In the following essay our attention will be mainly directed to these traces of independence, not so much in the domain of formal philosophy as in those regions where philosophy touches religion, where reason meets superstition, and where theology links itself with political theory. In the later period we shall limit ourselves exclusively to this last subject, to the attempts made to frame a political philosophy, and in particular to reconcile the notion of the state with the existence and the claims of an universal church, or to modify those claims by reference to the necessary exigencies of civil government.

The field therefore of our investigation is that of theology, but it does not follow on this account that its produce must also be theological. Theology is no doubt the mode of medieval thought: the history of the middle ages is the history of the Latin church. The overmastering strength of theology, of a clergy which as a rule absorbed all the functions of a literary class, gave its shape to every thing with which it came into contact. Society was treated as though it were actually a theocracy: politics, philosophy, education, were brought under its control and adjusted to a technical theological terminology. But when this characteristic is recognised, it is found to supply not only the explanation of the distance which seems to separate the middle ages from modern times, but also a means of bridging over the interval. Men thought theologically and expressed themselves theologically, but when we penetrate this formal expression we discover their speculations, their aims, their hopes, to be at bottom not very different from our own; we discover a variety beneath the monotonous surface of their thoughts, and at the same time an unity, ill-defined perhaps, but still an unity, pervading the history of European society. There was indeed never a

INTRODUCTION.

time when the life of Christendom was so confined within the hard shell of its dogmatic system that there was no room left for individual liberty of opinion. A ferment of thought is continually betrayed beneath those forms; there are even frequent indications of a state of opinion antagonistic to the church itself. The necessity of a central power ruling the consciences of men of course passed unquestioned, but when this immense authority appeared not a protection but a menace to religion, it was seldom that it was submitted to in complete silence.

When the church seemed to be departing from its spiritual dignity and defiling its ceremonial by the superstitions and the prodigies of heathenism, or when its pontiffs seemed to have adopted all the vices of secular princes and to have exchanged totally the church for the world, there were rarely wanting advocates of a purer Christian order, advocates whose denunciations might rival in vehemence those of a modern protestant. Even the doctrinal fabric of the church was not always safe from attack; for although no one impugned the truth of Christianity, the attempt was still repeatedly made to clear away the dust of centuries and reveal the simpler system of primitive belief. Such efforts, until we approach the border-line of modern history, were invariably disappointed. They rarely exerted even a momentary influence over a wide circle. In truth, however generously conceived, however heroically sustained, the aims of the premature reformers were often too audaciously, too wantonly, directed against the beliefs of the mass of their fellow-Christians to deserve success. We may admire their nobility or their constancy, but an impartial judgement can hardly regret that they failed. They troubled the world, it might be for a few years, and left their single memorial in their writings. Yet, though they may occupy but a small place in the history of civilisation, the light they cast upon the unusual tendencies of thought, the eccentricities, of the middle ages, makes them a not unfruitful subject of study.

INTRODUCTION.

A still more suggestive line of enquiry is opened in the general history of thought and learning. The masculine spirit and the confidence with which the philosophers of the period carried on their speculations is hardly suspected by those who are not familiar with the original literature. Men who were least of all inclined to oppose anything that bore the stamp of traditional authority, displayed a freedom of judgement which could not but tend to consequences in one way or another divergent from the established system. The methods by which they accommodated the two are indeed evidence of the imperfect grasp they possessed of the inexorable demands of the reasoning faculties: their theological consciences were equally inexorable in requiring the adjustment; or perhaps more truly, the necessary conformity of reason and authority was so regularly assumed that they were unaware of the act of accommodation; the theological correctness of the conclusion, however arrived at, was the inevitable consequence of this implicit identification of contradictory terms in the premises. We are often at liberty to leave the ultimate reconciliation out of account, as a mode characteristic of the time rather than an argument due to the individual writer. It is the road on which their thoughts travel that retains its interest for the student of philosophical history.

The continuous activity of the human reason in Latin Christendom has its witness partly in the opposition, conscious or unconscious, to the tradition of the church, partly in the spirit of its philosophy. Through these currents we may learn the deeper springs which existed in men's minds and which, however often dormant, frozen by the rigid strength of theology, were yet capable of welling forth to nourish the world. The position held by intellectual studies and by learned men is uniformly the measure of the prevalence of these liberal forces in society; yet since the greatest writers have usually exercised a more powerful influence over posterity than over their own generation, it is chiefly from their works that we can estimate the power which the stimulus once given to learning and thought could gain in a few minds outstripping their fellows. The history of learning therefore not only supplies the links that connect the several divisions of the first part of our enquiry, but also the groundwork on which its argument must be constructed.

It is well known that the rise of the western church was accompanied by a rapid decline in the study of classical letters.[1] Learning, such as it was, became restricted to the clergy and the monks, and these became more and more inclined to elevate their professional study at the expense, or to the condemnation, of every other. The rhetorical schools which had kept alive, however poorly, the tradition of classical learning were suffered themselves to die out, and their place was only in a small part taken by the seminaries which gradually grew up about different cathedral or monastic establishments. The *grammarian* was expelled by the *scholastic*, and the scholastic had little interest or little power to imbue his disciples with more knowledge than was required for the performance of the offices of the church. Those who aspired to lead others would seek to advance to an acquaintance, seldom profound or extensive, with the writings of the fathers; and might thus obtain an indirect and distant view of that country from which Augustin and even Jerome had not been able, however desirous, to shake themselves free. But since the day when the expiring paganism of Rome had entered its last conflict with Christianity, the church had granted no terms to the system she had displaced. It was not alone that the philosophical spirit had proved inimical

[1] In preparing the following section for the press I have derived much help from the first chapters of M. Hauréau's Histoire de la Philosophie scolastique, 1872, and of Mr. James Bass Mullinger's essay on The Schools of Charles the Great; 1877. I am also indebted to A. F. Ozanam's Civilisation chrétienne chez les Francs, ch. ix, 3rd ed., 1861 (being the fourth volume of his Oeuvres). See also S. R. Maitland's remarks on the attitude of the church towards secular learning, in The Dark Ages, xi, pp. 171–187 (cf. p. 403 n. 2), 1844.

INTRODUCTION.

[a] Adv. Hermog. viii, Opp. 295 B, ed. Cologne 1617 folio.

to orthodoxy: Tertullian's famous saying, [a] *Haereticorum patriarchae philosophi*, expresses but a portion of the truth. The entire classical tradition, all learning in its large sense, was treated not merely as irrelevant to the studies of the Christian, but as a snare from which he was taught to flee as from a temptation of the evil one. Such an antagonism inevitably tended to limit the aims and to narrow the character of the Christian church. It is not necessary here to trace its immediate result upon her doctrine and ceremonial; the fact by itself suffices to show that as Christianity extended its sway among the nations that had overwhelmed the empire, it could not bring with it those refining influences by which it would have been attended, had it absorbed and purified the culture of Rome. As it was, the church was built upon the ruins of a subjugated society; its fabric was but a step less barbarous than that of the Teutonic civilisation by which it was confronted.

If we confine our view to the literary aspect of the question, the marks of retrogression are clear and unmistakeable. Among the few who still cultivated learning oratory degenerated into panegyric, poetry occupied itself with mean or trivial subjects. With the rest the Latin language itself lost its nerve; idiom and even syntax were forgotten: it was enough if a writer could make himself understood at all. If down to the fifth century we find rare examples of an opposite tendency, the hostility of the church towards classical letters is thenceforth strongly marked. In the sixth century indeed Cassiodorus labours to prove that secular learning is good and profitable, *utilis et non refugienda cognitio*, and anxiously supports his argument by a catalogue of learned men downwards from Moses to the fathers:[2] but the apology itself implies the discredit into which

[2] De institutione divinarum litterarum, xxvii, xxviii; Opp. 2. 523 sq., ed. J. Garet., Venice 1729 folio. Quis enim, Cassiodorus concludes, audeat habere dubium, ubi virorum talium multiplex praecedit exemplum? scientes plane . . . rectam veramque scientiam Dominum posse concedere.

INTRODUCTION.

learning had fallen. A little later that discredit was completed when Gregory the Great employed his unrivalled authority to denounce all secular learning. The common story that the pope burned the Palatine library, because, as [b] John of Salisbury hints, he had a greater interest in the holy Scriptures, is no doubt false; but it not inaccurately represents the attitude Gregory took up in regard to classical studies. The [c] letter which he wrote on the subject to Desiderius, bishop of Vienne, has been often quoted, but it is too characteristic to be omitted here. The bishop, it seems, had ventured to teach grammar and read the poets. Gregory's remonstrance is as follows: *A report has reached us which we cannot mention without a blush, that thou expoundest grammar to certain friends; whereat we are so offended and filled with scorn that our former opinion of thee is turned to mourning and sorrow. The same mouth singeth not the praises of Jove and the praises of Christ.*[3] *Think how grievous and unspeakable a thing it is for a bishop to utter that which becometh not even a religious layman. . . . If hereafter it be clearly established that the rumour which we have heard is false and that thou art not applying thyself to the idle vanities of secular learning—nugis et secularibus litteris*, a significant hendiadys,—*we shall render thanks to our God who hath not delivered over thy heart to be defiled by the blasphemous praises of unspeakable men.*[4]

† 604.

[b] Policrat. viii 19 vol. 2. 370, ed. C. C. J. Webb, Oxford 1909: cf. lib. ii. 26 vol. 1. 142.

[c] Ep. ix. 54; Opp. 2. 1139 F, ed. Bened., Paris 1705 folio.

[3] The words, 'In uno se ore Iovis laudibus Christi laudes non capiunt,' have been misunderstood: see Mullinger, p. 77. I have no doubt that the phrase is borrowed from saint Jerome, 'Absit ut de ora Christiana sonet Iupiter omnipotens,' &c.: Ep. ad Damas., Opp. 4 (1) 153, ed. Bened., Paris 1706 folio.

[4] M. Hauréau, 1. 5, wittily compares the language of Jack Cade to lord Say: 'Thou hast most traitorously corrupted the youth of the realm in erecting a grammar-school: and whereas before our forefathers had no other books but the score and the tally, thou hast caused printing to be used; and contrary to the king, his crown and dignity, thou hast built a paper-mill. It will be proved to thy face that thou hast men about thee that usually talk of a noun, and a verb, and such abominable words as no Christian ear can endure to hear:' 2 King Henry VI. iv. 7. 'On le voit, l'imagination du poëte n'a pu rien ajouter au texte de la lettre pontificale.' *Unspeakable*, 'nefandus,' we may notice, was a favourite word with Gregory, to whom the Lombard was regularly *nefandissimus*.

INTRODUCTION.

This then was the policy, if we may so call it, of the church with regard to education, declared by him who has an undisputed title to be called the father of the medieval papacy, and whose example was law to his successors, as indeed it was to the whole of Latin Christendom for many ages. From this authority there was however one corner of Europe practically exempted.[5] Ireland had as yet remained free from the invasion of foreign barbarians, and had held its own tradition not only of Christian but also of classical culture. Although it did not receive Christianity until the middle of the fifth century,[6] the newly-planted religion had grown up with astonishing rapidity and strength.[7] The Irish, or, to give them their proper name, the Scots, had no sooner been enlightened by the preaching of a foreign missionary, saint Patrick, than they pressed forward to make all nations participators in the knowledge of their new faith. Already there was a steady emigration across the north channel into that country which was soon to borrow the civilisation, the very name, of the settlers.[8] Now, that emigration took a distinctively religious character. The little island of Hy off the coast of Mull became the head-spring from which Christianity was to penetrate among

[5] M. Hauréau's chapter on the Écoles d'Irlande, in his Singularités historiques et littéraires, 1861, is full of the interest which that author is peculiarly skilful in giving to whatever he writes. A good survey of the Irish missions is contained in a learned essay by Arthur West Haddan on Scots on the Continent, printed in his Remains, 258-294, Oxford 1876. [Cf. L. Gougaud, Les Chrétientés Celtiques, 134–174, 1911; and W. Levison, Die Iren und die Fränkische Kirche, in the Historische Zeitschrift, 109. 1–22, 1912.] For the character of the ancient Irish church see the introduction to J. H. Todd's Saint Patrick the Apostle of Ireland, Dublin 1864.

[6] That there might have been and probably were a few Christians in Ireland before saint Patrick's day is not of course denied: see Todd 197.

[7] 'It is recorded by chroniclers, as one might chronicle a good harvest, that A.D. 674 *Ireland was full of saints:*' Haddan 264.

[8] For a long time the name of Scotland continued to be common to the two countries. Thus saint Notker Balbulus speaks of an event as occurring *in Scotia, insula Hybernia:* Martyrolog. ad v. Id. Iun., in J. Basnage, Thesaur. Monum. eccles. et hist. 2 (3) 140, Antwerp 1725 folio. Compare the evidence collected by archbishop Ussher, Britann. Ecclesiarum Antiquit. 380–384, ed. 2, London 1687 folio.

the rude inhabitants of the Pictish highlands, or the English of Northumbria or Mercia. But the zeal of the Irish missionaries could not be confined within the compass of Britain. The Celt yielded not to the Northman in his passion for travel;[9] then as now the poverty of the land was the peremptory cause of emigration: but the ambition of the missionary supplied a far stronger incentive to distant enterprises than the mere love of adventure or the mere hope of gain; and those who had once been known but as the pirates whose terrible fleets ravaged the coasts of Britain or Gaul, became the peaceful colonists of Christianity in nearly every land where the Teuton in his advance westward had established himself. From Iceland to the Danube or the Apennines, among Frank or Burgundian or Lombard, the Irish energy seemed omnipotent and inexhaustible.

To account in any sort for this astonishing activity we have to go back to the form in which the Celtic church had grown up, and observe how its loose and irregular organisation left its ministers free to choose their own work where they would. In other countries the diocese had been the basis of Christian organisation: in Ireland it was the monastery. This was the centre of the religious community; the abbat, not the bishop, was its representative chief. When gifts were made to the church the monastery was the recipient; the abbat was their steward. Round the monastery then the clergy of the neighbourhood grouped themselves as a tribe or clan. The absence of any fixed endowment was an insuperable obstacle to the formation of an ecclesiastical constitution after the common pattern. Almost everywhere the [d] bishops were untrammelled by the cares of a definite diocese; often a band of many bishops is found settled at one place. The lesser clergy were driven to earn a living as they might, in the secular business of the farm or the plough. They had no hopes of ecclesiastical

[d] see Todd 1-7, 27, &c.

[9] Scotorum, quibus consuetudo peregrinandi iam paene in naturam conversa est: Vit. s. Gall. ii. 47 in Pertz 2. 30; 1829.

INTRODUCTION.

preferment to tempt them to stay at home: poverty was their natural lot, and it might be met with as little inconvenience abroad. Thus they poured forth upon the continent, the most devoted, the least self-seeking of missionaries: how poor they were we may learn from the fact that special hostelries were founded for their reception in many places of the Frankish realm by the charity of their wealthier fellow-countrymen.[10]

It is not however with the religious work of the Scots that we are immediately concerned: their literary tradition is still more remarkable and characteristic. Isolated in a remote island the stream of classical learning had remained pure while the rest of Roman Europe had suffered it to be corrupted or dried up in the weary decay of the empire that followed the Teutonic influx. In Ireland it was still fresh and buoyant; and from the Irish it passed back to the continent in greater and greater waves. Of the means by which their education was acquired at home we are but scantily informed. In the seventh century, [e] Bede tells us, the Northumbrian nobles, and others too of middle rank, flocked to the schools of Ireland; and *while some faithfully dedicated themselves to the monastic life, others chose rather to pass in turn through the cells of the masters and give their labour to study: and the Scots most readily received them, and provided them daily their food without charge, and books also to read, and free instruction.* But we have to guess from a variety of scattered notices and suggestions the precise way in which the Irish tradition of learning differed from that current on the continent. At one moment we read of saint Caimin, a teacher on an island

[e] Hist. eccl. iii. 27.

[10] At least these 'hospitalia Scotorum quae sancti homines gentis illius in hoc regno construxerunt et rebus pro sanctitate sua acquisitis ampliaverunt' were sufficiently numerous for the abuses by which the foundations had been diverted from their proper purpose, to call for the attention of the council of Meaux in 845, can. xl.: Mansi, Conciliorum amplissima Collectio 14. 827 sq., Venice 1769 folio. The ordinance for their reform was sanctioned by a capitulary of Charles the Bald a year later: Pertz, Leg. 1. 390 sq.; 1835.

of Loughderg, who made a critical edition of the Psalms;[11] INTRODUCTION.
and there is at all events [f] evidence to shew that the Scots possessed, in common with the Britons, a Latin version of the Bible distinct from the vulgate. It has been thought too that the [g] Greek language which had almost ceased to be known elsewhere in the west, was widely cultivated in the schools of Ireland.[12]

[f] cf. Haddan 271 sqq.

[g] cf. Ozanam 480–486.

But of greater significance is the fact that there reigned, not only among her professed scholars but also among the plain missionaries whom she sent forth to preach the gospel to the heathen, a classical spirit, a love of literature for its own sake, a keen delight in poetry. The very field of study of which the Latin was taught to say, [h] *This wisdom descendeth not from above, but is earthly, sensual, devilish,* was that to which the Scot turned with the purest enthusiasm. The gaiety of the Celtic nature made him shew his devotion to the classical poets by imitating them. Saint Columban, the apostle of Burgundy, whom men knew as the stern preacher of an austere discipline,[13] as the haughty rebuker of kings, was wont to seek refreshment from his religious labours in sending his friends

[h] James iii. 15.

[11] On this abbat Caimin of Iniskeltra who died in 653 see J. Lanigan, Ecclesiastical History of Ireland 3. 11, 2nd ed., Dublin 1829. Ussher says, Antiq. 503, that he saw a portion of the saint's work, said to be autograph. It was elaborately noted with the usual critical signs, and contained on the upper part of the page a collation with the Hebrew, and brief scholia in the outer margin. [Ussher's mention of Hebrew is a mistake. The Psalter, now in the Franciscan convent at Dublin, having been moved thither from the convent of S. Isidore at Rome in 1871, is assigned by J. O. Westwood, Facsimiles of the Miniatures of Anglo-Saxon and Irish Manuscripts, p. 88, 1868, to the eleventh or twelfth century. See also notes by Count Nigra in the Bibliothèque de l'École des Chartes, 46 (1885) 344 sq.; and by Mr. M. Esposito in the Proceedings of the Royal Irish Academy, 32. c. (1913) 78–88.]

[12] [The evidence for this opinion, at least so far as it relates to the time before the eighth century, is extremely scanty. Cf. M. Roger, L'Enseignement des Lettres classiques d'Ausone à Alcuin, 1905, 268–272.]

[13] The severity of the Rule put forth by Columban, in comparison with that of saint Benedict, is admitted, though Milman, History of Latin Christianity, 3rd ed., 1872, 2. 294, seems to imply an opposite judgement. Haddan, indeed, p. 267, goes so far as to claim an Irish origin for the substance of the entire penitential system. Compare William Bright, Chapters of early English Church History 96, Oxford 1878.

INTRODUCTION.

i Ussher, Vet. Epist. Hibern. Sylloge, 9–18, Dublin 1632 quarto.
k pp. 10 sq.

i letters in verse, now in the rhymed couplets of his own day, now in hexameters. Sometimes k the initials of the lines spell an acrostich: once the saint writes a long letter composed of a string of adonics.[14] Meagre as his performances may appear, if judged by ancient models, Columban's more serious poems are neither awkward nor ungraceful. All of them are full of conceits and mythological allusions; they read as the work of an entire pagan.[15] Equally they prove the breadth and freedom of the training which he had received at Banchor and which was the peculiar possession of the Scots. There is a vein of poetry running through the whole lives of these Irish confessors, a poetry of which the stories of their acts are indeed better witnesses than their practical essays in verse-making. They brought imagination, as they brought spiritual force, into a world well-nigh sunk in materialism.

Their lighter productions shew one side of the Scottish nature: their earnest, single-hearted pursuit of learning in the widest sense attainable, their solid hard work as

14 Accipe, quaeso,
nunc bipedali
condita versu
carminulorum
munera parva.

Afterwards he excuses the eccentricity of his metre:

Sufficit autem
ista loquaci
nunc cecinisse
carmina versu.
Nam nova forsan
esse videtur
ista legenti
formula versus.
Sed tamen illa
Troiugenarum
inclita vates
nomine Sappho
versibus istis
dulce solebat
edere carmen.

Then he explains the construction of the verse and concludes with a second apology, this time in hexameters, urging the weariness of old age and feeble health as a justification of his license: Ussher 13–18. [The genuineness of these verses has been questioned, but it is defended by W. Gundlach, in the Neues Archiv der Gesellschaft für ältere Deutsche Geschichtskunde, 15. 514–526, 1890.]

15 M. Hauréau, Singularités 12 sqq., rightly dwells on this characteristic. I have not noticed the poem ascribed to saint Livinus, whom tradition makes the apostle of Brabant in the seventh century; because the likelihood is that these elegiacs (printed in Ussher 19 sqq.) are as spurious as the biography, called saint Boniface's, with which they appear to stand plainly connected. The poetry of the Scots is however far from being limited to these two examples: Ussher prints another piece, pp. 36 sq.; and in later times instances, as that of John Scotus, are not uncommon.

scholars, is not less characteristic. Ireland was once the university, the [l] literary market not only, as we have seen, of northern England, but also [m] of the Frankish realm; and if its progress at home was arrested after the fatal inroad of the Northmen in 795,[16] the seed which the Scots had sown in other lands grew to a nobler maturity than it had ever reached on its own soil. [n] Wherever they went they founded schools. Malmesbury, the house of which saint Aldhelm was a scholar and ultimately abbat, took its origin from the company of disciples that gathered about a poor Scottish teacher, [o] Mailduf, as he sat in his hut beside the walls of the old castle of Ingelborne. The foundations of saint Columban, Luxeuil, and Bobbio,[17] long remained centres of learned activity in Burgundy and Lombardy; the settlement of his comrade, saint Gall, rose into the proud abbey which yet retains his name, and which was for centuries a beacon-tower of learning in western Europe; the sister-abbey of Reichenau, its rival both in power and in cultivation, also owed its fame, if not its actual establishment on its island in the lower lake of Constance, to Scottish teachers. Under the shelter of these great houses, and of such as these, learning was planted in a multitude of lesser societies scattered over the tracts of German colonisation; and most commonly the impulse which led to their formation as schools as well as monasteries is directly due to the energetic devotion of the Scottish travellers.

[l] cf. Camden, Britann. 730, ed. Lond. 1607 folio.

[m] Aldhelm. Ep. iii, Migne 89. 94 C, D; 1863: cf. Ozanam 487.

[n] cf. Haddan 267.

[o] W. Malmesb. Gesta Pontificum v. pp. 333 sq., ed. N. E. S. A. Hamilton, 1870. Cf. Bright 259; H. Hahn, Bonifaz und Lul 8 sq.; 1883.

[16] For the date see Todd, intr. to The War of the Gaedhil with the Gaill, pp. xxxii–xxxiv; 1867. The earlier invasion by the Northumbrian Ecgfrith (Bed. iv. 26) was little more than a momentary raid: the vikings on the contrary settled in Ireland, plundered the churches, and destroyed all the special tokens of Irish civilisation; see J. R. Green, Conquest of England, 65 sq.; 1883. From a poem describing how Sulgen, afterwards bishop of Saint David's *ivit ad Hibernos sophia mirabile claros*, written by the bishop's son John, Ussher, in his preface to the Sylloge, infers that there was a revival of the Irish schools after the Danish invasion; since the verse relates to about the middle of the eleventh century: but of this further proof is wanting. [Compare Dr. H. J. Lawlor's introduction to the Psalter of Ricemarch, I. pp. x–xiii, 1914.]

[17] On their foundation see Bede's life of Columban, x and xxix, Opp. 3. 283, 304 sq., ed. Basle 1563.

INTRODUCTION.

A new epoch in their labours abroad is opened in the empire of Charles the Great, whose hearty goodwill towards scholars and whose zeal for the promotion of learning are as characteristic and well-known as his skill as a warrior or as a king. If his reign marks the dividing line between ancient and medieval history, it is not only by virtue of its political facts but also because it begins the age of the education of the northern races, fitting them in time to rule the world as the Romans had done before them. In this great work the Scots, instead of toiling humbly by themselves, were now welcomed and recognised as indispensable coöperators. Their entry into the Frankish realm is related in the *Acts of Charles the Great*, written by a monk of Saint Gall[18] towards the end of the ninth century, whose account, however much coloured by legendary ornaments, may still [p] contain some features of a genuine tradition; at the least it points rightly to the main source from which the impulse of learning was communicated afresh to the continent.

p cf. Haddan 281.

[q] *When*, says the monk, *the illustrious Charles had begun to reign alone in the western parts of the world and the study of letters was everywhere well-nigh forgotten, in such sort that the worship of the true God declined, it chanced that two Scots from Ireland lighted with the British merchants on the coast of Gaul, men learned without compare as well in secular as in sacred writings; who, since they showed nothing for sale, kept crying to the crowd that gathered to buy, If any man is desirous of wisdom, let him come to us and receive it; for we have it to sell. This therefore they declared they had for sale, since they saw the people to traffic not in gifts but in saleable things, so that they thus might either urge them to purchase wisdom like other goods or, as the events following show, turn them by such declaration to wonder and astonishment. At length their cry being long continued was brought by certain that wondered at them or deemed them mad, to the ears of*

q Gest. Kar. Magn. i. 1 Pertz 2. 731.

[18] [Identified with Notker Balbulus: see K. Zeumer, in Historische Aufsätze zum Andenken von Georg Waitz gewidmet 97–118, 1886; and L. Halphen, in the Revue historique, 128 (1918) 293–298.]

Charles the king, always a lover and most desirous of wisdom: who, when he had called them with all haste into his presence, enquired if, as he understood by report, they verily had wisdom with them. Yea, said they, we have it and are ready to impart to any that rightly seek it in the name of the Lord. When therefore he had enquired what they would have in return for it, they answered, Only proper places and noble souls, and such things as we cannot travel without, food and wherewith to clothe ourselves. Hearing this he was filled with great joy, and first for a short space entertained them both in his household: afterwards when he was constrained to warlike enterprises, he enjoined the one, by name Clement, to abide in Gaul; to whom he entrusted boys of the most noble, middle, and lowest ranks, in goodly number, and ordained that victual should be provided them according as they had need, with fitting houses to dwell in. The other[19] *he dispatched into Italy and appointed him the monastery of Saint Austin beside the Ticinian city, that there such as were willing to learn might gather together unto him.*

Now, adds the biographer, *a certain Albinus*, the name is an accepted classical adaptation of Alcuin, *by race an Englishman, when he heard that the most religious emperor Charles was glad to welcome learned men, he too entered into a ship and came to him.* Here we are no doubt still wider of historical accuracy: it was not in this manner that Alcuin made acquaintance with the Frankish king, nor is it probable that the arrival of the Irish scholars was

[19] 'Alterum vero nomine:' two manuscripts add the name 'Albinum'; the rest of those collated by Pertz leave a blank space after 'nomine,' while the copies from which Jaffé prints, Bibliotheca Rerum Germ. 4. 632, 1867, omit 'nomine' as well. Possibly 'Albinum' stood in the original text, and was excluded because the sequel showed that the person intended could not be the same with the well-known Alcuin, while no contemporary scholar of the name was known. It may be observed that the 'Albinum' does not appear in the quotation of the passage given by Vincent of Beauvais, Speculum historiale, xxiii. 173, Nuremberg 1483 folio. I notice this because M. Hauréau, De la Philosophie scolastique, 1. 14, 1850 (the passage seems to have been omitted in the new edition of his book,—the Histoire), states the contrary. The legend therefore says nothing of the English Alcuin, certainly nothing of John Scotus, ornaments added by later writers, which even M. Hauréau, in his earlier work, confounded with the original story.

INTRODUCTION.

attended by the picturesque circumstances which the monk relates. Yet, however little there be of truth in the fable, it is still valuable as evidence of the clearness with which a subsequent generation seized the main fact of Charles's indebtedness to the British islands, and also with which it expressed, as an accepted and natural relation, the notion of affinity between learning and godliness which it [r] was the work of Alcuin and still more of the Scots to inculcate upon their age. Through their influence it was that the king sent forth the [s] famous capitularies of 787 and the following years, which enforced the establishment of schools in connexion with every abbey in his realm, and laid the new foundation of medieval learning.[20] *Amabat peregrinos* is said almost to Charles's reproach by his biographer [t] Einhard; yet the strangers whom he welcomed are in truth the first authors of the restoration of letters in Francia.

[r] cf. Mullinger 69.

[s] Encycl. de litt. colend., Pertz, Legg. I. 52 sq.; cf. Mullinger 97 sqq., 102.

[t] Vit. Car. xxi. Jaffé 4. 528.

The name of Alcuin introduces us to another element in this work. For England had also been for some time the scene of a literary life, less independent indeed and more correct in its ecclesiastical spirit, but hardly less broad than that of the Scots. A singular fortune had brought together as the second fathers of the English church, [u] a Greek of Tarsus and an African, Theodore archbishop of Canterbury, and Hadrian, abbat of Saint Peter's in that city, the one from Rome, the other from the neighbourhood of Naples. While Theodore worked to reduce the church of England into a nearer conformity with catholic discipline, the two friends had their school at Canterbury, where one might [x] learn not only the knowledge which made a good churchman, but also astronomy and the art of writing verses, and apparently even medicine.

A.D. 668–9.

[u] Bed. iv. 1: cf. Bright, Chapters 219 sqq.

[x] Bed. iv. 2; Bright 237 sq.

[20] A variety of notices respecting the schools of the time is collected by the Benedictines in the Histoire littéraire de la France, 4. 12 sqq.; 1738 quarto. They concern chiefly Lyons, Orleans, Fulda, Corbie, Fontenelle, Saint Denys, and Tours. It was to Tours that Alcuin withdrew, as abbat of Saint Martin's, in 796. A. F. Gfrörer comments on the importance of the schools of Aquitaine, Concha, Galuna, and Aniane: Allgemeine Kirchengeschichte, 3. 702 sqq., Stuttgart 1844.

But the previous experience of the teachers enabled them to extend their lessons into a field still less in conformity with the accustomed routine of monastic schools: they made their pupils learn Greek so thoroughly that more than half-a-century later Bede says that some of them still remained who knew Greek as well as their mother-tongue. [y] An Englishman too, Benedict Biscop, the friend of Wilfrid, who had attended Theodore on his road from Rome to Canterbury and had held for a while the abbacy to which Hadrian succeeded, helped forward the advancement of his countrymen in another way. He was a sedulous collector of books and took advantage of repeated journeys to Rome to return [z] laden with purchases or the gifts of friends, gathered thence or from places on the road. With these he endowed the abbey which he erected at Wearmouth; and among his last charges to the brethren of his house we read that [a] 'he enjoined them to keep jealously the precious and very rich library, indispensable for the learning of the church, which he had brought from Rome,—*bibliothecam quam de Roma nobilissimam copiosissimamque advexerat, ad instructionem ecclesiae necessariam*,—and not to suffer it through carelessness to decay or to be dispersed abroad.'

[y] Bed. hist. abbat. Vyramuth. iii.

[z] ibid.

[a] cap. ix.

The example of these three men was not lost upon the English. [b] Aldhelm who, pedant as he was, ranked among the most learned men of his time, passed from his Scottish master at Malmesbury to the school of Hadrian at Canterbury; and [c] a goodly band of other scholars (Greek is their peculiar qualification) went forth from this latter place to spread their knowledge over England. But it was in the north that the new learning took deepest root. At Jarrow, the offshoot of Benedict Biscop's monastery of Wearmouth, lived and died Bede, the writer who sprang at once into the position of a father of the church, and whose influence was by far the greatest and most unquestioned of any between saint Gregory and saint Bernard. He is a witness to the excellence of Benedict's collection of books: for though, [d] he says, *I spent my*

[b] Bed. Hist. eccl. v. 18.

[c] see Bright 237 sq.

[d] Hist. eccl. v. 24.

INTRODUCTION. *whole life in the dwelling of my monastery*, he shews an extent of knowledge in classical literature and natural science entirely unrivalled in his own day and probably not surpassed for many generations to come. Yet, be it remembered, it was first and foremost as a theologian and interpreter of the Scriptures that the middle ages revered him; and it is as an historian and the father of English historians that we now see his greatest distinction. Nor can the student of his works fail to recognise that Bede, like Aldhelm, combined the current which flowed eastward from Ireland with that which came with Benedict from Canterbury. His genial and versatile learning is no less characteristic than the loyalty in which he held fast to the strict tradition of the Catholic church. A child of Bede's in spirit, though he was probably not
A.D. 735. born until about the time of the master's death, was destined to take back his tradition to the continent at the moment when it was first ripe to receive the stimulating influence.

804. Alcuin faithfully carries on the current of learning in the north of England of which Bede is the headspring. In his poem *On the Pontiffs and Saints of the Church of York* [e] he describes his master's work in language which shews us the distinctive qualities for which his disciples valued him:

[e] ver. 1300–1317 Jaffé 6. 121: cf. ver. 684 sqq., 742 sq.

> Discere namque sagax iuvenis seu scribere semper
> Fervidus instabat, non segni mente laborans:
> Et sic proficiens est factus iure magister.
> Plurima quapropter praeclarus opuscula doctor
> Edidit, explanans obscura volumina sanctae
> Scripturae, nec non metrorum condidit artem;
> De quoque temporibus mira ratione volumen,
> Quod tenet astrorum cursus, loca, tempora, leges,
> Scripsit, et historicos claro sermone libellos;
> Plurima versifico cecinit quoque carmina plectro.

Alcuin, like Bede, was a teacher and an organiser of learning, a man of wide reading rather than of original thought. His position in the church at York had afforded him access to a library of unusual compass. [f] In the poem just quoted he gives a list of these volumes; it

[f] ver. 1535–1561 pp. 128 sq.

can only be a selection of what he thought the most important. Among them appear the Greek fathers, Athanasius, Chrysostom, Basil,—partly perhaps in their original tongue;[21]—with a good number of the Latins. Of classical poets are named Virgil, Statius, and Lucan; of their degenerate successors, Sedulius, Juvencus, Arator, and Fortunatus. History is represented by Pompeius Trogus, that is, in the abridgement which we know as Justin, and Bede; natural history by Pliny. Cicero is named only as an orator. For logic Alcuin mentions Aristotle,—certainly in a Latin guise,[22]—and the translators and commentators, Victorinus and Boëthius; for grammar Donatus, Priscian, and Servius. These are the better known of the authors recited in this interesting poem. Alcuin studied them with the simple purpose of fitting himself to be a teacher. He adopts and adapts, as he thinks most appropriate to his scope; but he creates nothing. On the problems which were so soon to agitate the schools, the nature of being, and the relation of objects to thought, he has little to say of his own; his [g] psychology is directly derived from saint Augustin, his logic from the abbreviators of Aristotle. Learning in England had indeed begun to decline, but before the process had gone too far, Alcuin transplanted it; and, whatever his intellectual limitations, just such a man was needed to set on foot a sound system of education in the Frankish realm.

[g] Hauréau I. 124 sqq.

It has been [h] maintained that Alcuin, at least in his later years, and the Scots with whom he worked held opposed positions in this movement; that Alcuin remained true to the tradition of saint Gregory, while the

[h] Mullinger 110–123.

[21] Bishop Stubbs thinks that the York library actually contained manuscripts both in Greek and Hebrew: Smith and Wace's Dictionary of Christian Biography, art. *Alcuin*, 1. 73 a; 1877. But Alcuin's words, de Pontif. 1535–1539, Jaffé p. 128, need not be pressed to mean more than the source from which the literature he mentions was derived; he does not speak of the language.

[22] Most probably the reference is to the abridgement of the Categories then ascribed to saint Augustin: cf. Hauréau 1. 93–97.

INTRODUCTION. Scots allowed too great a latitude in their learned ambition; that Alcuin treated them as rivals, almost as enemies to the truth. Nor is this view altogether groundless. There was without doubt a certain national jealousy subsisting between the English and the Scots; and Alcuin probably resented the predominance which the latter threatened to assume when, as an imaginative writer under Charles's grandson relates, [i] *almost all Ireland, regardless of the barrier of the sea, comes flocking to our shores with a troop of philosophers.* There were also differences of ecclesiastical detail. Even in matters of doctrine more than once the Scots had given cause of offence: [k] they had, it should seem, with their Greek learning, drawn more deeply from the wells of oriental theology than was approved by the cautious judgement of their age. One Clement, as [l] saint Boniface reports, had denied the authority of the fathers and canons of the church, and besides holding some views dangerous to morality, had gone so far as to teach that Christ by his descent into hell delivered all its prisoners, the unbelieving with the righteous; [23] and Virgil, bishop of Salzburg, had maintained the existence of dwellers in the antipodes [m] 'in defiance of God and of his own soul,' because thus apparently he limited the sphere of the Saviour's work of redemption just as Clement had enlarged it.

[i] v. infra, p. 74 n. 23.

[k] cf. Haddan 274, 284.

A.D. 744. [l] Ep. l. Jaffé 3. 140.

A.D. 748. [m] Ep. lxvi. p. 191.

There was clearly a repugnance between the plain, solid English temperament and the more adventurous, speculative genius of their neighbours. If it be said with truth now that the two peoples are incapable of understanding one another, it is manifest that they are not likely to have made that acquaintance at a comparatively early date after their first introduction. To hold however that Alcuin and the Irish stood apart in the matter of learning,

[23] 'Quod Christus, filius Dei, descendens ad inferos omnes quos inferni carcer detinuit inde liberasset, credulos et incredulos, laudatores Dei simul et cultores idolorum.' See saint Boniface's letter to pope Zacharias, ep. l., Jaffé 3. 140. Clement, we are informed, though a priest, apparently a bishop, was a married man with a family, and advocated marriage with a deceased brother's wife in conformity with the Jewish law: ep. xlviii, p. 133.

that Alcuin despised secular literature and forbade his scholars to cultivate it, appears to be an unfounded presumption: its sole positive basis lies in a [n] story told by a biographer who was not even a contemporary and who relates the affair simply in order to show the master's miraculous gift of clairvoyance. It was fitting enough that Alcuin should have [o] remonstrated with those who studied their Virgil to the exclusion or neglect of the Bible; but the fact proves nothing as to his general regard for letters, and the testimony of his writings and acts is more eloquent than such private admonitions. Alcuin and the Scots, we take it, laboured, with whatever transient [p] jealousies, in a common love of learning. The old temper which regarded religion and letters as irreconcilable opposites, was clean forgotten; the spirit is caught up by the rulers of the church themselves; and soon [q] a Roman council held under the pope, Eugenius the Second, can make a canon enjoining all diligence in the search for teachers to be appointed in all places to meet the necessities of the age, *masters and doctors to teach the study of letters and liberal arts, and the holy doctrines which they possess, since in them chiefly are the divine commands manifested and declared.*[24]

[n] Vit. Alchuin. x. Jaffé 6. 24 sq.

[o] Epp. ccvi. pp. 713 sq. ccxliii. p. 783; cf. epp. cxix. p. 485, cclii. p. 803.

[p] cf. Alcuin ep. xcviii. pp. 408 sqq.

A.D. 826. [q] Mansi 14. 494.

That such an ordinance as this should have been required proves how much the learning of the new empire

[24] See the dissertation of Wilhelm von Giesebrecht, De Litterarum Studiis apud Italos primis medii Aevi Saeculis, 11, Berlin 1845 quarto. The 34th canon of the Roman council, as re-enacted in an assembly presided over by Leo the Fourth in 853, is as follows: 'De quibusdam locis ad nos refertur non magistros neque curam invenire pro studiis litterarum. Idcirco in universis episcopiis subiectisque populis, et aliis locis in quibus necessitas occurrerit, omnino cura et diligentia habeatur ut magistri et doctores constituantur, qui studia litterarum liberaliumque artium ac sancta habentes dogmata, assidue doceant; quia in his maxime divina manifestantur atque declarantur mandata:' Mansi 14. 1008. For 'ac sancta habentes dogmata' there is a variant 'habentium dogmata': but though the 'sancta' seems required to justify the word 'dogmata,' the genitive 'habentium' is perhaps more suitable to the context than 'habentes.' The authoritative admonition was appealed to three centuries later by Abailard, as against the detractors of secular learning in his day: Theol. Christ. ii., Opp. 2. 442; Introd. ad theol. ii., ib. p. 69; ed. V. Cousin, Paris 1859 quarto.

INTRODUCTION.

A.D. 829.

r Conc. Paris. sext. iii. 12 Mansi 14. 599.

had lost its vigour and its wide diffusion in the troubled years that followed the emperor's death. Indeed barely fifteen years had passed since that event, when the prelates of Gaul appealed to Lewis the Pious to carry out the mandate issued by the Roman council, and to save the ruin into which the educational institutions of the country were already falling. r *We earnestly and humbly petition your highness*, they said, *that you, following the ensample of your father, will cause public schools to be established in at least three fitting places of your realm, that the labour of your father and yourself may not through neglect (which God forbid) utterly decay and perish*: *so*, they added, *shall great benefit and honour abound to God's holy church, and to you a great reward and everlasting remembrance.* Still the impulse given to civilisation by the work of Charles, however intermittent its effects may appear,—dying out, as it seemed, by degrees until the second revival of the eleventh and twelfth centuries,—was never wholly lost. Nor was the decline of literature so rapid as is frequently supposed;[25] the change is rather from an initiating to an appropriating age. In the eager life of Charles's day men had leisure for independent study and production: under his successors they were, as a rule, content with a reputation for learning. To be well-read and to reproduce old material, was all that was asked of scholars; and the few who overpassed the conventional

[25] For example, Dr. Hermann Reuter, Geschichte der religiösen Aufklärung im Mittelalter, 1. 16, Berlin 1875, has no justification in inferring from the words of Claudius of Turin, 'Nec saecularis litteraturae didici studium nec aliquando exinde magistrum habui' (praef. in Levit., Jo. Mabillon, Vet. Analect. 90, ed. Paris 1723 folio) that instruction was again becoming limited to the sphere of theology; since Claudius was brought up in Spain, when Christian letters were at a low ebb. Dr. Reuter is equally unfortunate in referring (ibid. 1. 15 and n. 7) to the same writer (praef. exposit. in ep. ad Eph., Mabillon 91) for evidence of the general decay of letters. Claudius is speaking of sacred learning; he has no interest in any other. On the state of literature under the later Carolings compare Carl von Noorden's Hinkmar Erzbischof von Rheims, 56, Bonn 1863; a dissertation written by an historical scholar who has but recently and prematurely passed from us, and for whose work and memory I would here express my gratitude and my personal respect.

boundary of the republic of letters found that they did it at their peril.

Nevertheless, even with these limitations, the age succeeding that of Charles the Great, partly from the very imperfection of its intellectual vision, was able to venture upon enterprises which had perhaps been suppressed in their birth under more regular and better organised conditions. In the first century of Christianity it has been said [s] that 'the disciples of the Messiah were indulged in a freer latitude both of faith and practice than has ever been allowed in succeeding ages.' A like criticism would be true with respect to the progress of thought after Charles's day. Not for many generations did philosophy assume that definite medieval guise in which it remained fixed until the dawn of modern history. The gates of theological orthodoxy were even less closely guarded. Hardly a century will elapse before we see, preparing or already matured, some of the characteristic problems of church-controversy, even then held of paramount importance, though none could foresee the sway they would hold over the minds of men hereafter. The sacerdotal basis of the church is attacked, the nature of the divine Trinity is subjected to cold analysis; the doctrine of predestination is revived, the doctrine of transubstantiation is formulated. Such were the unexpected fruit of Charles's and Alcuin's husbandry. In the two following chapters we shall examine a few specimens of the literature and the speculations of the ninth century. The first examples will be taken from a class of writings but indirectly connected with learned studies, and will illustrate the movement of thought with respect to religious, or, it may be, superstitious, usages and beliefs: the second chapter will attempt to delineate the character of the theology of the greatest philosopher whom Ireland sent forth to glorify the schools of continental Europe.

[s] Gibbon, ch. xv. vol. 2. 74, ed. Oxford 1827.

CHAPTER I.

Claudius of Turin and Agobard of Lyons.

Chap. I.

In the empire of Charles the Great the Latin church advanced to a clearer consciousness of her individuality, as apart from her oriental sister, than was possible before the state as well as the church had a western head. The old points of controversy which had once been common to all Christendom now vanish away. From the time of the British Pelagius, the heresies of the west had occupied themselves with a different class of speculations from those which convulsed the eastern church. Henceforward we shall find the former almost exclusively represented. The last of the eastern heresies, eastern in spirit if not directly in origin, is stamped out with the condemnation of the Spanish adoptians by the council of Frankfort, a [a] proceeding in which Alcuin took a conspicuous part. The last controversy between the churches is signalised by the repudiation of image-worship at the same council.

A.D. 794. [a] cf. Stubbs, Dict. of Christ. Biogr. 1. 73 b.

The immediate antecedents of this decision in the matter of image-worship are worthy of notice. The second council of Nicea, seven years earlier, had unanimously approved the practice. It had decreed, under penalty of excommunication, that images of the Saviour and of his Mother, of angels, and of all saints and holy men, should be everywhere set up, should be treated as holy memorials and worshipped; only without that peculiar adoration which is reserved for God alone.[b] In this ordinance the pope, Hadrian the First, concurred. The value of the pope's opinion was however now, and remained for several centuries, an extremely variable

A.D. 787.

[b] Milman 2. 391 sqq.; cf. C. J. Hefele, conciliengeschichte 3. 439 sqq., Freiburg 1858.

quantity. The famous Caroline Books, which (whatever be their actual authorship) indubitably proceed from the court of Charles the Great and from the closing years of the eighth century, [c] speak with quiet assurance of certain usages as *allowed rather by the ambition of Rome than by any apostolical tradition.* Nor was this feeling confined to the atmosphere of the court. In the matter of image-worship the council of Frankfort thought nothing of placing itself in direct opposition to the policy favoured by the pope. The council too was no mere Frankish diet; it was [d] attended by bishops from all the west, Spain and England, as well as by papal legates. But the authority of the latter was powerless against that of Charles, and the canons of Nicea were formally rejected. That the Greek contention in the end won acceptance is well known.[1] But the process was silent and without express enactment, just as in the [e] east the triumph over the iconoclasts was imperceptibly forgotten and images (in the strict sense) came to be unconsciously proscribed. At present, if the subject was discussed, as indeed it was with considerable vehemence, the question was how little, not how much, reverence could rightly be paid to images.

[c] Libr. Car. i. 3, Migne 98. 1015 D.

[d] Milman 3. 95.

[e] See H. F. Tozer in George Finlay's Hist. of Greece 2. 165 n. 3, ed. Oxford 1877.

The extreme party on this side is represented by Claudius, bishop of Turin.[2] A Spaniard, bred—if we may credit the testimony of his opponents—under one of the leading heretics whom the council of Frankfort condemned, he seems rather to have recoiled into a more decided, at least a more primitive, orthodoxy than to have been affected by his dangerous surroundings. He became a master in one of the royal schools of Aquitaine [3]

[1] Gfrörer has collected the early traces of this rapid change, Kirchengeschichte 3. 938 sqq.

[2] See especially Carl Schmidt's essay in Illgen's Zeitschrift für die historische Theologie, 1843 pt. 2.

[3] 'In Alvenni cespitis arvo, in palatio pii principis domini Ludovici, tunc regis, modo imperatoris,' are his own words, Epist. dedic. in enarrat. in epist. ad Gal., in the Maxima Bibliotheca Patrum 14. 141 A, Lyons 1677 folio; by the pages of which I regularly cite also Jonas of Orleans, Dungal, and Agobard. The school is conjectured to have been at Ebreuil, Histoire littéraire de la France 4. 223.

and was so much trusted by the king, Louis the Pious, that when the latter succeeded to the empire of his father Charles, he raised Claudius, about the year 818,[4] to the see of Turin. His reputation was that of an interpreter of the Bible.[5] He wrote commentaries on most of the historical books of the Old Testament, on the Gospel according to saint Matthew, and apparently on all the Pauline Epistles. Of these however but one, on the Galatians, has been printed entire. The others are known only by prefaces and extracts; and some are not edited at all.[6] It is not likely that we lose very much by our defective information about his works. He had not the faculty of lucid or graceful, or always even of grammatical, expression; and he repeatedly laments a defect which gave an irresistible opening to the ridicule of his literary enemies.[7] Far less did he bring the light of speculation or of original genius to bear upon the books he expounded. He compiled from the fathers—Augustin was his chosen

[4] Possibly a little earlier: Neander gives the date as 814, General History of the Christian Religion and Church 6. 216, transl. by J. Torrey, Edinburgh 1850.

[5] 'Claudium . . . cui in explanandis sanctorum evangeliorum lectionibus quantulacunque notitia inesse videbatur, ut Italicae plebis (quae magna ex parte a sanctorum evangelistarum sensibus procul aberat) sanctae doctrinae consultum ferret, Taurinensi subrogari fecit ecclesiae,' says his enemy, bishop Jonas, praef. in libros de cultu imaginum, 167 C, D; cf. 168 G.

[6] Few writers have their works scattered through such a variety of collections. The Enarratio in epist. ad Galat. is printed in the Max. Biblioth. Patrum, ubi supra; for the rest we have only specimens published in the Vetera Analecta of Mabillon, the Bibliotheca mediae et infimae Latinitatis of J. A. Fabricius, and in two collections of cardinal Mai. Some additional extracts are mentioned by Schmidt, who gives a detailed list of Claudius's known works and attempts a chronological arrangement, p. 44 n. 8, and in his article in Herzog and Plitt's Real-Encyklopädie: see too Mabillon p. 92, ed. 1723. All these pieces, I think, are collected in the hundred-and-fourth volume of Migne. How much besides lies hidden in the Vatican we cannot tell. Cardinal Mai's edition of the preface to Claudius's commentary on the Pauline Epistles is avowedly a specimen which he intended to follow by the whole work, Nova Collect. vet. Scriptor. 7. 274 n. 1, Rome 1833. He mentions also two codices at Rome of the Catena upon saint Matthew, Spicil. Roman. 4. 301, Rome 1840.

[7] See for instance his preface to the Lib. informationum litterae et spiritus super Leviticum, Mabillon, p. 90, and that to his commentary on the Ephesians, ib. p. 92, where he alludes to his 'rustic speech.'

master—for the benefit of those whose leisure or acquirements did not suffice for extensive reading. He commented with a view of edification; and seeking an ethical or a spiritual lesson everywhere, he fell willingly into the pitfall of allegory.[8] His fearless pursuit however of the principles he had learned in the course of a wide, if irregular, study of the fathers, makes Claudius a signal apparition at a time when the material accessories of religion were forcing themselves more and more into the relations between man and God. The worship of images, of pictures, of the Cross itself,[9] the belief in the mediation of saints, the efficacy of pilgrimages, the authority of the holy see, seemed to him but the means of deadening the responsibility of individual men. CHAP. I.

Claudius sought to quicken this sense. He is sure that if a man has a direct personal interest in his own welfare, if he does not rely on spiritual processes conducted by others on his behalf, nor tie his faith to material representations of the unseen, he can be the better trusted to walk aright. The freedom of the gospel he is never tired of contrasting with the bondage of the law, a bondage which he saw revived in the religious system of his day. Faith is incomplete without its corollary, action, or, as he prefers to call it, love. With the *works* of the sacerdotal law he will have nothing to do.[10] [f] *Let no man trust in the intercession or merit of the saints, because except he*

[f] Apologetic. ap. Jon. Aurel. p. 194 F. H.

[8] Claudius's allegorising tendency has however been exaggerated. He himself lays down the limit, 'scilicet ut manente veritate historiae figuras intelligamus,' in Galat. cap. iv. p. 158 B.

[9] Dr. Reuter, Geschichte der religiösen Aufklärung 1. 17, is surely guilty of an anachronism in speaking of the 'crucifix,' of the existence or possibility of which neither Claudius nor any of his opponents seem aware. See for example Jonas 168 H. Pictures of the crucifixion there doubtless were, and perhaps crosses bearing a painted figure; but these are not what we call 'crucifixes.'

[10] De admonitione et exhortatione unde rogasti quod scriberem, ut votum quod voverunt domino reddant; . . . nullam admonitionem meliorem potui invenire quam epistulae primae Pauli apostoli, quam misi, quia tota inde agitur ut merita hominum tollat, unde maxime nunc monachi gloriantur, et gratiam Dei commendat, per quam omnis qui vovit, quod vovit domino reddat: praef. in epp. Pauli, Mai, Nov. Coll. 7. 275 sq.

CHAP. I.

hold the same faith, justice, and truth, which they held, he cannot be saved. Men choose the easy way before the hard one which consists in self-sacrifice.[11] [g] *God commanded men to bear the cross, not to adore it: they desire to adore that which they will not spiritually or bodily to carry with them. So to worship God is to depart from him.* The only acceptable service is that, born of faith and supported by the divine grace, which issues in an all-embracing love. The following short passage contains the sum of his ethical principles. [h] *Charity,* he says, *or love, is comprehended in four modes. By the first we must love God, by the next ourselves, by the third our neighbours, by the fourth our enemies. Unless we have first loved God, we shall not be able to love ourselves; that is to say, to abstain from sin: and if we love not ourselves, what standard have we to love our neighbours? and if we love not our neighbours, much less shall we love our enemies. Whereof this is the proof, that for the sake of God we despise even our salvation, yea, and our very souls. Faith therefore alone sufficeth not for life, except a man love his neighbour even as himself, and not only not do unto him the evil which he would not unto himself, but also do unto him the good which he would have another do unto him; and so fulfil the universal law, namely, to abstain from evil and to do good.*

[g] ibid. p. 183 D, H.

[h] Enarr. in Galat. iv. p. 161 C, D.

With these thoughts in his heart, and longing to impress them upon his generation, Claudius passed to his diocese of Turin. His fiery and uncompromising temper met opposition and peril as inducements rather than obstacles to action. We are told that he often took up the sword with his lay comrades to drive back the Saracens when they pressed forward from their strong places on the coast of Spain or Gaul to overrun his country.[12] But the paganism, as he held it, which reigned everywhere around him,—the offerings and images that defiled all

[11] Quia videlicet nisi quis a semetipso deficiat, ad eum qui super ipsum est non appropinquat, nec valet apprehendere quod ultra ipsum est si nescierit mactare quod est: Apol. ap. Jon. p. 184 C. The sentence, according to Jonas, is adopted from saint Gregory.

[12] Compare his reference to such expeditions, Mai, Nov. Coll. 7. 275.

the churches,[13]—formed the more present evil against which he set himself to do continual battle. [i] He called for the utter destruction of all images and pictures throughout his diocese. [k] He forbade the observance of saints' days, and the very mention of saints in the liturgy. Foremost in executing the work, he raised a storm about him: his life was not safe.[14] [l] The people were passionately excited, but the protection or favour of higher powers was probably with him, and his name is not to be added to the roll of martyrs who have perished for lack of sympathy with the grosser needs of their contemporaries.

i Jon. 168 G.

k Dungal. Responsa contra perversas Claudii Taurin. episc. sententias, p. 223 F.

l Dungal, ibid. p. 199 D: cf. infra pp. 31 sqq.

Yet the truth is that, with all his fanaticism, Claudius alone of his age grasped the inevitable consequences of its spiritual condition. It was an age of materialism, and there was no possibility that the images could remain in churches without the people worshipping them, or that if they worshipped them they would understand the nice distinction between this worship and that of God laid down by the second Nicene council.[15] Claudius denounces this inevitable polytheism. *If*, he says, *they worship the images of saints after the fashion of demons,*—that is, of course, in the manner of the old gods of the country,—*they have not left idols but changed their names.*[16] He was accused of inventing a new heresy. [m] *Nothing*, he replies, *can be falser. I preach no sect, but hold the unity and expound the verity of the church. Sects and schisms, heresies and superstitions, I have ever, so far as in me lay,*

m Apol., ap. Jon. 169 F, 170 A.

[13] Inveni omnes basilicas, contra ordinem veritatis, sordibus anathematum et imaginibus plenas: Apol. ap. Jon. 170 D.

[14] See his complaints in the Apologetic, ap. Jon. p. 171 C, and in a preface addressed to Theodemir as late as 823, ap. Mabillon, Vet. anal. 90; cf. p. 91.

[15] Προσκύνησις was decreed, not λατρεία; cf. supra, pp. 27 sq.: a distinction which modern protestants find difficult to appreciate. The English language indeed allows great latitude to the signification both of 'worship' and 'adoration'; and the unique relation is only implied in 'idolatry' and certain hypothetical derivatives like 'Mariolatry.'

[16] Saint Agobard expresses himself in almost the same words, De imag. xix. p. 291 C. Claudius proceeds: Si scribas in pariete vel pingas imagines Petri et Pauli, Iovis et Saturni, sive Mercurii, nec isti sunt dii nec illi apostoli; nec isti nec illi homines: ac per hoc nomen mutatur, error tamen et tunc et nunc idem ipse permanet semper: Apol., ap. Dungal. 201 G and Jon. 174 B. C.

CHAP. I.

stamped upon and crushed; I have fought with them and taken them by assault, nor will I ever, so far as in me lies, cease to combat them with the help of God. He turns to his accuser: [n] *Why dost thou humble thyself and bow to false images? why bend thy body a slave before vain likenesses and things of earthly fashion? God made thee erect. Other animals are prone and look earthward, but thy face is raised towards God. Thither look, raise thine eyes thither; seek God above, so shalt thou have no need of things below.* This is the basis of his teaching. Following closely in the track, often quoting the very words, of Augustin, he repeats that [o] a spiritual religion is independent of the sensuous, is dragged down by any attempt to make it intelligible to the outward eyes: it looks directly towards God. For this reason he refuses to dwell even upon the humanity of Christ. The man Jesus did his work once for all: Claudius would turn men's thoughts to their glorified Lord. [p] *When these worshippers of a false religion and superstition say, For the memory of our Saviour we worship, reverence, adore a cross painted and carved in his honour, they take no pleasure in our Saviour except that which pleasured the ungodly, the shame of his passion and the scorn of his death. They believe of him what the ungodly, Jews or heathen, believed, who believed not in his resurrection; and they know not to think aught of him save as in anguish and dead; they believe and hold him in their hearts to abide continually in passion, nor consider nor understand that which the apostle saith,* [q] *Though we have known Christ after the flesh, yet now henceforth know we him no more.*[17]

[n] Apol., ap. Jon. 175 G: cf. lib. super Levit., Mabillon 90 sq.

[o] Praef. in Levit., Mabillon 91: cf. Reuter I. 19 & n. 17.

[p] Apol., ap. Jon. 176 C, 177 C.

[q] 2 Cor. v. 16.

Claudius attacks every visible symbol and memorial of the life of Jesus. [r] *You worship all wood fashioned after the manner of a cross, because for six hours Christ hung upon a cross. Worship then all virgins, because a virgin bare him. Worship stables, for he was born in one; old rags, for he*

[r] Apol., ap. Jon. 177 H sq.

[17] This verse, it is interesting to note, was also a favourite with Berengar of Tours, who, in his resistance to materialistic opinions, was in many respects the unconscious disciple of Claudius: De sacra coena 45, 94, 200, ed. A. F. and F. T. Vischer, Berlin 1834.

was swaddled in them ; ships, for he ofttimes sailed in them ; asses, for he rode thereon. There is no end to his mockery. He excuses himself for it by the bitterness of the facts he has to withstand. [s] *Ridiculous these things all are, and to be mourned rather than written. We are compelled to allege foolishness against the foolish ; against hearts of stone we must cast not the arrows of the word, not sage reasons, but volleys of stones.* Thus he traverses and assails the whole circle of the popular religion of the Latin world. About pilgrimages alone he is more reserved. The fashionable pilgrimage to Rome he cannot indeed approve, but he admits that [t] *it does not hurt every one, nor benefit every one.*[18] But for the peculiar claims of the see of saint Peter he has nothing but derision. [u] The authority of the apostle ceased with his death :[19] his successors possess it just so far as their lives are apostolic. [x] *He is not to be called apostolic who sits in the seat of the apostle, but he who fills the office of the apostle. Of them that hold that place and fulfil not its office the Lord hath said,* [y] *The scribes and the Pharisees sit in Moses' seat : all therefore whatsoever they say unto you, that observe and do ; but do not ye after their works : for they say and do not.* With equal clearness Claudius [z] expresses the distinction between the ideal church and the imperfect copy which represents it on earth.

[s] ibid. p. 178 G, H.

[t] ibid. p. 189 A.

[u] ibid. p. 193 G : cf. Dungal 211 B.

[x] Apol., ap. Jon. 195 H sq.

[y] Matth. xxiii. 2 sq.

[z] Enarr. in Galat. i. p. 142 E.

It was probably opinions like these last which saved Claudius from any rebuke from the emperor for the greater part of his career.[20] They pass almost without question even in the controversy raised by the publication of his *Apologetic.* His other views, too, if they went further than those accepted at the court, were at all events errors

[18] The reprint of Jonas's extracts (see below, p. 33 n. 23), p. 198 E, presents a variant still more guarded in language.

[19] It seems doubtful whether 'aliis' or 'aliis succedentibus,' just after, can be pressed (with Gfrörer and Milman) to mean the whole episcopal order : I have therefore omitted the clause, and interpreted the whole sentence in the light of what follows.

[20] I find this inference anticipated and extended by Gfrörer, Kirchengeschichte 3. 733. Schmidt, ubi supra, p. 62, thinks it implied by a passage in Jonas, p. 175 F, G, that Claudius had at one time come under the censure of the pope, a supposition not improbable in itself and rather confirmatory than otherwise of the suggestion which I have made in the text.

CHAP. I.

on the right side; iconoclasm was less reprehensible than the 'idolatry' of the Greeks. Those who were hottest in their repudiation of Claudius, used very similar language with regard to the other extreme. [a] Walafrid Strabo, who became abbat of Reichenau in 842, holds a scrupulous balance in the controversy; and Walafrid had been a pupil of Rabanus Maurus, and was in some sort a representative theologian of his age. How little, too, the style of argument adopted by his antagonist Jonas commends itself to modern catholics may be gathered from the cautions and expostulations with which his Benedictine editors have thought it necessary to accompany him.[21] Claudius was in fact carrying to their logical issues principles which were virtually recognised by the council of Paris in 825, and which even fifty years later were mentioned by the papal librarian Anastasius, in a dedication to John the Eighth, as still holding their ground among *certain persons in Gaul* [22] at a time when the Greek practice had won nearly universal acceptance in the west. We can therefore hardly take bishop Jonas at his word when he speaks of Claudius as an enemy of [b] *all the sincerest churchmen, the most devoted soldiers of Christ, in Gaul and Germany:* we know indeed from a [c] friend who was also Claudius's opponent in this respect, that in spite of his action in the matter of images, his commentaries on the Bible were received with eager enthusiasm by not a few of the highest prelates of Gaul.

Claudius therefore took no pains to defend himself until he had carried on his warfare during a number of years. His *Apologetic*—a defiant proclamation of his views—he at last addressed to his former friend, the abbat Theodemir, who had warned him of the perilous course he was taking. The answer was a [d] council of bishops held at Lewis's court, and a condemnation; but Claudius can hardly have been much awed by what he is reported to

[a] De eccl. rer. exord. viii. Migne 114. 928.

[b] p. 169 C.

[c] Theodemir. epist. ad Claud., ap. F. A. Zachari. Biblioth. Pistor. 60, Turin 1752 folio.

[d] Dungal 223 H, Jonas 167 D.

21 See pp. 166, 167 H, 193 mg., and the pregnant note, *Caute lege*, p. 195 H, marg.

22 Quibusdam dumtaxat Gallorum exceptis, quibus utique nondum est harum [imaginum] utilitas revelata; Mansi 12. 983 D.

CHAP. I.

have termed [e] *an assembly of asses.* Nor was his refusal to attend followed by any measure to reduce him to obedience The emperor, more, it should seem, to conciliate these prelates than from any serious intention of controlling Claudius, sent [f] extracts of the offending book to Jonas, bishop of Orleans, with the desire that he would refute it. These extracts are all that remain to us of what to the historian is Claudius's most valuable work: [23] the refutation did not appear until after his death. Meantime, Dungal, a Scottish teacher of Pavia, issued a vehement *Reply*, [g] earnestly invoking the imperial aid in suppressing the new heresy. Theodemir also returned to the controversy. Perhaps we may [h] infer from Jonas's unwillingness to publish his polemic, that Claudius as he aged had tempered his fire: more probably Jonas himself found that the act would not increase his favour with the emperor. Be this as it may, the bishop lived more than ten years after he had sent forth his defence, to all appearance without let or molestation from any one. [i] His strenuous career was closed not earlier than 839, but he [k] left behind him disciples enough to stimulate controversy. His writings too, with the exception of the *Apologetic*, were rapidly multiplied and diffused. His fame as a commentator secured the survival of a good deal of his peculiar teaching; but it is hazardous, if not impossible, to connect him in any direct way with the appearance of similar opinions, whether in the congregations of the Waldenses centuries later, or in those isolated puritan outbreaks which repeatedly confront us in the course of medieval history.

[e] Dungal, l. c.

[f] Jonas 167 D, E.

[g] Dungal 199 F.

[h] cf. Schmidt ubi supra, p. 64.

[i] F. Ugheil. Ital. sacr. 4. 1432 A, B, Rome 1652 folio.

[k] Jon. 167 E, F.

In his protest against the invocation of saints Claudius perhaps stood alone, but in the other points in which he separated himself from the current doctrine he had a

[23] The fragments are collected in two pages of the Maxima Bibliotheca Patrum 14. 197 sqq., which give an appearance of continuity to what is really a string of extracts by no means regularly consecutive. Moreover the text is so inaccurate and the punctuation so bewildering that I have preferred to seek the originals in the pages of Dungal and Jonas themselves.

CHAP. I.

supporter (there is, indeed, no evidence to place them in actual association) of far greater ability and far wider influence in the person of saint Agobard. Like him, born in Spain, Agobard was more fortunate in his education. He was brought up from an early age in the south of Gaul, at a time when the impulse given to learning by Charles the Great was in its first vigour: of that civilisation Agobard remained the representative when its founders were dead, and its spirit was falling into decay. Leidrad, archbishop of Lyons, bred him for his successor, made him coädjutor, and after some years secured his appointment to the see when he retired to a cloister in 816.[24] Agobard's life as archbishop corresponds closely with the reign of Lewis the Pious; he died on the 8th June, 840, in the same month as the emperor.

A.D. 779.

Success was prepared for him by others: he deserved it by his contribution to the defence of the orthodox belief against the heresy of the adoptians. But he continued always entirely unaffected by the circumstances of his high position. Independent and regardless of consequences, he held to the principles which he enounced, with unconquerable audacity. He saw the masses around him sunk in a state of sluggish credulity, and instead of leaving them there, as others did, in the opinion that a debased people is the easiest to govern, he laboured hard for their liberation and attacked unsparingly every form of superstition wherever he found it. His thoughts were wider than Claudius's, but in the matter of images the Gallic and Italian prelates were of one mind. If Agobard was the less active in carrying his views into practice, it was not for want of firm conviction. Certainly he was not withheld by the risk of any opposition he might encounter in the Frankish church. He wrote

[24] I take the date from a manuscript notice quoted by Mabillon, Iter Italicum 68, Paris 1687 quarto. [So too Monsignor Duchesne, Fastes épiscopaux de l'ancienne Gaule, 2. 172; 1899.] Bouquet, 6. 190 B marg. and note (1749), infers from the chronicle of Ado of Vienne, a. 815 (so also in Pertz's edition, 2. 320), that Agobard's elevation took place a year earlier.

in the same strong spirit, now of persuasion, now of rebuke, as Claudius; but no controversy ever arose over his utterances. The heads of the church were with him; but at the same time the masses were fast bound by superstition. Agobard may have calculated the injury which the character of an iconoclast would inflict upon his personal influence over them. He may have felt the hopelessness of the undertaking, and held it wiser, and in the end more effectual, to elevate the people gradually by the voice of reason.

The difference, therefore, between him and Claudius regards chiefly the means to carry out their common aims. But Agobard is always guided by a calmer and clearer perception than his vehement ally. [l] He desires, indeed, the removal of all pictures from the churches, but he admits that they are essentially innocent and only rendered pernicious by abuse. [m] *The ancients*, he says, *had figures of the saints, painted or carved, but for the sake of history, for record not for worship; as, for example the acts of synods, wherein were portrayed the catholics upheld and victorious, and the heretics by the discovery of the falsehood of their vile doctrine convicted and expelled, in memorial of the strength of the catholic faith, even as pictures stand in record of foreign or domestic wars. Such we have seen in divers places: yet none of the ancient catholics held that they should be worshipped or adored.* [n] The pictures in churches should be looked at just as any other pictures. Only the faithlessness of the age, which will find some special virtue in them, forces him to condemn them utterly. [o] God must be worshipped without any sensuous representations. [p] *Whosoever adoreth a picture or a statue, carved or molten, payeth not worship to God nor honoureth the angels or holy men, but is an idolator:* he is beguiled to evil under the fairest disguises of devotion; [q] *Satan transformeth himself into an angel of light.* The opposition of spirit and matter is as real to him as to Claudius. He, too, held that [r] visible objects were a hindrance not a help to the perception of the invisible. [s] *When faith*

[l] Lib. contra eorum superstitionem qui picturis et imaginibus sanctorum adorationis obsequium deferendum putant, xxxiii. 294 F.

[m] Cap. xxxii. p. 294 E.

[n] cap. xxxiii. p. 294 F.

[o] cap. xxiv. p. 292 D.

[p] cap. xxxi. p. 294 D: cf. ep. ad Barthol. vii. p. 282 C.

[q] 2 Cor. xi. 14.

[r] capp. xv., xvi. p. 290 B, D.

[s] cap. xxxiii. p. 294 F.

CHAP. I.

is taken from the heart, then is all trust set on visible things.

The rule thus stated Agobard proceeds to apply to the 'vulgar errours' of his day. Want of faith is the root of superstition: it is nurtured by unreason. [t] *The wretched world lies now under the tyranny of foolishness: things are believed by Christians of such absurdity as no one ever could aforetime induce the heathen to believe, who knew not the Creator of all.* Of the various works which he wrote upon this subject, not the least interesting, and certainly the most curious, is the treatise *Against the absurd Opinion of the Vulgar touching Hail and Thunder.* It appears that [u] there was a class of impostors who assumed to themselves the office of 'clerk of the weather.' These *tempestarii*, or weather-wizards, claimed the power not only of controlling the weather, and securing the fields from harm, but also of bringing about hail and thunder storms, [x] and especially of directing them against their private enemies. [y] Plainly they derived a goodly revenue from a blackmail forced by the double motives of fear and hope. [z] *We have seen and heard*, says Agobard, *many who are overwhelmed by such madness, carried away by such folly, that they believe and assert that there is a certain region called Magonia*—no doubt the Magic Land—*whence ships come in the clouds: the which bear away the fruits of the earth, felled by hail and destroyed by storms, to that same country; and these sailors of the air forsooth give rewards to the weather-wizards, and receive in return the crops or other fruits. Certain ones have we seen, blinded by so dark a folly, who brought into an assembly of men four persons, three men and a woman, as having fallen from the said ships; whom they held in bonds for certain days and then presented before an assembled body of men, in our presence, as aforesaid, that they should be stoned. Howbeit the truth prevailed, after much reasoning, and they who brought them forward were confounded.* He condescended to seek evidence of the power of the weather-wizards, but could obtain no account at first hand. [a] People were confident that such or such a thing had

[t] Lib. contra insulsam vulgi opinionem de grandine et tonitruis, xvi. p. 275 B.

[u] capp. i., xv. pp. 271 D, E, 274 G.

[x] cap. iii. p. 272 H.

[y] cap. xv. p. 274 G.

[z] cap. ii. p. 271 F, G.

[a] De grand. vii. p. 272 H sq.

been done, but they were not present at its performance. It was this credulous habit of mind that irritated Agobard. He disdained to allege scientific reasons to overthrow what was in its nature so unreasonable. He could only fall back on the same broad religious principles which had guided him in his repudiation of images. There he says that our relation to God must be direct and without the intervention of sensible objects: [b] here, conversely, that God's relation to nature is immediate and least of all conditioned by the artifices of men. He acknowledges that [c] *almost every one, in these regions, noble and simple, citizen and countryman, old and young,* believes that storms are under human control, and attributes the work of God to man. [d] He spares no words in condemning this infidelity which [e] *believes partly in God, partly that God's words are of men; hopes partly in God, partly in men.*

[b] capp. ix., xiv. pp. 273 D, 274 F.

[c] capp. i., xiv. pp. 271 D, E, 274 F.

[d] cap. xi. p. 273 H.

[e] cap. xv. p. 274 H.

With equal vigour he opposed superstitions which tended to the profit of the church. To his straightforward vision they were the more dangerous, since they degraded the church with the people, instead of maintaining it pure, as a light shining in darkness. [f] There was an epidemic at a place, so he writes to bishop Bartholomew of Narbonne, the causes of which were traced to the activity of evil spirits. The terrified people crowded to the church and lavished offerings of silver and gold and cattle, whatever they possessed, at the feet of saint Firmin. The bishop in perplexity wrote to Agobard for advice: his answer was a warning against the faithlessness implied in trusting to the power of the saint to ward off visitations which proceed from the hand of God. The devil no doubt is at work, but not in the way these people supposed: his action is far less physical than mental: *he is seen to prevail over some men, not so much for the purpose of striking them down as of deluding them.* It is difficult to overestimate the change which the acceptance of Agobard's view would have caused in the popular beliefs of the middle ages. The continual visitations of evil spirits of which the history is full would then have

[f] Ep. ad Barth. episc. Narbon. de quorundam illusione signorum, i. p. 281 D, E.

CHAP. I.

resolved themselves into the creatures ot a disordered imagination; the latter, not the former, being the work of the devil: those who believed in his direct visitation, not its supposed victims, were really under his influence. [g] For his success, Agobard explains, requires a receptivity on men's part, *lack of faith or delight in vanity;* and with these favourable conditions he can indeed lead them helplessly to destruction and death. Agobard gives elsewhere a remarkable illustration. [h] *A few years since,* he says, *a certain foolish story went abroad when there was a murrain of oxen: it was said that Grimoald, duke of Benevento, sent out men with powder to scatter over the fields and mountains, meadows and springs, forasmuch as he was enemy to the most Christian emperor Charles; by reason of which powder the oxen died. For this cause we have heard and seen many persons to be apprehended and certain slain.* Agobard comments on the absurdity of the tale. He asks why only the oxen and no other animals suffered, and further how the murrain could extend over so large a tract of land, when if all the inhabitants of Benevento, men, women, and children, each with three wagons full of powder, had been employed, they could not possibly have sprinkled powder enough. *But, what,* he adds, *was most strange, the prisoners themselves bare testimony against themselves, affirming that they had that powder, and had scattered it. Thus did the devil receive power against them by the secret but righteous judgement of God, and so greatly did he prevail that they themselves were made false witnesses unto their own death.*

[g] cap. vii. p. 282 C.

[h] De grand. xiv. pp. 274 H sq.

But the influence of the devil, in Agobard's mouth, is actually little more than the conventional expression —for Agobard was before all things orthodox—for men's proclivity to unreason and faithlessness.[25] Superstition

[25] Dr. Reuter, 1. 30, confesses himself unable to harmonise the account in the place last quoted and in the epistle to Bartholomew, vii, of the appearance of the devil 'als wirklich handelnder,' with the other passages in which his activity seems conditioned by the self-deception of men. But he has certainly drawn too definite an inference from Agobard's words when he represents him as saying, 'people are deceived because they deceive themselves.' Agobard in

might take the form, as we have seen hitherto, of their claiming powers which really belong to God. It was none the less superstition to postulate the intervention of God in cases where human judgement alone was necessary. For men to disregard the evidence of ascertained facts,[26] and to call for perpetual [i] miracles at their behest was impiety of the worst kind, making God in fact the servant of man. It is this argument, supported by copious citations from the Scriptures, that Agobard alleges against the popular customs of ordeal by fire or water and of wager of battle. Of the two usages the ordeal was [k] discouraged and prohibited by the emperor;[27] and Agobard may have deemed it unworthy of serious argument. He applies his forces mainly to the exposure of the wrong—[l] *nex*, not *lex*,—involved in the test of combat. The ordeal indeed was destitute of any feature except the superstitious, while combat, as [m] Hallam observes, might be held to be partly redeemed by 'the natural dictates of resentment in a brave man unjustly accused, and the sympathy of a warlike people with the display of skill and intrepidity.' At Lyons, the old Burgundian capital, the 'wager of battle,' resting as it did on a law of the Burgundian king Gundobad, is [n] thought to have been resorted to with peculiar frequency. [o] Agobard addressed one of his two treatises on the subject to the emperor and implored him to suppress the evil. [p] He urged not only the religious objections,

i Lib. de divinis sententiis digest. contra damnabilem opinionem putantium divini iudicii veritatem igni vel aquis vel conflictu armorum patefieri, ii. p. 301 E.

k Capit. Wormat., a. 829, Pertz, legg. I. 352 § 12.

l Lib. adv. leg. Gund. xi. p. 266 C.

m Middle ages, 3. 294, ed. 1872.

n Gfrörer 3. 751.

o Lib. adv. leg. Gundob. vii. p. 265 C.

p De div. sent. v. p. 302 B.

fact nowhere expresses himself without qualification, either on this head or on that of the devil's actual interference in human affairs. The words with which he closes the story given in the text, offering it as an example 'de inani seductione et vera sensus diminutione' (p. 275 B), shew how closely connected in his mind the two ideas were. It is uncritical to link a number of detached phrases or epithets, chosen from different places, and to take credit for realising, when one is only confusing, an author's system.

[26] Utilitas iudiciorum constat in discussione causarum et subtilitate investigationum: Lib. adv. legem Gundobadi et impia certamina quae per eam geruntur, x. p. 265 H.

[27] It is significant that so representative a churchman as archbishop Hincmar of Rheims opposed this ordinance: Noorden, Hinkmar 173. Gottschalk also challenged the ordeal as a test of the truth of his opinions: ibid. p. 67.

CHAP. I.

that God's judgements are unsearchable and not lightly to be presumed, but also the arguments of common sense. The combat declares not the judgement of God but the right of the strongest, and gives a criminal encouragement to strife. [q] The vanquished is cast into despair and loss of faith, while in many cases the conqueror proves his innocence by adding the guilt of murder. [r] If the test is worthy of confidence, how came Jerusalem into the hands of the Saracens, Rome to be pillaged by the Goths, Italy by the Lombards? The martyrs of the church, *the witnesses of truth, waxed strong by dying: the upholders of iniquity by killing perished.*

[q] Lib. adv. leg. Gundob. l. c.

[r] cap. ix. p. 265 E, F.

With these various weapons, drawn from the armoury of reason, of experience, of religion, Agobard made war upon the superstitions of his age. He took his stand upon the unassailable ground of Christian verity, but he had his own opinions even in matters like the inspiration of the Bible. Thoughtful men over whose minds the authority of the Bible is supreme have always endeavoured to temper its severity by one of two modes of viewing it. Some enlarge its field by erecting an ample superstructure of allegory upon the literal text,—thinking that they are laying bare its deep, underlying truths,—a method which allows the utmost freedom or license of interpretation upon a servile and uncritical basis. In this way Claudius, and far more John Scotus, were able to bring the words of Scripture into harmony with their own teaching. Others, with a greater fidelity to the scope of the Bible, insist that the letter is subordinate to the spirit, to the general bearing of the book. Among these is Agobard. He rebukes Fredegisus, abbat of Tours, for the *absurdity* of holding that the actual words of Scripture are inspired:[28] its

[28] Quod ita sentiatis de prophetis et apostolis ut non solum sensum praedicationis et modos vel argumenta dictionum Spiritus sanctus eis inspiraverit, sed etiam ipsa corporalia verba extrinsecus in ora illorum ipse formaverit: Lib. contra obiectiones Fredeg. abbat. xii. p. 277 E: an argument against all organic theories of inspiration.

sense is no doubt divine but its form is human.[29] The same rule must be our guide in its interpretation. We must make it intelligible, even against the grammatical sense, so long as we preserve its spirit;—*ut sacramento rei concordaret.*

To this wide-reaching liberality there is one exception in the hostility which Agobard bore towards the Jews. But the archbishop's action was not simply that of a bigot, and the motive of the controversy in which he engaged was entirely honourable to him. He set his face against a flagitious custom of which the Jews, the great [s] slave-dealers of the empire, had the monopoly. [t] He forbade the Christians of his diocese to sell slaves to the Jews for exportation to the Arabs of Spain, and sought also to place a variety of restrictions upon the intercourse of the two races. The emperor however supported the Jews, and Agobard could only resort to passionate appeals to the statesmen of the palace and to the bishops, in the hope of reëstablishing a state of things more consonant with the principles of the church. We are not concerned to defend the curious slanders he repeats in his letter *On the Superstitions of the Jews*: it is sufficient that he believed them. But the truth was that under Lewis the Pious, particularly after his marriage with his second empress, Judith, the position of the Jews might fairly be held to menace Christianity. Charles the Great had shewn them tolerance; Lewis added his personal favour; and under him they enjoyed a prosperity without example in the long course of the middle ages.[30] They formed a peculiar people under his own protection, equally against the nobles and the church; and their privileges

[s] H. Graetz, Gesch. der Juden 5. 246, Magdeburg 1860.

[t] De insolentia Iudaeorum, p. 255 C.

A.D. 826.

[29] Usus sanctae scripturae est verbis condescendere humanis, quatinus vim ineffabilis rei, humano more loquens, ad notitiam hominum deduceret et mysteria insolita solitis ostenderet rebus: ibid. vii. p. 276 E.

[30] For the following outline I am chiefly indebted to Graetz, 5. 245–263 [pp. 230–247 in the fourth edition, Leipzig, 1909.] His remark as to the dishonesty of Agobard in baptising the slaves of Jews and thus emancipating them may be just: but Christians have at all times been not unready to stretch their loyalty to honour at the call of religion, and Agobard asserts that the slaves begged to be baptised, De baptismo Iudaicorum mancipiorum, p. 262 E, F.

CHAP. I.

were guarded by an imperial officer, the Master—he even claimed the title of King[31]—of the Jews. Free from military service, the Jews were indispensable to the commerce of the empire; on account of their financial skill it was common to trust them with the farm of the taxes. Nothing was left undone which might gratify their national or religious prepossessions. They had rights from which Christians were excluded, entire freedom of speech was allowed, and the very weekly [u] markets were postponed to the Sunday in order that the alien race might observe its sabbaths. The Jews built their synagogues, and held lands and pastures; they planted vineyards and set up mills, in perfect security. At the court of the emperor they were welcomed with marked distinction. They went there with their wives, and were only known in the throng by the more sumptuous display of their apparel. The empress Judith was singularly attached to them, and the courtiers, taking up the fashion, attended the synagogues and admired the preaching in them above that of their own clergy.

[u] De insol. Iud., p. 255 G.

It is evident that some motive nobler than jealousy or intolerance might actuate a churchman in resisting what he was bound to consider inimical to the interests of religion. Agobard's view of it was confirmed by the distrust he felt in the emperor's advisers, and in the empress. But we have not here to do with his position as a leader in the revolt which attempted to place Lothar on his father's throne, [x] instructive as it may be as illustrating Agobard's application to the field of politics of that clear perception of right and wrong, that fearless and unswerving adherence to his beliefs, that we have found elsewhere.[32]

[x] cf. Reuter I. 36.

[31] The chief rabbi of the synagogue of Narbonne asserted that Charles had granted him this dignity; certainly a street in this place was named Rey Juif: G. B. Depping, Les Juifs dans le Moyen Âge 110, 1845.

[32] I am not sure that we can affirm, with Noorden, pp. 38 sq., that Agobard's preference for the power of the ecclesiastical over the secular estate was caused by his conviction of the feebleness of Lewis's government. This may have decided him, but his moderation has not the tone of a convert: see for instance his letter to the emperor, De comparatione utriusque regiminis, ecclesiastici et politici, especially p. 315 E.

For his courage, as [y] Gfrörer notes, is even more astonishing than the freedom of his vision. In the light of ten centuries we may think his arguments truisms and wonder at the pains he took to demonstrate what seems to us to need no demonstration, to expose what is unworthy of exposure. But the fact remains that he stood absolutely alone in his generation, with the single exception of Claudius of Turin; and Claudius's interest was limited to a single branch of superstition, while Agobard undertook the destruction of the whole.

[y] vol. 3. 753.

In both alike the influence of saint Augustin is paramount. It is, indeed, the continual interruption of long extracts from the fathers, and above all from Augustin, that too often defaces to our modern eyes the impression of lucidity and vigour which are the just attributes of Agobard's style. Whether or not in direct quotation the presence of the father's treatise *On true Religion* and of the *City of God* is seldom wanting. Doubtless Claudius and Agobard were here simply following the universal habit of the scholars of their day, with whom Augustin ranked second alone to the Bible; to contradict him, as Paschasius Radbert said, was impiety.[33] But there were few who accepted his spiritual force and left out of account his extravagance of fancy; there were few who chose only his good part and wrought it with such wisdom, as these two did. [z] While others in the generation immediately following heard only the appeal of his less worthy utterances, the incongruous children of his genius, and were led into the opposite extreme, superstition,[34] they used precisely those elements of his teaching which had a practical tendency. They found in him a beacon to shed light upon the deepening obscurity of the age, a weapon

[z] cf. Reuter 1. 41 sq.

[33] Augustinum quem contradicere fas non est: De partu virginis ii, in Luc d'Achery's Spicilegium sive Collectio veterum aliquot Scriptorum, 1. 51 a, ed. F. J. L. de la Barre, Paris 1723 folio.

[34] The curious treatises of Paschasius Radbert and Ratramnus relating to the manner of Christ's birth will be found in d'Achery, ubi supra, pp. 44 sqq., 52 sqq. Paschasius addressed his disquisition to the matron and virgins of the convent of Vesona in the diocese of Périgord.

to assail and overthrow its resistance to vital religion; and with this they were content. To enquire deeper into their master's thoughts, to speculate upon the mysteries of being and of God, was foreign to their purpose.

Agobard does, indeed, once venture upon the field of controversy in theological metaphysics; he wrote a book against Felix of Urgel, the adoptian: but here, too, he is still the theologian, not a philosopher. He recites the testimonies of the fathers, but he cares not to add to them his independent criticism. His reticence was justified by the experience of the years after him, when the attempt was made to [a] accommodate the spiritual system of Augustin to the concrete doctrines of the church, and the amalgam proved the strangest product of that materialising age, the definition of the doctrine of transubstantiation. No innovation could have been better calculated to promote the decay of the moral individualism of Christianity, and the growth of a servile dependence upon the priestly order. It succeeded, not because it professed a conformity with saint Augustin, but because the age was tending towards intellectual degradation. When, however, some years later, Gottschalk, the medieval Jansen, revived from the same father an unconditional doctrine of predestination, the result was quite different. For this doctrine was as subversive as Claudius's puritanism of the newer theory of the church. A stimulus was given to controversy, but the issue was foregone. Latin Christianity had come to acquiesce in a belief which admitted God's predestination of the good, his foreknowledge only of the wicked; in the technical phrase of Calvinism, predestination but not reprobation. When Gottschalk affirmed both, the language of saint Augustin had to be explained away. It was impossible that his authority could support tenets which, it was seen, struck at the root of the power of the clergy, not only by the implied denial of the efficacy of the sacraments, but also of the value of human absolution. Augustin's unseasonable restorer appeared to be guilty of the most hopeless,

[a] cf. Reuter I. 43.

unpardonable heresy. It was discovered that his opinions included the most opposite errors, the denial of the freedom of man's will, and of the necessity of divine grace. CHAP. I.

Few disputes ever had a more accidental origin. Gottschalk, the son of a Saxon noble, was forced as a child into the monastery of Fulda. When he grew up he rebelled, and denied the obligation of his father's vow. A council at Mentz, to which he appealed against the authority of his superior, reversed the sentence. The powerful abbat, it was none less than Rabanus Maurus, brought the case before the emperor and won his cause. The youth was condemned for life to the rule of saint Benedict. But the high-spirited ambition of his birth was quickened, not quenched, by his bondage. The fame he would have made in the active life of a noble, he now sought in the adventurous paths of speculation. He removed to the monastery of Orbais near Soissons, and buried himself in saint Augustin. The theory he developed in this seclusion had a natural affinity with the morbid cravings, the vindictive passions, of a disappointed man. It assuaged his regrets for lost earthly prosperity by the confidence of eternal happiness hereafter. It gave him a weapon with which to assail his opponents: their reward was already decided for them. He pressed the certainty of their doom with fanatical violence. The controversy which followed is too purely theological, too unrelieved by any warmth of human sympathy, by any real sense of human needs, to detain us in its dark and weary progress.[35] It is of importance as introducing us to that astonishing thinker whose aid was rashly invoked against the monk of Orbais. The theological dispute was for a moment merged in the deep sea of philosophy: when it rose again the monk Gottschalk was forgotten; the voice of orthodoxy on all sides was directed against Johannes Scotus, the belated disciple of Plato, and the last representative of the Greek spirit in the west.

A.D. 829.

[35] The history here only glanced at is related in an admirably luminous chapter of Noorden's Hinkmar 51–100.

CHAPTER II.

JOHN SCOTUS.

CHAP. II.

A.D. 849.

THE dispute about predestination had long perplexed the Frankish world when Hincmar, the great archbishop of Rheims, applied to John Scotus[1] for help. Gottschalk had received his sentence from the council of Quierzy, and died after a long confinement in the monastery of Hautvilliers. But the controversy had failed, as controversies usually fail, to secure conviction to either side, and John gladly assumed that the fault lay in the incompetence of theology by itself to decide the profound questions involved. He began his book on the subject[2] by the announcement that true philosophy and true religion are identical; a solution of religious problems can only be effected by the aid of philosophy; and true philosophy rests on the basis of the unity of God. The oneness of his essence implies also a oneness of will, a will that can tend only towards good. To conceive a predestination to evil is to conceive a duality, a contradiction, in the divine nature. But predestination of any sort can only be

[1] The biography of John Scotus, which resolves itself mainly into a criticism of scanty and conflicting materials, was first attempted by F. A. Staudenmaier, a catholic professor at Giessen, whose Johannes Scotus Erigena und die Wissenschaft seiner Zeit, Frankfort 1834, was left unfinished. Its biographical conclusions are for the most part reproduced in the Leben und Lehre des Joh. Scotus Erigena, Gotha 1860, of Dr. Theodor Christlieb, of Bonn. A more sceptical criticism is applied, in the biography, Johannes Scotus Erigena, Munich 1861, by Dr. Johannes Huber, well known for his spirited action in connexion with the oecumenical council of 1869–1870. [See also my article in the Dictionary of National Biography, 51 (1897) 115-120.]

[2] Of the tract De praedestinatione, to which I had not access when I wrote the present chapter, Huber has given an elaborate analysis in his work cited above, 60–92. See also the summary in F. C. Baur's posthumous Christliche Kirche des Mittelalters 50–55, Tübingen 1861; and Gfrörer, Kirchengeschichte 3. 867 sqq.

improperly asserted of God, since he is independent of time. If we connect it with any notion of necessity it cannot be asserted of him at all; since his will is absolute freedom; and man, as the highest image of God, possesses this same entire freedom of will, which he can use as he pleases for good or evil. There remains but one sense in which we can speak of God's predestination; that is, his permission of what happens in the creature by reason of his free will. He suffers this freedom of will, but when it moves to evil he knows it not; for God is ignorant of evil. If he knew it he would be the cause of it: we cannot separate his knowledge from his will, which *is* cause. For God, therefore, evil exists not; it has no cause, it is simply the negation of good. Sin, therefore, and its punishment come not from God. Every misdeed bears its punishment in itself, in the consciousness of lacking good. The eternal fire is a necessary part of God's universe. The righteous will rejoice in it; the wicked suffer, because they are wicked, just as (he quotes the simile from the *Confessions* of Augustin) the sunlight hurts the weak while it is harmless to sound eyes. The order of the world sets a limit within which each creature moves and which it cannot overpass. It sets a bound to the possibility of wickedness, but for which the wicked would fall into that nothingness which is the nature of evil. In this sense alone is punishment fore-ordained, *that wickedness be not able to extend itself, as it would, into the infinite.*

These are some of the arguments which the Scot brings against the contention of Gottschalk. We see at once their startling character. They were no doubt entirely unadapted to their purpose; it was no doubt vain to argue on philosophical grounds with men who relied exclusively on theology and on a one-sided selection of 'scriptural proofs.' But it is on this very account that the reasoning is memorable. There is nothing in it of the commonplaces of controversy or of theology. It has a terminology of its own. Outwardly, indeed, John Scotus appeals, like his opponents, to the Bible, to Augustin, to

CHAP. II.

the common church tradition. But these strains are actually those which give colour to a web of thought quite different in texture. Its material, indeed, is only partly Christian,—and this, as we find it in his matured system, is drawn from the Greek fathers, Origen, Basil, Gregory of Nazianzus, and Gregory of Nyssa, more than from the Latins,—but most of all it comes from the heterogeneous manufacture of the latest Neo-Platonists, the men who sought to combine a religion which failed to satisfy the speculative instinct with the noblest philosophy of which they had information. The result was in any case a medley—'the spurious birth,' it has been [a] called, 'of a marriage between philosophy and tradition, between Hellas and the East'—but the attempt was so plausible, so enticing, that it has never wanted defenders from the beginnings of Christianity, from Justin Martyr, Clement of Alexandria, and Origen, to our own time.

[a] Jowett, Dial. of Plato 3. 524, ed. 2, Oxford 1875.

Among these Johannes Scotus, called Ierugena or Erigena,[3] is a figure unique not so much for the originality of his views as for the confidence with which he discovered them latent in Christianity. He is unrestrained by the habits of thought of his own age, in which he appears as a meteor, none knew whence. The mystery which surrounds him is appropriate for his solitary person. From the schools of Ireland he drifted, some time before the year 847, to the court of Charles the Bald, [b] like those former 'merchants of wisdom' with whom tradition

[b] supra, pp. 14 sq.

[3] As for the name the following facts may be accepted as ascertained: (1) he was known to contemporaries as Ioannes Scottus, Scotus, or Scotigena; (2) in his translation of Dionysius, and there only, he designates himself Ioannes Ierugena; (3) Ierugena is the oldest form that appears in the manuscripts, but it soon alternates with Erugena (in a copy of the beginning of the eleventh century, Saint John's college, Oxford, cod. cxxviii) and Eriugena; (4) Erigena does not make its appearance until later, while (5) the combination of the three names cannot be traced before the sixteenth century. See Christlieb 15 sq. On its meaning it is difficult to form a decided opinion. Probably it is derived from Erin or Ierne and modulated so as to suggest ἱερός. In any case Gale's notion (Testimonia, prefixed to his edition of the De divisione naturae, p. 8) that its bearer came from Eriuven or Ergene in the Welsh marches is to be rejected.

afterwards associated him. The [c] welcome he won from that liberal-minded prince and their intimate comradeship, the gaiety and sprightly humour of the Irish sage, his removal to England after Charles's death, and his new career as a teacher under the auspices of king Alfred, finally his murder at Malmesbury; [d] all these things are recounted by later annalists. His own time knows only that he was 'a holy man' who came from Ireland and had received no ecclesiastical orders.[4]

[c] Will. Malmesb. gest. pontif. v. 240 pp. 392 sq., ed. Hamilton.

[d] v. infra, p. 52: cf. append. i.

The king's regard for the sage, which we know also from John's poems and dedications, has its evidence in his employment in the palace school, but the story that this school was regularly established at Paris is a legend of a much later time.[5] Yet although the town on the Seine was by no means the ordinary seat of government, it was a favourite and not infrequent residence of the king—he was not yet emperor—whose capital lay at Compiègne or Laon. It owed its popularity at first no doubt to its neighbourhood to the abbey of Saint Denis, whose fame had attracted thither the dying Pippin and made his great-grandson Charles choose it for the burial-place of his house;[6]

[4] His birth is ironically touched on by an opponent, Prudentius of Troyes, 'Te solum omnium acutissimum Galliae transmisit Hibernia,' De Praedest. contra Io. Scot. xiv Max. Biblioth. Patr. 15. 534 E; 1677. [He describes him as 'nullis ecclesiasticae dignitatis gradibus insignitum,' iii. p. 479 E.] John's character appears from a letter of Anastasius the librarian, 'Ioannem . . . Scotigenam, virum quem auditu comperi per omnia sanctum,' Ussher, Epist. Syllog. 65.

[5] The statement is founded on a letter of pope Nicholas the First in which he calls for John's removal from Paris 'in studio cuius capital iam olim fuisse perhibetur,' ap. C. E. du Boulay, Hist. Univ. Paris. 1. 184, Paris 1665 folio. But this passage in the papal letter is not found in the recognised copies, e.g. Mansi, Concil. 15. 401 C; and du Boulay, p. 183, admits that he took it from the collectanea of Naudé. There is no doubt that it is merely one of those fictions invented for the glorification of the antiquity of the university of Paris, just as a later incident in John Scotus's life has been applied to that of the university of Oxford. Cf. Léon Maitre, Écoles épiscopales et monastiques 45, Le Mans 1866. [The words cited from pope Nicholas's letter are 'obviously interpolated.' See H. Rashdall, The Universities of Europe in the Middle Ages, 1. 273 n. 2, 1895; and L. Traube, Poetae Latini Aevi Carolini, 3. 519 n. 5 1896.]

[6] Mr. E. A. Freeman has well told the history of the revival of Paris in the ninth century: see his essay on The early Sieges of Paris, Historical Essays, 1st series, viii.

and it was possibly this same connexion which gave the Irish scholar the first opportunity for making his value felt. The belief that the foundation dated from the Areopagite Dionysius, the earliest Athenian convert of saint Paul, was at this time universally held; there was as yet no Abailard to contest it. The renown of the abbey added dignity to its supposed author; and when writings ascribed to him with an equal credulity, were brought into the west,[7] their purport aroused a natural curiosity, if only a translator could be found to reveal their treasures. Now Greek letters had never wholly died out in the Irish schools,[8] and John had skill enough to furnish the required version. How far the expectations of the votaries of saint Denis were satisfied by the work, we do not know. Perhaps the obscurity of the translation limited the number of its readers; at any rate it does not appear to have excited much attention. When [e] pope Nicholas the First objected to it and wrote to Charles the Bald demanding that the philosopher's work should be sent to him for correction, it was really not so much from suspicion of its contents [9] as from [f] hostility, in presence of an angry dispute between the churches, against anything Greek.

[e] v. supra, p. 49, n. 5.

[f] v. Ritter, Geschichte der christl. Philos. 3. 208 & n. 1, Hamburg 1844.

But the influence of the books upon the mind of the translator was momentous. The *Timaeus* of Plato he probably knew through the version of Chalcidius already; but now the bold forgery claiming the name of the Areopagite, which won currency in the sixth century, [g] though the actual date of its writing may be a little earlier, placed him in possession of a metaphysical system ostensibly founded upon works of Plato which were unknown to western Christendom, and elaborated with a speculative

[g] cf. Baur, Die christliche Lehre von der Dreieinigkeit und Menschwerdung Gottes 2. 205, n. 1, Tübingen 1842.

[7] It seems that before the present of the Byzantine Michael the Stammerer to Lewis the Pious in 827, Staudenmaier 1. 162 and n. 2, works attributed to Dionysius had already made their way westward. Such were sent by pope Paul the First to Pippin in 757 and by Hadrian the First to abbat Fuldrad of Saint Denis some years later: Gfrörer 3. 865.

[8] Compare a letter of Benedict of Aniane, the councillor of Lewis the Pious, in Baluze, Miscellanea 2. 97 b, ed. Mansi, Lucca 1761 folio.

[9] What suspicion there was, was probably inferred from the Scot's notoriety in the controversy about predestination.

fearlessness equally foreign to its spirit. Another Greek writer, the monothelete monk Maximus, supplemented the Scot's knowledge of the ultimate forms of Neo-Platonism, and from him too he translated a commentary on Saint Gregory which was likewise destined for the royal study. It should be remarked in passing that John, unlike the men to whom our attention has hitherto been given, addressed himself to a very select company; it might be to the king, whose intellectual sympathies were inherited from his father and grandfather, or it might be to his own hearers in the palace school. Twice only did he emerge into public view, and the estrangement, the public condemnation, which his utterances then on the subject of predestination [10] and of the nature of the Eucharist [11] provoked may have naturally confirmed his previous reserve. Of his further life little certain is recorded. He appears to have been in France in the year of the emperor's death.[12] The following year saw peace reëstablished in England, and [h] it is

CHAP. II.

A.D. 877.

[h] v. infra, append. ii.

[10] His predestination tract was twice condemned by church councils, at Valence in 855 and at Langres some years later. See Huber 97 sq. and the notes. To the former was due the contemptuous description of John's arguments as 'ineptas quaestiunculas et aniles pene fabulas, Scotorumque pultes' (Scots' porridge): cap. vi. Mansi, Conc. 15. 6 D.

[11] That John took part in the controversy raised by Paschasius Radbert is certainly to be inferred from the title of the work of Adrevald, De corpore et sanguine Christi contra ineptias Ioannis Scoti, printed in d'Achery, Spicilegium 1. 150 sqq.; ed. 1723. The conclusion is not invalidated but confirmed by the fact that in after years the book of Ratramnus on the subject was attributed to the Scot. It was known that he had written a treatise, and therefore the only appropriate treatise that came to hand was fathered upon him. This obvious argument seems to have escaped nearly all the modern writers who decide the point in the negative. The penetration of Noorden has further discerned certain peculiarities in the views ascribed by contemporaries to John Scotus which are inapplicable to Ratramnus: see his Hinkmar Erzbischof von Rheims 103, n. 2.

[12] This is inferred from a poem in which John commemorates the foundation of a church dedicated to the Virgin, which from several points of correspondence is believed to be that at Compiègne which Charles began in 877 on the model of his grandfather's church at Aix-la-Chapelle. As however the actual building was delayed by the emperor's death John seems to describe not what was really existing but the plan on which it was to be built. See the quotation in Huber 120 n.

CHAP. II.

difficult to resist a tradition which held currency throughout the middle ages that he sought retreat here when his old protector was taken away from him, and that his fervour of teaching was only closed when his scholars fell upon him and slew him. The monument that commemorated the *holy sophist* was soon destroyed, but repeated orders from pope or council have not succeeded in obliterating his truest memorial which remains to us in his writings, above all in the great work *On the Division of Nature*.[13] From this last we may, without attempting even in outline to portray his whole system, collect enough of its features to shew what a revelation he made of the dignity of the order of the universe; however much mixed with crude or fantastic ideas, however often clouded in obscurity, yet full of suggestion, full of interest everywhere.[14]

His reflexions upon the subject of predestination led John Scotus, as we have already seen, to trace his theory of the nature of sin. Augustin[15] and even Athanasius had been led to a similar explanation of the appearance of evil in the world, but how differently had they ap-

[13] Its proper title is Greek, Περὶ φύσεων μερισμοῦ. The editio princeps, which is far better reputed than Schrüter's reprint of 1838, was published by Thomas Gale (as appears from the appendix, p. 46), Oxford 1681 folio, whose pages I have added to my references to the work. In writing the present chapter I had not access to the edition by H. J. Floss, which forms the hundred and twenty-second volume of Migne's Cursus, and includes the rest of the Scot's works, namely (1) the translations of Dionysius and Maximus and the expositions on the former, (2) the tract on predestination, (3) a commentary and homilies on the gospel of saint John, (4) verses, and (5) a fragment on the procession and recession of the soul to God. The catalogue of lost works printed in the Testimonia prefixed to Gale's edition is not very critically compiled; it is corrected with various success by the biographers.

[14] The most profound exposition of the Scot's system with which I am acquainted is given by Baur, Lehre von der Dreieinigkeit 2. 263–344. Baur is especially complete in his analysis of John's relation to his Greek predecessors. I am also under obligations to the general works of Ritter 3. 209–296 and Gfrörer 3. 922–937. Of the biographers Huber is the most philosophical, while Christlieb loses himself in far-fetched speculations as to John's affinities to modern philosophy.

[15] Peccatum quidem non per ipsum factum est: et manifestum est, quia peccatum nihil est et nihil fiunt homines cum peccant: Tract. i in Ioh. evang., Opp. 3 (2) 294 c, ed. Bened., Paris 1689 folio.

plied it. With them it is found compatible with a belief in the eternity of punishment; to John it means that since all things proceed from good so in good they must all be one day absorbed. To this consummation he loves to apply the text, *Ero mors tua, O mors; morsus tuus ero, inferne.*[16] [i] To find the cause of sin in God's work he pronounces to be blasphemous.[17] [k] Sin, he repeats, has no cause because it has no real existence. How then does it arise? The answer is given in various forms which converge upon the central thought that sin is implied in the fact of man's free will. He takes the case of two men looking at a golden vase. There is no evil in the vase, but it may excite in the one feelings only of pleasure and admiration, in the other the passion of covetousness. The one receives the simple impression of a beautiful object; the other colours and deforms it by his own lawless desire. But this desire, this evil, is not indigenous to man's nature; it is the result of the irregular action of his reasonable and free will.[18] The senses are deceived by that which appears to be good, by *false good*, and the infection spreads inwardly to the intellect itself. [l] Thus the inner man wherein naturally *dwelleth truth and all good, which is the Word of God, the only-begotten Son of God*, becomes corrupt and *sins*. But this process does not originate in evil. The bodily sense does not desire a thing because it is evil but because it has the show of goodness. [m] *No vice is found but is the shadow of some virtue.*[19] Pride for instance is a perversion

CHAP. II.

[i] De div. nat. v. 36 p. 283.
[k] lib. iv. 16, v. 36 pp. 205 sq., 287: cf. August. de lib. arb. ii. 20 § 54, Opp. I. 608 F sq.

[l] lib. iv. 16 p. 205.

[m] lib. i. 68 p. 38.

[16] Hosea xiii. 14 in the Vulgate: the Hebrew has an important difference of meaning.

[17] Cf. 'Deus itaque malum nescit; nam si malum sciret, necessario in natura rerum malum esset. Divina siquidem scientia, omnium quae sunt causa est; . . . ac per hoc si Deus malum sciret, in aliquo substantialiter intelligeretur, et particeps boni malum esset, et ex virtute et bonitate vitium et malitia procederent: quod impossibile esse vera edocet ratio:' De divis. nat. ii. 29 p. 84. See above p. 47 and compare De div. nat. v. 27 p. 259.

[18] Non ergo in natura humana plantatum est malum, sed in perverso et irrationabili motu rationabilis liberaeque voluntatis est constitutum: ib. iv. 16 p. 206, cf. v. 36 p. 287.

[19] He adds 'by some fallacious likeness or contrariety,' giving however of the 'contrariety' the single instance 'as evil to good.' This can only be explained on the assumption that in his first book John was unwilling to force too

CHAP. II.

of a true sense of power—in good men it takes the form of a love of heavenly excellence and of a contempt of earthly weakness;—and [n] it was from pride that the sin of man began. It was the first exercise of his free will.

[n] lib. v. 25 p. 255.

In applying these views to the interpretation of the first chapters of Genesis, our Scot has practically to supersede its historical meaning by the allegorical. He explains any difficulties that he encounters in the narrative by the theory that it is accommodated to our lower understanding. It expresses truth by figures. [o] The order of time for instance, he says, is so often violated in the Bible itself that there can be no objection to our ignoring it in our exposition. [p] Adam must have sinned before he was tempted by the devil; else he would not have been accessible to temptation. The events that are related to have taken place in Eden, that is in the ideal state, really happened on earth and were consequential on Adam's sin. [q] *For if paradise is human nature formed after the image of God and made equal to the blessedness of the angels, then immediately he wished to leave his Creator, he fell from the dignity of his nature. His pride began before he consented to his wife.* By this act man came into the domain of time and space; [r] hence arose the physical distinctions of sex [20] and the rest of his bodily conditions, no less than the diversities of manners and thought that divide the human race. That which was single became manifold. We thus reach the ultimate result of the philosopher's conception of evil. [s] Sin is contemporaneous with the existence of the human body. [t] It marks the transition

[o] lib. iv. 20 p. 211.

[p] cap. 15 p. 197.

[q] ibid.; cf. v. 1 p. 224.

[r] lib. ii. 6, 7 p. 49.

[s] lib. ii. 9, iv. 10 pp. 51, 181.

[t] cf. Gfrörer 3. 929.

many novel thoughts upon the reader. The theory of evil waits for its complete development until the fourth book. As yet he is content to speak of evil in a general way as though it actually existed. The contradictions of his work have been exaggerated by critics and seldom fail to resolve themselves on a closer scrutiny.

[20] Baur, 2. 302, considers that the Scot held this separation of sex as 'the most important consequence of the fall.' I am inclined rather to think that he chose it as the most speaking example, the simplest way of denoting the material man. Who after Augustin could avoid regarding sex as the distinctive corporeal fact in man's nature? Compare on this salient principle of Augustin, Milman, Latin Christianity I. 151.

from the ideal to the actual, from the world of thought to the world of matter.

John's skill in fitting this theory within the framework of accepted doctrine cannot disguise its essential contrariety. He supplants the dark dogma of the natural corruption of man, his original destiny to perdition, by the conception of the negative character of evil. [u] It is, he would say with Plato, as little natural as the diseases of the body: it is the inevitable result of the union of flesh and spirit. But the primal dignity of man's nature must in the end reässert its sway. [x] *The soul may forget her natural goods, may fail in her striving towards the goal of the inborn virtues of her nature; the natural powers may move, by fault of judgement, towards something which is not their end*: but not for ever. For the universal tendency of things is upward; [y] *and thus from evil is wont to turn good, but in nowise from good evil. . . . The first evil could not be perpetual, but by the necessity of things must reach a certain bound and one day vanish. For if the divine goodness which ever worketh not only in the good but also in the wicked, is eternal and infinite, it follows that its contrary will not be eternal and infinite. . . . Evil therefore will have its consummation and remain not in any nature, since in all the divine nature will work and be manifest. Our nature then is not fixed in evil; . . . it is ever moving, and seeks nought else but the highest good, from which as from a beginning its motion takes its source, and to which it is hastened as to an end.* As all things proceed from God, so in God they find their final completion. He is the end of things, the last of the four forms of nature which make the foundation of the Scot's system.

This fourfold division is absolutely John's own property and discoverable [z] elsewhere only in the Indian doctrine of the Sankhya: '[a] in the simplicity of his general plan,' it has been truly said, 'he surpasses all the philosophers of the middle ages.' The scheme breaks into two by the distinction of creator and created. The first and fourth forms are the [b] two aspects of the uncreated

[u] De div. nat. ii. 5 p. 49; cf. Plat. Tim. p. 86.

[x] De div. nat. v. 26 p. 256.

[y] cap. 25 pp. 254 sqq.

[z] H. T. Colebrooke, On the Philos. of the Hindus, in Misc. Essays, 2. 256, ed. 1873.

[a] Ritter 3. 211 cf. p. 294, n. 1

[b] De div. nat. ii. 2 p. 46.

CHAP. II.

unity, according as we consider it as the beginning or as the end of things. The one creates: the other creates not, it is the [c] *rest* for which nature strives and which consists in the restoration of things to their original unity. Between these terms lie the two forms of created things. They have the same division as the other two. The second creates: the third creates not. The one is the world of ideas, the pattern upon which the other, the sensible universe, is made. It contains the abstractions: [d] goodness—the first of things,—essence, life, wisdom, truth, intellect, reason, virtue, justice, health, greatness, omnipotence, eternity, peace, and all the virtues and reasons which the Father created once for all in his Son, and according to which the order of all things is framed, each considered by itself and apart from sensible objects. These are the primordial causes of things, the [e] effects of which are manifested in time and place in the third form of nature. But it is impossible to keep the effects apart from the causes; [f] they are involved in them, and with them eternal, though not eternal as God; for [g] eternity, like every other attribute, can only be predicated of him in an improper sense, he is more than eternal. [h] Place and time exist not with him: he has nothing accidental, cause and effect with him are one. Therefore the [i] universe, as his creation, is eternal: *non erat quando non erant.* In such fashion this clear-sighted idealist represented the accepted belief, according to which creation is bringing into being in the sense of bringing into the sensible world: his opinion was perhaps an inevitable deduction from the premises of formal Platonism, and something very like it was [k] maintained by so correct a theologian as saint Anselm. To John Scotus thought is the only real being, and, philosophically speaking, [l] body has no existence except as dependent on thought.[21] But he chooses to express

[c] cf. lib. iii. 10 p. 111.
[d] lib. ii. 36 p. 94.
[e] lib. i. 1, ii. 2 pp. 1, 47.
[f] lib. iii. 5, 6 pp. 105 sq.
[g] lib. i. 16 p. 10.
[h] cap. 23 p. 15.
[i] lib. iii. 8, 15 p. 106, 119.
[k] Monolog. ix. p. 7 D, E, ed. 2. G. Gerberon., Paris 1721 folio.
[l] De div. nat. i. 6, 35 pp. 3, 20.

[21] It has often been remarked that John has in plain terms the argument of Descartes: 'When I say *I understand that I am,* I prove that I am, that I can understand that I am, and that I do understand that I am;' Dum ergo dico, *Intelligo me esse,* nonne in hoc

truth by alternate affirmation and negation, confirmatory when they appear most contradictory to one another; and so he couples with the assertion that there was no time when the universe was not, the contrary assertion that there was a time when it was not. In a sense that transcends intelligence it exists eternally; in another sense [m] it began to be when it passed into the sphere of time and place. The meaning is in strict correspondence with that which we have found in John's theory of evil. Evil arises by the passage from the spiritual to the material: objective creation by the passage from the eternal to the temporal. Good in the one argument, eternity in the other, is the positive element in the universal system; [n] matter is the mere *concourse of the accidents of being.*

CHAP. II.

[m] lib. iii. 15 p. 119.

[n] lib. i. 62 p. 34.

Such is John Scotus's world. To him as to [o] Plato its goodness is its essential significance: it begins and ends with thought, with pure being, with God. He fills in the outline with a confidence, a certainty, of the truth of his speculations. Yet, as though half conscious of their strangeness to the understanding of his age, he is ever anxious to prove that he is continuing, not breaking off from, the line of thought sanctioned by the greatest of the fathers and by the Bible itself. Authority is still a power with him, but limited, expanded, refined. The [p] name of the fathers, of Augustin himself, cannot deter him from forming his own conclusions on any subject. [q] Even the Bible, though necessarily containing nothing but truth, presents that truth with so much accommodation to the bodily senses that it is the [r] duty of the philosopher to endeavour to penetrate beneath its metaphors and bring forth the substance that underlies them. For

[o] Timaeus 29 sq.

[p] De div. nat. iv. 14, v. 37 pp. 192 sq., 296.

[q] lib. i. 66 p. 37.

[r] lib. iii. 30 p. 140.

uno verbo, quod est *intelligo*, tria significo a se inseparabilia? nam et me esse, et posse intelligere me esse, et intelligere me esse, demonstro. Num vides verbo uno et meam οὐσίαν, meamque virtutem, et actionem significari? De divis. nat. i. 50 p. 27. Saint Augustin's statement of the syllogism, though less clearly expressed, appears to me to be virtually identical with John's; so that the latter will hardly deserve the distinction claimed for it by M. Hauréau, Histoire de la Philosophie scolastique I. 183 sq.

CHAP. II.

its sense is infinite, because it is the reflexion of the divine reason; but reason stands above it, is man's sure guide in interpreting the written message of revelation. [s] If the authority be true, neither can contradict the other, since both proceed from the same source, namely from the divine wisdom. To appreciate this position we must remember that its object was in no wise to lower the dignity of the Bible, but solely to elevate the conception of the human understanding. Nor was it a new or unheard-of thing. Fredegisus, Alcuin's scholar at York and his successor in the abbacy of Saint Martin at Tours, had made a very similar statement of the relation of reason to authority, and he had felt it compatible with the most literal view of inspiration.[22] Neither he nor the Scot had any doubt of the irrefragable truth of the Bible. But while Fredegisus found it in the literal sense, John sought for the larger meaning concealed within its depths. [t] *For the sense of the divine utterances is manifold and infinite, even as in one and the same feather of the peacock we behold a marvellous and beautiful variety of countless colours.* Like principles, as one applied them, might lead to a submissive dependence on the letter, or to amplest freedom of rational enquiry. [u] For in the one writer, reason without the support of authority is weak, in the other it stands firm [x] *fortified by its own virtues, and needs not to be strengthened by any prop of authority.*

[s] lib. i. 68 p. 38.

[t] lib. iv. 5 p. 164.

[u] v. Reuter 1. 40 sq.

[x] De div. nat. i. 71 p. 39.

If we examine more closely the Scot's view of reason it appears that authority is actually related to it as a species to its genus. In both God reveals not himself but the forms in which we can conceive him. The [y] human reason is the dwelling-place of the word of God. This manifestation, this *theophany* (John's technical name for God's revelation to man), is coëxtensive with the reign of reason and therefore, since reason is every-

[y] lib. iv. 16 p. 205

[22] See above pp. 40 sq. The correspondence is plain if we accept the emendation of the place in Fredegisus proposed by Dr Reuter, Geschichte der religiösen Aufklärung im Mittelalter 1. 274 n. 21: 'primum ratione, in quantum hominis ratio patitur, deinde auctoritate, non qualibet sed rationali (*edit.* ratione) duntaxat.'

thing, it is universally diffused. [z] It is *the cause and substance of all virtues,* [a] it is a stream that runs through all nature. [b] *Intellect . . . and the rest of things that are said to be, are theophanies, and in theophany really subsist; therefore God is everything that truly is, since he makes all things and is made in all things.* The pantheism of the last sentence must be interpreted by John's view of God as apart from nature, a view as important in his system as that of revelation. It is [c] impossible for any one who fairly weighs his opinions on this subject not to feel that the charge of pantheism has been premature and warranted only by one set of statements, contradicted and at the same time justified by another set no less necessary to the complete understanding of his doctrine. If the reconciliation appear paradoxical we have but to remember that paradox in the philosopher's view is inevitable when we attempt to conceive the eternal.

[z] lib. i. 9 p. 5.
[a] lib. iii. 12, 18 pp. 117, 126.
[b] cap. 4 pp. 103 sq.
[c] cf. Ritter 3. 242, 286.

The statement that God is everything stands in juxtaposition to the statement that God is the supreme unity. The one bears relation to the world, the other to God himself. The latter is therefore the only strict mode of expression. The central thought of John Scotus's system is that God's being is absolute, it cannot be described by any of the categories to which creation is subject; for he transcends them all. [d] We cannot without a misuse of language affirm of him essence, quantity or quality, relation, position, or habit, place or time, action or passion. For to affirm these or any of these of God is to limit the illimitable: they are only applicable by way of accommodation to our earthly understanding, they have a literal meaning to the simple, [e] to the philosopher they are figures of speech. The rule is stated universally, and can admit no exception [f] even in the theological relation of Father and Son. His honesty forbade our philosopher to ignore a difficult consequence of his position, even when it seemed to oppose a cardinal point of piety. [g] He is indeed reluctant to dwell upon the subject, but not from any mistrust of his own

[d] De div. nat. i. 17 p. 12.
[e] capp. 69, 75 pp. 38 sq., 42; cf. Reuter 1. 60 sq.
[f] De div. nat. i. 18 p. 13.
[g] capp. 14, 18 pp. 8 sq., 13.

CHAP. II.

[h] capp. 14, 16, 78 pp. 9, 11, 44; cf. Baur, Lehre von der Dreieinigkeit, 2. 274 sqq.
[i] De div. nat. i. 14 p. 8.

conclusions. The truth lay, he felt, in a double form: we can only express our thoughts about God by contradictions; [h] we affirm and deny the same things of him, and so aim at a higher harmony in which the contradictions of our human understanding are reconciled. For the mystery of the divine Trinity [i] *passes the endeavours of human reason and even the purest understandings of celestial essences. We infer from the essence of the things that are, that it exists; from the wonderful order of things, that it is wise; from their motion, that it is life. As, saith saint Dionysius the Areopagite, 'The highest and causal essence of all things cannot be signified by any signification of words or names, or of any articulate voice.' For it is neither unity nor trinity, such as can be contemplated by the purest human, by the clearest angelical, understanding*[23]. . . . *Chiefly for the sake of those who demand a reason for the Christian faith . . . have these symbolical words been religiously discovered and handed down by the holy theologians. . . . Beholding, in so far as they were enlightened by the divine Spirit, the one unspeakable cause of all things, and the one beginning, simple and undivided and universal, they called it Unity; but seeing this unity not in singleness or barrenness, but in a marvellous and fertile multiplicity, they have understood three substances of unity.*

[k] lib. ii. 23 p. 70.
[l] lib. iii. 20 p. 128.
[m] lib. ii. 9 p. 51.
[n] lib. iv. 7 p. 171
[o] lib. ii. 5 p. 49.

John Scotus traces this trinity in unity in the nature of the universe,—[k] in the Creator, the idea, and the fact of things; in another aspect, in οὐσία, δύναμις, and ἐνέργεια,—and in its final resolution into unity. He traces also its reflexion in man, [l] in reason, understanding, and sense. For [m] man is the summing up of nature: [n] he has both a heavenly being and a sensible being, [o] combines the highest and the lowest elements. He is the meeting-point between creation and Creator, and this meeting is summed up in the two-fold nature of Christ. As all nature is contained in man, so all humanity is contained in the Word

[23] He repeats this almost in the same words in chapter 35 of the second book, p. 93, adding 'quaecunque de simplicissimae bonitatis trinitate dicuntur seu cogitantur seu intelliguntur, vestigia quaedam sunt atque theophaniae veritatis.'

of God.[24] When we speak of the incarnation, we do not mean an individual, historical fact, but [p] the eternal connexion of the ideal and actual. Cause and effect, as has already appeared, cannot be separated in God; they are implied in his single creative will. This union is revealed in the incarnation, by which [q] the Word of God passed from the region of cause to that of effects, and descended into the sensible world. It was not a temporal act, but the expression of the necessary reciprocity of temporal and eternal, the immanent relation of God and the world. It is the supreme theophany. [r] By it *the light to which no man can approach opened access to every intellectual and reasonable creature. . . . In Him the visible things and the invisible, that is to say, the world of sense and the world of thought, were restored and recalled to unspeakable unity, now in hope, hereafter in fact; now in faith, hereafter in sight; now by inference, hereafter in experience; already effected in the manhood which he assumed, hereafter to be fulfilled in all men without distinction.*

CHAP. II.

[p] v. Baur 2. 307 sqq.

[q] De div. nat. v. 25 p. 252.

[r] ibid. p. 253.

This restoration of the world is the great subject of the Scot's fifth book. The fourth *division* of nature is its return to primal unity. The body of man is restored to the elements; these elements coalesce in the resurrection into a new body; and this turns to spirit, the spirit reverts to its original causes, the causes to God. [s] *For God shall be all things in all things, when there shall be nothing but God alone.* Is this restoration asserted of man alone or also of his brother animals? of the good or also of the evil? finally, of the individual or only of the race? To these three questions John has his answer. The first gives him no difficulty. Immortality holds good not only of man, but of the whole animated creation. He will conclude this on *a priori* grounds: the lower animals have their 'natural virtues,' [25] they have souls, albeit irrational. But the decisive argument is that man is simply

[s] cap. 8 p. 232.

[24] Christ therefore united all the elements of humanity, of creation: he was not 'vir' but 'homo.' Cf. lib. ii. 6 p. 40.

[25] See the curious instances of the memory and the chastity of animals, and of the piety of storks, lib. iii. 41 p. 158.

CHAP. II.

a species of the animal kingdom, and that if the genus perish, the species must perish with it. The immortality of man is the warrant for the immortality of the whole creation. All nature will return to its first causes.

The question about the survival of evil is more embarrassing, and it cannot be concealed that the Scot does in some places seem to affirm something like a relique of the doctrine of eternal damnation. But in the first place this doctrine is much less plainly declared in the books of *The Division of Nature* than in the treatise *On Predestination;* and the latter is an occasional work, written for a special purpose and hampered by its conditions; the former is the representative book of the philosopher's life. In the second place, when a man makes use of conventional language and also of expressions entirely opposed to it and strikingly original, we cannot hesitate as to which is the genuine utterance of his own opinion: and [t] the declaration that eternal torment is totally incompatible with the truth that the whole world is set free by the incarnation of the divine Word, is made in distinct terms and closely interwoven with the fabric of John Scotus's reasoning. An eternity of suffering and evil is irreconcilable with an eternity of *goodness and life and blessedness.* There is no room for it in his system. He files away its edges and rounds off its corners until its orthodox shape has disappeared. [u] First he denounces the 'irrational' folly of trying to combine a sensible hell with a spiritual existence: the punishment of the wicked must stand solely in their memory of past wrong. New evil cannot arise then; they will be pained by the phantasies of their old misdeeds. But, proceeds John, though they be deprived of blessedness, something will yet remain to them: [x] the 'natural goods' in which they were created cannot be taken away. Doubtless all gifts are made in proportion to man's capacity of receiving; but the philosopher is sure that this capacity can and will grow and develop until evil is all swallowed up in good. [y] There may be degrees and stages in happi-

[t] cap. 27 pp. 257 & 260.

[u] capp. 28, 29, 31 pp. 264 sq., 272.

[x] cap. 38 p. 310.

[y] cap. 23 p. 248.

ness, in the progress toward perfection; but there is a certainty of the final victory of good. If it be otherwise, if there be a sensible world of torments, [z] *then have we laboured in vain, and the sentences of the holy writers which we have alleged will be turned into derision: which God forbid.* [z] cap. 28 p. 265.

The third question involved in John Scotus's view of the return of creation into the Creator concerns the immortality of the individual. He answers it by analogies. [a] The air is still air though it appear to be absorbed into the light of the sun and to be all light. *The voice of man, or of pipe or lyre, loses not its quality when several by just proportion make one harmony in unity among themselves.* Nor is it reasonable to suppose that man will subsist in a spiritual state without a body. [b] The body of our present humanity will disappear, but it will be exchanged for the spiritual body inseparable from the idea of man, the body which he had before he entered into the world of matter. [c] The whole man is eternal. *This therefore is the end of all things visible and invisible, when all visible things pass into the intellectual, and the intellectual into God, by a marvellous and unspeakable union; but not, as we have often said, by any confusion or destruction of essences or substances.* It is here, in the profoundest and the most original part of his scheme, that the Scot shows most evidently how impossible it would be for him to rest in a purely pantheistic belief. His nature forced him to hold that those virtues, that will, which make man the image of God upon earth, those qualities which exalt one man above his fellows, will not become perfect by 'remerging in the general soul.' Perfection implies their survival 'unconfounded and undestroyed.'

[a] cap. 8 p. 234.

[b] cap. 13 pp. 236 sq.

[c] cap. 20 p. 242

His entire conception of the recovery of all things, of a unity into which the trinity of nature is resolved, is certainly the most original feature in the system of the Irish thinker. In dividing up theology on a philosophical basis he achieved a greater discovery than he was perhaps conscious of. He discovered that the doctrine of

CHAP. II.

the church was not stationary but progressive; it was susceptible of development, of indefinite expansion. He discovered in Christianity the germs of all truth. Not only the idea of Christ but all those understood in dogmatic Christianity he applied and enlarged in such a manner that the result was rather a philosophy of religion, than a philosophy of Christianity: and thus to theology he contributed little that it could accept; to philosophy he added not a few of the salient ideas which we connect with the modern schools of metaphysics. His own views were doubtless buried with his writings: they were found out afresh by other men before their publication proved how they had been anticipated. Essentially his system would suffer little if we deducted from it all those Christian elements upon which he supposed it rested; we should find a philosophy in which the idea of God, the idea of evil, and many of its central features, resemble in a remarkable way the thoughts of Spinoza. Yet it would be as dishonest to regard these Christian elements as adventitious, as it would be to ignore the Hebrew antecedents of the great Dutch philosopher. They were necessary to the Scot because he lived in a tradition of Christian theology, because this was the framework in which his thoughts were trained to move and from which he could not wholly free himself. Nevertheless he advanced so far in the direction of giving new meanings to old phrases that he was, speaking generally, unintelligible to his age.

At the same time the fact of his appearance in the ninth century, the fact of his apparently unbroken favour at the imperial court, is a remarkable evidence of the liberal spirit which remained with the successors of Charles the Great. It is not as though John was kept at the royal school, just as a miracle of learning, in ignorance of what he actually taught. On the contrary, Charles the Bald had received from his mother the empress Judith, the friend of the Jews, the double elements of a complete education, wide learning and the scholar's instinct of openness to conviction. He was not a mere patron of scholars, he was their friend to whom they deferred on difficult points;[26] he liked to enter into disputation with them, laid down theses and invited them to discuss them without reserve. [d] As emperor he wished to appear a loyal son of the catholic church, but he refused to condemn opinions unless they were plainly shewn to be hostile to it, and he was generally discreet enough to hesitate about the proof and to hold his judgement free. The keenness of his intelligence conspired with a natural elasticity of temper to produce in his political action what certainly degenerated into an habitual irresolution and infirmity of purpose. But the vices of a statesman are often virtues in private life, and in this view Charles's indecision bears the character of a judicial tolerance, a tolerance to which his continued intercourse with John the Scot is a speaking witness; although it would be unsafe to infer from the scanty notices we have of their relation, that he shared with the philosopher more than a general sympathy with his spirit of free enquiry.

CHAP. II.

[d] cf. Reuter 1. 48 sqq.

John certainly had [e] disciples, but they cannot have been numerous. Among near contemporaries [f] Heric of Auxerre, and his pupil, saint Remigius, both teachers of great repute, may be proved to have been indebted

[e] Gfrörer 3. 873, Huber 50.

[f] see Hauréau, Hist. 1. 182–193, 201–204; & in the Not. ex Extr. des Manuscr. 20 (2) 5–20; 1862 quarto.

[26] Heric of Auxerre's epistle dedicatory to the emperor, prefixed to his Life of saint Germanus of Auxerre, shows us, in however exaggerated terms, what contemporaries thought of Charles as a patron of learning. Part of it is well-known (cf. supra p. 22), but a larger extract will not come amiss here: Id vobis singulare studium effecistis, ut sic ubi terrarum magistri florerent artium, quarum principalem operam philosophia pollicetur, hoc ad publicam eruditionem undecumque vestra celsitudo conduceret, comitas attraheret, dapsilitas provocaret. Luget hoc Graecia, novis invidiae aculeis lacessita, quam sui quondam incolae iam dudum cum Asianis opibus aspernantur, vestra potius magnanimitate delectati, studiis allecti, liberalitate confisi: dolet, inquam, se olim singulariter mirabilem ac mirabiliter singularem a suis destitui: dolet certe sua illa privilegia (quod numquam hactenus verita est) ad climata nostra transferri. Quid Hiberniam memorem, contempto pelagi discrimine, pene totam cum grege philosophorum ad littora nostra migrantem? Quorum quisquis peritior est ultro sibi indicit exilium; ut Salomoni sapientissimo famuletur ad votum: Actt. SS. mens. Iul. 7. 221 F sq., Antwerp 1731 folio. An admirable characterisation of the emperor is given by Noorden, Hinkmar 116 sqq.

CHAP. II.

for more than they cared to acknowledge, to the materials provided them in the works of the Scot. But in the dark age that followed, those writings seem to have been almost unknown. Early in the tenth century, indeed, we meet with an [g] extract from a poem apparently of John's composition, and a passage from the *Division of Nature* is cited in a theological treatise written a little later; [27] but in neither case is the source of the quotation indicated. Then, again, when the Scot's book *On the Body and Blood of Christ* obtained a sudden notoriety in the dispute raised by Berengar of Tours on the nature of the sacrament, the importance attached to his authority by the opponent of transubstantiation is valuable as evidence of the power that his name still possessed; but it is nearly certain that the [h] work to which Berengar appealed, and which was burnt by the council of Vercelli, was the production not of John but of his contemporary the monk Ratramnus. A solitary trace of John's influence may be found in the fact that, probably through some [i] glosses of his, the *Satyricon* of Martianus Capella soon came to take once more that recognised place in the schools which it had held centuries earlier in the dark days of [k] Gregory of Tours; but the acceptance of this meagre compendium only shews how incapable his heirs were of appreciating the treasure he had left them in his own works.[28]

[g] Invectiva in Romam, E. Dümmler, Auxilius und Vulgarius 46 n.; 1866.

[h] cf. supra, p. 51 n. 11. A.D. 1050.

[i] cf. Hauréau, Not. et Extr., ubi supra.

[k] Mullinger, Schools of Charles the Great 35, 65.

[27] In the tract De corpore et sanguine Domini commonly ascribed to Gerbert. See Carl von Prantl, Geschichte der Logik im Abendlande 2. 57 [58] n. 227; 1861: cf. Huber 434. Neither of these writers adverts to the doubt which hangs over the authorship of the book. See below p. 77 n. 12.

[28] It has been supposed that the book, of which the full title is De nuptiis Philologiae et Mercurii, a tasteless allegory descriptive of the seven liberal arts—was the exclusive possession of the Irish: cf. Haddan, Remains 273 sq., 280. In Alcuin the very name does not occur, and Mr Mullinger, pp. 64 sqq., 111, 118, has elaborated a theory of this writer's studied hostility to Martianus. Had however such a motive existed I feel confident that it would have appeared somewhere in Alcuin's writings. His silence has much rather the look of ignorance. Nor can it be said that the work was only read 'wherever pious scruples did not prevent' (p. 65), in face of abundant instances of its use from Remigius of Auxerre to John of Salisbury.

On the other hand, John has been claimed as in some sense [l] the author of the scholastic debate of the earlier part of the middle ages. He was the first writer in the west who systematically adopted a regular syllogistic form of argumentation, and he was continually reproached with this peculiarity by antagonists such as Prudentius of Troyes. Forgotten for a while, the tradition should seem to have somehow revived, possibly through the studies of Roscelin, and by such an one to have been applied to trains of reasoning widely diverse from anything suspected by John Scotus. On one side he is reputed the father of nominalism, on the other he is thought to have exerted no slight influence on the theological speculations of Gilbert of La Porrée. When, further, we observe that [m] the *Division of Nature* was associated in the condemnation of the heresy of Amalric of Bène,[29] and that it was this work which called forth a [n] bull of Honorius the Third in 1225, enjoining a strict search for all copies of the book or of any parts of it, and ordering them to be sent to Rome to be solemnly burnt,—any one who knowingly kept back a copy being declared obnoxious to the sentence of excommunication and the brand of heretical depravity,—we shall be able to form some estimate of the variety and the intensity of danger which was subsequently discovered in the teaching of the Scot.

CHAP. II.

[l] cf. infra. append. ii. 6, iv.

[m] Huber 435.

A.D. 1209.

[n] Alberic. Chr., ap. Mansi 22 1211–1214; 1778: [cf. H. Denifle, Chartul. Univ. Paris., 1 (1889) 106 sq.]

That such a judgement was warranted by the principles of correct catholic opinion will hardly be denied; but we must not omit to place beside it the fact that there was also literary tradition respecting John, so soon as his memory had been recalled to notice, of a gentler and more appreciative character. His translation of Dionysius was not only widely read, as we know from the numerous manuscripts of it that exist, but also commented on by a man of the saintly reputation of Hugh of Saint Victor, not to mention many others; and it is

[29] See Charles Jourdain's examination of the evidence of Martinus Polonus, in the Mémoires de l'Académie des Inscriptions et Belles-Lettres 26 (2) 470–477; 1870.

CHAP. II.

o Hist. of Lat. Chr. 4. 334.

p Gest. pontif. v. 240 p. 393, ed. Hamilton.

possible, as o Milman supposes, that it contributed not a little to the growth of 'Christian mythology.' William of Malmesbury, who was singularly well informed about John and his works, has a good word to say even of the *Division of Nature*, which he describes as p *very useful for solving the difficulty of certain questions, albeit he have to be pardoned for some matters wherein, holding his eyes fast upon the Greeks, he has deflected from the path of the Latins.* The acuteness of this criticism enhances the value of William's opinion; he was well aware that John had been deemed a heretic, and he confessed that *there are truly very many things in his book, the which, unless we carefully examine them, appear abhorrent from the faith of the catholics.* This temperate judgement is repeated by the most popular of the encyclopaedists of the middle ages, Vincent of Beauvais. There is also evidence that the name of John Scotus was known and honoured not only at Malmesbury but also in that Saxon monastery of Corvey which preserved its Carolingian culture longer perhaps than any other: so late as the middle of the twelfth century, its abbat, Wibald, writing to Manegold of Paderborn, commemorates the philosopher as closing the line of great masters of the age which began with Bede the Venerable, and went on with Haimon of Halberstadt and Rabanus Maurus,—*men most learned, who by writing and reasoning left in the church of God illustrious monuments of their genius.*[30]

q D. 1149.

[30] Quid loquar de caeteris viris doctissimis qui post predictos in aecclesia Dei scribendo et disserendo preclara ingenii sui monimenta reliquerunt? Bedam, dico, et Ambrosium Aupertum, Heimonem, Rabanum, Iohannem Scottum, et multos preterea, quorum opera legimus; nec non illos quos vidimus, Anselmum Laudunensem, Wilhelmum Parisiensem, Albricum Remensem, Hugonem Parisiensem, et alios plurimos, quorum doctrina et scriptis mundus impletus est: Epist. clxvii, in Jaffé, Biblioth. 1. 278; 1864. See other instances in Hauréau, Hist. 2 (1) 59; 1880.

CHAPTER III.

THE DARK AGE.

If the attempt of John Scotus to change Christianity into a philosophy failed to make an impression upon the succeeding age, it is the less surprising when we consider that he failed in company with all the wise men of the ninth century. Their religious and their philosophical aims were alike forgotten, the practices and beliefs they combated won a gradual acceptance. In the interval between the decline of the Carolingian house and the reformation of the eleventh century, Christendom sank into a grosser view of religion, into an abasement of morals that pervaded the clergy equally with the laity, into an ignorance all but universal. In this Dark Age, as it is well described, it is a thankless task to seek for the elements of enlightenment of which the vestiges are so scanty. Their existence, however, is proved by the life they manifested as soon as the spirit of religion was reäwakened. It was the divorce between religion and learning, between religion and morality, that signalised the time; a divorce that, just as in the seventh century, was conditioned by the helpless confusion of the external order, its effect in turn reäcting upon itself.

Yet to speak of the age as consciously reverting to paganism,[1] is to misread its character. When the church surrendered her charge of intellectual things, she assimilated herself no doubt to the returning barbarism of the civil state; and in this process she absorbed a variety of pagan elements which came to be identified with the

[1] This is a conclusion which vitiates much of Dr Reuter's view of the period, Geschichte der religiösen Aufklärung I. 67–78: to his references however I am frequently indebted.

CHAP. III.

essence of her religion, and from which her rebellious children in the sixteenth century were by no means able entirely to liberate themselves. The service of God was merged in ceremonial on the one hand, in superstition on the other. Even those men who had the wish to uphold the principles which the nobler minds of the ninth century had professed, had not the strength to carry them out consistently. Ratherius, bishop of Verona, a good example of the cultivated churchman of his day and a sturdy enemy of the worldliness and profligacy of his contemporaries, repeats the declamations of saint Agobard against magic. He denounces the credulous spirit of those who assume its efficacy, and yet he himself [a] recommends for some ailment a remedy of an entirely superstitious nature. He has a just contempt for the fashion in which fasts, penances, and pilgrimages were undertaken, and a very slight opinion of their value at all unless controlled by a high spiritual motive: yet his protests against materialistic views of religion are compatible with so hearty an adhesion to the doctrine of transubstantiation that [b] the treatise of Paschasius Radbert, which first formulated it, was often ascribed to him.

† 974.

[a] A. Vogel, Ratherius von Verona I. 69, Jena 1854.

[b] ibid. I. 234 sqq., 2. 180 sqq.

Religion was fast subsiding into mere superstition or into its kindred opposite, materialism. The claim to mysterious powers was the means by which the clergy were enabled to maintain their hold upon the people. Insensibly they were enveloped in the same shadow, and we have actually evidence of a body of Christian priests [c] in the diocese of Vicenza who worshipped a God with eyes and ears and hands; they were branded as a distinct order of heretics, anthropomorphites: such was the result of the popular and authorised image-worship. Nor was it only in the ceremonial of the church or in the medley of Christian and heathen manners and thoughts that the collapse of religion made itself felt. Ambitious churchmen found their only opening, now that the ambition of Christian learning was forgotten, in the service of the secular state, where they were the more indispensable,

A.D. 939.

[c] Rather. serm. i. de quadrag. xxix. sqq., in d'Achery's Spicilegium I. 388 b sqq., ed 1723.

since in the north, at least, they formed the only class that received any sort of mental culture. But it is one of the contrasts between the northern and southern civilisations that while in the former what schools there were, existed solely for the clergy and did not travel beyond their meagre professional requirements, in Italy the degradation of the church and papacy (the more felt because near at hand) produced so general a contempt for their ordinances and prescriptions that educated men turned away from theology to the more tangible interest of classical learning.

The candidates for ecclesiastical orders here mixed with the sons of nobles at [d] schools which were established and conducted, more often than otherwise, by lay *philosophers*, for the exclusive purpose of teaching *grammar*, and which to the stricter churchman appeared directly pagan in their bias. One of these teachers, Anselm of Bisate, [e] complains that he was shunned as a demoniac, *almost* as a heretic; and Anselm, *the Peripatetic* as he styles himself, is a good, if late, specimen of his class. He was a highly connected Milanese clergyman, a travelled man too, who had visited Mentz and Bamberg. The *Rhetorimachia*, which he wrote between the years 1049 and 1056, and dedicated to the emperor Henry the Third, is a masterpiece of laborious futility. How little the pedant's vein was in keeping with catholic notions may be learned from a vision which he relates that he once saw. [f] The saints and the muses, he tells us, struggled for possession of him, and he was in the greatest perplexity to which side he should ally himself, *for so noble, so sweet, were both companies that I could not choose either of them; so that, were it possible, I had rather both than either.*

[d] see Giesebrecht, de litt. stud. ap. Ital. 12–19: cf. Vogel I. 40 sq.

[e] Epist. ad Drogon., Dümmler, Anselm der Peripat. 19, Halle 1872.

[f] Rhetorim. ii., ibid. pp. 39 sqq.

Under such training as Anselm's, the future clergy of Italy gave themselves up to their humanistic studies with an enthusiasm which the theology of the day was impotent to excite in them. There are even a few symptoms of a declared hostility to Christianity. One Vilgard of Ravenna is said to have reverenced Virgil, Horace, and

CHAP. III.

Juvenal as infallible authorities;[2] but we cannot draw too broad an inference from this assertion in an age which, we know from the example of [g] Ratherius, was apt to consider the canons of the church and the forged decretals of Isidore as equally with the Bible and the fathers, the *discipline of God.*[3] The patriotism of the Italian seduced him into an error possibly more innocuous than that which approved itself to the orthodoxy of the time. There was a mysterious sanction inherent in written documents which it did not occur to men to criticise or distinguish.

[g] De contemptu canonum i. d'Achery, Spicil. I. 351 a.

In the same way, if any of these scholastics chanced to engage in the controversies of the church, he was inevitably entangled in a motley confusion of sacred and profane. [h] Eugenius Vulgarius exhausts his classical vocabulary, in language recalling the most servile rhetoric of the brazen age of the empire, to express the [i] *divinity* of that pope whose pontificate is marked by the deepest ruin of order, the vilest abandonment of decency, that Rome ever witnessed. Yet he dismisses the claims of the apostolic see with a confidence worthy of Claudius of Turin or of a modern protestant, and maintains that a man can only obtain the authority of saint Peter by deserving it.[4] The contradiction would be inconceivable but for the mixture of heterogeneous ideas which marks the barbarism of the age. The church refused to be

[h] Dümmler, Auxilius und Vulgarius, 44 sqq.
[i] see his letter to Sergius III, ibid. 143 sq.

[2] See the somewhat fabulous account of Rodulph Glaber, Hist. ii. 12 in Bouquet 10. 23, 1760.

[3] Compare the Discordia inter Ratherium et clericos: Quod vero scriptum invenitur in lege Moysis et prophetis et psalmis, quod in evangelico, actibus et praedicationibus apostolorum, decretalibus pontificum et constitutionibus canonum, non rursum a Deo tibi elucet inspiratum: d'Achery 1. 364 a.

[4] Debuerat certe erubesci homo velle Deo tollere quod suum est. Pater enim omne iudicium dedisse Filio dicitur, non Romae: neque Filius dixit, Tu es Roma et super hanc Romam aedificabo ecclesiam meam, sed *Tu es Petrus et super hanc petram*; non dixit Petrum sed petram, intelligi volens eius fidei et confessionis soliditatem aedificare et firmare immeritorum subsequacium consimilem, non quidem sequacium sine merito: alioquin non est sequax Petri, si non habeat meritum illius Petri. Quid igitur? ostende mihi fidem sine operibus, et ego ostendam tibi sequacem Petri sine merito illius Petri. . . . Num dicendum est profuisse summis sacerdotibus super cathedram Moysis sedisse? &c. De causa Formosiana xi., Dümmler, Auxilius und Vulgarius 130.

taught, and suffered accordingly. The clergy who were educated in the Italian rhetorical schools formed the purely secular portion of their order, and led it into more grievous disrepute. If the training of the scholastic was associated with the function of the clerical politician, the union was but external: by the assumption of literary arms the church as a religious body lost more than it gained.

It is moreover significant that the schools of Italy preserved a tradition of Roman law possibly uninterrupted from ancient times.[5] [k] The special law-school of Pavia dates from the tenth century, and early in the eleventh the study of law is spoken of in a way that gives the impression of its being a long-established institution in the ordinary schools. Milo Crispin records that Lanfranc, the famous archbishop of Canterbury, [l] *was trained from boyhood in the schools of liberal arts and civil law, after the custom of his country;—in scholis liberalium artium et legum saecularium ad suae morem patriae.* [m] Other circumstances too make it highly probable that law formed a regular subject of instruction in many schools from a much earlier period. It would obviously engage the attention of those churchmen who promised themselves a future of political activity. The principles of Roman law would combine themselves with their theological ideas, and it is difficult not to trace in this connexion one of the opportunities through which, in the judgement of competent lawyers, [n] the phraseology and argumentative methods of the old jurisprudence were enabled to penetrate the theology of western Christendom.

In the north, as we have said, the state of the clergy was different.[6] They had their professional colleges in

[k] see Giesebrecht, Gesch. d. Deutschen Kaiserzeit 1. 358, 4th ed., Brunswick 1873.

[l] Vit. Lanfr. v. § 11 Migne 150. 39 A; 1854.

[m] F. C. von Savigny, Gesch. d. röm. Rechts im Mittelalter 2. 119, 224 sqq., Heidelberg 1816; Vogel 1. 41: cf. Prantl, Gesch. d. Logik. 2. 69.

[n] see sir H. J. S. Maine, Ancient Law 354–364, 5th ed., 1874.

[5] [Cf. Rashdall, The Universities of Europe in the Middle Ages, 1. 95–108.]

[6] There is a curious and ancient gloss in the margin of the codex containing Gerbert's treatise De rationali et ratione uti, itself nearly contemporary with the author, which deserves quotation. 'Italia,' it runs, 'fertilis in ferendis est frugibus, Gallia et Germania nobilis in nutriendis militibus. Nesciunt Itali quid sapiunt Galli. Itali denarios cumulant, Galli sapientiam corradunt'; Bernhard Pez, Thesaurus Anecdotorum novissimus 1 (2) 151 mg., Augsburg 1721 folio.

CHAP. III.

the schools attached to the greater monasteries and cathedrals. But these, even if a few, especially in Lotharingia, retained something of their vital force, had long lost their popularity and become appropriated to a class. The slender tradition of learning and thought lay hidden in their libraries rather than shone forth in the mechanical instruction of their teachers. The rare pupils who sought for knowledge were left, as we may learn from the experience of o bishop Ratherius, to discover it by their own labour. The pursuit of the few was looked on with suspicious jealousy by the many, and the most tentative steps towards enlarging the compass of education were mistrusted as though they had been directed against religion. An excellent illustration of this attitude of mind is afforded by the history of Bruno the Saxon, known by the time-honoured name of saint Bruno. His brother, Otto the Great, was never more consciously the successor of the great Charles and the second founder of the medieval empire, than when he set himself to organise a body of ministers specially educated for the duties of government. The chancellorship had by this time become a mere titular appendage to the archbishops of Mentz, Cologne, Trèves, and Salzburg, whose work was done by the royal chancery or *chapel*, the staff of clergymen of the household. It was of the first importance not only to train these into efficiency but also to bring up a new generation of administrators qualified to manage the affairs of what was soon to be an empire. This task Otto entrusted to the young abbat Bruno,[7] who wisely recognised the necessity of promoting the widest learning attainable. Among his studies p Greek is specially mentioned. It is an interesting circumstance that now, as in the first foundation of the Palace School by Charles, it was to the British islands that the German looked for help; and Israel, a Scottish bishop,[8] was called from his cloister

o Vogel I. 24.

† 965.

p Ruotger, iv, vi.

[7] See Giesebrecht, 1. 321–331 and Vogel 1. 154–173.

[8] Ruotger calls him *episcopus Scotigena*, Vit. Brunon. vii, Pertz 4. 257; 1841. Flodoard, a. 947, ib. 3. 394 (1839) and Richer, Hist. ii. 66, ib. 602, say *Britto* or *Brittigena*: he was no doubt an Irishman.

at Trèves to be his teacher. The coöperation of the Celt is [q] recognised as of singular and indispensable importance. [q] Giesebrecht I. 325 sqq.

Bruno's learned ardour and the pains he took to secure the fittest masters and to collect the choicest classical manuscripts that could be found in Italy, are celebrated with wondering admiration by his biographer.[9] [r] *He restored the long ruined fabric of the seven liberal arts;* history, rhetoric, poetry, philosophy, especially the more mysterious problems of metaphysics, were the subjects he loved to discuss with the doctors whom he brought together. He joined in the disputations, ready to give counsel, readier to receive it; he would always rather himself be a learner than a teacher. A man of his receptive nature was sure to exercise a personal attraction over those around him, and the power which Bruno possessed he used with a single purpose of leading them through learning to a wisdom that should raise them into another world than that gross and corrupt society in which they lived. His own example, much like king Alfred's, was a model of the union of a scholar and a statesman. Himself continually occupied with every sort of official business he always reserved his early morning hours for study. He withdrew from the noisy mirth of the supper-table to find relief in his books, his energies apparently freshened by the labours of the day. Wherever he went he carried about his library with him [s] *as it had been the ark of the Lord.*

[r] Ruotger v. vi. pp. 256 sq.

[s] ibid., cap. viii.

Yet the age which gloried in the character of archbishop Bruno, could only find in that love of learning which was his special virtue, a reason for doubting whether he were really the saint men called him. The difficulty was resolved in a legend that soon won currency. A certain Poppo, says Thietmar, [t] *fell into a trance and was led to an high mountain, whereon he beheld a great city with beautiful buildings: then approaching a lofty tower he climbed*

[t] Chron. ii. 10, Pertz 3. 748

[9] Non suffecit ei in gazophilatium cordis sui colligere quod in promptu habebat; peregrina insuper conduxit aenigmata, et quicquid phylosophicum terrenisque sensibus remotissimum sensit, hoc undecumque contraxit: Ruotger v. p. 257.

CHAP. III.

its steep ascent and upon its spacious top obtained the vision of Christ seated with all his saints. There was Bruno archbishop of Cologne, being accused by the supreme Judge for his vain pursuit of philosophy: howbeit saint Paul was his advocate and he was restored to his throne. To us looking back at Bruno's work, it is difficult to exaggerate its value whether to his nation or to the church at large. Under his guidance the royal palace became the centre also of intellectual life in Germany. Bruno's aim was to fit the clergy to spread this new civilisation over the country, and when they departed to higher offices afterwards, as when he himself was raised to the see of Cologne, to form each one a fresh centre of learning. In this way he seconded the measures which the wisdom of his father and brother, Henry and Otto, had directed to the revival of the political state. The example was taken up by the religious houses, and their schools—those of Reichenau and Saint Gall are particularly distinguished —entered upon a new course of learned activity. The clergy of Lotharingia and Germany became marked out from the rest of Christendom no less by their education than by its fruit, their moral excellence.[10] To such seed the German popes owed their distinction, and through them the restoration of the papacy signalised by Leo the Ninth and Gregory the Seventh was made practicable.

A.D. 953.

It was long before the intellectual revival which began to shew itself from the middle of the tenth century, was sensibly felt. Guitmund, archbishop of Aversa, speaking of the time when Fulbert, who died in 1029, came to govern the school of Chartres, which he made the chief home of learning in Gaul, confesses that [u] *at that time the liberal arts had all but become extinct* in the land. A single name illuminates the literary record of the age, and Gerbert the Aquitanian, pope Silvester the Second, owes his

[u] De corp. et sang. Christi verit. i. Max. Bibl. Patr. 18. 441 B: cf. Gozechin. scholast. epist. ad Valcher., Mabillon. Vet. Anal. 437–446, ed. 1723.

[10] This is recognised by bishop Arnulf of Orleans (if the author be not Gerbert) in his famous speech before the council of Saint Basol near Rheims in the year 991: 'In Belgica et Germania . . . summos sacerdotes Dei religione admodum praestantes inveniri,' Act. conc. Rem. xxviii, Pertz 3. 673.

unique position less to his writings than to his personal influence as a teacher; as a teacher too not of moral but of natural philosophy, as a master not of theology but of statecraft. The stores of his knowledge,—v were they acquired from the Arabs during his stay in the Spanish march, or won by long practice and research in every library accessible to him,—were no doubt unequalled. Gerbert was a mathematician, a natural philosopher, and a pioneer of natural philosophers; his learning was believed to be universal: but, except in the domain of positive science, he was but the ready accumulator and diffuser of what was actually within the range of any well-read student of his day. In theology and metaphysics he produced little or nothing. If we exclude the necessary official productions of a dignitary of the church, sermons and speeches addressed to synods and similar gatherings, and these too concerned not with theology but with ecclesiastical politics,[11] we shall find that Gerbert composed x not one theological work, or, if he wrote any, they have been lost; for the only treatise of this class which has been ascribed to him is certainly not his.[12]

v [cf. Julien Havet, Oeuvres de Gerbert, p. vii. n. 1; 1889.]

x cf. infra, append. iii.

It was indeed in practical affairs that Gerbert's interest

[11] It would be more accurate to say, one sermon (De inform. episc., Migne 139. 169–178) and one speech of a substantive character and of undisputed authenticity (that delivered before the council of Mouzon in 995, Mansi 19. 193 D–196 B; 1774): see the bibliography in Fabricius, Biblioth. Lat. med. et inf. Aet. 3. 43 sq., ed Florence 1858.

[12] The book De corpore et sanguine domini (Migne 139. 177 sqq.), at first printed as anonymous, was reëdited by Pez from a manuscript at Goettweih which bore Gerbert's name: see the editor's dissertatio isagogica to his Thesaurus Anecd. noviss. 1 pp. lxviii, lxix; and the ascription has been generally admitted. See the Histoire littéraire de la France 6. 587 sq., 1742; Neander, History of the Christian Religion and Church 6. 308; Gfrörer, Kirchengeschichte 3. 1585; cf. supra, p. 76, n. 24. Long ago, however, the laborious Mabillon found reason to attribute the work to Heriger abbat of Lobbes; see his preface to the Actt. SS. O. S. B. 4 (2) pp. xxii–xxiv, Paris 1680 folio: and this opinion was favoured by Dr R. Koepke (praef. in Herigeri et Anselmi Gest. episc., Pertz 7. 146 sq.) and Dr Vogel, Ratherius 2. 46 sqq. [Neither view seems to be tenable, for Heriger's own work, which is altogether different from that printed by Pez, has been discovered in MS. 909 in the University Library at Ghent: see E. Dümmler, in the Neues Archiv 26 (1901) 755–759, and A. Hauck, Kirchengeschichte Deutschlands, 3. 319 n. 2, ed. 3, 1906.]

CHAP. III

was engaged, and his thoughts no more than his actions were disquieted by any considerations of religion. From a teacher Gerbert became a politician. We discern his character in the arts by which he obtained the archbishoprick of Rheims.[13] Full of resource, unscrupulous in intrigue, he had the shrewdness, the practical sagacity, of a man of the world: moral difficulties were no difficulties to him. His record lies not in a fancied inauguration of the crusades (this was to all appearance but the y hasty conclusion from a letter in which he laments the spoliation of the holy city, drawn by those who knew the potency of such an appeal a century later[14]); but in the imperial projects which he impressed on the boy Otto the Third and whereby he hoped to restore to Rome her ancient glory. Gerbert the magician is an imagination of later growth, but the currency of the fable bears witness to the uniqueness of his position.[15] A scholar who did not concern himself with the higher questions of faith and thought could only, it appeared, be susceptible of influences of an opposite and infernal origin.

y H. von Sybel, Gesch. d. ersten Kreuzzuges 458, 2nd ed., 1881.

[13] The Acts of the synod of Saint Basol by which his predecessor was deposed are printed in Bouquet 10. 513 sqq., and in Pertz 3. 658–686. The remarkable speech of Arnulf bishop of Orleans, which depicts the degradation of the papacy and fearlessly proposes an entire secession from its authority (Pertz 672 sq., 676), has been substantially reproduced by most of the historians: see Gfrörer 3. 1476 sqq., cf. vol. 4. 508; Milman 3. 338 sqq.; Giesebrecht 1. 654 sq. It deserves mention in this place because the Acts, if we are to believe Richer, Hist. iv. 51 Pertz 3. 648, and Gerbert's own preface, were edited by the latter; and, the province of an editor being undefined, we may reasonably give him a considerable share not only of the diction but of the spirit of the speech: cf. Neander, 6. 132 n. 1.

[14] [The letter seems to be merely an ornamental circular sent out to invite contributions for the charitable foundations established by the Christians in the Holy Land: 'Quod armis nequis consilio et opum auxilio subveni. Quid est quod das aut cui das? nempe ex multo modicum et ei qui omne quod habes gratis dedit nec tamen ingratus recipit.' Cf. Havet, Oeuvres de Gerbert, p. 22 n. 3.]

[15] It is significant that Gerbert was too much of a personality to be lost in his pontifical title. Thus in the Fleury chronicle, a. 1002, we have his obituary as *Girbertus Papa*, Baluze, Miscell. 2. 307; 1679. On the genesis of the story about Gerbert's magical powers and league with the devil, see J. J. I. von Döllinger, Die Papst-Fabeln des Mittelalters, 155–159, Munich 1863.

Yet the studies which Gerbert avoided were in fact the more dangerous, and it is hardly perhaps a coincidence that the contemporary reäwakening of interest in intellectual things was accompanied by a strange crop of heresies. [z] In a time of mental ferment, now as often in the history of Christianity, it was impossible to restrain the speculations of men with undisciplined faculties, and living, as most of the scholars of the middle ages lived, a cloistered life. The relief which some monks would find from the routine of devotion in works of husbandry or handicraft, the more cultivated would seek in meditation on the mysteries of religion or the secrets of philosophy. If they were teachers such enquiries might be initiated by the questions of pupils. The ambition of novelty, of originality, would be another stimulus to metaphysical exploits; and novelty of this sort would seldom lie within the bounds of the traditional dogma. Men of a less independent spirit, whose minds were just opening to the apprehension of difficulties in the doctrinal system of the church, would be content to accept any new solution of their doubts that was offered to them. In the present instance it was probably contact with the dispersed heretics of the oriental church that kindled the flame,[16] and henceforward in various lands and under various forms there is a constant current of opposition to the authorised belief of Christendom. Unlike the properly intellectual movement, it affected the easily excited people even more than the clergy. The character of the sectaries, their temperance, their earnestness, their devotion, which appeared in a noble contrast with the greed, the profligacy, the worldliness, of the orthodox, were readily accepted

[z] cf. Milman 4. 326 sqq., 335.

[16] The historical review prefixed to Mr [now Sir] Arthur J. Evans's travels Through Bosnia and the Herzegóvina, pp. xxiv–xliii, 1876, abundantly shews that such an influence was possible as early as the tenth century; it is admitted by Neander, 6. 429, 439; and the fact that it existed later may justify the conclusion that similar results were produced by similar means at the time with which we are here concerned. The firm hold too which the name Bulgarian, as a term of infamous import, has taken both in the French and English languages, points in the same direction.

CHAP. III.

as credentials for the truth of their tenets. The history of these heretics has, however, less interest than some of their peculiarities might seem to promise. What, for instance, can be said of the story told by Rodulph Glaber of a countryman of Vertus near Châlons who had a vision, at its warning put away his wife, went to the church, there destroyed a cross and a picture of the Saviour, and declaimed to the people on the wickedness of paying tithes?[17] It is added that he sustained his assertions by passages from the Bible, while explaining that what the prophets said was *in part not to be believed:* whence we may gather that he had imbibed some of the special doctrines of the eastern Paulicians, whose loyalty to the New Testament is supposed ([a] though the evidence is conflicting) to have been balanced by their repudiation of the Old. An extreme case like this betrays, with however much exaggeration, the characteristics of medieval heresy, an incongruous mixture of heterogeneous elements, a dualism borrowed from the religion of Zoroaster, ill-compacted with a rationalism that claimed to represent the teaching of saint Paul.

A.D. 1000

[a] see Evans pp. xxix, xxx.

From the first ages of Christianity there had always been a tendency more or less widely operative, to free the religion from its burthen of Jewish principles and traditions. The puritanism of the Hebrew scriptures was exchanged for another puritanism resting upon the idea of the essential evilness of matter. Marcion and Manes at different epochs framed systems of which the uniting principle was the double reign of good and evil. The authority of the prime God was confronted by a restless malignant power whose rule was coëval with the existence of the universe. The opposition of spirit and

[17] As 'omnimodis superfluum et inane,' Rodulph Glab. hist. ii. 11, Bouquet 10. 23 The chronicler is sure that the man (his name was Leutard) was out of his mind; and it is remarkable that the bishop to whom the scene was reported felt satisfied with the explanation and let him go free. Leutard proceeded to drown himself in a reäction, it was said, of despair. At the same time, as Neander hints, p. 445, it is not improbable that the suicide was a figment and that the enthusiast fell a victim to the fanatic zeal of the populace.

matter, of good and evil, was so fundamental that it was impossible, in their view, to conceive the incarnation of the Deity in a human body or his liability to the sufferings of man: such facts, they held with the primitive docetists, were illusions to the senses; they were true only in an ideal acceptation. The same principle forbade their allowing any spiritual, or at least any perfecting, virtue to the material act of baptism or to the sacramental elements of bread and wine. They rejected every emblem of religious worship, the image, the painted cross, the reliques of saints. The human soul was deprived of all accessory aids to salvation, of all that interposed between spirit and spirit: celibacy, the proof of its conquest over matter, was the one indispensable condition to eternal happiness. The schemes of the Manicheans and the Marcionites came to diverge in the idea of the church. Manes inaugurated a priestly caste; his theory was sacerdotal: the later Marcionites on the other hand adopted a congregational system.

From Syria the Marcionites, or as they were afterwards known, the Paulicians, [b] spread over the eastern provinces of Asia Minor. They seem to have absorbed the remnant of the Manicheans; at least they inherited their ill-repute: original differences of doctrine may have been forgotten in community of oppression.[18] They grew strong and resisted, for a while were victorious; it was attempted to break their strength by a policy of transportation, and numbers were carried over at different times into Thrace, where they came to form a powerful and aggressive community. Extending from Bulgaria among the strictly Slavonian populations of Servia and Bosnia, the [c] Bogomiles, as they are now called, appear to have found the

[b] see Finlay, Hist. of Greece 2. 243, &c.

[c] ibid., p. 67

[18] In this way it appears possible to reconcile the title usually applied to the heretics of western Europe with their known lineage from the Paulicians whose teaching in regard to the church was plainly opposed to Manichaism: cf. Evans pp. xxxiii, xxxiv. The distinction is pointed out by Mosheim, Instit. Hist. eccles. 312, ed. 2, Helmstädt 1764 quarto; and by Gfrörer 3. 199. See on the whole subject of the history of the sect, Gibbon's fifty-fourth chapter [with Mr. J. B. Bury's notes, and appendix vi., in vol. 6. 540 sqq., 1898].

CHAP. III.

[d] cf. Evans pp. xxxii–xxxiv.

[e] cf. Gibbon 7. 138 sq.

soil already [d] partly prepared for the reception of their teaching by the primitive beliefs and customs of the people; and from these lands, by channels of which we are imperfectly informed, [e] they passed into Sicily, Italy, France, and even Germany; and from the end of the tenth century onward there is hardly a generation in which the catholic church was not troubled by the appearance of their spiritual offspring which it confused under the familiar and infamous name of Manicheans.

The success of the heretics was assisted by several circumstances in the ecclesiastical condition of the west. Their views of Christian brotherhood were eagerly welcomed by people who groaned under the pretensions of an unworthy priesthood; their other heresy, the enforcement of celibacy, was already the kernel of faith among the stricter churchmen. That horror for the married state which the saint Augustin had retained from his youthful Manichaism, had already subverted the Christian idea of family life. It was the instrument which the reformers of the tenth and eleventh centuries again borrowed from the heretics, and by which they strove to purify the priesthood; for however the doctrine of celibacy was theoretically admitted, the authority of the church had hitherto interfered but little with the domestic relations of the clergy. Pope Hadrian the Second in the ninth century was himself a married man. (A.D. 867.) The clergy of Milan claimed their right as depending on the express rule of saint Ambrose. In Germany, England, and France the parish priests lived openly and without blame with their wives.[19] The reversal of this state of things, the work of Hildebrand, was undoubtedly designed with the sagacity of a statesman; but if his success established the church as a political power, it did not promote the morality of the clergy.

The defenders of the old custom at Milan were quick

[19] See the vigorous description of Milman 3. 440–447, 468–477; 4. 17–24 (the pages following about Dunstan contain a variety of errors of fact and inference); also pp. 61 sqq.

to see the dangers that would arise if married persons were excluded from holy orders.[20] The historian Landulf has preserved a remarkable record (if to some extent imaginary, hardly less valuable as expressing opinions current in Milan not long after the event took place) of a disputation they held with their opponents on the subject. CHAP. III.

[f] One declared that to deprive a priest of his wife meant simply to multiply his mistresses: *vetando unam et propriam uxorem, centum fornicatrices ac adulteria multa concedis.* Another, the archdeacon Wibert, recited the praises of married virtue from the Bible and from saint Ambrose, and [g] boldly declared that whatever was lawful to a layman was lawful also to a clergyman; *for all are priests, whosoever be sons of the church, be they laymen or clerks.* They invoked the freedom of the apostolic age, and charged the upholders of celibacy with the taint of *those of Montforte*, a castle not far from Asti which afforded shelter to a sect whose heresy was a matter of common notoriety at the time.[21] The Milanese had chosen a telling argument. The reproach was so far a just one that the party of Peter Damiani and of Hildebrand, and these despised sectaries were in this regard equally fallen from the primitive humanity of their religion.

[f] Landulf iii. 25 p. 92.

[g] cap. 23 p. 9

The fortunes of the western Paulicians need not detain us long. There was no principle of development in their creed; it reflected no genuine freedom of thought. It

[20] This was the only point at issue: it was admitted that no one could marry after ordination: cf. Landulf, Hist. Mediolan, iii. 26, Pertz 8. 94; 1848. Gerbert's profession at Rheims, *Nuptias non prohibeo, secunda matrimonia non damno*, Mansi 19. 108 A, was only the extravagant pledge of a political aspirant: cf. Gfrörer 3. 1462.

[21] Forsitan adhuc illa sententia implicitus ea qua olim illi de Monteforti te imbuerant; qui omnem Christianitatem mulierem non tangere et genus humanum sine semine virili, apum more, nasci dicentes, falsis sententiis affirmabant: Landulf iii. 26 p. 93. Milman has related this singular debate at some length: vol. 3. 470 n. 2. On the Milanese usage with respect to marriage, compare Anselm the Peripatetic's language: 'Nobis enim clericis quibus licet liceat; in uxoribus et filiis libera est potestas. Usus quidem prestat, ipsa defendit auctoritas:' Rhetorimach. ii. p. 45.

CHAP. III.

took root among the obscurest and rudest orders of society, in the ignorant villages of Lombardy or in the low suburbs of the French or Flemish trading towns. An enthusiast, generally an Italian, might stir up the common people and expose them to the vengeance of the church: such were the victims of catholic zeal at Toulouse,[22] at [h] Arras, Cambray, and Liège, in the course of the eleventh century. But the influence rarely as yet extended deeper into society, as when, [i] in the case just alluded to, the heretics (here they were clergy as well as laymen) enjoyed the alliance of the countess of Montforte.[23] In one single instance, if its source be not wrongly traced, we find a whole religious foundation in an important town, a widely frequented clerical school, pervaded by the dangerous current.

[h] see Neander 6. 435–439.

[i] cf. ibid., pp. 430–435 A.D. 1031.

Perhaps the most singular fact in the history of these canons of Saint Cross at Orleans is the silent and unsuspected way in which their sect grew. [k] A member of it had been dead three years before his character was discovered. [l] One of the two leaders, Stephen,[24] had been confessor to the queen of France; [m] he and his colleague Lisoius, or Lisieux, were familiars of the court and of the king. The very council which condemned them admits that they were [n] *distinguished among all for wisdom, surpassing in acts of holiness, bountiful in almsgiving.* At length their opinions were detected, and a synod convened to examine them. They were charged with nameless atrocities in their secret meetings, calumnies of the same class as those with which the early Christians were wont to insult the heretics of their day, and possibly as

[k] Ademar iii. 59 Pertz 4. 143.

[l] Gest. syn. Aurel., Bouquet 10. 539 D.

[m] Rod. Glab. iii. 8 ibid., p. 35.

[n] Gest. syn. Aurel. p. 537 A.

A.D. 1022.

[22] Ademar of Chabannais connects the execution of certain Manicheans at Toulouse in 1022 with the appearance of these *heralds of Antichrist* in many parts of the west: Hist. iii. 59 Pertz 4. 143 (or Bouquet 10. 159 D).

[23] Milman's treatment of them, 3. 442 sq., 5. 402, is exceptionally perfunctory. It may be noticed that they, unlike the eastern Paulicians, were covetous of martyrdom. The Albigenses after *their* overthrow returned to the primitive custom of the sect, and dissembled their opinions.

[24] Rodulph Glaber calls him Heribert by a mistake that has been often corrected. Heribert was in fact the traitor of the heresy.

false.[25] The judgement, we may be sure, was the more exemplary on account of their previous favour in high places. The persons whose intimacy with the arraigned canons might seem to commit them too deeply to their errors, attested their own innocence by the savage joy with which they heard the sentence,—[o] the queen, according to one account, plucked out the eye of her old confessor as he passed from the hall;—and thirteen of the number, two others recanting, perished at the stake.

CHAP. III.

[o] Rod. Glab., l. c.

The *Acts* of the synod of Orleans suggest no clue as to the origin of this sect. Among contemporaries [p] Ademar of Chabannais alone describes it as Manichean. He traces it to the teaching of a certain Rusticus—or was he only a *rustic?*—of Périgord. [q] Rodulph Glaber, on the contrary, says it was imported by a woman from Italy. Both these writers, however, betray too plainly their ignorance of the characteristics and motives of the heretics for us to be at liberty to accept their testimony without corroboration. If we examine the indictment against them, we find a variety of articles shewing kinship with the Paulician beliefs. They denied, it was alleged, all the facts of the human life of Christ, the miracles of his birth, his passion, and his resurrection; [r] all miracles, they said, were madness, *deliramenta*. They assailed doctrines not less closely bound up with the life of the church, [s] the regenerating virtue of baptism, and the presence of the body and blood of the Saviour in the eucharistic species; they denounced the vanity of invoking saints, the superfluity of the Christian works of piety. Rodulph adds that they held the universe to be eternal and without author, and if the specification be true it would place the canons of Orleans in a position by themselves; but the tenet is little in keeping with

[p] Hist., l. c.; cf. vv. ll. in Bouquet 10. 159 c & P. Labbe, Nov. Bibl. mss. Libr. 2. 180, Paris 1657 folio.

[q] Hist., ubi supra.

[r] ibid., p. 36 A, B.

[s] Gest. syn. Aur. p. 537 E.

[25] Milman's remark that they 'were, if their accusers speak true, profligates rather than sectarians' (he enters into no detail in the matter) may be contrasted with the judicial impartiality of the Benedictine editors of the acts of the synod, p. 538 n., from whom I have borrowed the parallel in the text. Gibbon has given a lively picture of the corresponding passages in the history of the ancient church, ch. xvi, vol. 2. 155 sq.

CHAP. III.

the spirit of their creed. Its general resemblance to the oriental heresy is plain, but it has long been acknowledged that, however probable the relationship may be, there is no necessity to explain its origin in this way; [t] it might have sprung up by itself, as the result of a rational speculation, tinctured with mysticism: and even if the first impetus was given from abroad, it remains likely that its dissemination at Orleans was assisted by the reviving spirit of enquiry which was already becoming powerful in France.

[t] see Mosheim 380 sq., Neander 6. 430 sq., Milman 5. 399 n. 1.

On the other hand, it would undoubtedly be improper to class these extravagancies with the other manifestations of opinion divergent from the general tenour of catholic belief which we meet with in the eleventh century. They indicate at most a link between the profession of an heresy which seemed to the world repulsive, and the assertion of individual views which might be startling, perhaps on that very account attractive, but which excited the anger of rivals rather than of enemies. To the latter order belong the opinions of Berengar of Tours and of Roscelin, who less by the issues to which they pointed than by the intellectual activity which they roused, are counted among the heralds of the scholastic philosophy. Through their resistance the medieval realism grew into the matured form which it retained until the introduction of the complete works of Aristotle in the thirteenth century. The debate, it is well known, rests upon the problem of the nature of being, a question no doubt insoluble because to all time each man will answer it, spite of argument, according to the special constitution of his own understanding. Existence might be held to reside more truly in the highest and broadest conceptions of which the mind is capable, in truth, in goodness, in every abstraction furthest removed from ocular observation; according to the technical terminology, in the *universals*. To the realist the ideal was the only true existence; [u] every conception of the mind had necessarily a corresponding reality.[26] The

[u] cf. Hauréau, Hist. de la Phil. scol. 1. 289 sq.

[26] I have purposely described the theory by an illustration of its practical issue, since for our present purpose we are hardly at all concerned with its technical definition.

school of Roscelin proceeded from the opposite extreme, from experience. Our senses, it was felt, are the only certain warrant for existence, and they only reveal to us the individual. The universals, therefore, the cardinal point of dispute, could only be our own generalisations from observed facts.

Roscelin, who brought the latter view prominently into the field of discussion, was not, however, as is commonly presumed, nor was Berengar, the first nominalist of the middle ages. This position, [x] according to an early chronicler, belongs to John the Sophist, whose identification with John Scotus, long suspected, has been made probable by the acute arguments of [y] Dr von Prantl. So hearty a Platonist as the Scot could not but be a realist in his ontology: but equally little could a logician escape the influence of Aristotle, the philosopher to whom he owed his method; and John's view of language and of the scope and functions of logic is far removed from the arid tradition of Isidore and Alcuin.[27] Dialectic, he admitted, had kinship with grammar and rhetoric, in so far as it dealt with human speech pure and simple. But words and thoughts, and therefore words and things, were definitely if imperfectly correlative. John therefore claimed for dialectic a higher dignity than that of a mere mechanical instrument: it was *the searcher out of the common conceptions of the mind*,[28] the guide of reason.

[x] cf. supra, pp. 76 sq.

[y] cf. infra, append. ii. 6, iv.

It was easy to carry this train of reasoning a stage further, and to argue that the general terms with which logic occupies itself are not its source but its product. The universals, the Scot had agreed, are words; what if they be mere words? Already in his lifetime the suggestion was taken up by Heric of Auxerre,[29] whose pupil, however, saint Remigius of Auxerre, reverted to a declared

[27] [Cf. Prantl, Geschichte der Logik im Abendlande, 2. 36 sq., in the second edition, 1885; and E. K. Rand, Johannes Scottus, p. 19, Munich 1906.]

[28] Communium animi conceptionum rationabilium diligens investigatrixque disciplina: De div. nat. i. 29 p. 19.

[29] [On Heric, see L. Traube, in the Neues Archiv, 18, 71–105; 1892.]

CHAP. III.

cf. infra, append. iv.

realism. [z] The party division may therefore be dated from the close of the ninth century. Remigius was a far more important person than Heric. At Rheims, and afterwards at Paris, he was unrivalled as a teacher of grammar, dialectic, and music; and the rapidly advancing greatness of the Paris school, assisted by the reputation not only of the teacher but of such of his pupils as [a] Odo, the second abbat of Cluny and the creator of its fame, would naturally tend to fix the principles of Remigius in an age which had no mind for independent thought. Thus, with apparently the single exception of the learned centre of [b] Saint Gall, realism held everywhere an undisputed reign. Gerbert, whose dialectical activity is represented for us by a debate in which he took part before Otto the Third, and by a slight treatise in which he pursued a little further one of the points raised on that occasion, was hardly at all in sympathy with the subjective aims of metaphysics; although [c] probably his literary interest and his energy as a teacher were the means of restoring to the use of the schools some of the materials for logical study which had fallen into neglect in the century before him. [d] Otherwise his practical temper was satisfied to accept the tradition as he found it. It was not until thought was again turned to religious questions, and doctrine subjected to the test of reason, that the opposition was revived.

[a] see Gfrörer 3. 1335 sqq.

[b] Prantl, Gesch. d. Log. im Abendl. 2. 61–67, 1861 [2nd ed. 1885.]

[c] Hauréau 1. 212 sq., & in the Not. et Extr. des Manuscr. 20 (2) 2 sq.

[d] cf. Prantl 2. 53–57 [58].

The principles of the realist combined readily with a Christian idealism: he relied upon the safe foundation of authority—the various elements of the church tradition, the Bible, the fathers, the canons of councils, and the decretals of popes;—and treated logic as its useful but docile handmaid.[30] The nominalist on the contrary, though he might not wish to overthrow the ancient and respectable fabric of authority, reduced its importance

[30] 'Quae tamen artis humanae peritia,' says saint Peter Damiani, Opusc. xxxvi. 5, 'si quando tractandis sacris eloquiis adhibetur, non debet ius magisterii sibimet arroganter arripere, sed velut ancilla dominae quodam familiatus obsequio subservire, ne si praecedit oberret.

by giving, [e] as John Scotus gave, an equal if not a superior place to reason. Reason was the basis on which he rested, and logic, as the method which controlled the exercise of its powers, became the science of sciences. It was therefore natural that the dialectical reaction should ally itself with the protest of reason against the dogma of transubstantiation. [f] Berengar of Tours, who maintained what may be called the Zwinglian view of the Lord's supper, is therefore so far the beginner of the new movement that the rationalism of the opinions he put forth set the whole catholic world thinking, questioning, disputing. Himself ready enough to recant under pressure, the number of his immediate disciples may not have been large: but the stream of speculation once let loose, could not be restrained at will. It was a time of religious reform, and reform went hand in hand with the promotion of education. Monasteries and their schools were restored or founded in a continually expanding circle. They busied themselves with the rudimentary 'arts' of the Trivium, grammar, rhetoric, and dialectic; and the last, because of its universal applicability, remained the most popular study even for those who proceeded to the higher branches of the Quadrivium, or to the faculties of theology or law. The disputations which in the English universities only died out at the end of the eighteenth century, and retained much later a formal existence in the superior faculties, are the shadowy survivors of a system which was in its fresh ardour in the eleventh century. To the enthusiastic dialectician everything would seem to depend upon the turn of a debate; a challenge to a disputation was as serious as a challenge to the combat: logic became the centre round which all speculation revolved, and the question about its metaphysical basis became the absorbing one for all who pretended to share in the commonwealth of scholars.

[e] supra pp. 57 sqq.

[f] cf. Hauréau, Hist. i. 222 sqq.

Nevertheless the suspicion with which theologians regarded the new study was not soon averted. Apart from antecedent principles it was not likely that they

CHAP. III

1089. should look with approval upon an art in which they were usually outmatched by their opponents. Archbishop Lanfranc, a learned man and a good lawyer, was greatest in the practical affairs of the state: in dialectical warfare he shewed but poorly. He vanquished Berengar by transparent sophisms. Logic in his hands was an imperfect instrument which he had not fully learned to use.[31] The difference between this controversy and that which was provoked by Roscelin towards the close of the century is worth noticing. Whereas [g] Berengar seems to have been led by moral doubts in reference to the miracle of the Lord's supper, to investigate minutely its claims to belief and thus to open the whole question of the meaning of authority,[32] while the dialectical form in which his polemic was cast was the last stage in his intellectual process; in Roscelin's case the order was reversed. The conclusion of the one was the starting-point of the other. By the sheer honesty and consistency of his logic Roscelin came to dispute the accepted dogma of the holy Trinity. He refused to exempt any fact from the jurisdiction of reason, and fearlessly applied his nominalistic principles to the supreme problem. *If in God*, he argued, *the three Persons are one thing and not three things, then the Father and the holy Ghost must have been incarnate with the Son*: if on the contrary they are *three things each by itself severally, as three angels or three souls, yet so as in will and power they be altogether one, then, did usage permit, we ought to speak of three Gods.*[33] The terms of the dilemma are those

[g] cf. Reuter 1. 92 sqq.

[31] On Lanfranc's controversy with Berengar see the extracts in Prantl 2. 75 [76] n. 308, and compare Rémusat, Abélard 2. 162 sq. Dr von Prantl, vol. 2. 73, note 302, accepts Lanfranc as the author of the Elucidarium. This text-book of theology has been variously ascribed to Augustin, to Guibert of Nogent, and to Honorius of Autun; as well as to saint Anselm, among whose works it has even appeared in print. See the Histoire littéraire de la France, 12. 167; 1763. [The book is generally believed to be a compilation by Honorius Augustodunensis, but whether he was of Autun or of Augsburg is still disputed.]

[32] Dr Reuter remarks, 1. 93, of the tendency of the doctrine of transubstantiation, 'Das Mirakel hörte auf Mittel zu sein, es wurde Zweck.'

[33] The argument as reported to Anselm (Baluze, Miscell. 2. 174, ed. Mansi) and stated by him in the De fide Trinitatis, i. p. 41 b, presents but one horn of the dilemma. Both are given, but

which in the early history of Christianity had been inspired only by the venom of enemies. Rejecting the error charged to the patripassians, Roscelin frankly accepted the reproach of tritheism. But we may learn from the extreme rigour with which he stated the alternatives, that with him there was not a religious principle but simply a speculative position at stake.[34]

If it was almost an accident of time that connected Roscelin with a theological debate, it was certainly nothing more that involved saint Anselm in one of dialectics. A thinker of immensely larger capacity than Lanfranc, Anselm, like his predecessor in the see of Canterbury, belongs in spirit to the past. He is, it has been finely said, [h] the last of the fathers. Unlike Lanfranc, he belongs also to the far future: as a philosopher, he is in at least one notable train of reasoning the parent of Descartes. His serene vision overlooks the chasm of scholasticism; he is not engulphed in it. Some of the questions on which he meditated are so alien from the temper of his time that one cannot but ask whence he derived the impulse. To this question, however, [i] no answer has yet been given, and for the present we may still believe that the idea of constructing an argument for the existence of God originated in his solitary thought. At first indeed Plato, through the channel of saint Augustin, supplied him with the suggestion that the existence of relative good upon earth implies the existence of an absolute Good of which it is a reflexion. To this purpose he wrote the *Monologion*. But he was not content until he had perfected an argument the profoundness of which might, he felt, appeal to every reasonable man. Such he discovered in the

[h] Hauréau I. 269.

[i] cf. infra, append. v

in a somewhat involved form, in Anselm's letter to Fulk of Beauvais, Epp. ii. 41 p. 357 b. I have extracted the statement in the text from a comparison of these three passages.

[34] This was long ago seen by the candid Mosheim, p. 382, 2nd note. Still the charge of blasphemous heresy long clung to Roscelin; see Abailard's letter to the bishop of Paris, written about 1120, Opp. 2. 150, ed. Cousin: and Roscelin's reply, ibid. pp. 796–801, still insists, in however modified language, upon the Three in preference to the One.

CHAP. III.

famous 'ontological' argument of the *Proslogion*, that the existence of God is proved by our thought of him.[35] It is the very subtilty of the conception that makes the reasoning silent to mere logicians; but among philosophers it has commanded a wide-spread sympathy. Anselm's confidence in its truth has been justified by the manner in which his argument has been woven and re-woven into the systems of modern thought.

k Prantl 2. 86.

j Herimann. Narr. restaur. abbatiae s. Martin. Tornac. i. d'Achery, Spicil. 2. 889 a, ed. 1723.

Thus Anselm's interest lay in a field above the controversies of logic; his thoughts did not readily move within that formal circle. He joined of necessity in debates to which one cannot be brought to believe that he devoted his best faculties.[36] The [k] technical victory in his controversy with Gaunilo lay with his opponent, and although our scanty information of the literary proceedings of the time tells us nothing relevant of the reception of his other writings, we may be fairly sure that the realists, or traditionary party, had not yet trained themselves to the same expertness in the manipulation of logic which the nominalists already possessed. A story told by a chronicler of the abbey of Saint Martin at Tournay, and relating to the last years of the century, throws a curious light upon this relation. [j] There was a master there, Odo, afterwards bishop of Cambray, whose fame was so eminent *that not only from France, Flanders, and Normandy, but even from far distant Italy, Saxony, and Burgundy, divers clergymen flowed together in crowds to hear him daily; so that if thou shouldst walk about the public places of the city and behold the throngs of disputants—greges disputantium—thou wouldst say that the citizens had left off their other labours and given themselves over entirely to philosophy*. But after a while a check came. Odo, who

[35] The argument has been spoken of as derived from Augustin and Boëthius, but it is clearly shown by F. R. Hasse, Anselm von Canterbury 2. 240 (1852), that this statement rests upon a confusion of the motive of the Proslogion with that of the Monologion.

[36] Cousin justly remarks, 'il retombe dans la barbarie de son temps dès qu'il quitte le Christianisme et s'engage dans la dialectique scholastique. . . . Ce n'est pas là qu'il faut chercher saint Anselme :' Fragments philosophiques 2. 102, 5th ed., 1865.

was an old-fashioned realist, found his position menaced by the increasing popularity of a certain Raimbert and a whole school of nominalists at Lille; since [m] it was observed that the lectures of the latter had a much more practical result in training men to reasoning and to readiness of speech; *maxime quia eorum lectiones ad exercitium disputandi vel eloquentiae, imo loquacitatis et facundiae, plus valere dicebant.* Yet there could be no fault in Odo, *for he departed not from the doctrine of the ancients.* Thus exercised in his mind, therefore, one of the canons of the church had recourse to a wizard, who unhesitatingly declared in favour of the realist. To him realism had indeed the support of authority; and the fact expressed under this grotesque guise still holds good in a more reasonable form when we approach the master to whose credit is usually assigned the establishment of realism. The distinction of the parties is still the same; the realism of William of Champeaux, like that of saint Anselm, [n] proceeds from a metaphysical rather than a logical starting-point.

CHAP. III.

[m] ibid. ii. p. 889 b.

† 1121.

[n] see Prantl 2. 128 [130].

But the dialectical spirit was now too strong to endure a subordinate rank: it animated the realists, now that [o] William of Champeaux had given them a tangible formula, just as vigorously as the nominalists. But the formula was no sooner discovered than the appearance of Abailard, and his criticism first of one side and then of the other, drove each to its defences. The immediate effect of this disturbance was to break up the parties into manifold subdivisions. [p] John of Salisbury, the acutest historian of the movement, reckons no less than ten distinct positions on the main dialectical problem, and this enumeration is not exhaustive.[37] With this universal outburst of criticism the intellectual history of the middle ages enters into its second youth. The interval of darkness is now quite past. The age of the church schools is about to be succeeded by the age of the universities. The nature

[o] see Cousin 2. 123, Hauréau 1. 320.

[p] Metalog. ii. 17 pp. 814 sqq., Policrat. vii. 12 vol. 1. 141 sq.

[37] A lucid summary of the principal points of difference will be found in Carl Schaarschmidt's Johannes Saresberiensis nach Leben und Studien, Schriften und Philosophie 319 sqq.; 1862. See also the analysis given by Dr. von Prantl, vol. 2. 118 [119] sqq.

of the discussion indeed takes it out of the sphere of any but a professed history of philosophy, not merely because of its extremely technical form, which it is difficult to render into modern language, but also because the apparent minuteness and triviality of its distinctions, unless subjected to a long and searching examination, tend rather to conceal than to disclose the ferment of thought from which it sprang. But we shall learn perhaps more of the real character of the age and of the forces at work in it by studying the manner in which men learned and taught, and had their controversies, and making acquaintance with some types of its culture, than by a direct analysis of its dialectical theories.

CHAPTER IV.

THE SCHOOL OF CHARTRES.

At the beginning of the twelfth century three schools are distinguished in the contemporary literature above the multitude which had sprung into new life in France and were connected with so many of her cathedrals and religious houses. These three were at Laon, Paris, and Chartres.[1] It would be more accurate to say, they were the schools of Anselm and Ralph, of William of Champeaux, and of Bernard the Breton. For in those days the school followed the teacher, not the teacher the school. Wherever a master lived, there he taught; and thither, in proportion to his renown, students assembled from whatever quarter. Thus it had been at Tournay, as we have seen, under Odo, at Bec under Lanfranc and Anselm, and still earlier under Fulbert at Chartres. The tie was a personal one, and was generally severed by the master's death. A succession of great teachers in one place was a rare exception.

The eminence of William of Champeaux drew logical students to Paris, but not because he taught at Paris. The success of one of them, Abailard, [a] in forcing his master to modify the basis of his system added a peculiar notoriety to a school whose fame was already established: for William's action heralded the downfall of the old-fashioned realism, and the orthodox system, heretofore so solid and substantial, came to acknowledge sects whose number and division might contrast unfavourably with the comparative unity of their rivals. Moreover the

[a] Abael. hist. calam. ii. Opp. I. 5, ed. Cousin 1849.

[1] [Rheims under Alberic should be added to the number: cf. supra, p. 68 n. 30, and infra, p. 129.]

exciting presence of Abailard tended to give Paris a permanent importance as a seat of learning. The natural pugnacity of youth gathered crowds of students to a scene where an endless encounter was going on, in their several lecture-rooms, between the heads of the opposing parties. Paris became the centre of the dialectical struggle, and in another generation we see it filled with the noise of a new populace of schools set up in every part by ambitious teachers. But the schools of William of Champeaux flourished only with their master. We are not even certain who occupied his place at Notre Dame; for it is only a hazardous guess that identifies his successor with [b] Robert of Melun: nor is the celebrity of Saint Victor, where the later years of William's life as a teacher were passed, any the more connected with him. He left the priory, on his elevation to the see of Châlons, a name for dialectic: but that which made the enduring reputation of the abbey ([c] it obtained this dignity in the year of his removal, or the year after) was something quite different. It was an impulse of reaction from the dialectic movement, due to the presence among its canons of Hugh of Saint Victor. The spirit which Hugh infused was more theological and religious, less instinctively literary, far less secular. This was the stamp of the mystics of Saint Victor which long remained their common tradition; but it was not the legacy of William of Champeaux.

[b] Schaarschmidt, Johannes Saresberiensis 72.

A.D. 1112.

[c] Duchesne, not. xii. in hist. calam., Abael. opp. 1. 42; Hist. litt. de la France 10. 308, 1756; C. de Rémusat, Abélard, 1. 16 sqq.; 1845.

† 1141.

The two other great schools of France have this likeness to William's, that they were rigorously realistic; but in neither were dialectics the main interest of the place in the way they were at Paris. Of the school of Laon we know little besides its renown. Its history is comprised within the lifetime of the brothers Anselm and Ralph, whose celebrity attracted scholars from all parts of western Europe. At one time we see a band of clergymen from Milan, the rival of Rome, prouder in her religious tradition than any other church in Christendom, journeying to Laon that they might sit at the feet of the acknowledged masters in theology.[2] At another [d] it is Wicelin, a mature teacher at Bremen, who gives up his school and spends some years in France, learning the interpretation of holy Writ from the same masters. Anselm, the 'doctor of doctors,'[3] the pupil perhaps of his more famous namesake at Bec,[4] was at different times the master both of William of Champeaux, who seems to have been in some sort regarded as his legitimate successor,[5] and of Abailard, [e] who characteristically despised him as an eloquent man without much judgement; not to speak of Alberic of Rheims, Gilbert of La Porrée, and many more of the theological students of the time. [f] He died as early as 1117, and the [g] school was thenceforward directed by his brother alone; but it seems to have soon lost its peculiar eminence, and with Ralph's death in [h] 1138 it sank again into the obscurity from which their single efforts had raised it.

CHAP. IV.

[d] Helmold. chron. Slav. i. 45 Pertz 21. 46 sq.; 1869.

[e] Abael. hist. cal. iii. Opp. 1. 7: cf. Hug. Metell., ubi infra.

[f] [Sigebert] Auct. Laudun. ad ann., Pertz 6. 445.

[g] Herimann. de miraculis s. Mar. Laudun. iii. 4, Pertz 12. 656.

[h] Hist. litt. 10. 191.

Apart from the personal weight of the teachers, the school had acquired a peculiar and almost unique name for the stedfast fidelity with which it maintained and handed on the pure theological tradition of the church.[6]

[2] Landulf de s. Paulo, Hist. Mediol. xxv, Pertz 20. 30 sq. One of these visitors is mentioned in a letter by an Italian student at Laon, perhaps a little later, printed in the Bibliothèque de l'École des Chartes, 4th series, 1. 465 sq. Another letter, ibid., p. 466, shews how largely the school was frequented. Compare the Histoire littéraire 10. 173–176, where an extensive list of its disciples is given.

[3] The title seems an accepted one: see one of the supplements to Sigebert of Gembloux, Auctar. Affligemense, a. 1100, Pertz 6. 400; John of Salisbury, Epist. ccxi, Opp. 2. 54, ed. J. A. Giles, Oxford 1848.

[4] Histoire littéraire 10. 171. The statement that Anselm of Laon had previously taught at Paris appears, so far as I can discover, to rest upon the patriotic sentiment of du Boulay and the authors of the Histoire littéraire rather than upon any positive testimony.

[5] 'Mortuo Anselmo Laudunensi et Guillelmo Catalaunensi,' wrote Hugo Metellus in his bombastic style to Innocent the Second, 'ignis verbi Dei in terra defecit:' ep. iv, C. L. Hugo, Sacrae Antiquitatis Monumenta 2. 331, Saint Dié 1731 folio. Compare Reiner, a monk of Saint Laurence at Liège, writing about the year 1190, who couples the names together as 'opinatissimos tunc Franciae magistros:' De ineptiis cuiusdam idiotae i, Pertz 20. 596. Later still Vincent of Beauvais, Speculum naturale xxxiii. 93, speaks of Anselm as 'magister nominatissimus scientia morum, et honestate clarus.'

[6] [Anselm's Sententiae are now printed by Dr. F. Bliemetzrieder, Münster 1919].

CHAP. IV.

A generation after Anselm, many years after Ralph, had passed away, their authority is appealed to in the same unquestioned manner as an English clergyman might appeal to Hooker or Barrow. [i] It is relied on as irrefragable by Robert de Bosco, archdeacon of Châlons, in connexion with the trial for heresy of Gilbert of La Porrée in 1148; and later still in 1159 [k] John of Salisbury avers that no one would dare to detract in public from the lustre of those *most splendid lights of Gaul, the glory of Laon, whose memory is in pleasantness and blessing.* It is supposed that while Anselm devoted himself to the field of theology, Ralph instructed the school in the 'liberal arts' generally; but as to the sort of teaching he gave we have no information.[7] Our ignorance appears all the greater in comparison with the amplitude and vivid detail of our knowledge of the school of Chartres, which has a remarkable individuality among the schools of the time. Its interest was not theological nor principally dialectical, but literary: its character was that of a premature humanism. The golden age of the school is nearly contemporary with that of Anselm of Laon and William of Champeaux; but it is carried on to a later date through its master Bernard, whom John of Salisbury signalises as [l] *in modern times the most abounding spring of letters in Gaul.*

[i] Joh. Salisb. Hist. pontif. viii, Pertz 20. 523: cf. Gaufrid. Claraevall. Libell. contra capp. Gilleberti, Bernardi Opp. 2. 1338 c, ed. Mabillon, Paris 1690 folio.
[k] Metalogic. i. 5 p. 746.
[l] Metal. i. 24 p. 782.

The cathedral school of Chartres had early in the preceding century been famous as a house of religious learning. Its president, the saintly Fulbert, a pupil of Gerbert, was one of those quick-souled teachers who, just as saint Anselm two generations later, gave so powerful an impulse to the reviving civilisation of the time. Even [m] after his elevation to the bishoprick of his own city, Fulbert still continued to follow his chosen calling among the scholars of the cloister. The position he won as a teacher—Berengar of Tours was among his pupils,—and the name of 'Socrates' by which his scholars delighted to remember him, bear

[m] Bouquet 10. 466 note e.

[7] [His treatise on the abacus, published in 1890, marks a stage in the history of mathematics in the west. See my work on The Exchequer in the Twelfth Century, pp. 47, 51, 53; Oxford 1912.]

witness to the attractive force of his personality.[8] At his death, says the biographer of saint Odilo, [n] *the study of philosophy in France decayed, and the glory of her priesthood well-nigh perished.* But Fulbert's learning was that of a divine, though he was a scholar and a mathematician too. He was wont of an evening to take his disciples apart in the little garden beside the chapel, and discourse to them of the prime duty of life, to prepare for the eternal fatherland hereafter. Without this presiding thought there was infinite danger in the study of letters by themselves: they were only worth cultivating in so far as they ministered to man's knowledge of divine things.

[n] Iotsald. [Lotsald.] vit. Odil. viii. 32, Actt. SS. 1 Jan. p. 68 a; 1643.

We have little information concerning the fortunes of the school of Chartres after Fulbert's death in 1029;[9] but it is natural to presume that the literary tradition of the city, if not unbroken, was before long restored by the presence, whether his influence was actively exercised or not,[10] of its bishop, the great lawyer Ivo, [o] *a religious man*, as he is described, *and of great learning*, who *in his youth had heard master Lanfranc, prior of Bec, treat of secular and divine letters in that famous school which he had at Bec.* Certainly some time towards the close of Ivo's life (he died in 1115[11]) the school emerges again

[o] Rob. de Monte, Chr., a. 1117, Pertz 6. 485.

[8] Adelman, scholastic of Liège and afterwards bishop of Brescia, writing to Berengar of Tours, recalls prettily 'dulcissimum illud contubernium quod . . . in academia Carnotensi sub nostro illo venerabili Socrate iucundissime duxi . . . Sed absque dubio memor nostri, diligens plenius quam cum in corpore mortis huius peregrinaretur, invitat ad se votis et tacitis precibus, obtestans per secreta illa et vespertina colloquia quae nobiscum in hortulo iuxta capellam de civitate quam Deo volente senator nunc possidet, saepius habebat, et obsecrans per lachrymas . . . ut illuc omni studio properemus, viam regiam directim gradientes:' Ep. ad Bereng., Max. Biblioth. Patrum 18. 438 D, E.

[9] The date I give according to the modern reckoning: see Mabillon, Vet. Anal. 231 ed. 1723; Gall. Christ. 8. 1116 B, Paris 1744 folio. The old account makes it 1028: Max. Biblioth. Patrum 18. 3 A, B.

[10] 'Scholas fecit' in the Martyrologium Ecclesiae Carnotensis prefixed to Juretus' edition of Ivo's letters, Paris 1610, and in Gallia Christiana 8. 1133 A, is so far as I am aware a solitary notice: nor need it mean much. The Histoire littéraire 10. 112 says that Ivo rebuilt the schools.

[11] The year is certain See the Martyrologium and Gallia Christiana 8. 1132 A. Other dates, 1116 and 1117, are probably to be explained by the slowness with which news travelled in those days.

CHAP. IV.

into notice under the rule, first, it should seem, of Bernard, and then of his brother Theodoric; and thenceforward, down to near the middle of the twelfth century, it enjoyed a peculiar distinction among the schools of France. The names of the two brothers are taken by [p] Otto of Freising as a typical instance to illustrate the dangerous nimbleness of Breton wits, a characteristic of which Abailard furnished a still more striking example: [q] Abailard himself adduces them (if it be really to them that he refers) in proof of the perverse theological views that could be maintained by persons holding the highest rank as teachers. Unlike Abailard, however, neither came into conflict with the ecclesiastical authorities.

[p] De gest. Frideric. i. 47, Pertz 20. 376.

[q] Theol. Christ. iv. Opp. 2. 522 sq.; cf. Rémusat, Abélard 2. 210 n. 1.

[r] Bernard and Theodoric were both canons and in turn chancellors of the church of Chartres. The latter, though his activity lasted long beyond his brother's lifetime, may be mentioned first. John of Salisbury distinguishes him as [s] *a most diligent investigator of the arts*, and [t] expressly as a logician; of his skill as a teacher of rhetoric, John [u] speaks in less favourable terms. If we are to credit a [x] curious story, which may not be altogether without authority, it will appear that it was this same scholar who attempted to instruct Abailard in the rudiments of mathematics. Tirric, as he is here called (the name is already softening into Thierry), is again doubtless one with the Terric, [y] *a master of the schools*, who took part in Abailard's trial at Soissons, and the [z] Theodoric of Chartres who was present many years later at that of Gilbert of La Porrée at Rheims. [a] Midway between these two dates he appears as an eminent teacher at Paris. A single treatise, one on the six days of creation, represents for us Theodoric's literary production; and of this only a few extracts have been printed.[12] These suffice, however, to shew us how boldly he pushed the

[r] Hauréau, Comptes rendus, l. c., p. 75.

[s] Metalog. i. 5 p. 745.
[t] lib. iv. 24 p. 905.
[u] lib. ii. 10 p. 804.
[x] v. infra, append. viii.

[y] Abael. Hist. calam. x. opp. 1. 22.
A.D. 1121.
A.D. 1148.
[z] Mabillon. Ann. o. s. B. 6. 435, Paris 1739, folio.
[a] Vit. Adelb. II, in Jaffé, Bibl. rer. Germ. 3. 589 sq.; 1866.

[12] See Hauréau, Hist de la Philos. scol. 1. 393–403 [and Notices et Extraits de quelques Manuscrits Latins de la Bibliothèque Nationale, 1. 51–69; 1890. On Theodoric's unpublished Heptateuchon see A. Clerval, Les Écoles de Chartres au moyen Âge, pp. 172, 221 sqq.; 1895].

principles of realism to their furthest issues, and argued from the doctrine of the unity of all being, that all being is God, and that God is the form of being of all things. How far the author's influence was exercised in the school of Chartres, we are left to surmise from that of his elder brother, whose philosophy was of a similar complexion. For it is to Bernard in all probability that the restoration of the school to its old repute was due. Yet there is little beyond the external relation to connect the teaching of Bernard with that of Fulbert or, for that matter, of Lanfranc. Perhaps the single link is to be discovered in its conservative character, its aversion from modern innovations; but even this attitude marks the great difference between Bernard and his predecessors. They looked back and relied upon Christian doctrine as it had filtered through the dark ages; he sought his models beyond Christianity in the reliques of classical antiquity, and emulated neither the theological weight of Fulbert nor the dialectical prowess, such as it was, of Lanfranc.

Bernard [13] was a devoted Platonist,—[b] *perfectissimus inter Platonicos seculi nostri*, says John of Salisbury,—but instead of for that reason attacking nominalism, he rather sought to win his opponents over to his side by a demonstration of the essential harmony of Plato and Aristotle. We may believe [c] John of Salisbury when he says that the proof was unsuccessful; but he gives no details, nor is it likely that he entered into a minute examination of the different theories current in his day. He stood by the ancients and took little heed of what appeared to him ephemeral controversies. It is indeed

[b] Metalog. iv 35 p. 918.

[c] Lib. ii. 17 p. 816.

[13] [In the first edition of this book I followed the prevailing opinion and took Bernard of Chartres to be the same person as Bernard Silvester or Silvestris, the author of the treatise De mundi universitate. But M. Hauréau, revising his earlier view, has shewn that the latter's connexions were with Tours, not Chartres: Mémoires de l'Académie des Inscriptions 31. (2.) 99 sq.; 1884. Moreover the abbé A. Clerval, Les Écoles de Chartres au moyen Âge, p. 161, gives reasons for believing that Bernard of Chartres died before 1130; whereas his namesake wrote in the time of Eugenius the Third. See my article on The Masters of the Schools at Paris and Chartres, in the English Historical Review, 35, 326-331; 1920.]

a relief in this tempestuous time to make acquaintance with a man holding a distinguished place as a teacher, who nevertheless pursued his quiet way in the study of the classics, and seemed unconscious of the surrounding tumult. [d] *We are*, he would say, *as dwarfs mounted on the shoulders of giants, so that we can see more and further than they; yet not by virtue of the keenness of our eyesight, nor through the tallness of our stature, but because we are raised and borne aloft upon that giant mass.*

[d] ap. Joh. Salisb. Metalog. iii. 4 pp. 855 sq.

In this reverent dependence on the ancients lies therefore the main peculiarity of the school of Chartres. Learning, Bernard took it, was the fruit of long and patient thought, careful study of worthy models, and a tranquil life free from distracting circumstances. In his own words,

[e] Mens humilis, studium quaerendi, vita quieta,
Scrutinium tacitum, paupertas, terra aliena,
Haec reserare solent multis obscura legendo.

[e] ap. Policr. vii. 13, vol. 2. 145.

Grammar, the necessary staple of a school, was thus to be a discipline as well as a technical acquirement. Now we have to bear in mind that in the middle ages boys learned grammar, that is Latin, not commonly as an accomplishment or piece of training, but as an indispensable vehicle of communication. Fluency more than depth was required, and elegant scholarship was nearly unknown. To meet this demand therefore it was usual for the schoolmaster to drill his boys simply in books of rules and abstracts. Priscian, Donatus, and Alcuin supplied the common text-books, and the classical authors, if heard of at all, were only heard of through delectuses. Bernard's method was a protest directed against this hurried unintelligent system. He maintained that grammar was the basis of all culture and must be learned slowly, leisurely, thoroughly; above all it must be gathered from the classics themselves, and not from all authors alike, but from the best authors.

[f] John of Salisbury has given a large and most interesting picture of what he found in practice under Bernard's disciples. [g] Gilbert of La Porrée followed him as chan-

[f] Metalog. i. 24 pp. 780 sqq.

[g] Metalog. i. 5 p. 745.

cellor, but Bernard's tradition was handed on mainly by William of Conches and Richard l'Évêque. How powerful it was may be illustrated from a number of passages in John of Salisbury's writings. In the account to which we have referred, it is the choice of reading that stands out as the salient characteristic of Bernard's method, and marks it as aiming at a totally different level of excellence from that which had hitherto been deemed sufficient. The primary rudiments of the art were certainly not neglected. The pupil went through all the routine of *metaplasm, schematism, and figures of speech;* but this was only the groundwork. As soon as possible he was introduced to the classical texts themselves; and in order to create a living interest in the study, Bernard used not merely to treat these grammatically, but also to comment freely upon them. He would point out for instance how the style of prose differs from that of verse, *so that what are vices in the one may be even counted virtues in the other.* Nor did he confine himself to the form of what was being read; he was still more anxious to impress upon his pupils its meaning. It was a principle with him that *the wider and more copious the master's knowledge, the more fully will he perceive the elegancy of his authors and the more clearly will he teach them.* For in them, explains John, the bare material is so refined and perfected by knowledge drawn from every possible source *that the finished work appears in some sort an image of all arts. . . . Ransack Virgil or Lucan, and whatever philosophy thou profess, thou wilt find there its quintessence.* This method of illustration, of bringing all forces to bear upon one's subject, is noted by the same writer as characterising Gilbert of La Porrée, the most famous scion of the Chartres school. *He used,* says John, *the help of all sciences, as the matter demanded; for he knew that the general consists, by mutual service, in the particular.*[14]

[14] Utebatur, prout res exigebat, omnium adminiculo disciplinarum, in singulis quippe sciens auxiliis mutuis universa constare: Historia pontificalis xii p. 526. The authorship of this invaluable record, which was published for the first time in 1868, as an anonymous

CHAP. IV.

Bernard carried out his system in a way that suggests the routine of a much later age. He set his boys, or young men (for, if John of Salisbury's case be typical, the course was rather that of a university than of a school), to do daily exercises in prose and verse composition, and prepared them by explaining the qualities in the orators or poets which they should imitate; his great rule being that they should be brought up on the best models and eschew the rest. *Among the virtues of the grammarian*, says John, *the ancients justly reckoned this: to be ignorant of some things.* The pupils passed round their copies of verses to one another for correction, and the healthy friction helped to keep up the stimulating influence of their master. Nor was composition the only practice which they were given. They had also to learn by rote, and every day keep a record of as much as they could remember of the previous day's lesson; *for with them the morrow was the disciple of yesterday. . . . After this wise*, adds John of Salisbury, *did my preceptors, William of Conches and Richard surnamed the Bishop, now by office archdeacon of Coutances, a man good both in life and conversation, instruct their pupils awhile. But afterwards, when opinion did prejudice to truth, and men chose rather to seem than to be philosophers, and professors of arts undertook to instil the whole of philosophy into their auditors more quickly than in three or even two years,—they were overcome by the onset of the unskilled crowd and retired.*[15] *Since then less time and less care have been bestowed on grammar, and persons who profess all arts, liberal and mechanical, are ignorant of the primary art, without which a man proceeds in vain to the rest. For* [h] *albeit the other studies assist literature, yet this has the sole privilege of making one lettered.*

[h] cf. Metalog. i. 27 pp. 777 sq.

---

work, by Dr. Wilhelm Arndt in Pertz's twentieth volume, was proved by Dr. von Giesebrecht in the Sitzungsberichte der philosophisch-philologischen und historischen Classe der königlichen Bayerischen Akademie der Wissenschaften, 3. 125 sq.; Munich 1873.

[15] I have commented on the interpretation of this passage, which seems to me to have been generally misunderstood, infra, Appendix vii.

A competitive system such as that John refers to, was a natural result of the [i] intellectual restlessness of the time. The aim of the school of Chartres was directly opposed to this. Grammar, according to Bernard, was not to be treated as a mere technical study, as an instrument to be used in philosophy or theology: it was an end in itself. In a word he endeavoured according to his lights to substitute for grammar philology in the large sense. The level to which he attained may appear to us very imperfect; but we have at least this testimony to his success, that John of Salisbury, who followed his method, wrote indisputably the purest, if not the most graceful, Latin of the middle ages. He has a taste in style and a breadth of reading for which no previous period has prepared us. The idea of learning which he reveals is something quite different from what we meet with in the preceding centuries, whether in the eleventh, in the verbose inanities of [k] Anselm the Peripatetic, or even at the close of the ninth, in the childish unconsciousness of saint Notker Balbulus, himself an inmate of the renowned monastery of Saint Gall. The latter, after discoursing at length [l] *Of the famous Men who have expounded the holy Scriptures*, thinks it necessary to say a word about secular literature. *For the rest*, he says (he is writing to Solomon, afterwards bishop of Constance), *if thou desirest to know also the authors of the gentiles, read Priscian. Moreover, the histories of Josephus the Jew and of our Hegesippus should be read. And I set an end to my book. Amen.*

[i] cf. cap. 3 p. 741.

[k] v. supra, pp. 81 sq.

[l] De illustr. viris qui s. scripturas exponebant sub fin., Pez, Thes. anecdd. noviss. 1 (1) 14.

From what has been said of Bernard's conservative temper, and of the way in which he held aloof from the popular wrangle of dialectical controversies, it may fairly be surmised that his school did not attract so great a number of pupils as some other schools which had sprung up with the dialectical movement, and which devoted themselves to the novel vogue. Such, as we shall see, were those of Melun, and of Saint Geneviève and the Petit Pont at Paris. At the same time we may reasonably infer that Chartres attracted a distinctly higher class

CHAP. IV.

of students than these, at least after the retirement of William of Champeaux, and the death of the brothers of Laon. John of Salisbury may again be called as witness. After two years under famous dialecticians at Paris, he was glad enough to spend three more under the masters of Chartres. The teachers he names in this connexion are William of Conches and Richard l'Évêque : a third distinguished disciple of Bernard, Gilbert of La Porrée, who was perhaps still resident at Chartres when he arrived, John did not attend as a master, so far as we know, until later. These successors of Bernard illustrate the tendencies of his teaching in several ways; but it is remarkable that only one of them, William, and William only in a modified degree, can be regarded as Bernard's heir in what we take to be his special characteristic, namely his indifference to, if not his negation of, theology as a branch of scientific study.

m Metalog. i. 5 p. 745.

n v. Metalog. i. 13 pp. 758 sq.

William of Conches is ranked after Bernard [m] as the most accomplished, *opulentissimus*, grammarian of his time. With him, as with Bernard and with [n] John of Salisbury, the rules of speech which comprise grammar, dialectic, and rhetoric, and are together included under the name of *eloquence*, are the first things which the philosopher must possess : *with them equipped, as with arms, we ought to approach the study of philosophy*, first as learned in the sciences of the Quadrivium, and finally in theology, *since by the knowledge of the creature we attain to a knowledge of the Creator*.[16] But the basis of the whole is grammar : *in omni doctrina grammatica praecedit*. This is the mark of the school of Chartres; and it is unfortunate that William's comprehensive work, the *Philosophia*, remains a fragment at the end of the fourth book just at the point where he is about to introduce the characteristic subject.

[16] Philosophia iv. 41 Hon. p. 1020 F. The work to which I refer under this title I quote either from the edition printed as the work of Honorius of Autun, in the twentieth volume of the Lyons Max. Biblioth. Patr., 1667, or from that to be found among Bede's works, vol. 2, in the edition of Basle 1563 folio; which recensions I distinguish as Hon. and Bed. On the various intricate questions relating to William's bibliography see below, Appendix, v, vi.

Hence we know the author principally as a natural philosopher, it would be more accurate to say, as a cosmologer; and in this quality his writings are a good sample of the freedom of thought that issued from the classic calm of Chartres.

Bernard had found in his philosophy an adequate explanation of all the phaenomena of life, ethical and metaphysical as well as physical: and William was his true disciple; but with this difference, that he expanded the definition of philosophy so as to include theology. His views on this subject, there can be no doubt, he derived almost exclusively from the writings of Abailard; but if he was only a theologian at second hand, this was because his interest was still confined to the outward facts of nature. He borrowed from theology just so much as was necessary to elucidate the genesis and order of the universe, and beyond this he did not care to go. For the same reason he parted company with the realists before accepting that doctrine of ideas which others found the most attractive feature in Platonism. Alike in his [o] commentary on Boëthius's *Consolation of Philosophy*, a work of a comparatively early date, and in the [p] *Dragmaticon* which he wrote long afterwards with an avowedly apologetic purpose, we find the same reluctance to admit conclusions which, he plainly felt, did not belong to his proper field of enquiry. His business was with the external and tangible. The root of his system is disclosed in the sentence above quoted: *By the knowledge of the creature we attain to a knowledge of the Creator.* Nor was this any but a legitimate application of the habits of thought current in the schools of the time. Realism no less than nominalism, as Bernard and Theodoric are witness, had its [q] inevitable issues running counter to the accepted religion: yet the realists as a rule were disposed rather to compromise Christianity in favour of Plato than to loose hold of the universal truth of their philosophical theories. William of Conches treats the two authorities as practically coördinate, and, with the one exception to which we have

[o] v. Jourdain, Not. et extr. des manuscr. 20 (2) 54 n. 3.

[p] v. infra, p. 129.

[q] cf. Tr. de gener. et spec., Cousin, Ouvr. inéd. d'Abél. 517, 1836; Rémusat 2. 97 sqq.

CHAP. IV.

[r] Philos. i. 19 Hon. p. 999 E.

referred, confidently adapts his interpretation of the letter of Scripture to the principles which he had learned, through whatever indirect channels, from Plato. [r] *The wisdom of the world,* he repeats, *is foolishness with God: not that God esteems the wisdom of this world to be foolishness, but because it is foolishness in comparison of his wisdom; nor does it follow on that account that it is foolishness.*

William therefore seeks God through nature: he proves his existence from the good design and government of the world, and scruples not to find a different explanation of the mystery of the Trinity from that which is sanctioned by the fathers of the church. *There is,* he says,[17] *in the Godhead, power, and wisdom, and will, which the saints call three persons, applying these terms to them by a sort of affinity of meaning, and saying that the divine power is Father, the wisdom Son, the will the Holy Ghost. . . . The Father,* he continues, *begat the Son, that is the divine power begat wisdom, when he provided how he would create things and dispose them when created: and since he provided this before the ages, before the ages he begat the Son, that is, wisdom; and this of himself not of another, because not by the teaching of another nor by experience, but of his own nature, he had this knowledge. From the time he was (if it be lawful to say it of eternity), from that time he knew these things, nor was there any else to know them. If therefore he is eternal, his wisdom also is eternal. Thus the Father begat the Son, coëternal with him and consubstantial.*[18] In

[17] Est igitur in Divinitate potentia, sapientia, voluntas: quas sancti tres *personas* vocant, vocabula illis a vulgari per quandam affinitatem transferentes; dicentes potentiam divinam *Patrem*, sapientiam *Filium*, voluntatem *Spiritum sanctum*: Philos. i. 6 (Bed. 2. 312; Hon., p. 998 A). Cf. infra, Appendix vi. 6.

[18] Pater ergo genuit Filium, id est, divina potentia sapientiam, quando providit qualiter res crearet et creatas disponeret: et quia ante secula hoc providit, ante secula Filium, id est, sapientiam, genuit; et hoc ex se non ex alio, quia neque alicuius doctrina neque usus experientia, sed ex propria natura hoc scire habuit. Ex quo autem fuit (si fas est dicere de aeterno), ex eo [*edd.* quo] haec scivit, nec [*al.* non] fuit qui [*al.* quin] ista sciret. Si [*al.* Sic] ergo aeternus est, et [*al.* quia] sapientia eius aeterna est. Hic [*al.* Sic] Pater genuit Filium coaeternum sibi et consubstantialem: Philos. i. 8 Bed. 2. 313. I add in the last three sentences the variants from Hon. p. 998 C; in one word I have conjectured an emendation.

another place [s] William expressly rejects the notion that Eve was created out of Adam's rib, as a crabbed, literal interpretation. *How*, he asks, *are we contrary to the divine Scripture, if concerning that which it states to have been done, we explain the manner in which it was done?* [19]

CHAP. IV.

[s] Philos. i. 23; infra, append. vi. § 6.

Such independent utterances not unnaturally made William an object of violent dislike to his more cautious or more pious contemporaries. His works are full of complaints of his detractors. He accounts for the opposition he met with, as the venom of envious rivals: *Because they know not the forces of nature, in order that they may have all men comrades in their ignorance, they suffer not that others should search out anything, and would have us believe like rustics and ask no reason; so that now the word of the prophet should be fulfilled, The priest shall be as the people. But we say that in all things a reason must be sought, and if it fail we must confide the matter, as the divine page declares, to the Holy Spirit and to faith.*[20] These envious monks, however, *if they perceive any man to be making search, at once cry out that he is a heretic, presuming more on their habit than trusting in their wisdom.*[21] William takes them to be altogether the same class of teachers who compounded for the slenderness of their knowledge by the pace at which they could carry their pupils through the whole of philosophy. [t] He is never tired of inveighing against these glib smatterers.

[t] v. infra, appendix vii.

At length, however, as he advanced in years, William

[19] Nam in quo divinae scripturae contrarii sumus, si quod in illa dictum est esse factum, nos qualiter factum sit explicemus: Hon. p. 1002 E (*Nos* I supply from Bed. 2. 318).

[20] Sed quoniam ipsi nesciunt vires naturae, ut ignorantiae suae omnes socios habeant, nolunt eos aliquid inquirere, sed ut rusticos nos credere nec rationem quaerere; ut iam impleatur propheticum, *Erit sacerdos sicut populus.* Nos autem dicimus in omnibus rationem esse quaerendam: si autem alicui deficiat (quod divina pagina affirmat) Spiritui sancto et fidei est mandandum: ibid. Cf. infra, p. 149 n. 6.

[21] Si inquirentem aliquem sciant illum esse haereticum clamant, plus de suo caputio praesumentes quam sapientiae suae confidentes: ib., p. 1002 F.

CHAP. IV.

came to see that there was this justice in the objections raised against him on the score of orthodoxy, that even though every doctrine he maintained was capable of defence, he had erred in the novelty of the terms in which he had stated them. Some time after John of Salisbury had quitted Chartres, William of Saint Thierry, the prime mover in the final attack on Abailard, [u] detected the danger that lurked under the innocent form of Conches's *Philosophy*. It was enough, he said, to have had a new theology to extirpate in the case of Abailard, without the addition of a new philosophy.[22] He wrote a strenuous letter on the subject to Bernard of Clairvaux; and the influence of the autocratic saint conspired, it seems, with the hostility which William of Conches had excited among rival teachers, to determine the latter to withdraw from the wrangle of the schools. His Norman birth perhaps helped to find him protection in the household of [x] Geoffrey the Fair, count of Anjou, who was now in occupation of Normandy, and who had himself endured the edge of saint Bernard's vigorous denunciation.[23]

[u] Ep. ad Bern. de error. G. de Conch., B. Tissier, Bibl. patr. Cisterc. 4. 127–130, 166e folio.

[x] cf. infra, append. vi.

To this prince William addressed a new edition of his *Philosophy*, rewritten in a more docile spirit, and distinguished from the earlier book by its dialogue form. He confesses in it [y] the errors and omissions which experience had discovered to him in the work of his youth, *imperfectum, utpote imperfecti*, and is resolved to make ample amends by striking out not only *things contrary to the catholic faith*, but also everything at all connected with it which, though capable of defence, might savour dangerously of novelty. It was better, he felt, to be silent than to risk the possibility of falsehood. His former work, therefore, he suppressed, and begged everyone who possessed the book to join him in condemning

[y] Dragmaticon, praef., pp. 5 sq., Strasburg 1567: cf. infra, append. iv. 2.

[22] Etenim post Theologiam Petri Abäelardi Guillelmus de Conchis novam affert Philosophiam, confirmans et multiplicans quaecunque ille dixit: Epist., ubi supra, p. 127.

[23] 'Comes Andegavensis, malleus bonorum, oppressor pacis et libertatis ecclesiae,' says Bernard in a letter assigned to the year 1141: Ep. cccxlviii. 2, Opp. 1. 317.

and destroying it. *Not words*, he protested, *make a heretic, but their defence.* It is a strange commentary on his judgement, and on the criticism of William of Saint Thierry, that the work thus disowned should have lived to be printed in three several editions as the production of the Venerable Bede, of saint Anselm's friend, William of Hirschau, and of Honorius of Autun; the taint of heresy plainly cannot have been long perceptible to medieval librarians. Nor, indeed, was the change that transformed the *Philosophy* into the *Dragmaticon* a very extensive one: substantially the two books are for the most part the same. To the ideology of Plato he had never committed himself: now he takes the opportunity of emphasising his correct position with respect to a pitfall into which, in fact, he had never stumbled; [24] in such matters, he says, [z] *Christianus sum, non academicus.* He remained a Platonist so far as the external and rational elements of the philosophy were concerned, but he went to orthodox theology for the rest.

[z] Dragm. vi. p. 306.

It is likely that the moderation with which he had learned to express his views restored his credit in the eyes of the stricter churchmen. Certainly his *Dragmaticon* enjoyed a remarkable popularity, and a wide diffusion attested by a multitude of manuscripts at Vienna, Munich, Paris, Oxford, and other places. The favour in which he was held by Geoffrey Plantagenet we know only from William's own scanty notices, and of his later years nothing is recorded. If it be true that he died at Paris about 1154,[25] we may find here a possible kernel of truth in the old tradition which has been constantly repeated from du Boulay, Oudin, and the other literary historians,

[24] The Dragmaticon, or Dialogus de Substantiis physicis, has been carefully analysed in an interesting paper by professor Karl Werner, in the seventy-fifth volume of the Sitzungsberichte der philosophisch-historischen Classe der kaiserlichen Akademie der Wissenschaften, Vienna 1873. See especially pp. 400 sqq.

[25] The date is given among the notices of 1154, but with the prefix 'hoc tempore,' and only in the chronicle of Alberic, called of Trois Fontaines, who died nearly a century later: Bouquet 13. 703 D; 1786.

CHAP. IV.

and which makes William from first to last a distinguished figure in the 'university' of that city.[26]

The meagre facts thus elicited concerning the philosopher's external biography are abundant in comparison with those recorded of his colleague at Chartres, Richard l'Évêque, whose virtues as a man and a scholar are,[a] celebrated in no ordinary terms by his pupil and friend, John of Salisbury. Richard, so far as is known, left no memorial as a writer. Unlike William he advanced from teaching to the active service of the church; he became archdeacon of Coutances, and finally in [b] 1171 bishop of Avranches. The situation of his ministry brought him also into connexion with the house of Anjou, and it was his city of Avranches that witnessed the readmission of Henry the Second to the communion of the church after the murder of Thomas Becket. He died in 1182, the last survivor of the masters of Chartres.

[a] Metalog. ii. 10 p. 804, &c.

[b] Hist. litt. 14. 215 sq.; 1817.

A.D. 1172.

Gilbert of La Porrée has a more important place in the philosophical history of the age even than William of Conches, partly because his studies lay in departments of learning to which a greater relative weight was attached than to natural philosophy or grammar. A contemporary panegyrist proclaims him lacking in no one of the seven liberal arts, save only astronomy;[27] but in sober history he appears as a theologian and a dialectician. In dialectics he holds in one way a quite unique position; for

[26] Dr. Schaarschmidt, who was the first, I think, to combat this theory, is inclined, Johannes Saresberiensis 22, to question William's connexion with Paris at any time. The epitaph however, or rather the panegyric, upon him, which says,

> Eius praeclaret natu Normannia, victu
> Francia, Parisius corpore, mente polus,

is stated to have been the composition of Philip Harveng, abbat of Bonne Espérance, who died perhaps thirty years after William: Du Boulay, Historia Universitatis Parisiensis 2. 743. It appears indeed that M. Charma disputes this evidence and discovers the philosopher's grave in a village near Évreux: see Hauréau, Singularités historiques et littéraires 266. This, if proved, would be a welcome solution of a vexed question.

[27] Temporibus nostris celeberrimus ille magister,
Logicus, ethicus hic, theologus atque sophista,
Solaque de septem cui defuit astronomia :—Du Boulay 2. 736.

his *Book of the Six Principles*, a supplement to the *Categories* of Aristotle, was accepted through the middle ages as second only in authority to the works of the founder of logic (among which, both in manuscript and print,[28] it held its place until the Latin versions of Aristotle were exchanged in general use for editions of the Greek), and it was made the basis of extensive commentaries by Albert the Great and several other schoolmen. Gilbert is thus the first medieval writer who was at once taken as a recognised authority on logic, the immediate successor of Boëthius and Isidore; for Alcuin's *Dialectic*, although a very popular text-book, had only been admitted as a convenient summary, and had by this time been rendered practically obsolete by the higher proficiency which was now expected of logical students: and even if Gilbert's treatise is hardly worthy of its reputation, it undoubtedly indicates a remarkable advance in the notions men had of scientific necessities, that anyone should venture to complete a section of a work of so unapproachable an eminence as Aristotle's *Organon*.

If dialectics made Gilbert's lasting fame, theology was the rock upon which his fortunes were nearly shipwrecked. He is the one man whom saint Bernard of Clairvaux unsuccessfully charged with heresy. This singular experience may be conveniently treated in another connexion; at present it will suffice to notice the few facts which are known about his life. Born in Poitiers about the year 1075,[29] he left his native city to become successively the scholar of [c] Bernard of Chartres and of the illustrious Anselm of Laon.[30] It was doubtless the attraction of the former teacher that recalled him to Chartres, where he

[c] Otto Fris. de gestt. Frid. i. 50 p. 379.

[28] I have used the Venice folio of 1489.

[29] John of Salisbury, writing of the year 1148, speaks of Gilbert as one who 'circiter annos 60 expenderat in legendo et tritura litteraturae:' Historia pontificalis viii. Pertz 20. 522.

[30] M. Hauréau, Histoire de la Philosophie scolastique 1. 448 [following Mabillon, praef. in Bernardi Opp. i. § lviii.], rightly exposes the error by which Otto of Freising describes Hilary of Poitiers as Gilbert's first master. *Saint* Hilary was in fact the father to whose writings Gilbert constantly professes himself peculiarly indebted.

CHAP. IV.

settled and was made chancellor of the cathedral. After perhaps twenty years of this life he removed to Paris, and gave lectures in dialectics and theology. He did not, however, stay long in the capital, for in 1142 he was raised to the bishoprick of Poitiers.[31] Possibly he was not sorry then to obtain an honourable office in the country, for we are told that [d] Abailard, when approaching condemnation at the council of Sens, turned to Gilbert with the line of Horace,

[d] Gaufrid. Vit. s. Bernardi v. 15, Bern. opp. 2. 1122 F.

[e] Tunc tua res agitur, paries cum proximus ardet.

[e] 1 epist. xviii. 84.

Gilbert must therefore have already been pointed at as a fellow-heretic with the victim of Sens. The presage, as the sequel shews, proved true; but it was four years after his preferment that the crisis of his life came. A charge of heresy which was brought against him occupied and perplexed the deliberations of two successive councils; and to this day it is debated whether he was condemned or acquitted. It will suffice for the present to observe that the visible result of the second council was that the bishop returned untouched to his diocese, where for the few years remaining of his long life he ruled in peace. [f] He died in 1154. The fact that his alleged offence related to the detail of theological metaphysics takes it out of the atmosphere of that school of which we have attempted to discern the peculiar elements. His theology is a legacy not from the teaching of Bernard of Chartres, but from Anselm of Laon, who, [g] we know, had suggested, though he did not countenance, at least one of the theses which brought Gilbert into trouble.[32] It is also necessary to bear in mind that the

A.D. 1148.

[f] Rob. de Monte Chron. a. 1154 [Chron. of Stephen, &c., 4. 181, ed. R. Howlett, 1889.]

[g] Jo. Salisb. Hist. pont. viii. p. 523.

[31] Compare my article in the English Historical Review, 35. 325 sq., 332 sq.

[32] A special point of connexion between Anselm and Gilbert lies in the fact that the latter wrote a series of glosses in continuation and extension of his master's Glossa interlinearis et marginalis, itself a supplement to the standard Glossa ordinaria of Walafrid Strabo. 'Considerato quippe magistri Anselmi Laudunensis glossandi modo, quod videlicet nimia brevitate non nisi ab exercitatis in expositionibus patrum posset intelligi, glossam proliχiorem eoque evidentiorem fecit:' Appendix to Henry of Ghent, De scriptoribus ecclesiasticis, cap. viii., A. Miraeus, Biblioth. eccles. 174, Antwerp 1639 folio. Gilbert thus

latter would in all probability never have attracted hostile notice, had not the party of tradition first tasted blood in the person of Abailard. Ignorance, prejudice, an incapacity of criticism, coupled the two men together; and Gilbert suffered from the tail of the storm which had overwhelmed Abailard. CHAP. IV.

became a joint author of what was practically the authorised body of notes on the Bible current in the middle ages. The 'glosatura magistri Giliberti Porretani super Psalterium quam ipse recitavit coram suo magistro Anselmo,' Psalms (cod. coll. Ball. Oxon. xxxvi, f. 144 D), appears to have been held in particular esteem: cf. Alberic, a. 1149, Bouquet 13. 702 B; Robert de Monte, a. 1154; William of Nangy, who also refers to Gilbert's comments on the Pauline epistles, ibid., vol. 20. 736 B. See too du Boulay 2. 734 (who accidentally writes *Petri* for *Giliberti*), and the Histoire littéraire de la France 10. 181, 12. 474. [That Gilbert was the author of the commentary on the Pauline epistles, which has also been attributed to Gilbert of St. Amand, is proved by Denifle, Luther und Luthertum, 1. (2), Quellenbelege, 334–346, Mentz, 1905.]

CHAPTER V.

PETER ABAILARD.

CHAP. V.

WITH Abailard we turn again to the schools of dialectic, but Abailard is much more than a dialectician. He is the commanding figure in the intellectual history of his age,

[a] Epitaph. ii, sub fin., Opp. 1.717, ed. Cousin.

[a] Cui soli patuit scibile quidquid erat.

It is his general attitude towards the study of philosophy and of theology that demands our examination, far rather than those technical points in which he was suspected of departing from catholic Christianity. If he was, as he consistently maintained, the devoted son of the church, he was none the less a herald of free thought by virtue of his bold assertion of the duty of private judgement and his contempt of those who take everything on trust. [b] *By doubting we are led to enquire; by enquiry we perceive the truth*: this is the method which Abailard professes. It is not that he doubts that the two roads, of reason and authority, must ultimately converge: only he will not start from any but the direct questionings of his own mind. Self-reliance is his special characteristic. It shews itself in his personal history even more than in his writings, so that his entire life is an exemplification of the force of a Titanic personality in revolt against the spirit of his time.

[b] Sic et non, prol. p. 17, ed. E. L. T. Henke et G. S. Lindenkohl; Marburg 1851.

Abailard,[1] like so many of the great men in the earlier

[1] With reference to the name, it is hardly necessary to say that from the first its spelling fluctuates. In the editions it is commonly normalised as *Abaëlardus*; the diphthong is altogether a modern invention, disproved by every instance in which it occurs in verse. On the whole it seems that *Abaielardus* is the earliest form. This appears, e. g., in the facsimile of the Munich manuscript of the Sic et non given at the end of Henke's edition, as

middle ages who have been given the highest place in the literary history of France, was not a Frenchman. He was born [2] in Brittany, at [c] Palais, or Le Pallet, in the neighbourhood of Nantes. Although the eldest son of a good house, he early abandoned his birthright to his brothers and resolved to make himself a name in learning. He became a pupil, [d] *discipulorum minimus*, of Roscelin, the daring nominalist whose doctrine was condemned in its theological issues by the council of Soissons in 1092, but who appears to have submitted to the sentence and to have been allowed to hold a scholastic post at the church of [e] Saint Mary of Loches in Touraine.[3] Roscelin, if we are to give credit to an old [f] legend, soon excited a spirit

CHAP. V.
A.D. 1079.
[c] Hist. calamitatum i. Opp. 1. 3 sq
[d] Rosc. ep. ad Abael., Abael. Opp. 2. 794.
[e] Hauréau, Singul. hist. et litt. 228.
[f] v. infra, append. viii.

well as in Otto of Freising (ed. Pertz) and John of Salisbury (in his Historia pontificalis), although the former alternates with *Abaiolardus*. Of the Paris manuscripts of the thirteenth century, edited by Cousin in the Ouvrages inédits d'Abélard, one gives *Abailardus* (intr. p. viii.), the other two *Abaelardus* (see the facsimile facing p. 434). Other rare forms need not be quoted, some of them are uncouth enough; but the fact that the initial *a* was frequently dropped (see an instance below, Appendix viii.) may be taken as evidence of where the accent lay. It was natural that the word should become softened in common use; and *Abailardus* and *Abalaërdus* were no doubt practically undistinguishable in pronunciation. I adopt the former, partly because it approaches nearest to the original (though it needs no apology even to the French, since it is accepted in Firmin-Didot's Nouvelle Biographie générale), partly because it avoids those associations with eighteenth-century sentimentalism which surround the name of *Abélard* and obscure the philosopher's true significance. The popularity of this last spelling seems to date from its selection by Pierre Bayle in his Dictionnaire historique et critique, s. v.

[2] For the biography my principal guide has been Abailard's own correspondence, though this has necessarily to be taken with reserve. Besides the contemporary literature, I have derived very great help from the biography of Charles de Rémusat, the first piece of genuine scholarly work ever devoted to Abailard. Still it should be observed that Bayle, in the article above referred to, has the credit of introducing order into the narrative of Abailard's life; in which respect Milman, for instance, History of Latin Christianity 4. 342–365, is not seldom far less trustworthy. From all the authorities—Cousin, Ritter, Hauréau, and Prantl should be added—I have ventured to differ seriously in my general estimate of Abailard's character. While preparing this and the following chapters for the press I have had the advantage of reading Dr. S. M. Deutsch's Peter Abälard, ein kritischer Theolog des zwölften Jahrhunderts; 1883.

[3] Dr. von Prantl identifies this *ecclesia Locensis* with Locmenach, now Locminé, near Vannes, in Brittany: Geschichte der Logik im Abendlande 2, 77 [78] n. 314.

CHAP. V.

[g] ibid., sub fin.

of resistance in his pupil, and in a year Abailard left the school. After spending perhaps a short time at [g] Chartres, where he attempted in vain to acquire the rudiments of mathematics,—though this experience may belong to a later period in his career,—he made his way to Paris, to the cathedral school, where his master was the representative realist, William of Champeaux.

The abruptness of the transition from Roscelin to William, the extreme views held by the two masters, may explain how it was that Abailard set himself in turn to combat the logical position of both; but his subsequent career sufficiently shews how little inclined he was under any circumstances to subject his intellect to the authority of a teacher. The nominalistic principles which he had learned from Roscelin, he took with him to Paris and used with signal effect against the hierophant of realism. He at once aspired to the rank and influence of an acknowledged master, but the not unnatural hostility of William seems to have prevented his opening a school in Paris itself. The history of the relations of the two rivals is like John Scot's account of logic; it was a flight and a chase, [h] *quaedam fuga et insecutio*. The same city was not large enough to hold them both. Abailard therefore began by teaching at some distance from Paris, in the royal fortress of [i] Melun; he soon ventured a little lower down the Seine, to Corbeil. But the severity of his studies had told upon his health, and he was forced to take rest. For a few years he lived in seclusion, possibly with his family in Brittany; but so soon as his strength was recovered he hastened again to Paris.

[h] Heric. Autissiod. gloss., ap. Cousin, Fragm. philos. 2. 320.

[i] Hist. calam. ii. pp. 4 sq.

By this time William of Champeaux also had withdrawn from the active work of the cathedral school and had retired to the priory of Saint Victor. But the pressure of his friends had not left him long in his religious leisure: he was now lecturing at Saint Victor on the old subjects, and Abailard was once more found among his auditory, less a pupil than a critic. Abailard pressed the master with objections: he boasts that he compelled him to seek a new formula for his logical theory,[4] and the success of this feat made the adventurous disputant for the time the hero of the schools. He set up a school for himself; he was even invited by William's successor at Notre Dame to take his place. But William, though at Saint Victor, was not out of hearing of what went on in the city. He did not risk a personal encounter with Abailard, but attacked him through the master who had offered him a post of so dangerous an authority. The too compliant master was disgraced, and Abailard judged it prudent to transfer his school to his old quarters at Melun. Soon, however, William for other reasons also quitted Paris. Abailard was at once on the spot. He established himself upon the hill of Saint Geneviève within a short distance of the city, and determined to brave the consequences. When William once more returned, it was too late. His old fame as a teacher was almost forgotten, while Abailard's position was secured by a crowd of pupils whom the novelty and brilliancy of his discourses had fascinated into the sturdiest of partisans. Such at least is Abailard's account, which, coloured as it undoubtedly is by prejudice and avowed animosity, we have no means of contradicting from other sources. William indeed seems to have given up the long contest: after a while he was glad to subside into the quiet of a bishoprick.

The qualities by which Abailard won his unequalled popularity were not only a native gift for exposition, not only a singular [k] lucidity and plainness of statement so different from the obscure formalism usually inseparable from the handling of logic; but also an originality of thought which enabled him to make a serious revolution

[k] cf. Jo. Salisb. Metalog. iii. 1 p. 840.

[4] The exact nature of this change is doubtful on account of a various reading in the manuscripts of the Historia calamitatum, in respect to which Cousin, Fragments philosophiques 2. 115 sqq., and Rémusat, vol. 1. 20, adopt a different judgement from that generally received, e. g., by Ritter, Geschichte der christlichen Philosophie 3. 358, by M. Hauréau, Histoire de la Philosophie scolastique 1. 337 sqq., and by Dr. von Prantl, vol. 2. 129 sq. [130 sqq.] Dr. Deutsch, p. 103 n. 2, supports the opinion of Cousin and Rémusat.

[l] cf. infra, append. iv.

[m] cf. supra, pp. 86–90.

in the philosophical theory of the 'art.' [l] Traces of conceptualism there certainly are long before Abailard's time. We may find them in the ninth century in the glosses of Heric of Auxerre, if not in Rabanus Maurus: [m] in the eleventh the doctrine reappears in Berengar of Tours. But Abailard, though not the creator, was not the less the principal organiser and, for his own age, the founder of the school which lies intermediate between those of his two first masters. The system which he produced, if it was eclectic, was certainly nearer nominalism than realism: he conceded in fact the affirmations of both sides while denying the correctness of their negations. The main tenet of the nominalists, the absolute existence of the individual, he accepted; but he did not rigidly limit existence to that which is open to the senses. Genera and species, the categories and predicables, he refused indeed to endow with essence as things; they had no actual existence apart from the individual: nor was the universal, as William of Champeaux held, contained in its entirety within the particular. The process was the other way; it was from the particular that we arrived at the general by an effort of thought. On the other hand if the universals, if abstractions of all sorts, were the creations of the intellect, they were also its necessary creations; they were therefore so far real that the human mind could not do without them. In the same way Abailard found no difficulty in the *universalia ante rem*, the universals considered as anterior to the sensible world; since universals might equally be conceived in relation to the mind of God as to our own. The Platonic world of ideas was thus to be understood as existing in God's creative thought.[5]

Abailard's conceptualism was probably the most reason-

[5] See generally Rémusat 2. 119 sqq., Hauréau 1. 380 sqq., Schaarschmidt, Johannes Saresberiensis 319 sqq. The exposition of the two former writers, as well as that of Cousin, vol. 2 160–197, is partly vitiated by the stress they lay on the treatise De generibus et speciebus, the authorship of which is more than doubtful. [See Prantl, 2. 114 n. 49, 144 n. 148.]

able among the many proposals of his day which sought to frame a logical theory free from the revolutionary tendencies of Roscelin's nominalism, and yet better adapted than the elder realism to the more subtil and critical habits of thought to which men were now training themselves. This was virtually a return to the position of Aristotle, and in Abailard's case it is all the more remarkable because his direct acquaintance with the master was limited to the earlier treatises of the *Organon*; [6] he had therefore to [n] discover, to divine, for himself the issues to which Aristotle tended. From Abailard's time, probably through his immediate influence, the authority of the Greek logician grew uninterruptedly until the decline of the middle ages, and there is a strong presumption that [o] it was to the active encouragement of his pupil John of Salisbury that western Europe was indebted for a translation of the rest of the *Organon*. Within a century it possessed almost the whole of Aristotle in a Latin shape. Accordingly it is not surprising that Abailard's permanent reputation was founded upon his dialectical eminence. The [p] title of *Peripatetic*, by which he is regularly styled in John of Salisbury's writings, indicates this distinction, for the name had by this time acquired the same special meaning as [q] *sophist* had two or three centuries before, though it was already being superseded by the more accurate term *dialectician*. [7]

[n] Schaarschmidt 70.

[o] ibid., pp. 120 sq.

[p] cf. Prantl 2. 162 [163].

[q] cf. ibid., pp. 38 [37] n. 147, 76 [78] n. 312.

But Abailard was not contented with his reputation; he would not have his faculties circumscribed in a single field. He had an immense energy of mind, a restless ambition to dominate other minds; and in his age supremacy was only attainable by adding a mastery of theology

[6] How many of them is disputed. Schaarschmidt, pp. 70, 120 (cf. p. 305), says nothing beyond the Categories and the De interpretatione, with the Isagoge of Porphyry: Dr. von Prantl however, vol. 2. 100–104, shows that Abailard's knowledge extended to the Prior Analytics. [Cf. A. Hofmeister, Studien über Otto von Freising, in the Neues Archiv der Gesellschaft für ältere Deutsche Geschichtskunde, 37. 656–664; 1912.]

[7] Peripateticis, quos nunc dialecticos appellamus: Abael. Theol. Christ. iii. 1, Opp. 2. 448.

CHAP. V.

as a key-stone to unite and perfect the structure, in itself incomplete, of human knowledge. Nor would it be just to deny the natural significance of the connexion in which Abailard himself relates this passage in his life. He left his school on Saint Geneviève in order to visit his home in Brittany and to [r] take leave of his mother who was about to withdraw into a nunnery. *I came back to France,* he says, *principally that I might cultivate divine learning,—maxime ut de divinitate addiscerem.* He found his way clear before him: William of Champeaux was now bishop of Châlons, and Abailard might look with hopefulness to a career of influence in the future undisturbed by the evil eye, as he deemed it, of his enemy; rivals he had long ceased to fear. Nevertheless the impression made upon him by that last interview with his mother—we cannot misread the words, although the inference appears to have escaped the notice of his biographers—had taken so fast a hold of his mind that, even in the auspicious situation of affairs ready prepared, one would say, for him in Paris, he could not bring himself to break a solemn resolve. He passed through the capital and presented himself, this mature philosopher of four and thirty, as a disciple of the illustrious Anselm of Laon.

[r] Hist. calam. ii. p. 7.

Abailard has so much faith in himself that he describes every incident in his life as the result of careful planning; he leaves no room for emotion or sudden inspiration:[8] and yet it is these very rapid transitions in his mind that determined the crucial events which give his history so marked an individuality. [s] His self-confidence,—if we will, his vanity,—was opposed by an irresolution, an infirmity of purpose, which was no less characteristic an element in him. He surrendered his prospects in obedience to a religious impulse: doubtless he may have foreseen a wider potentiality of sway in the new field to which he betook himself; still for the moment he sank from the dignity of a famous teacher to the level of his own pupils,

[s] cf. Deutsch 50 sqq.

[8] Rémusat, vol. 1. 49, has made a similar remark in connexion with another incident in Abailard's life, on which see below, pp. 124 sq.

some of whom he perhaps might meet as fellow-scholars in the lecture-room at Laon. But it was one thing to form a resolution, another to have the courage or the humility to carry it out; and as a matter of fact Abailard's impatience of authority soon reasserted itself. He sat at the feet of a master whom he felt to be his inferior, and he despised him. Anselm's language, he says, [t] *was wonderful, but its sense was contemptible and void of reason. He kindled a fire not to give light but to fill the house with smoke.* Truly the genius of the two men lay in exactly opposite directions. Anselm was an erudite theologian, great in the 'case-law' of the fathers, believing what 'was written' and daring not to add to it. Reason, which to Abailard was the highest gift of man and therefore of the widest applicability, Anselm could treat as impotent in theology, just because it was a human faculty; as such, the things of God were beyond its competence. It is evident that the spirit in which Abailard approached the study was precisely the spirit which would be likely to lead to suspicion and danger in the twelfth century.

[t] Hist. calam. iii. p. 7.

His disgust with the [u] *barren fig-tree* whose delusive attraction had enticed him into visiting Laon, very soon became too strong for him to be able to continue his studies there. He ridiculed the notion that one could not teach theology 'without a master,' that is, without having gone through a course of instruction under a master; [9] and he provoked a challenge to put forth a specimen of his own skill. His fellow-students warned him against the temerity, but he would not be restrained. He gave an exposition of Ezekiel which, he tells us, so delighted his hearers that those who first came only from curiosity were joined in the subsequent lectures by a press of diligent students. Anselm was very wroth: his disciples Alberic of Rheims and Lotulf the Lombard,[10] urged upon him the duty of

[u] ibid., capp. iii, iv, pp. 7 sq.

[9] [See Denifle, Die Universitäten des Mittelalters, 1. 765 n. 31.]

[10] Otto of Freising gives the name as *Letald* or *Leutald* of Novara: De gestis Friderici i. 47, Pertz 20. 377. No doubt 'magister Luitolfus' in Gerhoh of Reichersperg, ep. xxi Migne 193. 576 c, is the same person.

interdicting a course of procedure which from being unauthorised was viewed almost in the light of rebellion. To the indignation of the rest of the scholars who had been glad enough to exchange the formal, if weighty, instruction of their old master for lectures into which Abailard threw all the energy and fresh vigour of his intellect, the course was suppressed; the interloper judged it wise to return to Paris. His stay at Laon had only proved to him in his own mind, that no learning, no eminence, was beyond his power: envy, he said, expelled him; rivalry was now out of the question.

x Hist. calam. v. pp. 8 sq.

x Abailard's reception at Paris confirmed his self-conceit. The former enmity there had vanished; only his reputation was remembered. He seems to have been at once made a canon of Notre Dame:[11] he resumed his lectures and became again the most popular teacher of his day.[12] While he was thus in the zenith of his career fate suddenly turned against him: he quitted the cathedral and entered the religious life in the abbey of Saint Denis; for the future he would be dead to the world. The circumstances of this crisis are familiar to all readers, whether of history or romance; and a good deal of mischief has been done by the solemn reproofs of the one, and the sentimentalities of the other, class of writers. Abailard himself, our sole informant of the particulars of his love for Heloïssa, was a man whose self-reliance, as we have said, required that every act of his should seem to be a skilfully devised link

[11] This is a surmise; Abailard is never actually spoken of as a canon of Paris, while different records seem to give him this title at Tours, Chartres, and Sens. See Rémusat 1. 39 n., and compare below p. 171 and n. 30.

[12] It was at this time, I am persuaded, with Cousin, vol. 2. 208 sqq., that Abailard wrote the Sic et non. A collection such as this, of discrepant opinions from the fathers on the principal points of theology, is just what an ambitious lecturer on the subject would prepare for his own use. My view of the date is not incompatible with the presumption raised by Dr. Deutsch, pp. 462 sq., that the prologue to it, naturally the last part of the composition, was written about the year 1121. [M. G. Robert, Les Écoles et l'Enseignement de la Théologie pendant la première Moitié de la xiie Siècle (1909) pp. 166–211, assigns the Sic et non to 1120–1122, the Dialectica to about 1121, the Theologia Christiana to about 1123–1124, the Introductio ad Theologiam to 1125, and the Letters to 1133–1136.]

CHAP. V.

in a consistent chain of policy; he almost writes as if to persuade us that from the outset he deliberately planned his mistress's ruin.[13] To those who read his words with a deeper perception of his character, and much more to those who go on to the long correspondence and the life-long interdependence of Abailard and Heloïssa, such an explanation will appear not merely inadequate but incredible. Abailard's account, written moreover under the oppression of enduring remorse, is too highly coloured by these mixed feelings to be taken as it stands: his interpretation of his error, or his guilt, is misleading. In the words of his wisest biographer, [y] 'he deceives himself; a noble and secret instinct bade him love her who had no equal:' and the same instinct kept the two in spiritual union, however far apart their lives might run, until the end.

[y] Rémusat 1. 49.

[z] Abailard privately married Heloïssa; but this step, a concession to the wishes of her family, was powerless to avert their vengeance. Here we must carefully observe that the marriage was in no wise thought of as an act unbecoming or forbidden to a clergyman. From Abailard's own writings we learn that he would be ready with arguments for such a case. The lower clergy, he held,[14]

[z] Hist. calam. vii. p. 15; epist. v. p. 98.

[13] A recent biographer of saint Bernard has supposed that Abailard began this stage in his career by a course of indiscriminate debauchery, and afterwards paid court to Heloïssa in obedience to a craving for a more select form of gratification: J. Cotter Morison. Life and Times of saint Bernard, 296; 1863. The single basis for the former part of this hypothesis, which is contradicted by Abailard's express statement, Hist. calam. v. p. 9, is a letter by Fulk, prior of Deuil (Abael. Opp. 1. 703–707), whose rhetorical flattery, and whose professed aim of consoling Abailard, cannot conceal the brutality of his satire: he is in fact merely retailing and magnifying whatever idle calumnies were current about Abailard among his enemies, besides adding not a few from his own gross imagination. [Not long before he died Mr. Morison assured me he was convinced that the view which he had expressed was without foundation.]

[14] The passage is in the Sententiae, cap. xxxi, published under the misleading title of Epitome theologiae Christianae by F. H. Rheinwald, Berlin 1835, p. 91 (or in Cousin's edition of the Opera 2. 582). The work is based upon the Introductio ad Theologiam, but unfortunately the particular chapter represents a portion of the Introductio which is now lost. It has been supposed that the Sententiae, although almost certainly not the production of Abailard himself,

CHAP. V.

were free to take wives so long as they were not in charge of a parish. He appealed to the established usage of the Greek church, to the exceptional privileges granted the newly converted English by Gregory the Great, in proof that celibacy was a law of expediency (and thus less or more restricted at different times and places), not one of universal obligation. Accordingly we do not find that either he or any one else objected to his marriage on this ground: it is certain that he was in orders, because he was a canon; but it does not appear that he was as yet even a subdeacon. When [a] Heloïssa argued against the proposal and urged the examples of gentile philosophers who remained unmarried in the interest of their labours, *unbound as they were by any profession of religion*, and concluded, *What does it become thee to do who art clerk and canon?*—the reasoning is simply that if marriage be an impediment to a philosopher's labours, how much more must it affect one with a religious obligation; but there is no hint of any further obstacle. Doubtless Abailard injured his position by his action; possibly [b] he might be conceived to be thereby disqualified from the functions of a theological teacher: but more it would be improper to assert. If there was any prejudice raised against him on this account it was quickly silenced when Fulbert, his wife's uncle, revenged himself with savage violence upon the invader of his home. [c] Fulbert, the

[a] Hist. calam. vii. p. 14

[b] Rémusat 1. 63.

[c] Hist. calam. vii, viii, p. 16.

are notes taken by a disciple from his lectures, and that they may be used with comparative confidence: see Rheinwald's preface, pp. xxvi–xxviii; Rémusat 2. 188, 243 sq.; Hefele, Conciliengeschichte 5. 410 n., 419 (1863); Deutsch 453–456. [This opinion has been decisively overthrown by Denifle, who has for the first time elicited the real meaning of Sententiae from a comparison of four contemporaneous collections: see the Archiv für Litteratur- und Kirchen-Geschichte des Mittelalters, 1. 402–469, 584–624; Berlin 1885.] In the passage referred to in the text it is evident that the manuscript, which is all through a very bad one, is seriously corrupt. The words are, 'Utrum clerici matrimonium contrahere possint, quaeri solet. Sacerdotes qui non fecerunt, possunt.' Rémusat, vol. 2. 249 n. 2, is disposed to understand *vota* with *fecerunt*; but the passage goes on to forbid marriage to any order above that of acolyte. Should we read *fiunt* instead of *fecerunt*?—'Those who do not become priests, may marry.'

champion of virtue, had to flee: his victim [d] was supported not only by the sympathy of his disciples and the clergy at large, but even by that of the canons and of the bishop of Paris himself. It was not then Abailard's marriage that set a period to his career as a teacher in Paris; it was the shock of the personal outrage to which he had been subjected and which it was a heavy task to survive. His honour in the city was in fact unimpaired. perhaps augmented: but the thread of his life was broken, He had no longer heart to continue his lessons: [e] he withdrew in bitterness to Saint Denis; his wife found shelter in the convent of Argenteuil.

[d] Fulcon. epist., Abael. opp. I. 706 sq.

[e] Hist. calam. viii. pp. 17 sq.

But Abailard found no rest in the abbey. The disorder, the loose manners, of his fellow-monks turned the religious quiet of the place into an uproar more jarring than the noise of the outer world. Abailard raised his voice in vain against these misdoings; at length he was permitted to remove to a cell in the country of Champagne. He had now rallied from his misery. The pressure of his former scholars roused in him again his old energy. He was once more a teacher, thronged by students of the arts whom it was his ambition to educate to the pursuit of *true philosophy*, in other words, of theology. He would be another Origen. [f] Theology, however, as he had learned at Laon was a dangerous profession unless the teacher had well authenticated credentials. To established masters, to [g] Alberic of Rheims and Lotulf of Novara, Abailard was an adventurer, all the more sternly to be suppressed because his popularity was draining their schools. They strained every nerve to effect his overthrow. But, to do them justice, it was not mere envy that prompted their opposition. Abailard's was a perilously exciting personality. His nature (this is a principal charge which [h] Otto of Freising makes against him) was too restless to endure subjection to any master. He committed himself to controversy with each in succession, and such was the defiant and contemptuous tenour of his argument that he made enemies of them all. The very qualities which delighted

c. 1119.

[f] ibid., cap. viii. p. 18.

[g] v. supra, pp. 128 sq.

[h] De gest. Frid. i. 47 pp. 376 sq.

CHAP. V.

his pupils, his dogmatism, his brave assurance, were just those which irritated his elders and contemporaries. In earlier years William of Champeaux had done everything in his power to keep his rival away from Paris: now it was Abailard's oldest master, the nominalist Roscelin, just closing his troubled career as a canon of Saint Martin's at Tours, who renewed the attack.

Abailard had indeed taken no pains to conceal his opinions. He had but recently published a work *On the divine Unity and Trinity*,[15] which appeared to his critics to contain grave errors with respect to the cardinal doctrine: for this he was to be called to account. Roscelin, eager no doubt to demonstrate his own innocence of a heresy for which he had suffered nearly a generation previously, and which he may have recognised as the object of certain pointed references in the new book,[16] came forward as the champion of the faith. He disseminated a rumour

i Opp. 2. 1 sq.

against Abailard's orthodoxy. [i] The latter reported the calumny to the bishop of Paris in a letter couched in language of indecent violence against his assailant. He reminded the bishop of Roscelin's past history and of the notorious contumely with which it had been attended. He also wrote, but the letter has not been preserved, in

[15] That this Tractatus de unitate et trinitate divina is the work that remains to us under the title of Theologia Christiana, was argued by H. Goldhorn, in the Zeitschrift für die historische Theologie 36 (30, of the new series) 161–229, Gotha 1866. Dr. Deutsch, however, pref., p. v. maintains, I think with good reason, that the Theologia is not identical with, but a new edition of, the Tractatus. [This is made certain by the discovery of the work in a manuscript at Erlangen by R. Stölzle, who published it under the title of Tractatus de Unitate et Trinitate divina, Freiburg 1891. I drew attention to the importance of the discovery in an article on Abailard as a theological Teacher, which appeared in the Church Quarterly Review, 41. 132–145; 1895.] Formerly the work had been considered to be identical with the Introductio ad Theologiam: see Rémusat, 1. 75 (cf. pp. 81 n., 88 n.), Cousin, Abael. Opp. 2. 1 sq., and Hefele, 5. 321 n. 1.

[16] At least such expressions are plainly given in the Theologia Christiana and in the Introductio ad Theologiam, which are on all accounts enlargements of the earlier work and in all probability follow its lines pretty closely in the part where they deal with the same subject. [These references are in fact found in the Tractatus de Trinitate, e. g., pp. 48, 54: see also Stölzle's preface, pp. xxvi–xxxii, and my article, pp. 137 seq.]

similar terms to Roscelin.[17] [k] Roscelin had his answer; in vituperation he was a match for his scholar: but possibly the taint attaching to his name prevented the affair from being carried further. The actual blow came from Rheims, where those same masters, Alberic and Lotulf, who had long before procured the discontinuance of Abailard's informal lectures at Laon, now presided over the cathedral school. In the seven or eight years that had passed since then they had risen to an influential position.[18] [l] They aspired to be the successors of Anselm and William of Champeaux, and their authority stood high in the counsels of Rodulph the archbishop of Rheims. The latter they prevailed upon to arrange with the papal legate, Conan, bishop of Palestrina, the assembly of a council to enquire into Abailard's errors: and so it came about. Abailard was tried before the council of Soissons in 1121, and he was condemned.

[k] Epist. ad Abael., Abael. opp. 2. 792–803.

[l] Hist. calam. ix. p. 18.

Of the details of this affair it is difficult to judge.

[17] This is evident from the fact that while Roscelin's rejoinder keeps pretty closely to the lines of Abailard's extant letter, it also animadverts in set terms upon some expressions not to be found in that letter. Everything moreover contradicts Cousin's notion, Abael. Opp. 2. 792, that Roscelin's letter drew forth that of Abailard to the bishop: for the latter, as appears from its beginning, is an answer not to a specific letter but to a report which Roscelin had circulated; while Abailard's countercharges are all presupposed in the letter of Roscelin. The discovery of this letter, it may be added, has finally settled an old controversy with reference to the authenticity and motive of Abailard's, and remarkably confirmed the prior arguments of André Duchesne, Abael. Opp. 1. 50 sq., and Rémusat, vol. 1. 81 n. 2. Hitherto it had naturally been questioned whether Roscelin could be alive at so late a date. The new fact has been skilfully applied to fill in the detail of his biography by M. Hauréau, Singularités historiques et littéraires 222–230, who had already discovered Roscelin's name (Roscelino de Compendio) among the signatories to a deed at Saint Martin's, Tours, about the year 1111, Gallia Christiana 14, instrum. 80 D; 1856.

[18] See the verses commemorating Alberic in the Life of Adelbert the Second, archbishop of Mentz, by one Anselm, ver. 599–606, Jaffé, Bibliotheca Rerum Germanicarum, 3. 586. Part of it describes the master as follows:

Qui nova pandendo, set non antiqua silendo,
Littera quae celat vetus aut nova scripta, revelat,
Dogmatis immensi dux primus in urbe Remensi,
Testamentorum pandens secreta duorum,—ver. 603–606.

For another sign of the regard in which Alberic was held, see the extract given above, p. 68 n. 30.

[m] Otto Fris. i. 47 p. 377.
[n] cf. supra, pp. 103 sq.
[o] Hist. calam. ix. p. 19.
[p] Epist. ad Abael., Abael. opp. 2. 796.
[q] cf. Deutsch 265.
[r] Theol. Christ. iii. opp. 2. 471; Intr. ad theol. ii, ibid., pp. 85–88.
[s] Intr., l. c., pp. 87, 88, cf. lib. i. p. 11; Theol. Chr. iii. p. 476.
[t] loc. cit.
[u] Epist. ad Abael., Abael. opp. 2. 798, 801.

Our principal witness is Abailard himself, and it would be too much to expect impartiality from one who suffered as he felt unjustly. [m]The charge against him was that he had imported his nominalism into the domain of theology. Since the time [n]when Roscelin first opened the discussion, the mystery of the Trinity had offered dangerous attractions to the students of logic. [o]Abailard tells us that the accusation was the same as an earlier council at Soissons had brought home to Roscelin: namely that he taught the existence of three Gods. If such were the charge it were easy enough for Abailard to answer it. [p]Roscelin had but now reproached him with precisely the opposite view; and no language can be clearer or more precise than that of his extant works (and [q]there is nothing to lead us to suppose that he changed his opinions in any material point), in which [r]he declares the substantial unity, the *singleness*, of the divine nature: [s]*where*, he says, *there is only a substance entirely one and individual, there is no plurality of things.* His real difficulty was to reconcile this absolute being with the tripersonal nature of God: and [t]Otto of Freising is probably right in asserting that the charge against him was that, *nimis attenuans*, Abailard effaced the discrimination of *the three Persons, which the church held to be not mere names but distinct things with separate properties;* in other words that he held, as [u]Roscelin had already insinuated, the proscribed tenet of Sabellianism, that the three Persons are the three aspects by which God reveals himself to us, Power, Wisdom, and Love (or Goodness).[19]

[x] Theol. Chr. iii. p. 477, Intr. ii. p. 87.
[y] Intr. l. c., pp. 88–93; lib. iii. p. 115.

There is no doubt that the description is partially just. [x]Abailard confesses that the attempt to prove the diversity coexistent with the unity, is one that baffles human reasoning. Philosophical terms are not merely inadequate to the expression of the supreme truth; [y]they are inapplicable to it. We are forced to use words in a

[19] [The incriminated passages were probably those in pp. 61–68 of the Tractatus, which do not reappear in the Theologia Christiana.]

special sense, to resort to metaphors and similitudes in order to bring it home to our understanding. It is true that the [z] illustrations and analogies which Abailard brought forward, to give, as it were, a glimpse of that which transcends thought, were liable to be perverted as though he intended them to be accurate representations of the truth itself: but setting aside this mistake, for which [a] there is little justification in his books, if we read them as a whole and do not pick out single sentences, there is no doubt that the main thesis may be, and has often been, held by orthodox Christians, who make a distinction between the essential nature of God and the forms by which we perceive it: and it has generally been held that, if imperfect, the doctrine is not necessarily heretical. Nor can it be doubted that it was not really Abailard's conclusions that formed the strength of the indictment against him, but the method by which he reached them.

[z] ibid. ii. pp. 93–100, 101 sq., 108

[a] cf. Rémusat 2. 304–343 (especially pp. 330 sq.), 381 sq.

It is, however, needless to speculate upon the right or wrong of the case, since [b] Abailard was by all accounts condemned unheard; there was no attempt, certainly no serious attempt, made at the trial to understand or confute him. If any step in this direction was taken, his superior knowledge and dialectical skill immediately drove his opponents back upon their material defences, the strong arm of the archbishop of Rheims and of his docile chief, the papal legate: [c] Abailard mercilessly exposed their vaunted championship of orthodoxy as involving commonplaces of heresy long ago exploded by the arguments of the fathers. Accordingly, although he had submitted his book to the jurisdiction of the council, with a promise that if there were anything in it that departed from the catholic faith, he would correct it and offer satisfaction, no one ventured to examine it. Bishop Geoffrey of Chartres therefore the most respected among the prelates of Gaul, seeing that there was no chance of a candid enquiry at Soissons, proposed an adjournment to a more learned tribunal to be assembled at a future

[b] Otto Fris. i. 47 p. 377; Abael. Hist. calam. ix, x. pp. 18–22.

[c] Hist. calam. ix. pp. 19 sq.; cf. cap. x. p. 22.

CHAP. V.

date at Saint Denis. The motion was agreed to, and for an instant Abailard had hope. But the legate was soon persuaded that a postponement would be a virtual admission of weakness. It was represented to him that Abailard's book was condemned by the very fact of his having *presumed publicly to lecture upon it without its having been authorised by the Roman pontiff or by the church* [20]; it must therefore be officially consigned to the flames as a warning to others. Bishop Geoffrey made stand no longer. He sorrowfully advised Abailard to yield: this violence, he said, could only recoil on the heads of its authors and assist the cause which it was intended to destroy. The book was burnt and its author was committed to the custody of the abbat of Saint Medard.

d Hist. calam. x. pp. 23 sqq.

Abailard was not long held in confinement. His sentence had become, [d] he says, a public scandal; and his restoration to Saint Denis was less an act of grace than a device for burying the consequences of the trial. But Abailard's second stay in his own monastery was as distasteful to him as the first. His unlucky discovery in the pages of the Venerable Bede that saint Denis, the Areopagite, the patron of the foundation, was bishop of Corinth and not of Athens, as maintained by the tradition of the abbey,[21] brought matters to a crisis. The brethren assembled in chapter, denounced the audacious statement, and threatened its perpetrator with further proceedings before the king. Abailard deemed it wise to flee; he made his way by night into the country of Champagne. But he could not always be a fugitive; he desired in no

[20] [The text as printed is corrupt. The true reading is cited by Denifle, Universitäten, i. 765 n. 31, from two French manuscripts, which are supported by the Bodleian MS. Add. C. 271 f. 92 A.]

[21] Saint Denis was no doubt bishop neither of the one place nor of the other, but of Paris; but this Denis was not the Areopagite. Abailard's critical sagacity led him to discredit the popular story, and he gladly accepted the first alternative he found. Still that the question arising with regard to the various persons who bore the name of Dionysius, can by no means be considered as settled may be gathered from the different articles in Smith and Wace's Dictionary of Christian Biography 1. 841 b, 842 a, 848 b, 849.

way to release himself from the obligation of his monastic vow, only to be free to exercise his own choice as to where he should live. To obtain such permission it was necessary to propitiate his religious superiors, whose irritation was hard to avert. [e] He explained in vain that he had discovered that the statement of Bede was outweighed by the superior authority of Eusebius and others.[22] At length the appointment of a new abbat of Saint Denis, the famous Suger, made matters easier, and Abailard was dispensed from residence in the house. He withdrew to a *solitude* in the neighbourhood of Troyes, possibly the same retreat whither he had gone on the occasion of his previous departures from Saint Denis.[23] There with a single companion he set up a hut of wattles and thatch, an oratory in the name of the holy Trinity. But it would certainly be a mistake to think that he now purposed to lead the tranquil life of a hermit. [f] Need, he says, forced him to teach; but it was not merely to supply his physical sustenance: his active brain must else have succumbed in the wild monotony of his new abode. No doubt he

[e] Epist. de Dionys. Areop., Opp. i. 682–686.

[f] Hist. calam. xi. p. 26.

[22] Dr. Deutsch, pp. 38 sq., satisfactorily excuses Abailard from the charge of sacrificing his own opinions to expediency; but it is possible that he had concealed the evidence of Eusebius in order to irritate the monks of Saint Denis.

[23] The first time 'ad cellam quandam recessi,' cap. viii. p. 17; the second 'ad terram comitis Theobaldi proximam, ubi antea in cella moratus fueram, abcessi,' cap. x. p. 24. These two are therefore the same; and the latter notice is brought into connexion with Privignum (Provins). Abailard's third visit was 'ad solitudinem quamdam in Trecensi pago mihi antea cognitam,' ib., p. 25. It seems natural to infer that the places were in the same neighbourhood, and this is certainly the old tradition. William Godell, who wrote as early as about 1173, expressly says that Abailard established the Paraclete on a spot 'ubi legere solitus erat,' Chron., Bouquet 13. 675 B, C; and the statement was evidently widely circulated, because it occurs in substantially the same words in the Chronologia of Robert of Auxerre, Bouquet 12. 293 E, 294 A, and in the Chronicle of Saint Martin's at Tours, ibid., p. 472 C. Bayle's objection to this record, Dict., s. v. *Paraclet*, n. A, vol. 3. 592, that Abailard did not teach there until after he had built the oratory, is therefore removed by the identification with the seat of his previous teaching. I notice that William of Nangy in repeating the story, Chr., sub ann. 1141, changed *legere* into *degere*. So at least the text runs in the received edition, Bouquet 20. 731 D, 1840: André Duchesne however read *legere* here as well, note xlv. to the Hist. calam., Abael. Opp. 1. 63

CHAP. V.

published the seat of his future lessons before he set out for it. At all events it was no sooner known where the master was than the story of his former sojourn in the same locality repeated itself. A concourse of students followed him, and the solitude was turned into an encampment. Abailard regained his old spirits. A school grew up about him, and the little oratory became the centre of a huddled mass of cabins and tents. Abailard rebuilt and enlarged it, and consecrated it afresh to the Paraclete, the *Comforter* of his hard-pressed life. He had the same learned ardour as ever; but more and more his secular teaching is becoming a necessity, not a chosen task; more and more he is growing absorbed in the study of spiritual things.

Was it this very fact, was it his presumed intrusion upon a field where only those who have not lifted up their mind unto vanity may dare to tread, that made this change in Abailard's life a signal for a renewal of suspicion against him? From this time, [g] Abailard says, he had to fear the slanders, the machinations, of the two men who boasted themselves the reformers of the religious life;—saint Norbert the *new apostle* of the regular canons, saint Bernard, of the monks;—the one the founder of the Premonstratensian order, the other of the abbey of Clairvaux. Abailard's fear is the only evidence of its cause. At the time when he dwelt upon it he had not to our knowledge come into personal conflict with either:[24] the day when Bernard should vanquish him at the council of Sens was yet far distant; in 1131 indeed he is found in friendly association with the abbat on the occasion of a high solemnity, in the presence of pope Innocent the Second at Morigny near

[g] Hist. calam., xii. pp. 28 sq.

Jan. 20, 1131.

[24] Bishop Hefele, vol. 5. 401, thinks that Abailard's reference to Bernard is an error of memory, but the critic forgets that Abailard had, so far as we know, no more reason for thinking of him when he wrote the Historia calamitatum than at the time of which he speaks. At least there is no evidence of the date of the composition of Abailard's letter to saint Bernard, Opp. 1. 618–624, or of the latter's treatise De baptismo aliisque quaestionibus, of which Dr. Deutsch, pp. 466–472, seems to have proved that Abailard was the object.

Etampes.[25] Still the presentiment of evil was so strong that Abailard meditated escaping altogether from the lands of Christendom and living alone, a blameless outcast. Soon, however, a middle path opened to him. About the year h 1125 the abbacy of Saint Gildas de Rhuys in Brittany became vacant: doubtless through his connexion with that country, he was called to assume the office. The invitation furnished the release he was seeking; and he gladly betook himself to the desolate coast, preferring to live among people of barbarous manners and strange speech, rather than to encounter daily suspicion of his beliefs on subjects which were now to him most sacred of all.

h Rémusat 1, 120.

For a course of years then, probably six or eight,[26]

[25] The names actually follow one another in the list of the notable persons present: Bernardus abbas Clararum Vallium qui tum temporis in Gallia divini verbi famosissimus praedicator erat; Petrus Abailardus, monachus et abbas, et ipse vir religiosus, excellentissimarum rector scholarum, ad quas pene de tota Latinitate viri litterati confluebant: Chronicum Mauriniacense, sub anno, Bouquet, 12. 80 c; 1781.

[26] I incline to the shorter period. Rémusat, vol. 1. 163 n., says that Abailard's departure from Saint Gildas 'fut antérieure à 1136 et probablement de plusieurs années.' Elsewhere, p. 139 n., he is disposed to place his removal from Brittany (some time after the final rupture with the monks) in 1134. But it must be borne in mind that the entire correspondence between Abailard and Heloïssa belongs to this interval. The latter first wrote when she had 'by chance' had a sight of Abailard's Historia calamitatum, composed in his retirement after, probably just after, he had quitted Saint Gildas; and we must allow some time for the news to have reached her. Moreover a correspondence of eight letters such as we possess supposes a considerable length of time. The last dates given in the Historia calamitatum are (1) the confirmation of the charter of the Paraclete by Innocent the Second, cap. xiii. p. 31; and this was on the 28th November 1131 (see the instrument, Opp. 1. 719 sq.): and (2) a legation from the pope to enquire at Abailard's request into the abuses at Saint Gildas, which we may reasonably conjecture was arranged during Innocent's visit to Gaul, October 1130–March 1132, and probably at the time, January 1131, when Abailard was in the pope's company at Morigny. Either we must be content to leave a blank interval of four or five years before Abailard reappears on Saint Geneviève, or else suppose him to have endured the intolerable life of Saint Gildas for as many as eight. I think it is more natural to abridge the latter. Let it be noticed that it is only the accident of the existence of the Historia calamitatum that makes the earlier part of his life so full of events, and only the incidental notice of John of Salisbury that commemorates his continued activity in 1136. But for this single mention Abailard's history from the termination of his own narrative to the council of Sens, remains a shadow.

CHAP. V.

Abailard dwelt at Saint Gildas, though it is difficult to understand how he could have lived there at all. Never before had he suffered such hardship, such unrelieved misery. He had now no longer any teaching to take his thoughts away from external cares. He was in the hands of violent men, unlettered, unruly, of unbridled passions and degraded lusts, robbers, would-be murderers: such were the monks of Saint Gildas. Abailard had no command over them; it was enough if he could preserve his personal safety. A single incident consoled him in this terrible period of his career. The convent of Argenteuil, where Heloïssa lived as prioress, had ceased to exist. [i] The abbat of Saint Denis had asserted on behalf of his house a legal claim upon it: he established his suit, and in [k] 1128 the nuns were dispersed. The news no sooner reached Abailard than he resolved to place his wife in possession of the deserted buildings of his oratory of the Paraclete. The grant was approved by the bishop of Troyes and [l] confirmed by pope Innocent the Second in 1131. From that day Abailard had a new interest to assuage his gloom. He visited the Paraclete frequently; he helped to remove the difficulties, even of the means of sustenance, that encompassed the infant nunnery; became the counsellor, the father, of the house. Each return to Saint Gildas made the tyranny of his own 'sons' more unendurable: [m] he sought every means of escape but was arrested by bandits hired by them. He engaged the aid of superior powers and had a number of the brethren expelled; but the act only exasperated the rest, flight became a necessity. At length he made good his escape; but not yet to security: [n] he long trembled lest his refuge should be discovered, and he fall a victim to the vengeance of the monks he had deserted.

[i] Hist. calam. xiii. pp. 30 sq.

[k] Brev. Chron. eccl. s. Dion., sub ann., Bouquet 12. 215 c.

[l] Gall. Chr. 12 instr. 259; 1770.

[m] Hist. calam. xv. pp. 34 sqq.

[n] Epist. iii., v., Opp. i. 79, 96 sq.

It is in this pitiable situation that the *History of his Misfortunes*, which has been our principal guide in the preceding narrative, was written: we do not know how long the crisis was protracted, but in the end he appears to have received permission to live free of the monastery while retaining his rank as abbat. The following years are filled only with his correspondence with Heloïssa. He is now the director of the fortunes of the Paraclete: he resolves the various problems that arose in respect of ritual and discipline; his thoughts are absorbed in the details, in the routine of practical religious life; he seems to have forgotten that he had ever been a master of worldly lore and a teacher to whom all men listened. Yet in fact this period was probably one of great intellectual activity. It seems that he was now engaged in collecting and putting in order his former works, in expanding and digesting the notes and glosses that had once stood him in such good stead at Saint Geneviève or at the Paraclete. It was now, unless the indications deceive us, that he mainly wrote, or at least brought into the form in which we now have it, the treatise on *Dialectic*, which holds a most important place in the history of learning, as well as that [o] *Theologia*, distinguished by editors as the *Introduction to Theology*, which furnished his enemies with a weapon for his final overthrow. Abailard had indeed lost neither the desire nor the power of subduing an audience, and twice again he was found on Saint Geneviève; twice again he became the centre of the dialectical world. How it was that he recovered his popularity we have no means of knowing, but it is a plausible conjecture [p] that the *History of his Misfortunes* was written not only with a view to publication, but also with the object of reminding the world of the position which he had once held among teachers, and which he was resolved to hold again. In 1136, when [q] John of Salisbury began his logical studies, it was to Abailard that he addressed himself; and if we may argue from the description of a keen young student, the master had lost nothing of his hold upon his hearers.

[o] cf. Goldhorn, ubi supra, pp. 185–190.

[p] Deutsch 44 sq.

[q] Metalog. ii 10 p. 802.

He appeared as a meteor, but soon vanished: his enemies had troubled themselves little about him, so long as he remained in obscurity. For fifteen years they had made no sign; but the mere dread of attack had driven him long

CHAP. V.

ago into the exile of Saint Gildas. His return to public work, and that in the immediate neighbourhood of Paris, aroused all the slumbering forces of jealousy, of personal dislike, of orthodox alarm. His former rivals indeed were either dead or had retired from the schools: of such opposition there was no longer any risk. But a new generation had arisen, and was now in full strength, of which the chieftain was Bernard of Clairvaux, a force which maintained permanent, implacable hostility against Abailard. Bernard stood for traditional authority; he held that to discuss the mysteries of religion was to destroy the merit of faith, and Abailard's whole method of analysis and exposition appeared to him fraught with the gravest peril. It was this, rather than any specific statements that might be quoted from Abailard's writings, which aroused Bernard's suspicion and enmity.

Abailard[27] had considered the problem of the relation between human knowledge and revelation, between reason and faith, in three successive theological treatises; in the work *de Trinitate* condemned at Soissons in 1121, in the revised edition of that work known as the *Theologia Christiana*, and in the *Introductio ad Theologiam*. In the first of these [r] he speaks of the impossibility of comprehending or explaining the Godhead; he cites Plato and saint Augustine on his side, and repeats the famous saying of saint Gregory the Great, *There is no merit in a faith whereof human reason furnishes the proof—Fides non habet meritum, cui humana ratio praebet experimentum.* He supports it by the words of saint Ambrose, *We are commanded to believe; we are forbidden to discuss. Nevertheless,* adds Abailard, *since we cannot by the authority of saints or philosophers refute the urgency of the arguments* which are wont to be used by the logicians, to whom in the context he has repeatedly addressed his reproofs, *unless, by human reasons we oppose them who rely on human reasons, we*

[r] Tr. de Trin. ii. pp. 26 sqq.

[27] [The substance of the two following paragraphs is reprinted, by the kind permission of the editor, from my article in the Church Quarterly Review, 41. 138–140.]

have resolved to answer fools according to their folly, and to destroy their attacks by the same arts with which they attack us. And on this ground alone Abailard declares that he will venture to expound the diversity of the Persons in one, individual, single Divine substance, and the incarnation of the Word, and the procession of the Spirit. But, he says, *I do not promise to teach the truth, which neither I nor any man can know; I shall only set forth something probable* (verisimile) *and nigh to human reason, at the same time not contrary to Holy Scripture, against those who boast themselves to attack the faith by human reasons, and find many easily to agree with them, since almost all men be sensual, and very few spiritual. It is enough for us to undermine in whatever way we can the strength of the chief enemies of the holy faith, especially since we can in no other way succeed, except we satisfy them by human reasons.* Nothing can be more evident than that Abailard adopts in this treatise the strictly orthodox, traditional view of the relation of reason and faith. Revelation is to be believed, not discussed; discussion is only permissible to refute the arguments of adversaries; we may use their own weapons against themselves. The whole passage is repeated substantially without change in the *Theologia Christiana;* all that Abailard has done is to add some fresh illustrations and arguments, which bring out still more clearly the firmness of his reliance upon authority. In one of these additions he says, [s] *Where reason is hidden, let authority satisfy us, and let that well-known and principal rule touching the strength of authority be upheld . . . 'Quod ab omnibus,' what is approved by all, or by most, or by the learned, is not to be contradicted.*

[s] Theol. Chr. p. 462.

There is a perceptible difference between Abailard's view in these earlier treatises and that maintained in the *Introductio ad Theologiam.* One passage indeed has been [t] cited from the latter in a directly opposite sense to those which we have found in the *De Trinitate* and the *Theologia Christiana;* but this interpretation rests first

[t] Reuter, Gesch. der rel. Aufkl. I. 227.

CHAP. V.

upon a corruption in the text, and secondly upon a mistake in punctuation.[28] Still a difference there is in Abailard's discussion of the matter which it seems to me can be most naturally explained on psychological grounds. Abailard was first and foremost a critic; the love of opposition was his normal stimulus to production; and the fact that the object of his attack held one view, led him inevitably to emphasise the contrary. We find him the hostile critic of both his masters in dialectics, Roscelin and William of Champeaux. When he became a monk of Saint Denis he was not long in discovering the accredited legend of that house to be unhistorical. And so in his theological writings, when in the earlier treatises he was addressing himself to the rationalism of Roscelin, he took pains to exalt the dignity of authority; but when many years later he found himself confronted by the rising forces of mysticism, as represented by saint Bernard and his school, Abailard took up the challenge and fought the battle of reason. Yet the difference between the earlier and the later works is more a difference of tone than of substance. In the one he attacks those who make reason the standard of faith, in the other he attacks those who rely exclusively upon authority. Consequently, in

[28] The manuscript at Balliol College, Oxford, ccxcvi. f. 29 *a*, from which Cousin printed his text, ii. 78, runs as follow: Novimus quippe ipsum beatum Gregorium saepius in scriptis suis eos qui de resurrectione dubitant, congruis rerum exemplis vel similitudinibus ratiocinando ipsam astruere, pro qua tamen superius dixit, fidem non habere meritum cui humana ratio praebet experimentum. Numquid [*a later hand has altered this into* Nam quid; *Cousin prints* Nunquam] hi quos rationibus suis in fide resurrectionis aedificare volebat, has eius rationes, secundum ipsius sententiam, refellere poterant, secundum quam scilicet astruere dicitur, nequaquam de fide humanis rationibus disserendum esse, qui nec hoc astruere dictis, ipse proprie exhibuit factis? Qui nec etiam dixit, non esse ratiocinandum de fide, nec humana ratione ipsam *discuti vel investigari debere, set non ipsam* [*these words in italics are omitted by Cousin*] apud Deum habere meritum, ad quam non tam divinae auctoritatis inducit testimonium, quam humanae rationis cogit argumentum; nec quia Deus id dixerat creditur, sed quia hoc sic esse convincitur, recipitur. Dr. Deutsch (p. 120) has acutely proposed an emendation bringing out substantially the meaning of what is in fact found in the manuscript. [M. G. Robert still quotes Cousin's misleading text: see Les Écoles et l'Enseignement de Théologie, p. 184 n. 2.]

the former he insists with greater emphasis upon the importance to be attached to authority than he does in the latter. Only in one point does his later treatment appear to differ seriously from his earlier; and that is where he [u] depreciates the virtue of belief before understanding. The change of opinion connects itself here also naturally with the change in his opponents: he had now to deal with theologians who accepted in the most literal sense the dictum of saint Anselm, *Credo ut intelligam.*

[u] Introd. ad theol. pp. 78 sqq.; cf. Deutsch, pp. 179 sqq.

We can however only surmise the reason which prompted Abailard, probably in 1137, to give up his lectures on Saint Geneviève. Perhaps he exaggerated the danger, it is even possible that some purely private consideration decided the step; at all events he soon returned. In 1139 he was again there, no doubt actively engaged in his old employment, when Arnold of Brescia, formerly, it is said, his scholar, now a fugitive from Italy, attached himself to him as his staunch ally and companion.[29] After Abailard for the last time quitted the place under the circumstances to which we shall immediately turn, Arnold remained his successor on the hill until he too was forced to leave France and take refuge at Zurich. Arnold's adhesion, however loyal, perhaps did harm rather than good. Abailard had no doubt given offence by exposing the morals of the clergy and attacking certain abuses of ecclesiastical discipline which subserved the interests of the order rather than of society at large: but his disciple went infinitely

[29] Ob quam causam a domino Innocentio papa depositus et extrusus ab Italia, descendit in Franciam et adhesit Petro Abaielardo, partesque eius . . adversus abbatem Clarevallensem studiosus fovit. Postquam vero magister Petrus Cluniaoum profectus est, Parisius manens in monte sancte Genovefe, divinas litteras scolaribus exponebat apud sanctum Hylarium, ubi iam dictus Petrus fuerat hospitatus: Historia pontificalis xxxi. p. 537. John of Salisbury thus does not state that Abailard was teaching at this time; it is however a natural inference, and is accepted by Dr. von Giesebrecht in the Sitzungsberichte der philosophisch-philologischen und historischen Classe der königlichen Bayerischen Akademie der Wissenschaften 3. 131; 1873. Otto of Freising, De gest. Frid. i. 48 p. 377, is ignorant of this visit of Arnold's to Paris; and it is probable that his mention of him, lib. ii. 20 p. 403, as in his youth a scholar of Abailard, is due to a confusion of dates.

CHAP. V.

further in denouncing all holding of property by the church and proclaiming a visionary revival of 'evangelical poverty.' The attachment of such an advocate was plainly not in Abailard's favour.

x Mabillon, not. in Bern. opp. I. pp. xxxiii, xxxiv.

It seems that in 1139 x William, once abbat of Saint Thierry near Rheims, now a humble monk at Signy, proclaimed, in a letter of passionate excitement, the horrible doctrines which he had detected in the theological works, and particularly in the new *Theologia*, of Abailard: y *Petrus enim Abaëlardus iterum nova docet, nova scribit.* The letter was addressed jointly to his friend Bernard and to Geoffrey of Chartres, whose influence had nearly succeeded in rescuing Abailard at the council of Soissons, and who was now papal legate. Geoffrey perhaps had no wish to take the matter up, and Bernard delayed. After a while, however, the latter, z *desiring with his wonted goodness and benignity that the error should be corrected and not its author confounded,* resolved to seek an interview with Abailard: so says Bernard's devoted biographer, afterwards his successor at Clairvaux, Geoffrey of Auxerre, who adds that Abailard was so much moved by the saint's temperate expostulations that he promised to amend his errors according as he should prescribe. The submission, however, if it was ever made, was shortlived. Abailard appealed to the archbishop of Sens, under whose metropolitical jurisdiction the diocese of Paris fell, and demanded an opportunity of defending his position. Geoffrey's account indeed cannot be true, for had Abailard been guilty of this tergiversation it would, as a Rémusat observes, not have escaped comment when the council was actually held: but there can be little doubt that the interview decided Abailard to a resolute assertion of his integrity. The opportunity he sought was conveniently chosen, for at b Whitsuntide in 1140 [30] the French king

y Epist. ad Gaufr. et Bern., Bern. ep. cccxxv. Opp. I. 302 B.

z Gaufr. Claraevall. vit. Bern. v. 13, Bern. opp. 2. 1122; cf. Bern. epist. cccxxxvii. 2, ibid. I. 309 B.

a Vol. I. 192 n.

b Gaufr. v. 13 col. 1122 C; Alan. Autissiod. vit. Bern. xxvi. § 71, ibid., col. 1267 B, C.

[30] [Whether the council was held in 1140 or 1141 has been disputed since the time of Baronius and Henschen. Deutsch, in Die Synode von Sens, pp. 50–54, Berlin 1880, argued in favour of 1141; while E. Vacandard in the Revue des Questions historiques, 50. 235–243 (1891) supported the earlier date. The words of Peter the

was about to visit Sens, and his presence would bring together a concourse of prelates to whose numbers and eminence the appellant could look with a greater probability of impartial judgement than it had been his lot to meet with at his trial at Soissons. Then too he had been the accused; now he was the challenger. The difference, it seems, truly characterises the change that Abailard's mind had undergone through his long years of suffering and disappointment. His confidence in his absolute orthodoxy had never failed him; but now for the first time was it a pressing need to him to bring it into clear publicity.

Fifteen years earlier Abailard had seen in Norbert and Bernard the two principal troublers of his peace: a monk himself, he had enough reason to distrust and rebel against the narrow and professional tendencies of his order. Now, Norbert was dead; but Bernard was still there, and all-powerful with a large section of the religious community. It was evident in Abailard's mind that the meeting at Sens was to be a duel, but Bernard was not equally eager to engage in it. [c] Such contests, he said, he disdained; it was not to their decision that the verities of faith were to be subjected: Abailard's writings were by themselves sufficient to convict him. None the less [d] did he circulate an inflammatory letter among the prelates who were about to take part in the council. At length he yielded to the representations of his followers and made his appearance at Sens. Abailard was also present;[31] but hardly had the council opened, hardly was the recital of his heresies begun,[32] when, by

[c] Ep. clxxxix. 4 Opp. I. 183 B.

[d] Ep. clxxxvii. col. 180 F, sq.

Venerable, Magistrum Petrum in ultimis vitae suae annis eadem divina dispositio Cluniaeum transmisit (Epist. ad Heloissam, in Abael. Opp. I. 713), seem to imply an interval of more than eleven months between Abailard's condemnation and his death.]

[31] In the dramatic account given by Rémusat, vol. I. 204, of the mien of the two combatants, the biographer has taken the rhetoric of Bernard, ep. clxxxix. 3, col. 182 F, 183 A, too literally.

[32] The order of the proceedings is somewhat obscure. [See the different explanations given by Deutsch, Die Synode von Sens, pp. 31–40, and by Dr. Wilhelm Meyer, of Spires, in the Nachrichten von der königlichen Gesellschaft der Wissenschaften zu Göttingen (Philol.-hist. Klasse),

CHAP. V.

a sudden revulsion of feeling, a failure of courage or a flash of certainty that the votes of the council were already secured,—perhaps that the excited populace would rise against him,[33]—he appealed from that tribunal to the sovereign judgement of the Roman pontiff, and quitted the assembly.

Thus at the close of his life as at every juncture in its progress, Abailard's fortunes turned upon the alternations of his inner mood. He believed his actions to be under the mechanical control of his mind; yet he was really the creature of impulse. At the critical moment, that lofty self-confidence of which he boasted would suddenly desert him and change by a swift transition into the extreme of despondency, of incapacity for action. He fled from the council, which proceeded to condemn his doctrines with as little scruple and as little examination as the council of Soissons,[34] but he never reached Rome. [e] He rested on

[e] Petr. ven. epist. ad Innoc. II, Abael. opp. I. 709.

1898, pp. 404–412.] In this particular I follow Bernard's letter just cited, § 4, col. 183 C: according to another, however, ep. cccxxxvii. 3, 4, col. 309 F sq., Abailard's opinions had been already condemned the day before he appealed. All the letters printed among Bernard's works which relate to this affair, I cite as his, although a certain number bear the names of the collective prelates assembled at Sens, or of some of them. Bishop Hefele considers, vol. 5. 405 sqq., that they are all of Bernard's composition, though authorised by the persons to whom they are ascribed. [Dr. Deutsch, however, thinks that ep. cccxxxvii is certainly not Bernard's, but probably the production of a clerk of the archbishop of Sens.]

[33] This last alternative is given by Otto, i. 48 p. 377. 'De iusticia veritus,' say two continuators of Sigebert, the Continuatio Praemonstratensis (Pertz 6. 452), one of the earliest of all our witnesses, and the Appendix 'alterius Roberti' (Bouquet 13. 331 A). Geoffrey tells us however that Abailard 'nec volens resipiscere, nec valens resistere sapientiae et spiritui qui loquebatur' (this too is the version which we find in some of Bernard's letters), had nothing for it but to appeal. He repeats a story that Abailard confessed that for the moment he lost his head: Vit. Bern. v. 14 col. 1122 D.

[34] Of neither council are the acts preserved in an official shape. Those of Sens we know from the letters of saint Bernard and from his biographers (Alan repeats from Geoffrey) who make little pretence to impartiality. On the other side we have the Apologetic of Peter Berengar, which is simply the invective of a passionate follower of Abailard: Abael. opp. 2. 771–786, especially pp. 772–776. Otto of Freising's is the account of a disinterested reporter acquainted only with the issue of the affair. I have preferred therefore to relate only the facts common to all our authorities. It is worth noticing that modern Roman catholics are unanimous

the road at Cluny; old age had suddenly come upon him, and he had no more strength to continue the journey. In the famous abbey he stayed, resigned and softened,—anxiously making his peace with Bernard, wearily repeating his protestation of innocence to the pope, who had lost no time in ratifying the sentence of Sens,[35]— until [f] increasing weakness made it necessary to remove him to the more salubrious climate of Chalons on the Saône. There [g] in the spring of 1142 his troubles ended. The violence of Bernard had rid the church of a spirit too high-minded and too sensitive to outlive the injury. Whether the saint was satisfied with his success we hardly know: but this at least is certain that, except to zealots of the circle of Clairvaux, the impression of the sentence of Sens was entirely effaced by the renown of Abailard's transcendent learning and of his pious merit as the founder of the Paraclete, now erected into an abbey and, under the rule of Heloïssa, preëminent in honour among the convents of France. To one who watched by him in his decline, to Peter the Venerable, abbat of Cluny, himself [h] no friend to new methods in learning, the memory of Abailard retained a sweet savour, pure from any stain of malice: he was [i] *ever to be named with honour, the servant of Christ and verily Christ's philosopher*.

July 16.

[f] Petr. ep. ad Heloiss., ib. p. 714.

[g] Duchesne in Hist. calam. n. liii. p. 71.

[h] Ep. i. 9. Biblioth. Clun. pp. 630 sq., Paris 1614.

[i] Petr. ep. ad Heloiss. p. 713.

---

in condemning the proceedings at Soissons and materially qualify their approval of the acts at Sens: see Rémusat, 1. 96 n., 218 n. 1. Dom Mabillon wrote, 'Nolumus Abaëlardum haereticum: sufficit pro Bernardi causa eum fuisse in quibusdam errantem, quod Abaëlardus ipse non diffitetur;' Praef. in Bern. Opp. 1. § 5. p. lv: while Bernhard Pez, the pious librarian of Moelk, judged Mabillon too *severe*; Thes. Anecd. noviss. 3. dissert. isag. p. xxi; 1721.

[35] The confirmation is printed among Bernard's epistles, nr. cxciv, vol. 1. 186 sq.; compare the postscript in Appendix, note 152 p. lxvi. How hard Bernard worked for this result and what scurrilities he thought proper to the occasion, may be learned from a budget of letters which he addressed to Rome, all written, I am persuaded, though Rémusat differs about some of them, *after* the council of Sens: Epistt. clxxxviii, cxcii (pace Mabillon's title), cxciii, cccxxxi–cccxxxvi (the 'abbat' addressed in this last epistle is surely a Roman), cccxxxviii. I am glad to find my view supported by Bishop Hefele, vol. 5. 404 sq., 409; with whom also I omit Ep. cccxxx (col. 304 E–305 E), accepting his hypothesis that it is a draught, of which Ep. clxxxix presents the final revision.

CHAPTER VI.

THE TRIAL OF GILBERT OF LA PORRÉE.

THE manifold directions in which the intellectual movement of the twelfth century exerted itself may be judged from the issues to which it led in the case of the Platonists of Chartres and of the Peripatetic of Palais. The same free spirit of enquiry animated both alike, only by Abailard it was not repressed within the proper domain of philosophy; it was applied without fear of the results to the most mysterious, the most jealously guarded, problems of theology. His doctrine was accepted unreservedly by the realist William of Conches; and the fruits of nominalist thought were enjoyed by those whose strict principles should have taught them to suspect the perilous gift. It is evident that the old distinction of the dialectical sects is fading away; and the present chapter will shew us a realist whose mind was permeated by theological metaphysics, and yet whose opinions were not secure from the charge of heresy. Nominalism was indeed the immediate product of the intellectual awakening which signalised the eleventh century; but it quickly reacted upon its rival, and both parties engaged with equal vigour in the advocacy of the claims of human reason. It would of course be absurd to imagine that any of these philosophical theorists had the least idea of supplanting the authority of the Scriptures and fathers of the church; it was simply a matter of interpretation. Few critics will pretend that if, for example, Abailard's views threatened directly or indirectly the doctrine of the Trinity as understood by Latin Christendom, they necessarily involved a denial of the doctrine of the Bible: for men had already discovered that the Bible, like the fathers, like Augustin especially, contained the germs of all heresies, of course in various degrees, just as truly as it did of the beliefs accepted as orthodox. On this point no controversy arose in the schools; every one agreed that the demands of reason and of authority, both rightly understood, could not but be in harmony. It was only in the heat of polemical detraction that one disputant charged another with contravening the authority of the Bible; and the charge was never in a single instance admitted: the answer was uniformly to explain how the opinions in question had been mistaken or wilfully wrested, and that in this respect conflict was impossible.

Authority, however, it must be remembered, was a very elastic term. It was generally understood as co-extensive with the church-tradition; but the uncritical habit of the medieval mind was also disposed to broaden it so as to include all documents bearing the stamp of antiquity, and we continually find the classical authors cited, even in theological treatises, with the same marks of reverence as the Bible or the fathers. Abailard himself indeed, though he might occasionally fall into the error, was far from countenancing it. The Bible, he said, must be true; if we find difficulties in it, either the text is corrupt or we have failed to grasp its meaning: but as to the fathers, *whose authority is much less*, we are free to exercise criticism.[1] Besides this, he drew a careful distinction between sacred and secular literature, and [a] applied himself with much elaboration to establish the dignity of the latter as an indispensable auxiliary to theological studies. How, he asked, can we reject its aid when the Bible itself

[a] Theol. Chr. ii. pp. 401–413; cf. Intr. ad theol. ii. ibid., pp. 62–73, & prol. pp. 2 sq.

[1] Sic et non, prol. p. 14, ed. Henke et Lindenkohl; cf. Theolog. Christ. iv., Opp. 2. 538 sq., ed. Cousin. [Abailard is almost repeating what saint Augustin said, ep. lxxxii ad Hieron. § 3, vol. 2. 190: 'Si aliquid in eis offendero litteris quod videatur contrarium veritati, nihil aliud quam vel mendosum esse codicem, vel interpretem non assequutum esse quod dictum est, vel me minime intellexisse, non ambigam. Alios autem ita lego ut quanta libet sanctitate doctrinaque praepolleant, non ideo verum putem quia ipsi ita senserunt, sed quia mihi, vel per illos auctores canonicos, vel probabili ratione, quod a vero non abhorreat, persuadere potuerunt. Cf. ibid., p. 245 E.]

CHAP. VI.

makes use of the books of the gentiles?[2] He closely argued the whole question, quoting and rebutting every objection that seemed possible; but the conclusion at which he arrived was far more moderate than that which many masters of his day postulated. The scholars of Chartres, for instance, following their natural tastes rather than any general principles, pursued the study of natural science or of the classics quite regardless of theology: in practice they even travelled beyond the borders of Christianity. Bernard Silvestris too in his Cosmography would only admit theological considerations under protest.[3] Abailard on the contrary was inclined to accept the rule of Plato who excluded the poets from his commonwealth: [b] the study of them, he said, however necessary as a part of education, was not to be indulged in too long.[4] But if the grammatical studies were chiefly valuable as a discipline, far different was his estimate of the higher branches of learning, and he decided that [c] all knowledge was either mediately or immediately useful and therefore to be encouraged. For learning is the vital force which multiplies a man's influence and makes it perennial. [d] Saint Paul has no greater merit than saint Peter, saint Augustin than saint Martin; yet one of each has *the larger grace in teaching* in proportion to his store of learned knowledge.

[b] Theol. Chr. ii. p. 445.

[c] Theol. Chr. ii. pp. 443 sqq., Intr. ad theol. ii. pp. 71 sqq.

[d] Intr. ad theol. ii. p. 72.

Abailard laid a particular stress upon the importance of the ancient philosophy, a department in which men

[2] I have translated 'quaedam assumpta de gentilium libris,' Theol. Christ. ii. p. 401, Intr. ad Theol. ii. p. 62, according to the sense, in order to avoid the extraordinary misunderstanding of Dr. Reuter, Geschichte der religiösen Aufklärung im Mittelalter 1. 187, that 'die Seher des Alten Bundes, die Apostel des Neuen haben—war die Meinung—aus den Werken der Hellenischen Weisen entlehnt.' Abailard refers simply to quotations from the classics, not to the borrowing of opinions.

[3] See the phrase, 'si theologis fidem praebeas argumentis,' De mundi universitate ii. 5, p. 40, ed. Barach and Wrobel.

[4] Dr. Schaarschmidt speaks, Johannes Saresberiensis 64 sq., as though Abailard had a special proclivity to classical studies, in the way John of Salisbury had; but the passage cited in the text leads to an opposite conclusion. Abailard had no doubt an immense interest in all literature, but it may be doubted whether his classical reading was equal to that of more than one of his contemporaries. This, I find, is also the opinion of Dr. Deutsch, Peter Abälard 69.

specially felt the need of a supplement to the Bible; and although his acquaintance with the former was, he confesses, [e] for the most part limited to the extracts he found in the fathers, he was not afraid to draw forth the great truth that there is a divine element in all noble thoughts, and that society has never been left destitute of divine enlightenment. [f] He held that Plato received a revelation.[5] He accorded to him the peculiar attribute of inspired workmanship, speech by means of mysteries, needing interpretation by means of allegories: [g] *for this manner of speaking is most habitual with the philosophers, even as with the prophets, namely that when they approach the secrets of philosophy, they express nothing in common words, but by comparisons or similitudes entice their readers the more cunningly.* [h] But for this gift *Plato the chief of philosophers we should reckon the chief of fools.* The principle was an old one, and Abailard was prepared to justify it on grounds of history and theology. [i] To him revelation was a far-reaching influence, not to be confined to the sacred records of any one nation. [k] The Bible was the revelation of the Jews; philosophy of the Greeks: the two ran on parallel lines until they were embraced, and absorbed, and united in Christianity. Even the cardinal doctrine of the being of God [l] *divine inspiration was pleased to unfold both to the Jews by the prophets and to the gentiles by the philosophers, in order that by it, the very perfection of the supreme good, each people might be invited to the worship of one God.*[6]

CHAP. VI.

[e] ibid., p. 66.

[f] ibid., lib. i. p. 55.

[g] ibid., p. 46.

[h] ibid., p. 48.

[i] Intr. ad theol. i. pp. 28–61.

[k] Theol. Chr. i, sub fin., pp. 399 sq.

[l] ibid., i. 2 p. 361; Intr. ad theol. i. p. 22.

Abailard's view is more or less that of the Alexandrine

[5] Augustin had gone no further than to explain an agreement with Christian doctrine which he found in Plato, on the supposition that the latter had either borrowed it from the recipients of revelation or else 'acerrimo ingenio invisibilia Dei per ea quae facta sunt, intellecta conspexerit:' De civit. Dei xi. 21, Opp. 7. 288 B, ed. Bened., 1685.

[6] 'Haec,' says he, Theologia Christ. iii p. 450, 'adversus illos dicta sufficiant, qui suae imperitiae solatium quaerentes, cum nos aliqua de philosophicis documentis exempla vel similitudines inducere viderint, quibus planius quod volumus fiat, statim obstrepunt quasi sacrae fidei et divinis rationibus ipsae naturae rerum a deo conditarum inimicae viderentur, quarum videlicet naturarum maximam a deo peritiam ipsi sunt a deo philosophi consecuti.'

CHAP. VI.

Platonisers in the early ages of the church: to his own generation, however, there was something new, striking, even alarming, in the manner in which he stated it.[7] m He seemed to efface the distinction between faith and unfaith, and to treat Christian doctrine almost as a species of philosophy. Yet, even had he done so, he would only have been formulating a proposition which after all was part of the tacit, unacknowledged creed of students of philosophy. Among them the dignity of *Plato the Theologian* [8] was certainly not allowed to suffer by comparison with the Bible. It was not merely that he furnished (by whatever crooked process of evolution) the materials for the accredited system of metaphysics: the accident that the middle ages as yet knew him only through the *Timaeus*,[9] made him also specially the authority in cosmology and theosophy. The trinity that was discovered there took the place for speculative purposes of the Trinity of the Christian church. n The Father and the Son became the ideal unities of Power and Wisdom, and there was a strong temptation to identify the Holy Ghost with the universal Soul. Abailard indeed never went this length, although o he was charged with the identification at the council of Sens: for himself he consistently distinguished the Third Person as Goodness or Love. But he liked to illustrate the prime doctrine by every possible analogy and was specially fond

m cf. Ritter, Gesch. der Christl. Philos. 3. 410.

n Theol. Chr. i. 2 p. 361.

o Otto Fris. de gest. Frid. i. 49 Pertz 20. 379.

7 [See saint Bernard's caustic remark, Ubi dum multum sudat quomodo Platonem faciat Christianum, se probat ethnicum: Tract. contra error. Abaelardi iv., Opp. 1. 650 A.]

8 According to the distinction of Cassiodorus: Through the work of Boëthius 'Pythagoras musicus, Ptolemaeus astronomus leguntur Itali; Nicomachus arithmeticus, geometricus Euclides audiuntur Ausonii [*ed.* Ausoniis]; Plato theologus, Aristoteles logicus, Quirinali voce disceptant,' &c.: Variorum i. epist. 45, Opp. 1. 20 a, ed. Garet.

9 A Latin version of the Phaedo and Meno was made, according to a manuscript of Corpus Christi college, Oxford, ccxliii. 14 & 16. (Coxe, Catal. Codd. mss. Coll. Oxon. 2. 101), by Euericus Aristippus,—no doubt the Henricus Aristippus mentioned by Hugo Falcandus, De tyrann. Sicul., Muratori, Rer. Ital. Script. 7. 281 C,—for Maio, great admiral of Sicily, and Hugh, archbishop of Palermo. This connexion gives a date of about 1160. There is however no symptom of the translation being used until the thirteenth century. Cf. Schaarschmidt 115 sq. [On the literary work of Euericus Aristippus see Valentin Rose, in Hermes 1. 373–389; 1866.]

CHAP. VI.

of dwelling upon the adumbrations of Christian truth which he found in Plato. [p] Plato, he says, conceived of God as of an artificer who planned and ordered everything before he made it: *in this wise he considers the pattern-forms, which he calls the ideas, in the divine mind; and these afterwards Providence, as after the fashion of a consummate workman, carried into effect.* Such a suggestion (Abailard does not mean it as an explanation, for the truth, [q] he avers, surpasses human understanding) may help to make us guess at the relation between the Father and the Son, and that of the Holy Spirit to both. In the same way our theologian took the doctrine of the universal Soul, the *anima mundi*, as a convincing proof of his favourite position that intimations of the divine mysteries were vouchsafed to the Greek philosophers. [r] He seeks to shew that it can be reconciled with the Christian faith in the holy Spirit; but he does not presume to identify the two ideas.[10] [s] The doctrine by itself, he says, is a dark saying veiled in a figure; taken literally it would be the height of absurdity: Christianity, he seems to infer, has supplied the means of solving the enigma and bringing it into harmony with the perfect truth. Abailard's prudence was however not followed by every one; and William of Conches, the uncompromising Platonist, who, [t] as we have seen, appears to have borrowed a good deal from a somewhat perfunctory study of Abailard, decided without hesitation that the Holy Ghost and the universal Soul were convertible terms,[11]

[p] Intr. ad theol. ii. p. 109.

[q] supra, pp. 130. sq.

[r] Theol. Chr. i. pp. 379 sqq., Intr. ad theol. i. pp. 37–40.

[s] Theol. Chr. i. p. 389, Intr. ad theol. i. p. 48.

[t] v. supra, pp. 107–111.

10 In his Dialectic, Ouvrages inédits, 475, he expressly repudiates the idea; but although it had previously had an attraction for him, I cannot agree with Cousin (ibid., intr. pp. xxxiii, xxxiv, or in the Fragments philosophiques, 2. 35) that he had ever 'professed' the doctrine.

11 Anima igitur mundi, secundum quosdam, Spiritus sanctus est. Divina enim voluntate et bonitate, quae Spiritus sanctus est, ut praediximus, omnia vivunt quae in mundo vivunt: Philos. i. 15, Bed. Opp. 2. 313, or Max. Biblioth. Patr. 20. 998 H. Here it is only stated as one of several opinions on the subject. But the decisive passage occurs in William's Commentary on the Consolation of Boëthius, of which specimens are printed by Jourdain in the Notices et Extraits des Manuscrits, 20 (2). The place in question to be quoted: Anima mundi est naturalis vigor quo habent quedam res tantum moveri, quedam crescere, quedam sentire, quedam discernere. Sed qui sit ille vigor queritur. Sed, ut mihi videtur, ille vigor naturalis est

and was only induced to withdraw the opinion by a threat and a reminder of Abailard's fate.

Thus, with whatever limitations and reserves on the part of professed theologians, there was a general tendency among scholars to take the motive of their theology from philosophy. Christianity was put into a Neo-Platonic setting; and if the result was in some ways fantastic, it was not the less a distinct gain, in an age when everything tended towards a coarse materialism, to have a philosophy which should bring into relief those spiritual and ideal elements of Christianity which have in all times been in danger of suppression under the weight of an organised dogmatic system. It was that characteristic of the Creator so emphatically seized in the *Timaeus*, namely his essential goodness, which was adopted as paramount by the Platonists of the twelfth century, as it had been by John Scotus in the ninth.[12] The thought passed into current theology and could not fail of influence as a counterweight to those dark theories of the divine government which lingered on, partly believed, never entirely disowned, from the predestinarianism of Augustin. Augustin has indeed

---

Spiritus sanctus, id est, divina et benigna concordia que est id a quo omnia habent esse, moveri, crescere, sentire, vivere, discernere. Qui bene dicitur naturalis vigor, quia divino amore omnia crescunt et vigent. Qui bene dicitur anima mundi, quia solo divino amore et caritate omnia que in mundo sunt vivunt et habent vivere. . . Quedam vegetat et facit sentire, ut bruta animalia, quedam facit discernere, ut homines, una et eadem manens anima; sed non in omnibus exercet eamdem potentiam, et hoc tarditate et natura corporum faciente, unde Virgilius: Quantum non noxia corpora tardant.

[12] It was in this way that Abailard could consider the unpardonable sin, the sin against the Holy Ghost, as consisting in a denial of God's Goodness: Heloïssae Problem. xiii. Opp. 1. 256 sq. No doubt the same sense of God' absolute goodness led him to reject the doctrine of redemption as elaborated by saint Anselm, and to maintain that the work of Christ consisted in attaching mankind to God by the bond of love. See especially the Sententiae (Epitome theologiae Christianae), cap. xxiii. Opp. 2. 569 sqq. Rémusat's treatment of the whole subject, vol. 2. 402–451, is full of interest. Compare Deutsch 367–387: 'Was bei Abälard wirklich fehlt, ist der Begriff der stellvertretenden Genugthuung in dem Sinne dass die Vergebung der Sünden dadurch bedingt war, dass die Strafe derselben von Christo anstatt der Menschen getragen wurde,' p. 383.

expressed this principle of goodness in the universe, often with persuasive force, sometimes in passages of exquisite beauty;[13] but at the same time this is too often obscured by his other doctrine which laid so heavy a stress upon the reign of sin, and it cannot be doubtful with which of the two tendencies his influence is historically associated.

Probably had not Abailard held so unique a position as a teacher, had he not exulted in publicity, his Platonic theology, which was singular only in its joyful recognition of a world of divine teaching of old outside the borders of Judaism, would never have excited suspicion: more intrepid views than his were promulgated without risk by a multitude of less conspicuous masters; Platonism was in fact the vogue of the day. But, the opposition once aroused, the church had to face a larger problem; she had to decide whether she would hold fast to the old moorings, or whether she could trust herself to sail at large, conscious of her intrinsic strength and fearless of any harm from without. The struggle between religion and science, or if we will, between authority and reason, broke out anew; and it seemed as though it were the object of the established powers to drive all professors of secular learning into the fellowship of those obscure and obstinate heretics who had now for a century or more been spreading discord among the churches of Christendom. In truth the principles of the heretics stood nearer to those of the guardians of catholic Christianity, than did the philosophy of the schools: they had a tradition, although it was not catholic, in which it was an obligation to place implicit, unreasoning faith. Yet it may be fairly argued that the church would have best consulted her own interests, had she conceded the scant latitude asked by the philosophers and allowed their invigorating force to turn the history of her progress into a new life.

The men whose opinions she proscribed were just those

[13] Nec auctor est excellentior Deo, nec ars efficacior Dei verbo, nec caussa melior, quam ut bonum crearetur a Deo bono: De civit. dei xi. 21 Opp. 7. 288 A. Cf. Confess. vii. 11 § 17 vol. 1. 140 C.

CHAP. VI.

whose activity was consistently devoted to the correction of the moral disorders from which he suffered. Roscelin, Abailard, William of Conches are unsparing in their exposure of abuses in the state of the clergy which it was equally the desire of every earnest member of the order to eradicate.[14] If [u] Abailard's life be thought to be vitiated by a single fault, his colleagues are invariably blameless. The learned clergy are the exemplars of the age; the unlettered are its reproof. It was owing to the latter, to their degradation in life because in mind, that the church stood in need of repeated, periodical revivals of religious discipline. The stimulus of learning was the least intermittent and therefore the most trustworthy motive for moral advancement: but instead of fostering the seed of promise, the husbandmen of the church rooted it up. Yet, be it observed, the good service and high rectitude of the philosophers were obvious and admitted: the errors were only suspected or guessed at. A complete examination was seldom attempted, never successfully carried out. Whereas the custom of the church, as [x] Abailard notes, had ruled that in such cases argument not force should be the constraining engine, the proceedings of their trials generally left it open to the accused to declare that his opinions had been misconstrued, that the quotations from his writings had been garbled. No council sat in judgement upon them that received, even among the most loyal catholics, unanimous assent: the sentence was the subject of apology not of congratulation.

[u] yet see below p. 171 n. 29.

[x] Intr. ad theol. ii. p. 76.

It is in the youth of an intellectual movement that antagonisms such as those to which we refer are sure to arise. The conservative instincts of a corporation, especially of a religious corporation, and most of all when that corporation has the splendid and sacred traditions of the catholic church, are immediately excited at the first whisper of possible competition; and not only so, or at least not

[14] Instances may readily be found in the Scito te ipsum of Abailard and in William's Dragmaticon: but the public action of the former is sufficiently declared. On Roscelin see Cousin, Fragments philosophiques 2. 96 sq.

so outwardly: it resents the bare idea that its position can be seriously threatened, and it opposes the new tendency because it is new. The text which we hear repeated incessantly through these disputes is that in which the [y] apostle warns Timothy against *profanas vocum novitates*. The ovelty is the profanity. In no example is this consideration plainer than in that of William of Conches, whose ready yielding to the pressure of orthodox objections has been [z] commented upon in a previous chapter. He withdraws, he condemns as blasphemous, opinions which he admits are capable of defence, solely because their terms are not to be found in the Bible. It is evidently a mere measure of prudence. He does not profess to abate a jot of his belief in the impugned statements: he suppresses the written record of them, and all parties are satisfied.

[y] 1 Tim. vi. 20.

[z] supra, pp. 110 sq.

Side by side with this hardly masked fear of novelty operated another instinct resting, like the first, upon a slavish acceptance of the words of Scripture. The line of demarcation which Christians have ever been disposed to draw between the word of God and the word of man, so as to distinguish between the absolute and the relative authority with which they speak, was insensibly confused with an altogether different division, that namely between the church and the world, which in essence is determined (in however varying forms) by the presence or absence of a high principle in life. 'Sacred' and 'secular' in this disastrous mode of thought were treated as the practical equivalents of 'good' and 'bad.' By the time with which we are concerned the phrases had indeed lost something of their significance. They consorted easily with the secure indolence of monasticism, and when such a man as saint Bernard ventured into the intellectual arena, they were almost the only weapons at his disposal: but when educated people (the distinction is [a] Gilbert of La Porrée's) took up the gauntlet, it was usually now as the champions of the old against the new.

[a] v. infra, p. 169.

It is needless to point out the disadvantages to the

attacked party of such terms of combat. Prepossessed with a blind reliance on their elders as by far the majority of medieval churchmen were (and it was the church which in all cases claimed the power of deciding questions which might more strictly belong to the cognisance of philosophy), the result was nearly certain before the argument began. At the same time, as we have said, it by no means followed that the verdict of a council commanded general acceptance: private sentiments of prejudice or favour,—a reluctance to assume nice points as irrevocably fixed, concerning which even the fathers were supposed to have allowed some latitude, and which few persons even pretended to understand,—all these motives, apart from the existence of personal attachment to the opinions condemned, coöperated to make such proceedings matters for criticism, a source of uneasiness to the faithful and a rock of offence to the hardier intellects among them. The trial of Gilbert of La Porrée furnishes a striking illustration of this, and it is the more deserving of close study since in it we have the rare advantage of three contemporary witnesses, of whom two speak to what they actually saw and all discourse at length on the general bearings of the transaction.

[b] supra, pp. 112 sqq.

[c] v. supra, p. 103.

Gilbert of La Porrée, bishop of Poitiers, has [b] already come before our notice as the most distinguished disciple of Bernard of Chartres; a man, it was considered, of universal learning, [c] who in the true spirit of his school gathered together every detail of accessible knowledge to illustrate and perfect his work. But unlike Bernard his principal interest lay in applying his acquirements to the investigation of theological problems; with him religion was the first thing. His theological activity is represented by a weighty and extensive Commentary on the *Books on the Trinity*, by Boëthius,[15] which were endued

[15] The five theological treatises, of which only the first is entitled de sancta Trinitate, were rejected as spurious by Dr. Friedrich Nitzsch, professor at Kiel, Das System des Boëthius und die ihm zugeschriebenen theologischen Schriften; Berlin 1860. [All the treatises except that De fide catholica (lib. iv. in R. Peiper's

with the unbounded authority that belonged to one who was [d] ranked with Cicero among the chief of Latin philosophers. Gilbert's general mode of approaching his subject suggests to a great extent, consciously or unconsciously, that of John Scotus.[16] He seeks to unite theology and philosophy, and he arrives at a similar result. Although he has not the affirmative and negative antithesis which forms so characteristic an element in the Scot's system, he is not the less precise in excluding the nature of God from the domain of human enquiry. [e] God is to him, on the one hand, the supreme abstraction, of which we can predicate nothing; on the other, he is the fulness of all being, which sums up and unites that which in the universe exists only in division and variety. The dominant idea, however, in Gilbert's mind is plainly the former.[17] He undertook to prove, just as [f] Abailard had done, that the highest truths of theology stand apart from and above the comprehension of our understanding, can only be hinted at by analogies and figures of speech. Yet in fact he started from a precisely opposite principle to Abailard's, since he held that in theology faith precedes reason, reason

[d] Abael. intr. ad theol. ii. p. 87; cf. lib. iii. p. 116.

[e] Lipsius, ubi infra, p. 212.

[f] Intr. ad theol. i. pp. 88 sq.

edition of the Philosophiae consolatio and Opuscula sacra, 1871) are expressly attributed to Boëthius in a brief notice contained in a Reichenau manuscript of the tenth century which there is reason to believe to be by Cassiodorus. See the edition of this Anecdoton Holderi by H. Usener, 1877. Dr. von Prantl however was not convinced by this evidence and adhered to the opinion of Nitzsch: Geschichte der Logik 2 (2nd ed.) 108 n. 35.]

[16] He has even the Scot's fourfold division of nature: 'Perfecta vero esset [Boëthii] divisio si ita dixisset, vel quod facere et non pati, vel quod pati et non facere, vel quod pati et facere, vel quod nec facere nec pati potest:' in Boëth. iv. p. 1227, ed. 1570.

[17] Those who wish to examine the intricate subject of Gilbert's views in detail will find some light in Ritter 3. 442–448, and still more in an article by Dr. Lipsius entirely devoted to Gilbert's theology, under his title, in Ersch and Gruber's Allgemeine Encyklopädie, sect. 1 vol. 67; 1858. Bishop Hefele's summary, Conciliengeschichte, 5. 446 sqq., cf. pp. 460 sq., is interesting; but he gives too much credit to the accounts of Gilbert's opponents, and would perhaps have been less adverse to the accused bishop in all respects, had the history of John of Salisbury been published at the time he wrote. Previously it was of course permissible to prefer the narrative of an eyewitness, Geoffrey of Auxerre, to that of Otto of Freising who knew what he records only by report. See below, pp. 161 sq.

CHAP. VI.

is impotent of itself to teach it us. Nevertheless Gilbert's exposition of his views is contained in one of the subtlest and most elaborate contributions to theological metaphysics that the middle ages have as yet given forth; and his opinions and Abailard's produced a similar effect upon their less inquisitive contemporaries. They appeared to render unmeaning that phraseology concerning divine things which had taken so deep a root in the pious consciousness of Christendom: this language, it would be inferred, could be possessed of but a partial and temporary truth, which to ordinary minds might seem not far removed from falsehood.

g Comm. in Boëth. i. p. 1154.

h cf. Lipsius pp. 214 sq., 221.

i Comm. i. pp. 1150 sqq., 1155 sq., 1167; cf. lib. ii. p. 1173.

Gilbert's real difficulty, however, concerned the Trinity. The being of God, he held, is absolute: we can predicate nothing of it; [g] not even substance, as we ordinarily understand the term, for substance is what it is by virtue of its properties and accidents, and God has no properties and accidents: he is simple being. It is incorrect therefore to say that his substance, divinity, *is* God; [h] we can only speak of the substance by virtue of which he is God.[18] It is evident that this thesis of an absolute Unity logically carried out, is of such a nature as to exclude the existence *within it* of a Trinity. [i] The three Persons must be something external and non-essential: in the substance *by which* they are God, in nature, they are one;[19] but as regards the substance or form *which* they are, they are three in number, three in genus, three distinct and individual beings; the three Persons, as such, could not be said to be one God. Gilbert thus hardly escaped the paradox of tritheism: and yet it is impossible to doubt that the heresy was one of expression, not of fact. The contradictions that make his study so con-

[18] [Probably it was the publication of Gilbert's work that led Abailard to revise his Tractatus de Trinitate in the form printed as the Theologia Christiana. Some of the additions appear to be expressly directed against Gilbert's doctrine. See my article in the Church Quarterly Review, 41. 140 sqq.]

[19] Quod dicitur illorum, . . . *quilibet esse Deus*, refertur ad substantiam non quae est sed qua est, id est, non ad subsistentem sed ad subsistentiam: Comm. in Boëth. i. p. 1161.

fusing are due to the presence in the writer's mind of an idea of a supreme Unity surpassing human thought or speech, a Unity which forbade the coëxistence of multiplicity. He could only apply the analogy of his own realistic philosophy and infer, or lead his readers to infer, that as humanity was a single essence by participation in which individual men were said to exist, so did the three Persons subsist, as individuals, by participation in the one absolute God.

On whichever side of Gilbert's theology we dwell, however innocent the one, however obscure the other, we cannot wonder that it startled many of his more timid or pious hearers, accustomed as they were to the definition and classification of the divine attributes authorised in the formularies of the church. [k] The bishop appears to have been drawn into a discussion with Arnald, one of his archdeacons, and then into a formal exposition of his views before the assembled clergy of his diocese. It is admitted by [l] John of Salisbury,—and the former part of the statement will not be denied by anyone who has read the commentary on Boëthius,—that Gilbert was obscure to beginners but all the more compendious and solid to advanced scholars. To the synod the doctrine was new, and therefore dangerous; and [m] the alarmed archdeacons hastened to report their fears, the bishop to defend his orthodoxy, to the pope Eugenius the Third. The latter was at Siena, about to visit France, and gave them a promise that he would submit the points in dispute to an ample examination on his arrival in that country [n] *because by reason of the learned men there resident, he would be the better enabled to make the enquiry* than in Italy. In the meanwhile the complainants secured a more formidable champion in the person of Bernard of Clairvaux. An unprejudiced contemporary, himself certainly no heretic, has passed a remarkable judgement upon the saint in connexion with his action in this affair. *The aforesaid abbat*, says the biographer of Frederick Barbarossa, bishop [o] Otto of Freising, *was from the fervour of his Christian*

[k] Gaufr. Claraevall. epist. ad Henr., ii. Bern. opp. 2. 1319 D.

A.D. 1146.

[l] Hist. pontif. xii. p. 526.

[m] Otto de gest. Frid. i. 46, Pertz 20. 376; Gaufr. ep., l. c.

[n] Otto, l. c.

[o] ibid., cap. 47 p. 376.

religion as jealous as, from his habitual meekness, he was in some measure credulous; so that he held in abhorrence those who trusted in the wisdom of this world and were too much attached to human reasonings, and if anything alien from the Christian faith were said to him in reference to them, he readily gave ear to it. In other words Bernard's constitutional distrust of the unaided human intellect conspired with a jealousy of those who had the power of turning it to account, to incline him to believe any talk discreditable to their Christian reputation.

Perhaps the verdict of history has hardly acquiesced in so injurious a view of his conduct: perhaps it was the very single-mindedness of his trust in spiritual things that made him recoil from any attempt to introduce into that sphere the reasons and questions of the world. They were tainted by their source, and to bring them into alliance with the spiritual was to pollute the faith and, as it were, to seek to unite Christ and Belial. But had Bernard's aim been realised, there could have been no more room for the rational development of the human mind, unless, were it possible, as an independent existence having no contact with its spiritual functions. Happily there was no excuse for the forcing into being of a premature secularism, a tendency as destructive of the intellectual powers as Bernard's spiritual absolutism. For he had no metaphysical theory of the unknowableness of the highest truths: on the contrary, they were the most certain, the only certain, knowledge. He had no wish to draw distinctions between the province of the spiritual and the intellectual, and leave the latter free within its own domain: he simply demanded its suppression; and against this blind claim on behalf of authority the better feeling of the age rebelled.

p capp. 47-50 pp. 376-379.

[p] Bishop Otto illustrates Bernard's nervous susceptibility to the danger of human speculation by the instance of his treatment of Abailard: thus he explains the motive that prompted the trial of Gilbert of La Porrée. He sets the two cases in skilful and artistic juxtaposition.

Yet he has certainly little sympathy with the philosopher whose personality has retained so unique an attraction for the modern world. To him Abailard appears, as he appears to a cynical [q] critic of our own day, as little more than a rhetorician. He distrusts his method and his self-confident temper: he cannot forgive him for his scorn of his teachers, and is persuaded that he engaged in dialectical disputes for the mere pastime of the thing. Yet even here Otto's judgement goes against his private aversion, and he is constrained to quote the story of Abailard's trial and condemnation as a proof of saint Bernard's credulity and morbid dislike of learned men. In fact the attitude of jealousy, of suspicion, produced in men's minds by Abailard's independent and arrogant bearing, is not the least justification of the treatment to which he was subjected. But these circumstances were wanting in the affair of Gilbert of La Porrée: [r] *the case,* says Otto, *was not the same, nor the matter kindred. For Gilbert had from youth submitted himself to the teaching of great men, and trusted in their weight rather than in his own powers.* He was on all accounts a serious and humble enquirer, and a man whose personal character stood as high as his reputation for learning. So undisputed indeed was his integrity that to attack him on points of faith might seem a hopeless undertaking. His archdeacons therefore were fain to resort to Clairvaux and rely on *the authority and weight of abbat Bernard* to accomplish Gilbert's overthrow as successfully as the same agency had been formerly employed against Abailard.

The calm narrative of the subsequent proceedings which Otto attempts has not been [s] universally accepted as history. It has been held to be invalidated not only by the fact that the writer was [t] at the time absent on the luckless enterprise of the second crusade, but also by a circumstance mentioned by his continuator Ragewin, namely that the bishop was haunted on his deathbed by a fear *lest he should have said anything in favour of the*

CHAP. VI.

[q] Prantl 2. 168 sq.

[r] cap. 50 p. 379.

[s] v. Mabillon, Annales o. s. B. 6. 434, Morison, S. Bern. 463 n. 1.

[t] De gest. Frid. i. 58 p. 385; cf. cap. 44 p. 375.

CHAP. VI.

opinion of master Gilbert that might offend any one;[20] and Otto's story certainly gives a very different presentment of the facts from that which we owe to the loyal industry of Bernard's secretary, Geoffrey of Auxerre, in after years himself abbat of Clairvaux. Geoffrey's account is contained in a set polemic against what he considered Gilbert's errors, and also in a letter which he addressed [u] more than thirty years later to Henry,[21] cardinal bishop of Albano, and the date of which by itself deprives it of a good deal of its value. The writer in both documents may be said to hold the brief for the prosecution: he does himself harm by the heat and passion of his language; and his candour has been a frequent subject of controversy in modern times as much among the allies of saint Bernard as among his detractors. At length the publication of John of Salisbury's narrative in his *Historia Pontificalis*,—the work, be it remembered, of a man of indisputable orthodoxy, a friend of both parties in the suit, and an eyewitness of its final stage,—has conclusively established the general correctness of Otto's report and goes far to justify the criticism, made by [x] an older scholar long before this confirmation could be appealed to, that Geoffrey tells so many falsehoods in so short a compass, that he must be judged entirely undeserving of credence.

[u] Epist., cap. xiii, ubi supra, col. 1324 C, D.

[x] Oudin de scriptor. eccl. 2. 1284.

[y] A council was summoned to examine Gilbert's heresy at Auxerre; it met at Paris in 1147. In his previous audience with the pope, the accused prelate had confidently denied the charges laid against him, and contradicted, or

[y] Otto, cap. 50 p. 379.

20 Inter caetera quae sollicitus de salute sua praevidebat, etiam hunc codicem manibus suis offerri praecepit, eumque litteratis et religiosis viris tradidit, ut si quid pro sententia magistri Gileberti, ut patet in prioribus, dixisse visus esset quod quempiam posset offendere, ad ipsorum arbitrium corrigeretur, seque catholicae fidei assertorem iuxta sanctae Romanae imo et universalis, ecclesiae regulam professus est: De gest. Frid. iv. 11 p. 452. It does not however appear whether these corrections were actually carried out. Can our present text be that of a *modified* recension? The 'ut patet in prioribus' rather implies, not.

21 The cardinal's name is given in the edition as Albinus, but it is shewn in the Histoire littéraire de la France 14. 339 n., that *A* is a mistake for *H*, and that the letter was written to Albinus's predecessor, Henry, who died in 1188.

perplexed by fine-drawn interpretations (this is the account of an enemy), the utterances to which he had publicly committed himself at Poitiers.[22] [z] At Paris however denial was not sufficient. [a] Adam of the Petit Pont, a practised logician who was specially noted [b] for the petty jealousy of his temper, and Hugh of Champfleury, [c] afterwards chancellor to the king of France and bishop of Soissons, came forward to declare the accuracy of the indictment against Gilbert. [d] The latter on his side called witnesses, *once his scholars, now his fellow-bishops*. He was confident in his orthodoxy, and overpowered the council by the subtilty of his distinctions. The judges demanded evidence which he could not traverse, his own book on Boëthius; but it was not to be found. Gilbert had it not with him, and his disciples thought it safer not to surrender it to the uncertain scrutiny of the council. Some extracts were however obtained, and Gilbert was confronted with them; but to no purpose. [e] The pope declared himself baffled. Gilbert's explanations were so unsatisfactory, so *violent*, Geoffrey says, that it was deemed advisable to adjourn the council to a fresh meeting to be held at Rheims in the following year. Meanwhile Gottschalk, abbat of Saint Éloy, was entrusted with the extracts, which he was to furnish with annotations for future use; and Gilbert was enjoined to attend on the occasion named with his Commentary for examination.

[z] Gaufr. libell., col. 1325 C.
[a] Otto, c. 51 p. 379.
[b] v. infra, pp. 208 sq.
[c] Gall. Chr. 8. 361; hist litt. 13. 537.
[d] Gaufr. l. c.; epist. ii., col. 1319 E-1320 A.
[e] Otto i. 54 p. 381.
A.D. 1148.

At Rheims Bernard's friends assembled in greater force. [f] Robert of Melun, Peter the Lombard, and other leaders of the schools of the day [23] were there as advocates for the prosecution. But opinion was as much divided in respect of their motives as of the subject-matter of the charge.

[f] Hist. pont. viii. p. 522.

[22] Elegit autem negare omnia, etiam quae Pictavis in synodo sua manifeste arguebatur fuisse confessus. Inter negandum tamen anfractuosis quibusdam, more suo, verborum cavillationibus utebatur: Gaufr. Libell. contra capitula Gilleberti, Bern. Opp. 2. 1325 A, B.

[23] John's list, some of the other names in which I have added below, p. 165, is supplemented by the enumeration taken from a manuscript of Ottoboni in Mabillon, Annales O.S.B. 6. 435. This includes names like Walter of Mortagne, Theodoric of Chartres, and again Adam of the Petit Pont.

John of Salisbury, who was present through the whole proceedings, leaves it an open question whether the offence lay in a substantial disagreement with 'the rules' or in the mere appearance of such a disagreement, arising from the unusual form of the words Gilbert employed:[24] for, he remarks, *it is certain that a good many things are now handled by scholars in public which when he put them forward were reckoned as profane novelties.* John's criticism of the character of the prosecution betrays well enough the general estimate of it among cultivated men outside the immediate circle of partisans. He doubts whether Gilbert's accusers were moved *by the zeal of faith, or by emulation of a more illustrious and deserving name, or by a desire to get favour with the abbat, whose authority was then supreme.* As to abbat Bernard himself, he adds, *there are several opinions, some thinking one way and some another, in reference to his having acted with such vigour against men of so great renown in letters as Peter Abailard and the aforesaid Gilbert, as to procure the condemnation of the one, to wit, Peter, and to use all his power to condemn the other.* How could a man of so singular a holiness have broken out into such intemperance as his conduct would seem to imply? We cannot think of jealousy as the moving principle here; Bernard must have been actuated by a righteous zeal. But as to the object of his assault, John could as little be persuaded that Gilbert had really committed himself to views from which Bernard was bound to dissent: *for*—the reason is curious and characteristic—*Gilbert was a man of the clearest intellect, and of the widest reading; he had spent some sixty years in study and the exercise of literature, and was so ripe in liberal culture as to be surpassed by no one, rather it was believed that in all things he excelled all men.*

There was thus a presumption in Gilbert's favour possibly not less powerful than the evidence against him.

[21] Cf. Otto i. 46 p. 376: 'Consuetus ex ingenii subtilis magnitudine ac rationum acumine multa praeter communem hominum morem dicere.' Compare too ch. 52, p. 379.

Even [g] Geoffrey has to confess that *though few were for the doctrine, very many were for the man, and did all they could to excuse and extenuate even opinions which they did not hold.* Bernard's party accordingly judged it prudent to organise their attack and to prepare for possible contingencies by a rehearsal, as it were, of the trial. [h] At this secret meeting were present the archbishops Theobald of Canterbury, Geoffrey of Bordeaux, and Henry of York, the influential abbat Suger of Saint Denis, and two future English primates, Thomas Becket and Roger of York. The fact transpired when the council met, and with it another fact not less unfavourable to the confederates, namely that the issue had broadened from a case as between Gilbert and the catholic church, to one [i] as between the pope and the cardinals on the one side and the prelates of France and England on the other. There was a risk of a schism. In effect it was not Gilbert, but the influence of Bernard himself, that was at trial; and [k] it was openly rumoured that the council was arranged *with the object of forcing the apostolic see to follow Bernard under a threat of withdrawing from the Roman communion.*[25] [l] All the cardinals but one united in resisting him: *these*, they said, *were the arts by which he had assaulted Abailard*, and they would have nothing to do with them. Bernard sought to win over the pope, *for he was a man*, says John, *mighty in work and speech before God, as it is believed, and as is well-known, before men:* but although usually successful, he was impeded in the present instance by the opposing unanimity of the cardinals.

[m] Gilbert therefore approached the struggle with confidence. [n] He brought not only the book on which he claimed to be judged, but his clerks followed with great tomes, presumably of the fathers, noted to support his arguments. He had evidently an advantage over his enemies who had only a sheet of selected extracts to go upon; and [o] Geoffrey was reduced to fetching as many

[g] Libell., col. 1325 D, E.
[h] Hist. pontif. viii. pp. 522 sq.
[i] Otto i. 57 p. 384.
[k] Hist. pont. ix. pp. 523 sq.
[l] cf. Otto, capp. 56, 57 pp. 382, 383.
[m] Hist. pont. x. p. 524.
[n] Gaufr. epist. iv. col. 1320 D, E; Otto i. 56 p. 382.
[o] Epist. v, vi. col. 1321 B, D.

[25] See John of Salisbury's words, 'Dicebant ad hoc esse convocatos, ut apostolica sedes metu schismatis cogeretur abbatem sequi:' cap. ix.

CHAP. VI.

books as he could from the church-library in order to persuade the council that his authorities were a match for the bishop's. The device, he thought, was an effective one; but [p] John of Salisbury assures us that the feeling of the council was all on Gilbert's side, and that the impression made by the wide reading he shewed was carried home by the eloquence of his language; for [q] he had a grave dignity both in voice and gesture. Every circumstance lent force to the earnestness with which he repudiated opinions which had been wrung and wrested out of his book. [r] *He declared that he was not to be called upon to agree with other men's works but with his own. . . He was not a heretic nor would be, but was and had ever been ready to acquiesce in the truth and to follow apostolical doctrine: for it is not ignorance of the truth that makes the heretic, but a puffing up of the mind that breeds contumacy and breaks out into the presumption of strife and schism.* The fourfold indictment which had been drawn up he entirely disclaimed: a supplemental count which [s] charged him with limiting the applicability of baptism, roused him to indignation; *that document*, he exclaimed, *I anathematise with him who wrote it, and all the heresies therein recited.*

[p] Hist. pont. x. p. 524.

[q] Otto i. 50 p. 379.

[r] Hist. pont., l. c.

[s] cf. Otto i. 50 p. 379.

[t] Gilbert's protest appeared to saint Bernard and his friends in the light of a mean piece of shuffling; but [u] the cardinals were satisfied that he had made out his innocence, and demanded the destruction of the bill setting forth the minor charges. The pope gave the order, which was at once [x] carried out by a subdeacon of the curia. Then followed a lively scene of disorder among the crowd of laity present, who were unable to follow the proceedings of the council and supposed that Gilbert was already condemned; and the pope had to explain to them in French that *it was not done to the injury of Gilbert, for that it was not his book, whereas he was found catholic in all respects and agreeable to the apostolical doctrine.* [y] The four principal accusations however still remained, and Gilbert's energetic repudiation of them could not exclude

[t] Gaufr. epist. v. col. 1321 C.

[u] Hist. pont., l. c.

[x] cf. Gaufr. epist. ix. col. 1322 D, E.

[y] Hist. pont. xi. pp. 524 sq.

the possibility that the *corpus delicti*, his Commentary on Boëthius, itself, really contained doctrines as objectionable as they; and it was not intended to give him the benefit of a flaw in the indictment. His opponents accordingly addressed their skill to the Commentary; but here they were still more obviously outmatched, for, however creditably they might argue on detached points for which patristic proofs and disproofs had been previously prepared for them, no one present was sufficiently qualified by his learning to criticise the whole book in detail.[26] The pope proposed that it should be handed to him that he might erase anything that might require erasure; but Gilbert repeated that his orthodoxy was assured and that it was [z] his own duty to alter whatever was amiss in the book, a declaration received with loud applause by the cardinals, who thought that now at last their work was nearly over.

[z] Gaufr. epist. viii. col. 1322 D.

But Bernard had one more shaft in his quiver. He, or his satellite Geoffrey of Auxerre, had constructed a set of [a] four formulas corresponding to and correcting the four heresies enumerated in the original indictment. This symbol was to be a test of Gilbert's obedience. But the fact that Gilbert had throughout unswervingly declared his adhesion to the catholic faith combined with the [b] cardinals' long smouldering jealousy of Bernard's influence to make its production the signal for an angry outcry. [c] The document was at length admitted, as it were on sufferance, but not so as to bind the council to its terms: nor can we tell with certainty how far Gilbert accepted it. [d] John of Salisbury says, he was admonished

[a] Otto i. 56 p. 383; Hist. pont. xi. p. 525; Bern. opp. 2. 1339 A–C; Gaufr. ep. vii. col. 1321 F, 1322 A.

[b] Otto i. 57 pp. 383 sq.

[c] Hist. pont. xi. p. 525.

[d] ibid.

[26] Helinand, Chron. xlviii., a. 1148, relates a conversation he had with an adherent of Gilbert, master Stephen of Alinerra (Aliverra, or Alvierra, Alberic. Chron., a. 1149 Bouquet 13. 702 B; cf. Pertz 23. 840, 1874), one of the clerks of Henry count of Champagne, and canon of Beauvais, who boasted that at the council of Rheims 'our Bernard could prevail nothing against *his* Gilbert,' and detracted in other ways from Bernard's reputation in the affair. Wherefore, conjectures the chronicler, master Stephen died in the very year of this interview: Tissier, Bibliotheca Patrum Cisterciensium 7. 186 b; 1669.

CHAP. VI.

that if there was anything in his book repugnant to the formulas, he should emend it in conformity with them, and that submitting to this injunction he was acquitted. [e] Otto of Freising on the other hand relates that owing to the confusion it was impossible to arrive at any decision on the last three points, it being doubtful whether there was any actual divergence of opinion among the parties. The pope however gave his ruling on the first head: *he directed that no reasoning in theology should make a division between nature and person, and that the essence of God should be predicated not in the sense of the ablative case only, but also of the nominative.*[27] The humour which [f] modern writers have discerned in the closing phrase, an anti-climax not unknown in the proceedings of ecclesiastical councils, did not disturb the gravity of the proceedings. *The bishop reverently received the sentence; he took back his archdeacons into favour, and returned with his order untouched and honour unabated to his own diocese.*

[e] capp. 56, 57 pp. 383 sq.

[f] Oudin 2. 1283 sq.; Hist. litt. de la France 12. 489.

It is right to add that Bernard and his followers did not own themselves beaten. [g] The former says that Gilbert expressly recanted, and [h] Geoffrey solemnly relates how, when judgement was given, the culprit *in fear and trembling, in the hearing of all, renounced with his own mouth those things which he had professed, refuted them severally, and promised for the future not to write or say or even think anything of the sort again.* But a curious fact is, that instead of Gilbert's book having been suppressed, it was the formal indictment against him that suffered this fate. The minor charges had been destroyed in public session of the council, and it was perhaps deemed discreet to make away with the rest. At least [i] John of Salisbury states positively that although he remembered hearing the indictment read, he could never find it either

[g] Serm. in cantic. lxxx. § 9, opp. 1. 1549 B.

[h] Libell., col. 1325 E; epist. ad Henr. i., viii. col. 1319 B, 1322 C, D; vit. Bern. v. 15 col. 1123 B.

[i] Hist. pont. xi. xii. pp. 525 sq.

[27] [See an interesting account in an anonymous Liber de vera Philosophia, which was written not long after 1179, printed by M. Paul Fournier in the Bibliothèque de l'École des Chartes. 47. 405; 1886. 'De qua [questione],' says this writer, '. . . sufficienter disputatum est: sed prorsus nihil inde diffinitum est; quia omnino sine iudicio, prudenti tamen consilio, dimissa est in dubio.']

in the papal register or in the Acts of the council, and only lit upon it at last in that work of Geoffrey's, which he temperately describes as written in an elegant style but vitiated by the singular bitterness of its tone. He proceeds to comment, with the same surprise as he expressed at the beginning of his narrative, upon the manner in which Bernard continued to attack Gilbert even after the latter's absolution by the council. Yet Bernard once made overtures to him,—and John, the friend of both, was the intermediary,—to hold a friendly discussion on certain questions raised by the writings of saint Hilary. The bishop declined with grave asperity: *it was sufficient that they had contended thus far, and if the abbat desired a full understanding of Hilary, he must first get better instructed in liberal learning and other matters pertaining to the discussion:* for, explains Salisbury, Bernard, however great as a preacher, *knew little of secular letters, wherein, as it is believed, the bishop was surpassed by no one of our time.*

Still the council had really decided nothing. Whether Bernard, says [k] Otto, *was deceived by human infirmity* or Gilbert outwitted the council, *it is not our place to enquire or judge.* The talk was, says [l] John of Salisbury, that the bishop was more adroit than candid. But John is loyal to his old master: because, he says, he could not be understood by his opponents, they maintained that he hid his perfidy in guile and obscure words. Nor did Gilbert profess himself satisfied with the result. [m] He wrote a new preface to his Commentary, to prove its substantial harmony with the confession of faith which Bernard had put before the council. It was impossible, he declared, to write anything that should not be open to misunderstanding. Is the Bible heretical because Arius and Sabellius read their heresies in it?[28] Was Gilbert to supply his readers with brains? There is no doubt that the apologist

[k] lib. i. 57 p. 384.

[l] cap. xii. p. 526.

[m] capp. xiii., xiv. pp. 527–530: cf. infra, append. ix.

[28] Se vero dicebat non maiori sapientia vel gratia praeditum quam apostolos et prophetas, qui, licet in eis loqueretur Spiritus sanctus, tamen aliis facti sunt odor vite in vitam et aliis odor mortis in mortem: Hist. pontific. xiii. p. 527.

touches the spring of the whole antagonism. It was not really a controversy between faith and error, but between ignorance and learning; and in this way we can understand how it was that the character and position of Gilbert, and nearly to the same extent of Abailard, remained unaffected by the obloquy to which they were exposed. The affair in fact interested only a very few outside the circle of Bernard's intimates. To these denunciation was a point of party honour, but to the rest of the world the proceedings or the results of the councils appear either unknown or else so questionable as to be practically put out of account. The latter alternative, however, hardly accords with the slender mental attainments of the monastic chroniclers who may be taken as reflecting the opinions of the average of churchmen their notices persuade us that they were simply ignorant that the great names they commemorate had ever encountered, or been overwhelmed by, the storm of religious hatred.

A few specimens will justify this statement. Their selection makes no pretence to an elaborate or critical examination, for all we seek is the popular report that won currency with reference to Abailard and Gilbert. It was usual when the news arrived of a famous man's death to enter it in what we may call the day-book of the monastery, and the epithet attached to the name would be that given to it by common rumour. In process of time these jottings would be dressed by a more ambitious member of the fraternity who would add details and specifications derived from other chronicles which circulated in the religious world of his day: so that though the work itself might be a century or more later than some of the events it relates, its evidence would still be carried back, through its secondary sources and through the acceptance which these latter had obtained, to that popular version of the original facts which we wish to discover.

The summary perhaps most often repeated of Abailard's career is that which appears in the [1] *Chronologia* of Robert, monk of Saint Marianus at Auxerre, who died in

[1] Bouquet 12. 293 E, 294 A.

1212, in a o *Chronicle of Saint Martin at Tours* of slightly later date, and in other compilations. It occurs under the date of the council of Sens, assembled, says the record, *against Peter Abailard;* but instead of even suggesting what the acts of the council were, it at once turns to a panegyric of the man: *he was of intellect most subtil, and a marvellous philosopher;*[29] *who founded a religious house in the land of Troyes*, famous as the abbey of the Paraclete. In the same way another chronicle, actually a chronicle of Sens itself, commemorates Abailard's death as that not of a convicted heretic but as of one of the canons of the church of Sens, *who established convents of nuns, particularly the abbey of the Paraclete, where he is buried with his wife.*[30] The multiplication of Abailard's good deeds shews how his local fame had grown with years: but that it was his religious work that survived, and the scandal of his opinions that was forgotten, is a fair proof of the relative notoriety of the two.

o ibid., p. 472 c.

Abailard's heresy, however, is not always ignored. An early chronicler, the English monk, William Godell, who wrote about the year 1173, enters into some detail on the subject; and his evidence is the more instructive since he is p particularly well informed about the affairs of the diocese of Sens, in which he is supposed to have lived. q *There flourished also*, he says, *in this same time* (he has just commemorated saint Bernard) *master Peter Abaelard, a man of very subtil intellect, and a great writer and teacher. Howbeit he was made by some the object of blame, and especially by the aforesaid abbat Bernard: for which*

p v. Bouquet 13. 671 n.

q ibid., p. 675 B.

[29] In his obituary in a Breton chronicle he is described as 'mirae abstinentiae monachus, tantaeque subtilitatis philosophus cui nostra parem nec prima [*leg.* priora ?] secundum secula viderunt:' Chron. Britann., a. 1143, Bouquet 12. 558 B. The first words of the sentence are very remarkable when we bear in mind the assertions commonly made as to Abailard's loss of credit in consequence of his relations with Heloïssa.

[30] 'Magister Petrus Abaulart, canonicus primo maioris ecclesie Senonensis, obiit; qui monasteria sanctimonialium fundavit, specialiter abbatiam de Paraclito, in quo sepelitur cum uxore': cited from the chronicle of Saint Pierre le Vif at Sens in the Histoire littéraire de la France, 21. 12 n. 1; 1847.

CHAP. VI.

cause a council was assembled, whereat he was present, and many things which were accused against him he steadily repelled, and very many he convincingly proved not to be his, which his opponents averred were his and said by him ; yea, and at length he repudiated all heresy, and confessed and declared that he would be the son of the catholic church, and thereafter in the peace of brotherhood finished his life. He proceeds to relate the foundation of the Paraclete in the same terms as those upon which we have commented in Robert of Auxerre.[31] The testimony, it may doubtless be objected, is that of a partisan, although written a generation after the events to which it refers : but it is at least remarkable that, except among his own biographers, Bernard has to wait a good half-century more before his case is admitted into history-books.[32] The Cistercian [r] Helinand, who died in 1227, is apparently the first to do this, in respect both to Abailard and to Gilbert of La Porrée; and those who follow him, [s] Alberic of Trois Fontaines (as he is commonly known), towards the middle of the century, [t] Vincent of Beauvais,[33] like Helinand a Cistercian, and others, all expressly rely upon

[r] Chr., a. 1142 & 1148, Tissier 7. 185 sq.

[s] Bouquet 700 A, B, 702 A, B.

[t] Spec. histor. xxviii. 17, 86.

[31] I conjecture that this concluding portion in William, p. 675 B, C, is not original, but that he and the others have taken it from a common source. Else I know not how the latter writers, supposing that they drew from William, should have passed over the question of Abailard's trial in silence. For the rest, William is, so far as I know, the first writer who gives the famous epitaph :

Est satis in titulo Petrus hic iacet Abäelardus :
Huic soli patuit scibile quicquid erat.

[32] This does not of course hold true of the proper theological literature. Compare below, appendix x.

[33] Vincent has elsewhere, Speculum naturale xxxiii. 94, a notice of the council of Sens in which he merely says that Abailard 'quadam prophana verborum vel sensuum novitate scandalizabat ecclesiam.' The phrase is characteristic, and recurs in some of the continuators of Sigebert, Appendix alterius Roberti, Bouquet 13. 330 E, 331 A, and Contin. Praemonstrat., Pertz 6. 452, who also apply it in modified terms to Gilbert of La Porrée. Gilbert's work, they say, a. 1148, Bouquet 332 D, Pertz 454, 'by reason of some new subtilty of words caused scandal to the church.' Robert however admits that it 'contained many useful things.' Among later writers William of Nangy, a. 1141 and 1148, Bouquet 20. 731 D, 733 D–734 A, is mainly dependent for his views upon Geoffrey, whose description of Abailard, 'celeberrimus in opinione scientiae sed de fide perfide dogmatizans' (Vit. Bern. v. 13 col. 1122 B) he substantially adopts.

his statement as an authority, whether singly or in combination with the biography of Geoffrey of Clairvaux and the Epistles of Bernard himself: they do not profess to write independently.

To return, however, to the more independent annalists, we find [u] a favourite combination, the very incongruity of which makes no small part of its significance, which grouped together the name of Abailard with that of Hugh of Saint Victor,—the master of sacred learning who held a place in the respect of the middle ages, with saint Anselm and saint Bernard, as an immediate successor of the fathers. The juxtaposition would be inexplicable but on the assumption to which we have been already led, namely that piety was an essential ingredient in the popular idea of Abailard. Even more extraordinary is a notice in the Tours chronicle to which reference has been made above, which [x] associates in the same sentence, as the representative churchmen of the age, Bernard of Clairvaux and Gilbert of La Porrée.[34] With reference indeed to Gilbert it is not necessary to collect testimony. On the one hand, he had not the European fame of Abailard; on the other, it is agreed that, whatever the issue of the council of Rheims, he left it acquitted or [y] absolved, and lived the rest of his days in honour. But there is one circumstance which we can hardly be wrong in connecting with that council of 1148, and which throws a curious light upon the feelings it should seem to have excited. The notice in the [z] *History of the Pontiffs and Counts of Angoulême*, a work which dates from a very few years later, may be quoted without comment. On the 15th of June, 1149, the clergy of the city chose for their bishop a certain Hugh of La Rochefoucauld, a man *well-trained in the liberal arts, who had attended master Gilbert in Gaul and most of all followed him in theology.* That, clearly, was his title to election.

If the religious character of Abailard and Gilbert

[u] Anon. chr. ad 1160, Bouquet 12, 120 C, D; Rich. Pictav. chron., a. 1141, ibid., p. 415 C.

[x] Chr. s. Mart. Turon., ibid. p. 472 B.

[y] Alberic. chr., a. 1149, Bouquet 13. 702 B.

[z] Bouquet 12, 399 D, E.

[34] Actually in William of Nangy the names thus occur, with that of the Irish saint Malachy inserted between them: Chron., a. 1138, Bouquet 20. 730 E.

CHAP. VI.

remained untouched by the suspicion of heresy, as little did their influence as teachers suffer on that account. [a] In the letters calling upon the pope to ratify the sentence of the council of Sens, the argument which Bernard pressed as of prime urgency was that Abailard's teaching was being diffused over the whole world by a large and enthusiastic body of disciples: and if he had no one legitimate successor, at least his opinions were thought worthy of a detailed refutation nearly forty years after his death by Walter of Saint Victor, a man who presented in his day, though with less authority, the same attitude of defiant hostility to secular learning as saint Bernard had done before him. Nearly forty years too after the trial of Gilbert of La Porrée the number of *his* disciples was so considerable as to draw the vehement [b] Geoffrey, now abbat of Clairvaux, once more into the fray, to denounce and to vituperate. The decision of the council of Rheims, he still found, was [c] powerless to restrain the ardour of his disciples: in spite of it, [d] Bernard himself had complained, the Commentary on Boëthius continued to be read and transcribed. [e] It was repeatedly averred by writers of the Cistercian following, that the disciples of Abailard and Gilbert had used their trials as a handle for attacking Bernard and the order at large. But only fanatics could speak of either as having founded sects. Neither sought to remove himself out of the comity of catholic Christendom, nor, as we have seen, did the learned or popular opinion of their day so remove them. By the world at large they were still honoured as philosophers and divines.[35]

[a] see Bernard's letters cited above, p. 145 n. 35; Otto i. 48 p. 377; cf. W. de s. Theod. ep. cccxxv. Bern. opp. I. 302.

[b] Epist. ad Henric. ix. col. 1322 D; cf. libell., col. 1325 A, 1326.

[c] cf. hist. pont. viii. p. 522; Reuter 2. 12; 1877.

[d] Serm. in cantic. lxxx. 9, opp. I. 1549 C.

[e] Helinand. chr., a. 1148 l. c.; Alberic. chr. a. 1149, l. c.; Vinc. Bellov. spec. hist. xxviii. 86.

It is thus too that John of Salisbury, the pupil of both, regards them. In his historical work he has occasion to relate the proceedings against Gilbert; but in all his other writings he appears simply unconscious that that trial

[35] Compare the significant way in which John of Cornwall, a most correct writer, refers to an opinion of Gilbert's: 'Magister Gilebertus Porretanus, ut multi perhibent, ea docuit. . . Sed quia super iis aliquod eius scriptum non legi et auditores sui etiam a se invicem dissentiunt, ad alios transeo:' Ad Alex. pap. III. ap. Martene et Durand, Thesaur. nov. Anecd. 5. 1665 A; Paris 1717 folio. One hardly suspects heresy here; yet John was a contemporary.

of which he had been an eyewitness ever took place. In the same way he admires Abailard as the master from whom he received his first lessons in dialectic. He criticises his philosophical system, but of anything further he is silent. Nor is his reticence in any degree attributable to delicacy; it is simply that John will not go out of his way to take notice of old wives' fables. To this writer, who has supplied so large a part of the materials for the last three chapters, we now turn. John of Salisbury reflects something of all the characteristics of the school of Chartres of which Gilbert of La Porrée was the most famous product, but his training is wider than the school itself. Before he went there he had caught the dialectical enthusiasm from Abailard: afterwards he brought his trained intellect under a new guidance, and his theology breathes the ethical spirit of Hugh of Saint Victor. He is thus a critic and a dialectician, a humanist and a divine; and it is the balance of his tastes and acquirements that makes him in many respects the fairest type of the learned men of his time.

CHAPTER VII.

JOHN OF SALISBURY.

CHAP. VII.

[a] Epist. ccii. vol. 2. 37.

[b] Metalog. ii. 10 p. 802, Leyden 1639.

[c] Policrat. ii. 28 vol. 1. 164.

JOHANNES PARVUS, John Little or Short—[a] *little*, according to his own paraphrase, *in name, less in skill, least in worth*—was born at Salisbury, it seems of English stock,[1] about the middle of Henry the First's reign. The year of his birth is commonly given as 1110; but this is evidently a mere calculation from the date of his death, 1180, on the presumption that he was then seventy years old, and it is contradicted by his own [b] statement that he was but a lad, *adolescens admodum*, when he went to Paris in 1136. Studies in those days began early, and it is nearly inconceivable that a man of six-and-twenty should enter, as John did, upon a course of education lasting ten or twelve years. We shall certainly be safer then if we place his birth between 1115 and 1120.[2] As a child, [c] he tells us, he was sent to a priest, as the manner was, to learn his Psalms. The teacher happened to have a

[1] This is a plausible inference from John's language in the Entheticus, ver. 137 sqq., in which he ridicules the courtier who is anxious to pass as a Norman; so that the authors of the Histoire littéraire de la France 14. 89, should seem to be in error in writing his name *Petit*. See the biography by professor C. Schaarschmidt, librarian at Bonn, to which reference has frequently been made in the foregoing pages; a model book to which I cannot too heartily express my obligations. My citations from the Entheticus refer to the edition by C. Petersen, Hamburg 1843, of the Entheticus de dogmate philosophorum, and not to the other poem bearing the same title which is prefixed to the Policraticus. Petersen's commentaries are learned and valuable, but vitiated by a constant endeavour to bring the author into connexion with Oxford, which is a pure delusion: cf. Schaarschmidt 11–21. [In the present edition I have adjusted the references to the Policraticus to the volumes and pages of the admirable edition of that work published by Mr. C. C. J. Webb; Oxford 1909. I have also altered the numbering of the letters so as to agree with that in J. A. Giles's edition of John's Works, vol. 1, 2; Oxford 1848.]

[2] Petersen, p. 73, thinks not before the latter date; Dr. Schaarschmidt, p. 10, between 1110 and 1120.

turn for magic, and used his pupils as assistants in his mysterious performances. John, however, proved a disturbing influence: he could see no ghosts, and his services were not again called for.

If this is all we know about his youth, we are very fully informed of his early manhood. The place in the *Metalogicus* in which he relates the progress of his learning when he went to France is one of those autobiographical passages rare in medieval literature which tell us even more of the life of the time than they do of their immediate subject. John was a witness of the disputes of the schools when they were in their first vigorous activity. [d] The impulse in dialectical questions which Abailard had excited in the early years of the century had been continually gaining strength since his retirement from Paris. [e] Now in the decline of his hard-beset life he was again teaching there, and it was from him that John received his first lessons in logic. But the student's thirst for all obtainable knowledge would not be satisfied with the expositions of a single master. John seems to have made it his object to learn from as many different sources as possible. He attended the masters of one and then the other side; but his critical faculty was always foremost. Except in politics, where a strong religious sympathy attached him to the hierarchical doctrine of his friend and patron, saint Thomas Becket, he never let himself become a partisan; and his notices of the intellectual struggle of his time are invaluable from their coolness and keen judgement. Hitherto we have used them as illustrating the careers and aims of several of his teachers: we have now to consider them as a part of the personal history of the scholar.

[d] cf. supra, p. 96.

[e] cf. supra, p. 137.

[f] *When as a lad*, John says, *I first went into Gaul for the cause of study (it was the next year after that the glorious king of the English, Henry the Lion of Righteousness,*[3] *departed*

[f] Metal. ii. 10 pp. 802 sq.

[3] The title occurs also in the Policraticus vi. 18 vol. 2. 48. It indicated the fulfilment of a prophecy of Merlin: see Stubbs, Constitutional History of England, 1. § 111, ed. Oxford 1880.

CHAP. VII.

from human things) I addressed myself to the Peripatetic of Palais, who then presided upon Mount Saint Genovefa, an illustrious teacher and admired of all men. There at his feet I acquired the first rudiments of the dialectical art, and snatched according to the scant measure of my wits,—pro modulo ingenioli mei,—whatever passed his lips with entire greediness of mind. Then, when he had departed, all too hastily, as it seemed to me, I joined myself to master Alberic,[4] *who stood forth among the rest as a greatly esteemed dialectician, and verily was the bitterest opponent of the nominal sect.* Thus Abailard was for a moment upon the scene of his early triumphs; but not now at Paris but near it (as Paris then was) on the hill of Saint Geneviève. When John of Salisbury heard him in 1136, he was once more, at the age of seven-and-fifty, lecturing as he had begun on dialectics. But his return again to public work doubtless reäwakened the hostility of teachers and churchmen to which he had previously been exposed. He left his school to Alberic, and John of Salisbury knew him no more as a teacher. His successor was a leading advocate of the logical system which he had spent his life in resisting.

[g] Metal. l. c., p. 803.

[g] *Being thus,* John continues, *for near two whole years occupied on the Mount I had to my instructors in the dialec-*

[4] It has been supposed that this Alberic of Rheims, Metalog. i. 5 p. 746 (if, as is probable, the reference there is to him), was the same person who took the lead in Abailard's prosecution at Soissons in 1121; Brucker, Historia critica Philosophiae 3. 755, Leipzig 1743 quarto; Schaarschmidt p. 71: and the identification has the colour of support from the terms in which John speaks of him, as though he had signalised himself by his opposition to nominalism. If, however, the facts stated in the Histoire littéraire, 12. 74 sq., are correct, there can be no doubt that Abailard's assailant is the same Alberic who was made archbishop of Bourges in 1136 and who is designated on the occasion of his preferment by pope Innocent the Second, as of Rheims, a specification which also appears in documents of 1128 and 1131. This is also the view taken by André Duchesne, In Hist. Calam. not. xxx, Abael. Opp. 1. 54, ed. Cousin. Alberic died in 1141. John of Salisbury's teacher on the other hand left Paris in 1137 or 1138 in order to continue his studies at Bologna, and M. Hauréau, Histoire de la Philosophie scolastique 1. 430, is certainly right in distinguishing the two persons. It is likely, though there is no proof, that John's master is the man whom he entitles, in one of his letters, nr cxliii. Opp. 1. 206, Alberic de Porta Veneris. Schaarschmidt is mistaken in saying that John speaks of him as archdeacon of Rheims.

tical art Alberic and master Robert of Melun (that I may designate him by the surname which he hath deserved in the governing of schools ; howbeit by nation he is of England) : whereof the one was in questions subtil and large, the other in responses lucid, short, and agreeable. They were in some sort counterparts of one another; if the analytical faculty of Alberic had been combined in one person with Robert's clear decision *our age could not have shewn an equal in debate. For they were both men of sharp intellect, and in study unconquerable . . . Thus much,* John adds, *for the time that I was conversant with them : for afterwards the one went to Bologna and unlearned that which he had taught ; yea, and returned and untaught the same ; whether for the better or no, let them judge who heard him before and since. Moreover the other went on to the study of divine letters, and aspired to the glory of a nobler philosophy and a more illustrious name.* Whatever may be the exact meaning of the reference to Alberic's defection there is no reason to suppose that there was any lasting estrangement between him and John. In after-years we gather from [h] the latter's correspondence that the master and scholar were good friends, when Alberic was archdeacon of Rheims and John a companion of Becket in exile. In his [i] *Metalogicus* too our author includes his old master in a list of the most highly reputed teachers in France. Of Robert of Melun he could not now foretell the future, when as bishop of Hereford, twenty-five years later, he proved a prelate after Henry the Second's own heart and a sturdy combatant against the archbishop's party. At present John knows only his achievements as a theologian, in which quality he was greatly esteemed as a systematic and most orthodox writer.[5] He appears to have set himself as a moderating influence against the reckless application of dialectical theories which was popular in his time. Like Gilbert of La Porrée he [k] placed the idea of God

CHAP. VII.

[h] Ep. cxliii. Opp. I. 206.

[i] lib. i. 5 p. 746.

† 1167.

[k] Summ. theol., MS. ap. Hauréau Hist. de la philos. scol., I. 492 n.

[5] He is mentioned for instance by John of Cornwall, Ad Alex. III., as one of those 'quos in theologia nihil haereticum docuisse certissimum est :' Martene et Durand Thes. nov. Anecd. 5. 1669 B.

CHAP. VII.

wholly outside the field of human reasoning, and by a careful definition of the relation borne by the universe to its Creator, [l] sought to erect an impassable distinction between the two. In thus guarding against the pantheistic issues to which realism was liable, he was obliged to divorce the two spheres of logic and theology which the schools had always been inclined to confuse.

[l] ibid., p. 493 n.

[m] *With these*, proceeds John, *I applied myself for the full space of two years, to practice in the commonplaces and rules and other rudimentary elements, which are instilled into the minds of boys and wherein the aforesaid doctors were most able and ready; so that methought I knew all these things as well as my nails and fingers. This at least I had learned, in the lightness of youth to account my knowledge of more worth than it was. I seemed to myself a young scholar, because I was quick in that which I heard. Then returning unto myself and measuring my powers, I advisedly resorted, by the good favour of my preceptors, to the Grammarian of Conches, and heard his teaching by the space of three years; the while teaching much: nor shall I ever regret that time.* John therefore turned to grammar after dialectic; he had by this time become conscious of an intellectual appetite which would not be satisfied by the formal routine of logical teaching. Alberic and Robert, he says, might have done good work in physical science *had they stood as fast upon the tracks of the elders as they rejoiced in their own discoveries.* It was their new-fangled system which he wanted to exchange for the less fashionable but more solid study of grammar. He was therefore glad when an opportunity presented itself for him to attend the master whose [n] writings shew him chiefly as a natural philosopher, but whom John distinguishes for his peculiar eminence as a grammarian.

[m] Metal. ii. 10 pp. 803.

[n] v. supra, pp. 106 sq.

John does not name the place where William of Conches taught, but the minute description which he elsewhere gives of the school of Chartres—a description to which particular attention has been directed in a preceding chapter,—not to speak of his many personal reminiscences of its former head Bernard and of Gilbert of La Porrée,

[o] *being at that time chancellor of Chartres, who was afterwards the venerable bishop of Poitiers*, leave us in no doubt as to the locality.[6] It was at Chartres therefore that John laid the foundation of his classical learning, and under Bernard's successors, William of Conches and Richard l'Évêque;[7] the latter, as he proceeds to explain, *a man whose training was deficient almost in nothing, who had more heart even than speech, more knowledge than skill, more truth than vanity, more virtue than show: and the things I had learned from others I collected all again from him, and certain things too I learned which I had not before heard and which appertain to the Quadrivium, wherein formerly I had for some time followed the German Hardwin. I read also again rhetoric, which aforetime I had scarce understood when it was treated of meagrely by master Theodoric*, the brother of Bernard, who also became in time chancellor of Chartres and who shared his philosophical, if not exactly his literary, interest. *The same I afterwards received more plenteously at the hand of Peter Helias*, a teacher who is known to us only as a grammarian, and as a grammarian of high repute;[8] his surviving [p] works being a Commentary

o Metal. i. 5 p. 745.

p Hist. litt. de la France 12. 486 sq.

[6] This connexion, the importance of which I have attempted to draw out in chapter iv, is due to the acute criticism of Dr. Schaarschmidt, p. 22. It may however be doubted whether John's words, 'Reperi magistrum Gilbertum,' Metal. ii. 10 p. 805, necessarily imply a previous acquaintance. I am glad to observe that M. Hauréau, who has devoted special attention to the literary history of Chartres, although he had passed the fact by in his two works on the scholastic philosophy and in his Singularités historiques et littéraires, now in the Comptes-rendus of the academy of inscriptions for 1873, 3rd series, vol. 1. 81, regards Dr. Schaarschmidt's hypothesis as conclusively established.

[7] The words 'Postmodum vero Richardum . . . secutus sum' might lead one to suppose that John attended this master *after* the three years of which he speaks in relation to William of Conches: but since those years run from 1138, and since his later master Gilbert of La Porrée left Paris in 1141, it is plain that there is no possible interval between the two periods and that Richard's lectures must be included in the former. Even so there remains but a very narrow margin for Gilbert's teaching, and I suspect that John's calculations are not intended to be understood too exactly.

[8] When Emo, afterward abbat of Werum (Wittewierum) in Groningen, went to study at Paris, Orleans, and Oxford, about 1190, he learned his grammar principally from Priscian and Peter Helias: see the Chronicon Menconis, in Hugo's Sacrae Antiquitatis Monumenta 1. 505.

CHAP. VII.

on Priscian and two metrical treatises, one a grammar, the other a glossary of rare words. It will not escape notice, as evidence of the breadth of training then demanded from scholastics, that hardly one of John's masters was lecturing on the subject which he had chosen for special and mature study: their general acquirements were such as to enable them to give competent instruction in almost any branch of what we may call the customary academical curriculum. In the later centuries of the middle ages such an experience would rarely indeed be attainable.

By the time at which John had now arrived he had ceased to be a mere pupil; he was also a private student, and a teacher as well. [q] *Since*, he says, *I received the children of noble persons to instruct, who furnished me with living—for I lacked the help of friends and kinsfolk, but God assuaged my neediness,—the force of duty and the instance of my pupils moved me the oftener to recall what I had learned. Wherefore I made closer acquaintance with master Adam, a man of exceeding sharp wits and, whatever others may think, of much learning, who applied himself above the rest to Aristotle: in such wise that, albeit I had him not to my teacher, he gave me kindly of his, and delivered himself openly enough; the which he was wont to do to none or to few others than his own scholars, for he was deemed to suffer from jealousy.* Adam of the Petit Pont was an Englishman who ultimately became bishop of Saint Asaph. He had his surname from the school which he afterwards set up on the little bridge connecting the City of Paris with what was perhaps [r] already known as the Latin Quarter. John had a genuine respect for the logician, whose [s] name he once associates with those of Abailard and Gilbert of La Porrée, as of the scholars to whom he owed most in this department of learning. But his opinion of Adam in his public capacity was very different. [t] Adam's book, the *Art of Reasoning*,[9] he says, was generally considered

[q] Metal. ii. 10 p. 804.

A.D. 1175.

[r] Schaarschmidt 13 n. 2.

[s] Metal. iii. prol., p. 839.

[t] ibid., iv. 3 p. 883

[9] What John calls the Ars disserendi is apparently the treatise entitled in an imperfect manuscript at Paris, De arte dialectica. Some extracts from this work, which do not immediately concern us, are printed by Cousin, Fragments philosophiques 2. 386–390.

to have been written with a wilful obscurity of language: *although his friends and advocates ascribe this to subtilty, most have explained it as proceeding from the folly or arrogance of a vain man.* Adam's pupils of course exaggerated his faults. [u] They gloried in their own inventions and had a great contempt for their elders. Adam encouraged them, having, it should seem, a purely mercenary principle of teaching. [x] *He used to say that he would have few hearers or none if he propounded dialectic with that simplicity of terms and easiness of sentences, with which it ought to be taught.* John emphatically disclaims being the pupil of such a man. *I was,* he adds immediately, *his familiar, by constant intercourse and exchange of books, and by almost daily discussion upon such topics of discourse as sprang up. But I was his disciple not for one day.*

CHAP. VII.

[u] Enthet. ver. 49–54.

[x] Metal. iii. 3 p. 853.

Thus before the end of five years of student life John was already entering on the career of a teacher: but to his earnest mind this resolve necessitated a further training at least equally extended. He returned to Paris and applied himself to the study of theology. The language in which he relates this movement leaves no doubt that the interval between his attendance on William of Conches and his masters in divinity was not all spent at Paris. For part of it he may have remained at Chartres; the spirit of that school has left an impress upon his mind so deep and uneffaceable that we cannot be persuaded but that his residence there was continued as long as possible; although a reference in [y] a letter which he wrote in later years to Peter of La Celle has suggested the [z] conjecture that he lived some time at Provins and perhaps [a] Rheims. Paris however was already tending rapidly to become the intellectual metropolis of Europe and a poor man like John would be sure to turn his steps thither in the hope of getting employment, for it was poverty that arrested him in the middle of the Quadrivium course to which he had been introduced by Hardwin and Richard. *From hence,* he says, *I was withdrawn by the straitness of my*

[y] Epist. lxxxii. p. 114.

[z] Schaarschmidt 23.

[a] Epist. cxliii. p. 206.

private estate, the instance of my companions, and the counsel of my friends, that I should undertake the office of a teacher. I obeyed: and thus returning at the expiration of three years, I found master Gilbert and heard him in logic and divinity; but too quickly was he removed. Gilbert left Paris, as [b] we have seen, when he was elected in 1142 to the bishoprick of Poitiers. *His successor*, proceeds John, *was Robert Pullus, whom his life and knowledge alike recommended. Then I had Simon of Poissy, a trusty lecturer, but dull in disputation. But these two I had in theologics alone. Thus, engaged in diverse studies near twelve years passed by me.*[10]

[b] supra, p. 114.

No doubt the reason why John adverts so perfunctorily to his theological studies is that the entire narrative upon which we have hitherto commented is inserted in the middle of a dialectical disquisition. Dialectics furnish its motive, and beyond them John does not think fit to pursue his story. Gilbert of La Porrée he heard in dialectics as well as theology: then he attended Robert and Simon; *but these*, he explains, as though to excuse his not continuing a digression from his principal subject, *I heard in theologics alone*. Nor can we allow ourselves to be detained by an enquiry as to the influence which these masters had upon him. [c] The character, the transcendental character, we should say, of Gilbert's theological system has been already sufficiently discussed; but John was his pupil but for a short time. Robert Pullen also (if this is to be preferred of the many forms in which his name is written) did not remain long at Paris; and of Simon of Poissy we know next to nothing. Robert, who became a cardinal and chancellor of the Roman church, was held by his contemporaries in singular honour as a theologian, although it has been suspected that his famous *Sum of Theology* borrowed something more than its method

[c] supra, pp. 156–159.

[10] The editions have *duodecennium* or *duodennium*; the former of which I take to be a gloss upon the latter. *Duodennium* however itself is considered by Dr. Schaarschmidt, pp. 24 sq., to be a corruption from *decennium*: yet compare above, p. 181 n. 7. [See also my article in the English historical Review, 35 (1910) 336.]

from Abailard:[11] but it is impossible to conjecture in what particular branch of his faculty John of Salisbury heard him. Probably enough the lessons which John attended were merely concerned with the exposition of the Scriptures. At any rate the tone of the scholar's theology is manifestly derived from another source than that of the teachers mentioned. The spirit of humanism, in fact, which was the distinctive essence of the school of Chartres, he brought into alliance with a totally different spirit derived unmistakably from the mysticism of Hugh of Saint Victor. The union was no doubt exceptional, for the ethical theology of the Victorines was rather calculated to recommend the life of a recluse than to countenance the wide interests and the wide reading of a man like John of Salisbury; yet as his writings shew, it is this ethical principle far more than any metaphysical or dogmatic system, that ruled his thoughts. To this characteristic of him we shall revert hereafter: at the present moment we notice it, as John notices his theological studies, just incidentally. Besides there is no evidence that Hugh, whom John only refers to twice in all his works, was ever actually his teacher; the current may have been communicated as effectively by private association with Hugh or with fellow-members of the abbey.

John concludes the record of his school-studies in a curious epilogue, half-humorous, half-grave, which shews how far his sympathy had been withdrawn, through his later training, from the absorbing religion of Saint Geneviève into which he had entered with such breathless ardour twelve years previously. [d] *And so*, he says, *it seemed pleasant to me to revisit my old companions on the Mount, whom I had left and whom dialectic still detained, to confer with them touching old matters of debate; that we might by mutual comparison measure together our several progress. I found them as before, and where they were before; nor did*

[d] Metal. ii. 10 p. 805.

[11] See Hauréau, Histoire de la Philosophie scolastique, 1. 484. The work in question, Roberti Pulli sententiarum libri viii, Paris 1655 folio, I have not had an opportunity of consulting.

they appear to have reached the goal in unravelling the old questions, nor had they added one jot of a proposition. The aims that once inspired them, inspired them still: they only had progressed in one point, they had unlearned moderation, they knew not modesty; in such wise that one might despair of their recovery. And thus experience taught me a manifest conclusion, that, whereas dialectic furthers other studies, so if it remain by itself it lies bloodless and barren, nor does it quicken the soul to yield fruit of philosophy, except the same conceive from elsewhere.

Such was John's final judgement on the ruling passion of his time: he felt that he had outgrown logic when he advanced to the study of theology. Still throughout his life, though he esteemed theology as the noblest subject on which the mind could exercise itself, his sympathies ran even more strongly to yet another branch of learning, the study of the classics. The external events of his career hardly concern us, and may be briefly summarised. On the completion of his theological course [e] he spent some time with his friend Peter, abbat of the Cistercian monastery of Moustier la Celle near Troyes, and afterwards his own successor in the see of Chartres.[12] Here in 1148 he had the opportunity of witnessing that council at Rheims in which saint Bernard failed to silence Gilbert of La Porrée, and of which we have [f] John's record, pointed with characteristic shrewd criticism. Here too he must have been admitted to friendly intercourse with the redoubtable abbat of Clairvaux, who [g] afterwards recommended him to the notice and favour of archbishop Theobald of Canterbury.[13] The latter had also been present

[e] Schaarschmidt 25 sq.

[f] Hist. pontif. viii, ix. Pertz 20. 522 sqq., 525.

[g] Bern. epist. ccclxi, opp. I. 325 B, ed. Mabillon.

[12] We need not suppose with Dr. Schaarschmidt, p. 25, that Peter was John's junior. He certainly survived the latter by seven years, but John died at no great age, and Peter as bishop of Chartres is described as old and infirm.

[13] Mabillon, in loc., dates the letter 1144; but Bernard says, 'Praesens vobis commendaveram eum,' and now that we know of an occasion on which the three were together, namely, at Rheims in the spring of 1148, it is needless to conjecture any other. The letter however cannot have been written very long after the council, since John in the autumn of 1159 speaks of having been nearly twelve years, 'annis fere duodecim,' occupied in

at the Rheims council and had there, it seems, made John's acquaintance. He accordingly received him on his return to England the more readily and at once attached him to his clerical establishment. For the next fifteen years or so John was constantly employed not only in the administrative routine of the primate's court, but also in delicate negotiations with the Roman curia. He was the firm and intimate friend of the English pope Hadrian the Fourth, and was the [h] agent by means of whom the latter's sanction was obtained to king Henry the Second's conquest of Ireland. Writing in 1159 he says, [i] *I have ten times passed the chain of the Alps on my road from England; I have for the second time*[14] *traversed Apulia. The business of my lords and friends I have often transacted in the Roman church, and as sundry causes arose I have many times travelled round not only England but also Gaul.*

CHAP. VII.

h Metal. iv. 42 p. 929.

i lib. iii. prol., p. 838.

John's position as secretary to archbishop Theobald, and afterwards to his successors, Thomas Becket and Richard, doubtless disposed him to form those hierarchical views which we find [k] expressed with such emphasis in his *Policraticus*. Nowhere could he find the conflicting claims of secular and ecclesiastical jurisdiction more clamorous for solution; nor had he any hesitation in deciding that the independence, the supremacy, of the church was essentially bound up with the existence of Christianity. Holding these principles, it does not surprise us to learn that [l] for some reason—the details have not survived—he fell into the king's displeasure. Whether for the time he had to give up his post we are not told; but it is certain that his income was withdrawn, and that he had to struggle with poverty and debt, as well as with danger menacing his personal safety. It is to this interval

k Policr. iv. 3 vol. I. 239; v. 2 pp. 282 sq.; &c.

l v. Schaarschmidt 32 sqq.

the business of the court: Policr., prol., vol. 1. 14. [It is probable that Eugenius when at Rheims took him into his employment and that for some time he was engaged as a clerk in the papal chancery. See my article on John in the Dictionary of national Biography, 29. 440 sq.; 1892.]

[14] John was in Apulia before 1154 'regnante Rogero,' Policr. vii. 19 vol. 2. 173; and again in company with pope Hadrian, i. e. between 1154 and 1159, ibid., lib. vi. 24 vol. 2. 67.

CHAP. VII.

m Policr., prol., vol. I. 17; viii. 25 vol. 2. 424; Metal. iv. 42 p. 929.
n Policr. viii. 23 vol. 2. 410; Metal., l. c.

of enforced idleness that we owe the production of his two most important works, the *Policraticus* and the *Metalogicus*. [m] Both were written during the time when the king was absent at the tedious siege of Toulouse in 1159: [n] the one was completed before, the other just after, the death of Hadrian the Fourth on the first day of September in that year. The storm which had impended over John of Salisbury seems soon to have passed by: but in 1161 his patron, archbishop Theobald, died, and the favour which was continued to him by Thomas Becket came to be a source of anxiety rather than of advantage. After an absence of more than four years king Henry was again in England in January 1163. The fact possibly determined John's withdrawal.[15] He left the country only to return with Becket seven years later, and to witness his murder. During this time of exile he was the truest, because the wisest, champion of the archbishop. The intemperate and wanton means by which the latter sought to promote his cause, John was the first to reprove. He did not spare his warnings, and, when necessary, would denounce Becket's actions not as impolitic but simply as unchristian.[16] Still his hearty adhesion to the hier-

[15] He again found hospitality at the hands of Peter of La Celle, who became abbat of Saint Rémy at Rheims some time after April 1162, Gallia Christiana 9. (1751) 234; and it was at this time that he composed the Historia pontificalis which has been assigned on internal notices to 1162 or 1163 (see Giesebrecht, Sitzungsberichte der philosophisch-philologischen und historischen Classe der königlichen Bayerischen Akademie der Wissenschaften 3. 124) and which is dedicated to the abbat. [But the work was not written until 1164 at earliest. See the Dictionary of national Biography, 29. 442.] Whether it was at this time or during his former stay with Peter of La Celle that John acted as the latter's clerk, 'quondam clericus noster,' as Peter wrote in 1176, Epist. vii. 6, Maxima Bibliotheca Patrum 23. 886 c, it is perhaps impossible to decide: Dr. Schaarschmidt, p. 26, seems to think it was on the earlier occasion.

[16] See a pointed example in a letter addressed to Becket, to which Dr. Schaarschmidt, p. 47 n. 3, draws attention. Among other things John says, 'Si enim litterarum vestrarum et ipsius [Becket's reply and his opponent's letter] articuli singuli conferantur, ex amaritudine potius et rancore animi quam ex caritatis sinceritate videbitur processisse responsio.' *He* would not treat the pope's courier with the contumely which Becket had thought fit to use towards a cardinal legate of the apostolic see: Epist. ccxx. Opp. 2. 72 sq.

archical principle with which Becket was popularly identified, made him stand firmly by his chief. In the revulsion of general feeling that followed his murder, John was reëstablished in the court at Canterbury, and finally [o] in 1176 his loyalty to the cause was rewarded by his elevation to the bishoprick of the city in which so large a part of his student-life had been passed, and to which he owed his introduction to classical learning. He was bishop of Chartres however only for four years; he died in 1180 and was succeeded by his life-long friend Peter of La Celle.

[o] Gall. Christ. 8. 1146; 1744.

[p] The quality that first strikes one in reading the works of John of Salisbury—and they stand nearly alone in medieval literature for the wide circle of readers to which they appeal—is what almost may be described as their modern spirit. It is this, we suspect, which has laid their author open to the charge of cynical indifference and insincerity. His judgement is generally so liberal that it is perhaps difficult for those who merely read him in snatches, as the older classical scholars used to do, to believe that it is genuine. Yet it is in this freedom of outlook that John's individual distinction as a writer lies. There are some things in respect to which nothing would induce him to relax his positiveness. These are the affairs, the interests, of religion; and these, especially in the political atmosphere of John's time, covered a large enough field: for all knowledge, all thought, all the facts of life were to be estimated by reference to the supreme arbitration of theology.[17] Yet even this restriction leaves a considerable space for free and irresponsible questioning, and John is evidently seen at his best when, having made the necessary stipulations and reservations in favour of catholic truth, he can range at pleasure among the memories of antiquity, and illustrate whatever comes to hand from the stores of his classical reading or from the shrewd observation of his own experience.

[p] cf. Schaarschmidt 295.

[17] Cum cunctas artes, cum dogmata cuncta peritus
Noverit, imperium pagina sacra tenet:
Enthet. 373 sq.

CHAP. VII.

The *Policraticus*, John's most extensive work, allows full play to his characteristic genius: indeed the multitude of digressions and episodes which enliven its course is apt to distract one from appreciating its real purpose. It cannot be fairly called a satire upon the society of the time; while on the other hand it is far from being a methodical treatise on morals. The former description has this excuse, that the author touches with a light hand the follies he sees about him; but the satire, like Juvenal's, is prompted by a deep underlying seriousness: nor is it in any way the motive of the book, in which the positive ethical element greatly preponderates. The title, according to the only plausible interpretation that has been put upon it, designates it as *The Statesman's Book*: [18] its alternative, *sive de Nugis Curialium et Vestigiis Philosophorum*, marks its two-fold aim. But the first part of the work is by no means mainly critical: the *vanities of courts* are thus styled by comparison with the more solid realities of philosophy which form the subject of the second part. The former deals with politics in the wide acceptation of the term, the latter with what one may term the internal polity of a man's self.

John begins in the first three books by clearing away the obstacles to the healthy life of the state, the vices and follies that impede its motion: in the next three he makes the first attempt since Augustin to frame an ideal system of government, on the basis of the necessary subordination of the secular to the religious state; a view to which we shall have occasion to return hereafter. In the second section of the work, the last two books, John passes to the individual: he proceeds from a review of the different schools of philosophy to lay down the principles of true knowledge, and seeks to determine the aim of philosophy, the assertion of the supremacy of the spirit over the senses, of the ideal over the material.

[18] Dr. Schaarschmidt's suggestion, p. 145, is that John knew the Greek name *Polycrates* and supposed it to be derived from πόλις. Hence he formed the title of his book, with no doubt an implied play on the meaning of the word *town*.

The latter part of the *Policraticus* covers substantially the same ground, although with far greater elaboration and relative completeness, as the elegiac poem, the *Entheticus*, which John appears to have originally written as an introduction to it. The latter is however by no means superseded by the prose work, and we can readily forgive the jejune rhythm of its imitation of Ovid for the pointed epigrammatic accuracy with which it depicts the learning and manners of the day. The framework of the *Policraticus* gives but a slight notion of the variety of its contents. It is to some extent an encyclopædia of the cultivated thought of the middle of the twelfth century. As an authority for the political history of the time, for the history of learning and philosophy, it is invaluable for the simple reason that it is not a professed history. The facts are introduced naturally, for illustration; and not on account of their intrinsic or obvious importance. The general liberality of sentiment to which the work bears witness is all the more significant because of its author's eminence in the religious world, which in turn gave his work a wider influence than if he had been suspected of making a compromise between orthodoxy and profane learning. Such men by their silent help towards raising the intelligence of their age have often done more than the ambitious protestant against established creeds or the wilful martyr of theological idiosyncrasy.

From the abundant materials offered by John of Salisbury's works we can only select two points for observation: one relates to his use of the classics, the other to his position in regard to the philosophy of the time. The distinctive mark of the *Policraticus* is a humanism which seems to remove it from medieval associations. Beyond dispute the best-read man of his time, no one is fonder than John of illustrating by quotation or anecdote every statement he makes; and the illustrations are taken, as if by preference, from the classics more frequently than from the Bible. No doubt

CHAP. VII.

q Policr. vii. 10 vol. 2. 133.

r Rom. xv. 4.

s Policr. vii., prol., p. 93.

t cap. 10 p. 134.

u ibid.

[q] he disclaims any idea of treating the two as coördinate: yet in ethical and even in theological matters he repeatedly confirms and, as it were, recommends the authority of Scripture by that of Plato or of Latin antiquity, just as though he had been the pupil of Abailard in other things besides dialectic. John's classical predilections assisted in his case a confusion of thought with which the happy ambiguity of the word *scriptura* had a good deal to do. [r] *Whatsoever things were written aforetime were written for our learning*, he would [s] like to understand of literature at large; and he quotes the maxim of saint Jerom, [t] *Love the knowledge of the Scriptures and thou wilt not love the lusts of the flesh*, in proof of the advantage that springs from all reading. He is speaking now of the study of the classics, and [u] warns us so to read them *that authority do not prejudice to reason*. Authority here is that of the masters of antiquity, and reason is the mental faculty considered as educated and enlightened by Christianity. The typical opposites have for the moment changed places; and the change is highly indicative of the regard in which the classics could now be held even by men the correctness of whose religious character was no less assured than was that, let us say, of the arch-enemy of learning, the champion of a 'rustic' faith, saint Peter Damiani, a century earlier.

John's classical tastes had no small share in determining his attitude towards the philosophy and especially the dialectics of his time. We have seen from the language in which he concludes the narrative of his youthful studies, how dissatisfied he was with the prevalent method of teaching logic. The nominalists had brought it into vogue as a means of asserting the rights of human reason; the realists had been driven to cultivate it in support of the religious tradition: but now both parties were subdued by the overmastering sway of argumentation. Dialectics had become not a means but an end; its professors were interested not to discover truth but to prove their superiority over rival disputants. The result was a competitive system of smatterers and sophists. The first period in the medieval study of logic had in fact passed its zenith and was already nearing its fall. A new one arose in the following century, far more important from a scientific point of view, but really less characteristic for the history of western culture because its materials were imported ready-made and in gross from Byzantine compilations and from the Arabic versions of Aristotle. It was not like the older western logic, of native growth, painfully preserved through dim ages, and in some remarkable cases depending for existence upon the chance survival of a single seed, which sent the acutest observer back upon his own mental resources even to guess at the form and structure of the mature organism. At the time however with which we are concerned logic had for the most part been degraded into idle casuistry and trifling; [x] it had fallen into the hands of inferior men. The name of Aristotle was dragged down by people who, in [y] William of Conches' phrase, were not worthy to be his scullions; and these conceited pretenders—even [z] Adam of the Petit Pont, who knew better—designedly made their lessons as obscure and intricate as possible, in order to attract pupils who learned only for display.[19] The more capable teachers were gradually forsaking the schools or else giving themselves up to theology, to natural science, or to some other study which was not so much infested by the noisy crowd.

[x] Metal. ii. 7 pp. 797 sq.

[y] Dragmat. iii. p. 80.

[z] v. supra, pp. 182 sq.

John of Salisbury, therefore, who had praise only for sound and honest work, and for the modesty and tolerance of the true philosopher, early parted company with the professional dialecticians. Afterwards at Canterbury, where though he did not perhaps actually occupy the post of a teacher, [a] he seems to have been regarded in

[a] Metal., prol., p. 732.

[19] William of Conches has more than one description of these coxcombs; see below Appendix vi and vii. Compare too the Dragmaticon (De substantiis physicis) iii. p. 63: 'In nugis sunt subtiles, in necessariis tardi et hebetes, sed ne nil fecisse cum repatriaverint videantur, ex pellibus vitulinis bene pumicatis et levigatis cum amplis interlineis libros componi faciunt, eosque coopertoriis rubeis et impressis vestiunt: sicque cum sapiente sacculo et insipiente animo ad parentes suos recurrunt.'

CHAP. VII.

some sort as the representative of learning in the archbishop's household, he was constrained to take up the defence of those principles of knowledge which he had acquired at Chartres, against the vain substitutes for it which were everywhere forcing themselves into notice. His *Metalogicus* supposes a state of things somewhat different from, somewhat more degenerate than, that to which we have just now alluded. His opponents were not solely the logical fanatics whose acquaintance he had made at Paris, although [b] they were as fond of splitting hairs. On the contrary they were animated by an impartial contempt for all the educational tradition of the schools: logic they scorned as heartily as they did grammar, and were confident of becoming philosophers by rule of thumb. John had no difficulty in combating this supercilious attitude, but the interest of his treatise is that it gives him occasion to discuss at large his favourite theme of the interdependence of the several 'arts' that relate to the laws and functions of language, in other words, of the Trivium: for he maintains it is only by a thorough study of grammar, rhetoric, and dialectic, considered as mutually connected and auxiliary, that we can lay the foundations of genuine knowledge. [c] Dialectic itself, valuable and necessary as it is, is *like the sword of Hercules in a Pigmy's hand* unless there be added to it the accoutrement of the other sciences.

[b] lib. i. 3 p. 740.

[c] lib. ii. 9 p. 801.

The *Metalogicus* has in one respect a peculiar value: [d] it is the first work in the middle ages in which the whole of Aristotle's *Organon* is turned to account. Having thus a surer basis to build upon than any of his predecessors, John relies entirely upon Aristotle for his logical theory. In reference to the crucial question of the universals he is the loyal disciple of Abailard, whose principles he elaborates from the newly discovered source. But even on a point to which supreme importance was attached by his contemporaries John declines to be positive: he chooses the conclusion of Aristotle not because of its absolute scientific truth but [e] *because it is the best*

[d] Prantl, Gesch. d. Logik 2. 238 [240] sq., Schaarschmidt 117–122, 215 sq., [Webb, prolegg. in Policr. 1. xxiii–xxvii.].

[e] Metal. ii. 20 p. 837.

adapted to the study of logic. For the same reason, except in this one department of learning, he avows his allegiance to Plato, whose general view of things he accepts by reason of the free range it concedes to enquiry and speculation. [f] *I am not ashamed,* he once says, *to number myself among the academics, since in those things about which a wise man may doubt, I depart not from their footsteps.* It is [g] not that he is in favour of a general scepticism, far less of a general indecision and vacillation. [h] Certain facts John conceives to be irrefragably established by authority; others stand on a secure foundation of reason: but there is a large class of problems in reference to which he holds his judgement in suspense, because they are not definitely solved by either of the prime arbiters of truth, nor yet verified by observation. Accordingly he gives a long and most curious list of *things about which a wise man may doubt . . . so* however, he prudently adds, *that the doubt extend not to the multitude.* The items are strangely mixed; they bring into vivid light on the one hand the immense interval between the certainties of modern knowledge and the vague gropings that had to serve for physical science in John's age, and on the other the eternal limitations of the human mind which forbid the elevation of metaphysics or theology to the rank of an exact science.

CHAP. VII.

[f] Policr., prol., vol. I. 17.

[g] lib. vii. 2 vol. 2. 95 sqq.

[h] vol. 2. 98 sq.

In reading this catalogue one cannot repress the thought, how many sects and divisions would have been spared the church in other ages and in our own time, had men been willing to confess with John of Salisbury that there are many questions which every man has a right to answer or to leave unanswered for himself. Among these John reckons providence and fate, chance and free will; even *those things which are reverently enquired about God himself, who surpasses the examination of all rational nature and is exalted above all that the mind can conceive.* Other questions which are included in the same large enumeration—the nature and origin of the soul; matter and motion; the causes and beginnings of things; the use and end of virtues and vices, and their source; *whether a man who*

CHAP VII.

has one virtue has all virtues, and whether all sins are equal and equally to be punished—may appear to have a less direct bearing upon theology; but it will not escape observation that hardly one of them but has come to make part, if not of the formal creed, still of the accepted tradition of some one of the sects of Christendom. In the middle ages the association was the more closely felt because theology was almost universally the standard of knowledge, the test by which the goodness of a philosophical tenet was tried. We do not indeed presume to say that John of Salisbury calculated the issues to which he committed himself; certainly if any connexion of the sort just named could be proved he would have been the first to withdraw the problem in question out of the class of 'doubtfuls.' Still it is his signal virtue, a virtue which, if we mistake not, he derived immediately from Bernard of Chartres, that, although he held as strongly as any man to the principle just mentioned, he distinctly limited it to facts with regard to which authority was precise, and left the rest open questions.

He did more than this: he enlarged the conception of authority; for the divine influence, he maintained with Abailard, is not to be sought only in the written revelation but in its indwelling in man's reason.

[i] Enthet. ver. 629–636.

[i] Est hominis ratio summae rationis imago
Quae capit interius vera docente Deo.
Ut data lux oculis tam se quam cetera monstrat
Quae sub luce patent et sine luce latent,
Claraque fit nubes concepto lumine solis,
Cum dependentes flatus abegit aquas:
Subdita sic ratio formam summae rationis
Sordibus expulsis induit, inde micat.

[k] Policr. iii. 1 vol. 1. 171 sqq.

[k] The reasonable soul is the habitation of God, by participation in whom all things exist: the good man therefore, for virtue is the antecedent of the right exercise of reason, may be trusted to *know*. It is thus that John is able to declare that [l] freedom is the most glorious of all things, because it is inseparable from, if not identical with, virtue.

[l] lib. vii. 25 vol. 2. 217.

John of Salisbury is the youngest exponent of a great and vigorous intellectual movement. The generation of its founders began in the last quarter of the eleventh century; John carries on its current past the middle of the twelfth. But the tide has been already long ebbing, and the thirteenth century hardly begins before [m] the *Physics* of Aristotle, now first made known to the Latin world, are solemnly interdicted by a council at Paris; a few years later [n] the proscription is extended to the *Metaphysics*.[20] That was in fact the meeting-time of two eras, and the opening of the new period of philosophical progress, created by the importation of the works of Aristotle, was threatened, as the efforts of Roscelin and Abailard had been, by the anathema of the church. Now, however, a reconciliation was soon arranged; and the church herself had the glory of claiming as her own the men who reared the stupendous fabric of the mature scholastic philosophy. Into this, the second and greater, period in the history of scholasticism we do not propose to enter; its magnitude and importance make it a subject by itself. In the following chapters our attention will be confined to a small department of it, one to which we are naturally led, since of the theories formed in the middle ages respecting the nature and functions of the state John of Salisbury's is the first that aspires to a philosophical character.

m [Denifle, Chartul. univ. Paris. I. 70.]
A.D. 1210.
A.D. 1215.
n [ibid., p. 78 sq.]

[20] The general fact of this condemnation is clear, though it is also certain that a confusion arose with John Scotus's work, on account, no doubt, of its title Περὶ φύσεων μερισμοῦ. See Jourdain in the Mémoires de l'Académie des Inscriptions 26(2) 486–489, Hauréau, Histoire de la Philosophie scolastique 2(1) 100–106.

CHAPTER VIII.

THE HIERARCHICAL DOCTRINE OF THE STATE.

Among the facts which make the eleventh century a turning-point in the history of society,—whether we look to the intellectual movement or to the consolidation of the feudal system, to the arousing of a national force in France and England under stress of northern invaders, or to the restoration of the imperial or the ecclesiastical dignity;—among the incidents in this general change, none was attended with such wide-reaching consequences as the new position claimed for the catholic church. It might seem as though, just at the moment when nations were beginning to realise their strength and to some extent acquiring even an individual consciousness, the church intervened and sought to merge them all in one confused mass, subject and submissive to her will. Yet evidently the churchmen were only doing their duty when they felt and confessed that the work of repairing society belonged of right to them; nor could they discover any secret for the efficiency of the church's action more natural than a lofty assertion of her right to control the secular state and make her counsels the guide of the world. The enunciation of this policy opened a new channel of thought and discussion quite independent of that stream of which we have observed the rise in the foregoing chapters: from it flowed a literature appropriated to the exposition of the theory of politics, and in special of the relations of church and state.[1] It is not our purpose here to examine

[1] In this and the following chapter I am largely indebted to the references contained in two very compendious tracts by professor Emil Friedberg of Leipzig entitled, Die mittelalterlichen Lehren über das Verhältniss von Staat und Kirche; 1874. [A collection of the treatises which were written during this long controversy will

in any detail the hierarchical scheme which is identified with the person and history of the archdeacon Hildebrand, the pope Gregory the Seventh; but there are some general considerations with regard to it which it is important to bear in mind, in order to understand the conditions under which men wrote. CHAP. VIII.

Whether or not we approve the methods by which Gregory laid anew the foundations of the papal power,[2] it would be idle to dispute the essential nobility of the conception, which ultimately rested on the necessity of reforming the church as preliminary to the reformation of the world. It was plain that society could not be purified by an instrument as corrupt as itself; and such had been the condition of the church, at least until the middle of the eleventh century. The crying evil was that it was becoming more and more a part of the state, the clergy entering more and more into the enjoyments, the luxury, the profligacy, of civil life. Reform, it was felt, must begin by severing this alliance and constituting the clergy as a class, a caste, by themselves, to offer a pattern of purity and self-devotedness to the laity. To us possibly, with the experience of eight centuries, it may appear that such a scheme was destined by its very nature to fail of its true objects, and that the character of the clergy and their spiritual and moral influence would have been better secured by placing them, with the intrinsic power of their office, not over but among the people. In fact there was perhaps[3] no surer means towards the degradation of an

---

be found in the Libelli de lite imperatorum et pontificum, published in the Monumenta Germaniae historica in three volumes, 1891–1897.]

[2] In the opinion of cardinal Hergenröther, Katholische Kirche und christlicher Staat in ihrer geschichtlichen Entwickelung 234 &c., 2nd ed., Freiburg 1876, Gregory did little more than carry into effect principles for which his predecessors had failed to find opportunity. [A luminous survey of more recent works on the subject is given by Dr. J. P. Whitney in the English historical Review, 34. 129–151; 1919.]

[3] John bishop of Lübeck at the council of Basle in 1434 made a proposition to the delegates 'ut sacerdotibus Christi nuptias restituerent: . . . inutiliter uxores esse praereptas sacerdotibus; vix inter mille unum reperiri continentem presbyterum, omnes aut concu-

CHAP. VIII.

order than to absolve it from social restraints and to enforce upon it a special code of morals which not all desired to keep and which many, if not most, found it easy to elude. At the same time the preponderant balance of church authority was precise against the toleration of a married clergy, and this part of the reform was rightly defended as a recurrence to patristic, if not to primitive, usage. Moreover the sharper the distinction, the separation, between clergy and laity, the more readily could the former be applied as an external and consolidated force against the disorders of civil society. On general grounds it is perfectly clear that if the church was to exercise that sway which all Christians agreed it ought to exercise, over the consciences of men, it must be as free as possible from those ties which bound it to the secular state; if, for instance, the churchman had to look to his king for preferment, he was not likely to be as vigilant or as courageous in the carrying out of his duty as if he depended solely upon his spiritual chief.[4] The isolation and independence of the clergy being then postulated, it was but a step further to assert their superiority, their right of controlling the state. [a] Gregory had a search made in the papal archives and found what he believed to be irrefragable evidence of the feudal dependence of the different kingdoms on the Roman see. Civil power,—so he wrote to bishop

[a] Epist. vi. 23 Jaffé 2. 468 sq.; cf. I. von Döllinger, Die Papst-Fabeln des Mittelalters 84.

binarios, aut adulteros, aut quod peius est, inveniri: . . . amicitiae vinculum inter laicos clericosque hac disparitate servari non posse; omnes sacerdotes quasi pudicitiae maritalis expugnatores a populo timeri . . . Res,' adds the narrator, Aeneas Sylvius, afterwards pope Pius the Second, 'erat complurimis accepta; sed tempori non convenire. . . . Quidam senes damnabant quod assequi non poterant. Religiosi, quia voto astricti erant continentiae, haud libenter audiebant, presbyteris concedi saecularibus quod sibi negaretur:' De rebus Basileae gestis commentarius, in C. Fea's Pius Secundus a Calumniis vindicatus 57 sq., Rome 1823.

[4] It is curious that Manegold in the treatise cited below, p. 203 n. 7, dwells upon the disadvantage to the people of *royal* patronage because kingdoms being extensive and including various nationalities, it might and did happen that persons were appointed to preferments in a district the very language of which they did not understand. See Hartwig Floto, Kaiser Heinrich der Vierte 2. 302, Stuttgart 1856. It is unnecessary to allude to the practices in regard to foreign preferments which resulted from *papal* patronage.

Herman of Metz,—was the invention of worldly men, ignorant of God and prompted by the devil [5]; it needed not only the assistance but the authorisation of the church. CHAP. VIII. March 15, 1081.

Viewing the new policy in its first rudiments, we cannot fail to detect an inevitable source of weakness, so far as its essential aims were concerned. It made demands on the clergy (and *a fortiori* on the pope, for whom was claimed a virtual omnipotence on earth) which could hardly be satisfied in a far higher stage of civilisation. In a word it was theoretical, ideal, visionary. As soon as it was brought into the sphere of practice, so soon as the church entered into conflict with the state, it became evident that the unworldliness assumed in the church only existed in so far that she had no material forces to rely upon; although the weapon of excommunication which she wielded was in fact more powerful than any forces that the secular state possessed. If the clergy were free from civil control, society on the other hand had little or no protection against their license. To make the high ecclesiastical officers proudly independent of the sovereign was to introduce the influence of the Roman see into every court, and to put canonical obedience in danger of becoming a matter of common politics. If ecclesiastical property was released from civil obligation, the church was as much as before subject to the cares and the temptations of wealth. The spiritual basis of the hierarchical pretensions in fact at once broke down on trial. The pope by aspiring to universal dominion, fell to the position of a sovereign among sovereigns; he became a disturbing influence in the political system of Europe, and the most religious of men were constantly troubled to reconcile their duty towards their

[5] Quis nesciat reges et duces ab iis habuisse principium qui, Deum ignorantes, superbia, rapinis, perfidia, homicidiis, postremo universis pene sceleribus, mundi principe diabolo videlicet agitante, super pares, scilicet homines, dominari caeca cupidine et intolerabili praesumptione affectaverunt?—Reg. viii. 21 Jaffé, Bibliotheca Rerum Germanicarum 2. 457.

CHAP. VIII.

country with what they believed to be their duty towards God.

The Hildebrandine policy thus contained within it the seeds of danger alike to society and to the church itself. But, over and above these intrinsic defects, the idea of a catholic church was confronted and menaced by another idea that did not yield to it in the magnificence and universality of its pretensions. The circumstances of the time brought the pope into peculiar relations with Italy and Germany, the inheritors of the title and traditions of the Roman empire. [b] Hitherto the emperor had been understood to represent on earth the unity and order of the divine government, holding in the secular estate a rank equal, and often very far superior, to that occupied by the pope in the spiritual. He was the vicegerent of God; that title had not yet been appropriated by the papacy. With such a doctrine Gregory would have nothing to do; his attitude with respect to it was unequivocally, defiantly revolutionary. He treated civil government at large as a human institution [c] so deeply polluted by its sinful origin,—Cain and Nimrod, it was commonly explained, were its first founders,—as to be by itself helpless and criminal. Between the two opposing principles no compromise, no lasting peace was possible. But the points on which we would dwell are not so much the broad issues raised in the interminable controversy, as the incidental consequences that were drawn from them. There are few facts more striking than the readiness with which the church admitted any form of civil government that would listen to her claims. Theoretically she had no preference for monarchical institutions; rather, it should seem, she was inclined to promote a democratic system. Granted only the superiority of the ecclesiastical power, there was no concession she would not make in favour of popular rights: and her advocates speak, now with the voice of 'revolution-whigs,' of the official character of kingship; now with the earnestness of Cromwell's independents, of the necessity, the duty, of

[b] cf. Floto 2. 286 sqq.

[c] cf. Aug. Triumph. de potest. eccles. xxxvi. 1 p. 212 b, ed. Rome 1582 folio.

tyrannicide.[6] Those passages of the New Testament which have been held to bespeak a divine right for kings are completely ignored, and the hierarchical pamphleteers, almost without exception, draw their lessons from the theocratic, or rather sacerdotal, teaching of the Hebrew scriptures or from the commonplaces of classical history.

A most interesting example of this method is to be found in a work written by Manegold, a priest of Lautenbach in Alsatia, in defence of Gregory.[7] [d] *King*, he says, *is not a name of nature but a title of office: nor does the people exalt him so high above itself in order to give him the free power of playing the tyrant against it, but to defend him from the tyranny of others. So soon as he begins to act the tyrant, is it not plain that he falls from the dignity granted to him and the people is free from his dominion? since it is evident that he has first broken that contract by virtue of which he was appointed. If one should engage a man for a fair wage to tend swine, and he find means not to tend but to steal or slay them, would not one remove him from his charge?* It is impossible to express the theory of 'social contract' more clearly than Manegold does: [e] *since*, he says, *no one can create himself emperor or king, the people elevates a certain one person over itself to this end that he govern and rule it according to the principle of righteous government; but if in any wise he transgresses the contract by virtue of which he is chosen, he absolves the people from the obligation of submission, because he has first broken faith*

[d] cap. xxx. ap. Floto 2. 289 n. [Lib. de lite 1. 365.]

[e] cap. xlvii., ap. Floto, ibid. [Lib. de lite 1. 392 sq.]

[6] The agreement has been often remarked. Sir Robert Filmer says of the doctrine that mankind is naturally at liberty to choose its government, 'This tenet was first hatched in the schools, and hath been fostered by all succeeding papists for good divinity. The divines also of the reformed churches have entertained it, and the common people everywhere tenderly embrace it,' &c. Then with reference to the 'perillous conclusion' drawn from this maxim, namely, that the people have power to 'punish or deprive' their sovereign, he adds, 'Cardinal Bellarmine and Calvine both look asquint this way:' Patriarcha i. 1 pp. 2 sqq.; 1680.

[7] It is preserved in a single manuscript at Carlsruhe, and has not, so far as I am aware, been printed. Extracts are given by Floto: see his account of the work, vol. 2. 299–303. [It has since been published in the Libelli de lite 1. 308–430.]

CHAP. VIII.

with it. But the writer was in fact going far beyond what his party required: for certainly nothing could have been more distasteful to Gregory the Seventh and his followers than to give subjects a general right of deposing their sovereigns. All that the pope maintained was that they should be ready to rise in arms against them at the bidding of the head of the church. Individual or popular liberty was the last thing Gregory wished to establish; absolute obedience was as much a part of his theory as it was of the imperialists: the only question was to whom, as the supreme lord, it was due.

It was not however until a considerably later date that the upholders of the independence of the civil state ventured to frame a counter-theory for their action. For the present [f] they were content to rely on the established usage of the Latin church and on the [g] formal recognition by Nicholas the Second of the emperor's right to ratify the election of the pope.[8] If they be held to have had the better of the argument, they limited themselves to the temporary demands of controversy. The first attempt to look apart from surrounding conditions and to produce a coherent system which should aspire to the character of a philosophy of politics came from the other side. When John of Salisbury applied himself to this subject in three books of his *Policraticus* there is nothing to remind us that the contest between Frederick Barbarossa and Hadrian the Fourth was just then ripening to a declaration of hostilities, or that the author himself was alienated from royal favour on account of his attachment to the policy of saint Thomas Becket. His treatment bears no reference to contemporary forms of government. His examples are those of the Old Testament or of the ancient Roman empire; there is not a trace even of the terminology of feudalism. John may now and then allude incidentally to modern customs, [h] but it is only by way of

[f] cf. Floto 2. 294–298.

[g] Pertz, Legg. 2 app. p. 178; 1837.

[h] Policrat. vi., prol., vol. 2. 1.

[8] It does not fall within my plan to go through the controversial literature of this time. A list of references will be found in Giesebrecht, Geschichte der deutschen Kaiserzeit 3.1049,1104;1865.

illustration.[9] The terms he employs for the officers of government and for the military organization are all foreign to feudal times and almost entirely classical. [i] His authorities for military affairs are Frontinus, Vegetius, and the rest; his general scheme of the state is drawn from the *Institutio Traiani* ascribed to Plutarch. There is no sign in it even of an order of nobility. All temporary matters John passes by, in order to attain what appear to him to be the eternal principles of civil right. Like the hierarchical doctrine which he expounds, his theory is entirely ideal, and bears almost an ironical complexion if we think of applying it to any monarchy of his own or indeed of any time.

CHAP. VIII.

[i] capp. 12, 19, vol. 2. 27 sq., 56 sq.

[k] John starts from the notion of equity as *the perfect adjustment of things,—rerum convenientia,*—of which there are on earth two interpreters, the law and the civil ruler. Having by a [l] previous definition excluded all bad kings, under the common name of 'tyrants,' from the field of his discussion, he is the more free to elevate the ideal grandeur of kingship. [m] *When,* he says, *we speak of the prince as released from the bands of the law, it is not that he has license to do wrong, but forasmuch as he ought to be moved not by fear of punishment but by the love of justice to observe equity, to further the advantage of the commonwealth, and in all things to choose the good of others before his private will. But who would speak of the prince's will in public matters? whereas he has no leave to will aught therein, save that which is counselled by law or equity, or determined by the consideration of general utility. In such concerns his will ought to possess the validity of judgement, and most rightly in them,* according to the maxim of jurists, [n] *his pleasure hath the force of law; because his sentence differs not from the mind of equity.* [o] Without this understood condition the maxim is false. The king therefore is

[k] lib. iv. 2 vol. 1. 237.

[l] cap. 1 p. 235.

[m] cap. 2 p. 238; cf. Ulpian., ap. Digest. i. tit. iii. 31, vol. 1. 80 B, ed. Antwerp 1575 folio.

[n] Ulp., ibid., tit. iv. 1 p. 84 C.

[o] Policr. iv. 7 vol. 1. 259 sq.

[9] Compare his reference to the corruption practised by sheriffs and by 'iustitiis quae, ut vulgari nostro utar, recte dicuntur errantes,' Policrat. v. 16. vol. 1. 352. Other notices of recent history are very interesting; see book vi. 6 vol. 2. 18 sqq., 18 pp. 47 sqq., &c.

CHAP. VIII.

so far independent of the law that his rank is coördinate with it: he stands on an equal level as an exponent of eternal right. Thus he can be described as [p] *an image of the divine majesty on earth . . . All power is of the lord God: . . . the power of the prince is therefore in such wise of God that it is still his, though it be exercised through the hand of a deputy.*

[p] Policr. iv. 1 p. 236.

We might think John of Salisbury to be the most fervent of imperialists; yet in fact his exaltation of the nobility of kingship is but a means towards the erection of a higher dignity still for the spiritual power. For the king's authority is only mediately derived from God. [q] *The sword,* the symbol of worldly power, *the prince receives from the hand of the church.* He is therefore *the servant of the priesthood,* merely exercising in its stead functions which it is too sacred to perform itself. [r] *Vain,* says John, *is the authority of all laws except it bear the image of the divine law; and useless is the decree of a prince unless it be conformable to the discipline of the church.* Yet here too the theory is purely ideal; John's conception of a state is that it depends upon the absolute principles of righteousness, and it was inevitable in his surroundings that he should identify these principles with the actual church of Christ, which stood as the symbol of them. No man was more outspoken in exposing the vices and abuses with which it was attended. [s] This unsparing denunciation was indeed usual with the heartiest upholders of church rights in the middle ages; and it tells strongly for their honesty and candour. But still there was no other institution in existence to which one could point as in origin dependent, and dependent solely, on principles higher than the common worldly rules of conduct. Accordingly John devotes the major part of his description to a [t] commentary on that passage expounding the duties of kingship which forms so remarkable a feature in the book of Deuteronomy. Thus far John's theory is just the conventional one which had been handed down through generations of churchmen. In principle it shows hardly

[q] cap. 3 p. 239.

[r] cap. 6 p. 251.

[s] cf. Friedberg 1. 5 sq.

[t] Policr. iv. 4–12 vol. 1. 244–279; Deut. xvii. 14–20.

any advance or development from that simple little manual which Jonas, bishop of Orleans, had compiled more than three centuries earlier for the instruction of Pippin, king of Aquitaine.[10] Jonas indeed is less ambitious and contents himself for the most part with stringing together extracts from the Bible and the fathers; but John of Salisbury's classical erudition did not lead him at all to modify the main point, of the supremacy of the church over the world. Both writers alike [u] find their best examples in Deuteronomy.[11]

[u] Jonas, cap. 3 p. 328 a.

The Bible however furnishes but scanty materials for determining more minutely the mutual relation of the several elements of the state, and John has recourse to a late Roman treatise, the *Institutio Traiani* already referred to, from which he draws the following simile. [x] The state, he says, has been likened to a living organism of which the soul is represented by religion, the head by the prince, and the other members by the various efficient classes of society. The hands are the soldiery, the feet the husbandmen and working people; the belly is the administration of finance, always inclined to surfeit and bring disorder upon the rest of the body; and the heart is the senate. John does not here enforce the principle, upon which indeed he has previously laid sufficient stress, of the subordination of the temporal state to the spiritual. He portrays religion as the 'soul' of government for the obvious reason that its care is for the interests of the soul; and if he recurs to the high estimation in which the priesthood ought to be held, it is simply as a [y] corollary from the reverence due to things in which

[x] Policr. v. 2 pp. vol. I. 282 sq.

[y] cap. 4 p. 295.

[10] The treatise to which dom d'Achery prefixed the title De institutione regia (Spicilegium 1. 323, ed. 1723) is a sort of special supplement to the bishop's three books De institutione laicali, his 'Holy Living,' we may say, printed ibid., pp. 258–323. I do not assert John of Salisbury's indebtedness to the book, for there is no evidence of the degree of popularity it enjoyed. The editors of it mention only two manuscripts, one at Rome, the other at Orleans, p. 324.

[11] I cannot therefore agree with Dr Sigmund Riezler, Die literarischen Widersacher der Päpste zur Zeit Ludwig des Baiers 136, 1874, that the use of the Old Testament forms a peculiar characteristic of the Policraticus.

CHAP. VIII.

they minister. There is no question here of the political duties of the church.[12] It does not therefore concern us to linger over the long didactic exposition which John writes upon the supposed text of Plutarch, and of which our only complaint is that it takes no account, except by way of illustration, of any of the facts and conditions of medieval polity. The classical ground-work gives a sort of individuality to John's treatment. He writes like an inferior Roman moralist of the silver age; but few would trouble themselves with his delineation were it not for the incidental allusions to, and observations respecting, contemporary or recent history.

There is one particular in which John's system is distinguished from that of almost every other political writer of the middle ages. It has already been noticed that John guards his theory of kingship by a careful distinction so as to exclude tyrants from all its privileges. Though he does not commit himself to the 'contract' notion which we have found in Manegold, it is clear that the ethical proviso which John requires, amounts in practice to the same thing and allows a large enough field for the exercise of popular opinion. But John extends the application of this check on misrule in a remarkable way. He inculcates with peculiar energy the duty not only of deposing but of slaying tyrants. [z] He wrote a book, now lost, *On the End of Tyrants*, devoted as it seems to this special subject, to which he [a] more than once recurs in the *Policraticus*. Tyrannicide is not only lawful, it is obligatory; we may resort to any means to effect this object except poison,

[z] lib. viii. 20 vol. 2. 373.

[a] libb. iii. 15 vol. 1. 232 sq., viii. 17–21 vol. 2. 345–396.

[12] I make this remark in order to guard against an inference which may naturally be drawn from Dr. Schaarschmidt's statement, p. 163,—also Dr. Riezler's, l.c.,—that John explains the soul of the state as 'the priesthood.' His words are: 'Ea vero quae cultum religionis in nobis instituunt et informant et . . . Dei cerimonias tradunt, vicem animae in corpore rei publicae obtinent. Illos vero,' it is true he adds, 'qui religionis cultui praesunt, quasi animam corporis suspicere et venerari oportet. Quis enim sanctitatis ministros Dei ipsius vicarios esse ambigit?' Lib. v. 2 vol. 1. 282. But the reference to old Roman usages which immediately follows is sufficient to persuade us that he is speaking only of the priest as supreme in his own, that is, in the spiritual, field.

[b] which is not justified by example and is [c] abhorrent from English customs. With this single exception any act overt or covert is allowable against the tyrant. [d] He is an enemy of the state and therefore those moral restrictions which bind society have no force in our dealings with him. We may flatter him, or employ any art, in order to lure him on to his destruction.[13]

CHAP. VIII.

[b] lib. viii. 20 p. 378.
[c] cap. 19 p. 372.
[d] libb. iii. 15 vol. 1. 232 sq.; viii. 18 vol. 2. 364.

It need not be pointed out how accurately John had learned the historical lessons of the Old Testament. All through the controversial literature relating to church and state, the hierarchical party, [e] as we have said, like the English puritans of a later age, rely on the precedents furnished by Hebrew history,[14] and pass by, or explain spiritually, those passages of the Christian Scriptures which insist with such emphasis on the universal duty of obedience to the temporal ruler. The doctrine that [f] *the powers that be are ordained of God* was held only with the reservation that God acted through the instrumentality of the church. Christianity in fact hardly influenced their political doctrine, except in so far as it considered life on earth as merely the preparation for another life hereafter, the 'road,' *via*, according to the expressive and constantly recurring phrase, that leads to the eternal 'home,' *patria*. Hence a new goal was set to human aspirations, and the nature of the civil state lost in worth by comparison of the supreme interests which lay beyond its cognisance. Nor did John of Salisbury at all rëadjust or discriminate the various factors in this

[e] cf. supra, pp. 202 sq.

[f] Rom. xiii. 1.

[13] It is a most curious coïncidence that another Johannes Parvus, Jean Petit, made this doctrine conspicuous in relation to the murder of the duke of Orleans in 1407. His arguments are identical: see M. Creighton, History of the Papacy during the Period of the Reformation 1. 372–376; 1882. The position was condemned in a general way by the council of Constance, 1415–1416.

[14] Thomas Aquinas, whose writings indeed stand apart from controversy, inverts this position. In the Old Testament, he says, where men looked only for temporary promises, the priests were subject to the king; but the New elevates the priesthood higher because in it men are directed to eternal goods: De regimine principum i. 14 Opp. 17. 166, ed. Venice 1593 folio; with the volumes and folios of which the edition of Antwerp 1612 agrees.

CHAP. VIII.

mixed tradition of Hebrew and Christian ideas. He enriched it by proofs and lessons from classical history, but the stuff of his system remained the same as that current in the common speech of churchmen. It needed another classical influence to be brought to bear upon politics to raise them from a medley of empirical axioms to something approaching the character of a philosophical theory. This influence was found in the thirteenth century in the *Politics* of Aristotle: its first exponent is the greatest and profoundest teacher of the middle ages, saint Thomas Aquinas.

The *Rule of Princes*[15] to which Aquinas devoted a special treatise, appears to him by no means a necessary form of government. Under the guidance of Aristotle, he approaches the subject with an entire absence of prejudice for it or any other form. [g] The supreme power, he says, may be confided to many, to few, or to one; and each of these arrangements may be good or bad. [h] He raises a presumption on quite general grounds that the unity of society—and this is the main object of government—is best secured by its subjection to a single ruler; but an aristocracy or a government by the people itself he allows to be equally legitimate, though not so well adapted to the necessities of the state. It is not the form but the character of the constitution that makes it good or bad. [i] As monarchy is the most perfect form, so on the other hand its opposite, tyranny, is the most corrupt and abominable. Aquinas distinguishes, as minutely as

[g] De regim. princ. i. 1, 2 Opp. 17. 161; cf. Baumann 121.

[h] cf. Summ. contra gent. iv. 76 Opp. 9. 513.

[i] De regim. princ. i. 3 ff. 161, &c.

[15] The four books De regimine principum which held their ground as the accepted textbook of political philosophy until the opening of modern history, are only in part the work of saint Thomas. His treatise is a fragment which breaks off in the course of the second book, and the remainder is the production in all probability of his disciple Ptolemy of Lucca: See Quétif and Echard, Scriptores Ordinis Praedicatorum, 1. 543; Paris 1719. With the help however of some others of Thomas's writings, and in particular of his commentary on Aristotle's Politics, we are enabled to fill up the most important gaps in his treatment of the subject and to gain a nearly complete view of his political theory. Dr. J. J. Baumann's Staatslehre des h. Thomas von Aquino 5 sq. (1873) contains a serviceable collection (in German) of the passages in Thomas's works, bearing upon the subject of polity.

John of Salisbury, between the king and the tyrant; like John, he postulates for the former an absolute devotion to the duties of his office, and thus exalts him to so ideal a dignity that he is empowered to speak of him as [k] holding the same position in his own domain as God holds over the universe; he stands to his realm (this is more than John would have allowed) as the soul to the body.

[k] cap. 12 f. 165.

But to this supremacy there are two limitations. In the first place while the end of all government is so to order human affairs that men may be the best prepared for eternal happiness, the special responsibility for spiritual concerns resides in the priests, who thus stand in the position of overlords to the civil ruler. The spiritual destiny of man requires a divine law over and above natural or human law. [l] *In order, therefore, that the spiritual be kept separate from the earthly, the office of this kingdom is committed not to earthly kings but to the priests, and above all to the chief priest, the successor of Peter, the vicegerent of Christ, the Roman bishop, to whom is due the subjection of all kings of the Christian people, even as to the lord Jesus Christ himself.* In the treatise *Of the Rule of Princes*, which he left a fragment, Aquinas hardly pursues the subject further; but elsewhere he propounds with the utmost decision the hierarchical theory of the church. [m] It is necessary, he says, to have some supreme authority in matters of faith: this authority resides in the pope, in whom is realised the unity of the church and the presence of the divine government. To him therefore is entrusted the power to control and to revise the ordinances of religion; [n] he has even competence to promulgate a new confession of faith *in order to prevent the rise of erroneous beliefs.* Those who have any acquaintance with medieval history know how elastic a term 'error' was in the mouth of the pope, and [o] Thomas pronounces that from the moment of the issue of an authoritative excommunication against a sovereign, he is deprived of the right to rule and his subjects are released from their oath of allegiance. It is of course a statement of the accepted doctrine among

[l] lib. i. 14 f. 166.

[m] Summ. contra gent. iv. 76 Opp. 9. 512 sq.

[n] 2 secund. i. 10 Opp. 11 (2) 7 sq.

[o] ibid., qu. xii. 2 f. 34.

CHAP. VIII.

the hierarchical party, and need not be further discussed; especially since Aquinas places by its side another check upon misrule the more interesting because of its approximation to modern ways of thought.

This second limitation upon royal power is that of the popular will. But let it be understood from the outset that the philosopher has no dream of looking to the capricious action of individual patriots as the instrument for setting things right; such is not his idea of maintaining order. [p] Tyrannicide in the common sense he altogether repudiates. *It is more seemly*, he says, *to proceed to the overthrow of tyrants not according to the personal presumption of one, but on public authority.* If the community has the right of electing its prince, it has also the right of deposing him; no oath of fealty, even though sworn in perpetuity, can stand in its way. If the prince be himself subject to a superior power, let the people invoke his aid; but if there be no earthly authority to appeal to, they can only trust to God and to patience. [q] Aquinas therefore allows no redress for misgovernment unless the redress sought be in conformity with law; he tempers the freedom of Old Testament examples by the rule of the New, [r] *Be subject to your masters with all fear; not only to the good and gentle, but also to the froward.* Yet he is so little satisfied with this conclusion that, while he [s] allows the advantage of hereditary monarchy in special circumstances, he strongly commends the elective form as a general rule, evidently because each new election gives an opportunity for placing restraints upon the royal power. Besides, as has appeared, an elected sovereign is legally subvertible. But Aquinas has no scheme to propound as to how the royal power is to be limited: [t] we are indeed told to contrive such a method of government as to leave the ruler no opportunity for violent measures but our philosopher gives no hint about the best means of arranging this, and insists mainly on the necessity for the community to choose their ruler wisely at the outset. [u] The prince, too, he explains, will find it

[p] De regim. princ. i. 6 f. 163.

[q] cf. Baumann 141.

[r] 1 Pet. ii. 18.

[s] Baumann 125 sqq.

[t] De regim. princ. i. 6 f. 162.

[u] Baumann 138.

to his own interest to moderate his actions in obedience to the popular will; otherwise he runs a risk of exciting his subjects to rebellion. His own prudence is thus the principal check on his conduct.

[x] Aquinas however only allows the title of king, in the strict sense of the word, to those who hold an absolute government, not in deference to the laws but according to virtue. It is John of Salisbury's notion in another shape. [y] He placed the king in a position external to law, because his acts were to be guided by the principles of eternal right; Aquinas substitutes the word 'virtue,' but the idea is the same: neither discusses the possibility of the two forces, of the law and the royal authority, coming into collision; or more accurately, they have already provided for the contingency by a definition of kingship which such conflict *ipso facto* changes into tyranny. [z] The king, in Aquinas' view, has to supplement the deficiencies of law by following the rule, or unwritten law, of his own will and his own reason. In opposition to this kingship which may be broadly distinguished in modern phrase as the theoretical imperial conception, [a] Thomas places the improper, what he terms the Lacedemonian, order. Such a king, he says, is bound to reign according to the laws and therefore is not lord over all. On the other hand [b] the less absolute he is, the more likely is his government to last, because there is the less chance of his stirring up illwill among his subjects. Yet even here we have to qualify the statement according to special circumstances. For instance, [c] in an advanced state of general civilisation, there is always a certain number of citizens possessing the governing spirit, who may therefore be expected to dispute the prince's authority, however much it be limited by prescription; whereas in a ruder state of society an absolute monarch has the better expectation of the permanent enjoyment of power, because there, the moral standard being in the average so low, it is easier for one man to stand out among his fellows with the special qualifications of kingship.

[x] ibid., p. 121.

[y] v. supra, pp. 234 sq., 238.

[z] Baumann 134 sq.

[a] Expos. in Arist. polit. iii. lect. viii. Opp. 5 (2) 52.

[b] Baumann 138.

[c] Expos. in pol. iii. lect. xvi. f. 57.

CHAP. VIII.

If Aquinas is evidently embarrassed in his attempt to combine the free politics which he read in the Greek examples with the existing specimens of monarchy in his own time, a difficulty which comes out curiously when [d] he finds himself compelled to restrict citizenship to the soldiery and officers of government, he makes amends by the clear and philosophic conception he forms of the nature of the state and of the sovereign's ideal relation to it. He rejects the popular 'spiritual' view which from Gregory the Seventh to Wycliffe regarded civil association as a consequence of the fall of man.[16] [e] Without the fall, he says, there would have been no slavery; but man's social instincts are an essential part of his constitution. [f] He cannot live alone as the beasts, nor is he like them provided with, or capable of supplying, the necessaries of life. He subsists by association and coöperation, and out of this need arises the necessity for a state, to unite and control individual action. The unity of society expressed in the formation of the state is given effect to in the person of the ruler. Following out this idea of the state as an organised unity, representing humanity in all its properties and therefore having [g] not only an economical but also a moral aim, Aquinas is able to arrive at some political results which are remarkably accordant with modern theories. Foremost among these is [h] his distinct preference for nationality, involving community of manners and customs,[17] as the basis of a state, a principle which helps him to the conclusion that [i] small states are *a priori* better than large ones. Nor can we omit to note the emphasis with which Thomas maintains that [k] it is the duty of the state to provide for the education of all its

[d] Baumann 147, 154.
[e] 1 summ. theol. xcvi. 4 Opp. 10. 317.
[f] De regim. princ. i. 1 f. 161.
[g] Baumann 108.
[h] ibid., pp. 144 sq.
[i] ibid., p. 152.
[k] ibid., pp. 161 sqq.

[16] In the Secunda secundae x. 10 fol. 30, he says 'Dominium vel praelatio introducta est [*ed.* sunt] ex iure humano: distinctio autem fidelium et infidelium est ex iure divino. Ius autem divinum quod est ex gratia, non tollit ius humanum quod est ex naturali ratione.'

[17] Neither in Aquinas nor in John of Paris, whose views on this point agree with his (see his treatise De potestate regia et papali iii, M. Goldast, Monarchia s. Romani Imperii 2. 111, Frankfurt 1614 folio), do I find any notice of the advantage of a common language.

members and [1] to see that no citizen suffers want. To these points we only advert in order to show that in them, just as in the optional or variable character assigned to the ultimate form of government, a churchman like Thomas Aquinas approaches nearer to the opinions of modern times than the generality of those who defended the claims of the emperor as against the pope, by a theory of the necessary, the indefeasible, the divine, basis of the imperial dignity.[18]

[1] ibid., pp. 155 sq.

With this idea Thomas had of necessity no concern. The empire might be held to have expired with Frederick the Second; and if Thomas wrote his book *Of the Rule of Princes* before the year 1266, it was at a time when the title of king of the Romans was disputed by two candidates neither of whom possessed, one of whom hardly aspired to, the shadow of real power. No emperor was again crowned until thirty years after Aquinas' death; and he was naturally led to the inference that the empire was absorbed into, or rëunited with, the mother-church: *it has not ceased*, he said, *but is changed from the temporal to the spiritual.*[19] It is indeed evident that his view of the

[18] It is needless to say that Aquinas has rudimentary notions of political economy (see the passages given by Dr Baumann, pp. 93 sqq. and the whole section, pp. 190–203) and repudiates the very thought of religious toleration: 2 Secund. x. 11, 12, xi. Opp. 11(2) 30 sqq., xxxix. 4 f. 101 (Baumann 185–189). Yet in both these particulars he shows insight and sound sense. See for example the objections he raises against the forcible baptism of the children of unbelievers, Qu. x. 12 f. 31 (Baumann 185 sq.).

[19] The coming of Antichrist, it was believed, would be heralded by a *discessio*, a departure from the faith and a secession from the Roman empire of part of its subjects. 'Sed quomodo est hoc?' asks saint Thomas; 'quia iamdiu gentes recesserunt a Romano imperio, et tamen necdum venit Antichristus. Dicendum est quod nondum cessavit, sed est commutatum de temporali in spirituale, ut dicit Leo papa in sermone de Apostolis: et ideo dicendum est quod discessio a Romano imperio debet intelligi non solum a temporali sed a spirituali, id est a fide catholica Romanae ecclesiae:' Expos. in 2 ad Thess. ii. opp. 16. 172 E. Cf. J. Bryce, The holy Roman Empire 114 n. 2. A curious gloss was given at an earlier time, during the contest concerning investitures, by Bonizo bishop of Sutri, namely, that the empire spoken of in the prophecy was the *eastern*; the western had already long been annihilated in consequence of the vices of its rulers. See Döllinger, Das Kaiserthum Karls des Grossen und seiner Nachfolger, in the Münchner historische Jahrbuch für 1865 pp. 387 sqq. [translated in Addresses on historical and literary Subjects, pp. 73–180; 1894.]

unique position of the church was one that could admit no rival to her in the secular state. But on the other hand the express preference which Thomas displays for nationality as the basis of the state, shows that he had learned, what the civilians remained ignorant of, that the world had outgrown the imperial conception; which notwithstanding still survived, always less and less of a reality, for upwards of five hundred years. Aquinas wrote in fact on the eve of a revolution in the history of European politics, not the less momentous because its results were defined in no external changes of government, dynasty, or frontier, were almost impalpable to contemporaries, and left all parties for the time as clamorous, as assertive, as before.

This change may be regarded in three sections. First, the opposition between the church and the empire became broadened into a general opposition between the church and the civil government of each individual kingdom. The consolidation of the French and English monarchies had raised up two forces with which it was far harder for the pope to grapple, than it had been, at all events in recent times, in the case of the empire. For apart from the fact that these powers were growing in solidity and in national feeling, while the German was declining, they had had no tradition which made them coördinate with the apostolic see, and which therefore might appear as a standing menace to the latter; they were in one sense beneath its dignity, and therefore all the freer to expand at their own will and to defy the intrusion of papal claims. The assertion of a national consciousness found imitators, and in Rome itself there were fitful and abortive endeavours (those of Arnold of Brescia in the twelfth, and of Rienzi in the fourteenth, century are notorious) to dissociate the city from the curia and to justify the lineage of the people by an idle claim to elect or to supersede the emperor. In the second place, when the empire did revive, it was but a shadow of its old self. The title of emperor, or of king of the

Romans (for the higher style was by no means regularly added), became insensibly a mere ornamental adjunct to a principality which had only a real existence, it might be, in Bavaria, in Austria, or in Bohemia: at best its holder was but a German sovereign, and each attempt to achieve the higher distinction of the empire, and to supplement the crown of Aix by those of Milan and Arles and Rome, ended in increasingly disastrous failure. It was exactly this period of decline that produced a literature in which the imperial idea was developed and glorified to a splendour unthought of hitherto. No less exaggerated are the claims now put forward for its rival. For in the third place, while the vitality of the empire was diminishing, the church was making rapid steps towards occupying the prerogatives left unclaimed or unrealised by it. As early as the middle of the twelfth century an anxious observer had remarked [m] that men spoke more of the Roman curia than of the Roman church. It was becoming a state among states while it aspired to be the supreme state that commanded and united all inferiors. Innocent the Third had made in his person the 'vicegerent of Peter' into the 'vicegerent of Christ'; and with Innocent the papacy reached its zenith. Nor did it for a long time exhibit any symptoms of decline. The conqueror of the empire fell beneath the defiance of the French king Philip the Fair, or more truly beneath the irresistible opposition of a strong national spirit in the kingdoms of Europe. The universal authority of Rome became confined within the narrow territory of Avignon: the means by which it was exerted became more and more secular, diplomatic, mercantile; and its spiritual efficiency was so far impaired that the loyallest servants of the catholic church could stand forth as the stoutest champions against the policy of the papacy, just because that policy was seen to be the surest means towards the destruction of the church.

[m] Gerhoh. Reichersp. Lib. de corrupto ecclesiae statu, ad init., Migne 194. 9 sq.

It is not a little remarkable that the secret of the reformation, namely, the incompatibility of the claims

CHAP. VIII.

of the church with the rights of the different nations that formed it, should have been so early discovered. But it was inevitable that, once the discovery was made, once the standard was raised against the encroachments (for so they were bitterly felt) of the papacy, the crusade should be extended to the abuses or deficiencies which were too obvious within the constitutional or dogmatic fabric of the church itself; and the heresies of Wycliffe or Huss were a natural outcome of the resistance provoked by Boniface the Eighth or John the Twenty-Second. It is not our purpose to follow the history to these issues: it is only necessary to observe that they were involved essentially in the conflict caused by the widened claims of the church. The political results of this conflict will come before us in the following chapter, but to make its precise conditions clear we have preliminarily to educe from the writings of the papal party the precise figure which the conception of the church took in their minds.

The time when Gregory the Ninth consolidated the canon law is well known to coincide with a general failure of historical insight and historical veracity, which operated well-nigh as strongly upon the actors in the events of this period as upon its chroniclers. Fictions were everywhere accepted as truth and used recklessly to explain existing facts; and among these fictions two had a diffusion and influence which it is difficult to overestimate. One of these, the [n] Donation, by virtue of which Constantine was alleged to have abdicated his imperial authority in Italy ([o] it was afterwards said, in all parts of the west [20]) in favour of the successor of saint Peter, had been used

[n] Decret. Gratiani, dist. xcvi. 13, 14.

[o] Döllinger, Papst-Fabeln pp. 73, 83; Friedberg i. 8.

[20] Thus Augustin Trionfo: Ad papam pertinet immediate imperii plena iurisdictio. Postquam enim Constantinus cessit imperio occidentali, nulla sibi reservatione facta, in civitate Romana, in partibus Italiae, et in omnibus occidentalibus regionibus, plenum ius totius imperii est acquisitum summis pontificibus, non solum superioris dominationis, verum etiam immediatae administrationis, ut ex ipsis tota dependeat imperialis iurisdictio, quantum ad electionem et quantum ad confirmationem: ita ut extunc nullus de iure potuerit se intromittere de regimine occidentalis imperii absque expressa auctoritate et mandato sedis apostolicae, nisi usurpative et tyrannice: De potest. eccl. xxxviii. 1 p. 224.

[p] as early as the middle of the eleventh century as a weapon against the German claim.[21] But by this time it had been discovered to prove too much, and Innocent the Fourth had to explain that the terms of this notable document were inaccurate: Constantine could not have granted to the papacy that which it possessed by the irrefragable gift of Christ; he could only have restored that which had been violently usurped from its legitimate owner.[22] Such was the view which found special favour among the churchmen of the fourteenth century, like Augustin Trionfo and Alvaro Pelayo.[23] Still whether it were a donation or an act of restitution, few (if any) questioned the reality of the fact or suspected the impudence of the fraud; and it exercised as much the wits of jurists and of those who were opposed to the temporal aggrandisement of the church, as it did of the defenders of that power.

[p] Döllinger 77.

A.D. 1245.

The second fiction to which we have referred is that of the Translation of the Empire, which, though [q] previously suggested by one or two controversialists, was not put into an authentic form [r] until the famous decree, [s] *Venerabilem*, of Innocent the Third. It gained a sudden and lasting publicity from the moment that it was included in Gregory the Ninth's collection of Decretals, and henceforward it was the shield behind which the popes fought; it entered into all polemics and all history-books down to and beyond the close of the middle ages. The problem was to explain how it came about that Charles the Great

[q] Döllinger, Kaiserth. Karls des Grossen 391.

[r] ibid., pp. 397 sq.

[s] Decret. Greg. IX. i. 6 cap. 34.

[21] The document is most likely as old as the years 752–774; see Döllinger, Papst-Fabeln pp. 67 sqq., 72–76; and compare Bryce, pp. 42 sq.

[22] Non solum pontificalem sed regalem [Christus] constituit principatum beato Petro eiusque successoribus, terreni simul ac coelestis imperii commissis habenis, quod in pluralitate clavium competenter innuitur: Epist. ap. F. von Raumer, Geschichte der Hohenstaufen 4. 120 n., ed. 2, 1841.

[23] Si inveniatur quandoque aliquos imperatores dedisse aliqua temporalia summis pontificibus, sicut Constantinus dedit Silvestro, hoc non est intelligendum eos dare quod suum est, sed restituere quod iniuste et tyrrannice ablatum est: Aug. Trionfo, i. 1 p. 3; cf. qu. xxxvii. 1–5 pp. 219–223. See also Alvaro Pelayo, De planctu ecclesiae i. 43, Ulm 1474 folio; and on the other side, John of Paris, De potest. reg. et pap. xvi, Goldast 2. 130.

CHAP. VIII.

obtained the imperial crown; how, in other words, the empire was *transferred* from the Greeks to the Franks. That this Translation was a reality no one thought of doubting. [t] The empire of Charles was no mere resuscitation of the extinct and forgotten empire of the west; it was the continuation of that universal empire, whose seat Constantine had established at Byzantium, but whose existence there was now held to have terminated by the succession of a woman, the empress Irene: the throne of her predecessor, Constantine the Sixth, remained unoccupied. The empire therefore went back to its rightful seat, and its title devolved upon Charles. His Lombard kingdom, added to the greatness of his Frankish domain, qualified him, without a competitor, for a supremacy to which he was called by the will of the Roman people, expressed through their spokesman, pope Leo the Third. Such was the conception admitted without dispute for centuries after the decisive event of the middle ages had taken place. [u] The only differences in its statement concern the relative shares of the emperor, the pope, and the Roman people in the transaction. It was well understood to be a sudden prompting of divine inspiration, the vehicle of which was necessarily the pope; but all accounts alike recognise the confirmation of the Roman people, and [x] the Frankish records narrate that the pope completed the ceremony of coronation by 'adoring' the emperor; thus recognising the sanctity of his person in a manner which is highly significant when we remember the ideas held of the relative positions of pope and emperor in later ages.

[t] Döllinger 351 sq.; cf. Bryce 47, 62 sq.

[u] cf. Bryce 53–57.

[x] cf. Döllinger 364 sq.

It is plain that any view which did not attribute the whole validity of the Translation to the official act of Leo the Third could not find favour with the new school of ecclesiastical politicians.[24] In the contest concerning

[24] It was common to seek the inception of the scheme in the policy of Hadrian the First (see Alvaro Pelayo i. 41) or even to throw it back to the time of Stephen the Second. The latter view owed its popularity to Bernard of Parma's gloss on the Decretals (see Döllinger, Kaiserthum Karls des Grossen 398) and was accepted by Martinus Polonus and a crowd of later chroniclers (ib. pp. 400–412).

investitures the difficulty of the common notion was already perceived. [y] Bonizo bishop of Sutri cut the knot by denying that the empire had ever passed into the hands of the Franks; it pertained still to the inheritance of the Greeks: the German claim was fictitious. Still its existence under the Franconian or the Suabian emperors was too pressing a reality to be explained away; and the extreme view taken by imperialists, that Charles's elevation was simply obtained by right of conquest,[25] was naturally enough balanced by an equal exaggeration on the other side, which saw in the event of the year 800, nothing less than a supreme example of the power inherent in the successor of saint Peter to displace and create empires. In such fashion it came about that Innocent the Third was able to state this audacious falsification of history as a cardinal fact in the relations of the church to the world. No discovery could have been more momentous. What the pope had given he could take away. [z] By the death of the emperor the jurisdiction of the empire reverted into the hands of the pope; and it lay in his power to decide when the vacancy should be terminated. If there was a double election it was for him to say which was the legitimate candidate; without his sanction the title of either remained null. The pope, in other words, had the right of controlling not the coronation of the emperor (that by universal consent rested with him), but the actual appointment of the king of Germany: and this advance took place just at a time when the emperor was gradually subsiding into something like a national German sovereign, and when the Avignonese pope had already sunk into a virtual dependent of the king of France. Never could the universality of the pretension be less justified, and never could the political character of the papacy be less disguised.

[y] supra, p. 215 n. 19.

[z] cf. Riezler 7 sq., 17 sq.

Perhaps the work that extols the papal prerogative to its highest pitch is the treatise [a] *Of the Power of the Pope*

[a] cf. Friedberg 2. 3–19.

[25] Compare Frederick the First's famous Roman oration reported by Otto of Freising, De gest. Frid. ii. 21 Pertz 20. 405.

by Augustin Trionfo, dedicated to that same pontiff, John the Twenty-Second, who put forward the claims to which we have just adverted. The substance of Trionfo's view is that the pope is in all respects the representative and plenipotentiary vicegerent of God. [b] If, he says, adoration is reserved for God alone, worship belongs to the pope, equal to that due to the saints, greater than that to the angels, in proportion to the universality of his prerogative. [c] The spiritual and temporal sway, symbolised by the 'two swords' of Scripture, pertains so inseparably to the successor of saint Peter,—by whom the one part of it is committed to secular princes to administer,—that [d] even if he be personally a bad man, his power is none the less 'of God.'[26] [e] Neither the emperor nor the laity have any right in his election; nor can any one depose him. [f] A general council may indeed declare his deposition in the event of his falling into heresy; but then it is not the sentence of the council that is operative against him, but [g] the act of heresy, by virtue of which he ceases *ipso facto* to be pope. Except in this single instance he calls for universal and unquestioning obedience. [h] From his will there is no appeal, not even to the judgement of God; for the utterance of the pope is identical with God's. [i] An appeal to God is therefore worse than futile, it convicts the appellant of rebellion against the divine government of the universe.

[b] De potest. eccl. ix. 1 p. 72.
[c] qu. i. 1 p. 3.
[d] art. 5 pp. 8 sq.: cf. qu. v. 3, 4 pp. 51 sq.
[e] qu. ii. 7, 8 pp. 25 sq.
[f] qu. v. 6 p. 54.
[g] cf. art. 1 p. 50.
[h] qu. vi. pp. 56 sq.
[i] art. 2 p. 58.

Being thus raised high above all earthly conditions, it is evident that the authority of the papacy altogether transcends that of the empire. The pope, says Trionfo, has the right not only of [k] deposing the emperor but also of [l] choosing one at his own discretion, supposing that there is a want of unanimity or other defect in the election, that the object of his choice is marked out by preëminent merit, or that the head of the church is able

[k] qu. xl. pp. 230 sqq.
[l] qu. xxxv. 1 p. 206.

[26] This position is not often favoured by the earlier writers on the subject. Thomas Aquinas (Baumann pp. 128 sq.) insists with as much force as Dante, De Monarchia i. 14, that a good ruler (or a good citizen) and a good man are convertible terms; and one would hardly apply a lower standard to the governor of the church.

by this exercise of his prerogative to secure her peace or the overthrow of her spiritual enemies. m He may thus in case of necessity deprive the established electors of their privilege and transfer it to whom he will, he may change the constitution of the empire; just as indeed he may transfer or change any other temporal government, being the representative on earth of the supreme Arbiter of kingdoms. n The existence of the civil state is only justified by the presiding presence of the priesthood, and o this authorisation obtains in the west by that Donation which restored its entire empire to the pope not only in sovereignty but in actual and immediate government, so that all the constitutions of its kingdoms are subject to his ordinance; p all the worldly possessions of kings depend from him:[27] q the emperor himself can issue no law without his concurrence. r His is the final court of appeal of the world. Such in brief outline is the matured statement of the relation of the pope to the temporal power, a statement which in no way exaggerated the pretensions avowed in the papal curia. Growing out of a confusion of ancient, and a disdain of the lessons of modern, history it aptly reflects the spirit of a time when the church had become immersed in the cares and interests, which she affected to control, of common worldly politics.

CHAP. VIII.

m art. 2–8 pp. 206–211.

n qu. xxxvi. 1 p. 212.

o v. supra, p. 218 n. 20.

p qu. xlv. p. 246 sqq.

q qu. xliv. 1 p. 240.

r qu. xlv. 3 p. 249.

[27] Thus also Aegidius Colonna (Aegidius Romanus) in an unpublished work De ecclesiastica potestate, from which extracts are given by Charles Jourdain in the Journal général de l'Instruction publique et des Cultes, 27. 122 sq., 130–133; 1858. 'Patet,' he says, 'quod omnia temporalia sunt sub dominio ecclesiae collata, et si non de facto, quoniam multi forte huic iuri rebellantur, de iure tamen et ex debito temporalia summo pontifici sunt subiecta, a quo iure et a quo debito nullatenus possunt absolvi:' Lib. ii. 4 (p. 131 n. 1). It is curious that this Aegidius should have long been regarded as the author of a certain Quaestio disputata in utramque partem pro et contra pontificiam potestatem, printed by Goldast, vol. 2. 96–107, and strongly hostile to the papal claims. The error is corrected by Jourdain, ubi supra, and by Dr. Riezler, pp. 139 sqq.

CHAPTER IX.

THE OPPOSITION TO THE TEMPORAL CLAIMS OF THE PAPACY.

THE eclipse of the empire in the latter part of the thirteenth century furnished an opportunity, of which we cannot wonder that the popes availed themselves, for augmenting and extending their political pretensions. Now however they were involved in a more difficult struggle, since an unsuspected obstacle had arisen in the growing national spirit of England and France. It is principally these changed conditions that make the pontificate of Boniface the Eighth a turning-point in the history of the medieval papacy; and it is an interesting study to watch the interworkings of the new motives in political speculation, now that the oppressive weight of the imperial conception was for the time removed.[1] One of the most curious essays in this regard is a treatise written in the latter part of the year 1300 by a certain royal advocate in Normandy, a person whom we may confidently identify with Peter du Bois, who held that office in the bailliage of Coutances, and is elsewhere known as a hot partisan of Philip the Fair in his contest with Boniface.[2] The professed aim of this treatise is

[1] In collecting materials for the present chapter I have derived very great assistance from the able work of Dr. Riezler on Die literarischen Widersacher der Päpste zur Zeit Ludwig des Baiers. I may notice that what I refer to as the second volume of Goldast's Monarchia s. Romani Imperii, 1614, appears as the *third* volume in the reïssue of that work, in which only the title-page and table of contents are new, dated 1621.

[2] See Natalis de Wailly, Mémoire sur un Opuscule anonyme intitulé *Summaria brevis et compendiosa Doctrina felicis Expeditionis et Abbreviationis Guerrarum ac Litium Regni Francorum*, in the Mémoires de l'Académie des Inscriptions et des Belles-lettres 18 (2) 435–494; 1849. M. de Wailly is able to fix the date minutely, pp. 471–476, and discourses with much acuteness and ingenuity about the author and his other works, pp. 481–493. [See also M. C. V. Langlois' introduction to du Bois' tract De recuperatione terre sancte, 1891.]

to give a short and easy method of avoiding wars so far as the king of France is concerned; and for this purpose, the author holds, [a] the best thing for society would be that the whole world should be subject to French rule. For, he explains, *it is a peculiar merit of the French to have a surer judgement than other nations, not to act without consideration, nor to place themselves in opposition to right reason.* To reap the full advantage of the arrangement it is necessary moreover [b] that the king should be born and bred in France, because experience teaches that there the stars present themselves under a better aspect and exercise a happier influence than in other countries.

CHAP. IX.

[a] Wailly 442.

[b] cf. p. 486 & n. 2.

These postulates being granted, du Bois proceeds to indicate the steps by which the desirable result might be attained. [c] He concedes the right of the papacy to all the territories comprised in the grant of Constantine, but adds that it is plainly beyond the power of the pope to carry his rights into effect. Being commonly an old and infirm person, and since he is not and cannot be a soldier, his very position is an incitement to the ambition of wicked men. *Wars therefore are stirred up; numbers of princes are condemned by the church with their adherents, and thus there die more people than one can count, whose souls probably go down into hell and whom nevertheless it is the pope's duty to guard and to preserve from all danger.* If however he should surrender his temporal domain, he would be all the freer to devote himself to the proper functions of his office, and a main cause of strife would be removed. But the means by which our speculator proposes to secure this end shew with singular directness how entirely the papacy had come to be regarded, not as a spiritual power standing apart from and above the temporal polity of Europe, but as a state to be treated with like any other state. The diplomatic agency, we read, of the king of Sicily might be employed to obtain from the church the title of senator of Rome for the French king, who should receive the holy patrimony, *the city of Rome, Tuscany, the coasts and the mountains,*

[c] pp. 443 sq.

Sicily, England, Aragon, and all the other countries, in exchange for an adequate pension to the pope, their present sovereign. [d] Lombardy itself, it is explained, although legally subject to the king of Germany, should offer no insuperable difficulties; since its nominal ruler is well aware of the hopelessness of undertaking its reduction to a state of real vassalage, and therefore everything might be easily arranged by a secret treaty either with himself or his electors.[3] This being secured it would perhaps be necessary to conquer the Lombards; any expedient would be lawful against them *since nothing could authorise them to refuse obedience to their prince;* and it is clear that they would in time yield to the force of arms assisted by the ravaging of their lands and the ruin of their commerce. The conquest of Lombardy would create so powerful an impression among other nations that the king of France could not fail soon to receive the submission of the rest of Europe; and thus a lasting peace would be secured for society.

[d] pp. 445–449.

A visionary scheme like this, the work of a layman and a lawyer, even with all its national vanity and exaggeration, is sufficiently indicative of the new horizon of political ideas that opened upon men in the end of the thirteenth century, to be deserving of comment. It shews us that the conception of the empire had already dwindled in the eyes of foreigners into that of a German kingdom, and that the temporal sway of the popes was seen to be the cause of endless mischief both to society and to the spiritual basis of the papacy itself. Nor can it escape notice that our theorist enunciates, as it were in a parenthesis, as a doctrine to which no one would think of objecting, that principle of necessary obedience to the temporal ruler which papal advocates had always been inclined to throw into the background or even formally to deny. It is in cases like this that the limitations of

[3] The former, our author specifies, on the supposition that it is true, as is reported, that the king possesses, or ought to possess, the right of transmitting his kingdom to his heirs, p. 445.

the medieval mind reveal themselves. To it only the two extremes are possible, absolute obedience to the sovereign or absolute obedience in all things to the church. When the supporters of the latter speak of civil rights they appear as though their single wish was to carry out what we should call a constitutional system; it is only when their correlative doctrine about the prerogative of the church is known, that we see how far they are removed from modern ideas: and in the same way it is regularly their opponents who are the defenders of pure, unrestrained absolutism, however much they may engage our approval when they [e] argue against the temporal pretensions of the spiritualty with all the attendant inconveniences of ecclesiastical exemptions and privileges, and [f] urge a far-reaching reform of the entire church-system, a return to primitive purity and primitive simplicity.[4]

[e] cf. ibid., pp. 450 sqq., 461 sq.

[f] pp. 465–468.

But it would be an error to suppose that the views of the French publicists, on the relations of church and state, of which du Bois is perhaps the earliest exponent, correspond in more than the object of their common attack with those of the imperial partisans. In the *Enquiry touching the Power of the Pope*,[5] also [g] probably the work of du Bois, we have a clear statement of the distinction between the relations of a kingdom like France [6] to the pope, and those of the empire. [h] The pope, he says,

[g] ibid., p. 492; cf. Riezler 143.

[h] Quaest. de potest. pap., p. 678.

[4] Compare the earlier instance of Robert Grosseteste in G. Lechler, Johann von Wiclif und die Vorgeschichte der Reformation 1. 192–200; 1873.

[5] This treatise is printed by Pierre Dupuy in the collection of Acts et Preuves appended to the Histoire du Différend d'entre le Pape Boniface VIII et Philippes le bel, Roy de France, pp. 663–683, 1655 folio.

[6] Dr. Riezler speaks of 'Frankreich und England,' as though the author had abandoned his previous notion (see above, p. 226) of the English vassalage. The difference indeed might lead one to conjecture that the hypothesis of the common authorship of this work and of the Summaria brevis just now described, was not so well grounded as we have affirmed. But the truth is that, instead of ranking England in the same class with France, du Bois expressly distinguishes its position: 'Aliquae causae sunt in imperatore quare subditus sit papae in temporalibus, quae non inveniuntur in aliquibus regibus, sicut in regibus Franciae et Hispaniae, et fuit etiam aliquando in rege Angliae, videlicet, usque ad tempus regis Ioannis, qui dicebatur *Sine terra*,' &c.: p. 681.

is evidently the temporal lord of the emperor; for the latter needs to be confirmed and crowned by the pope, whereas no such authorisation is required in France. Undoubtedly this freedom from traditionary, even though disputable, restraints upon the title of their sovereign. helped to give a broader and bolder scope to the speculations of French writers; and the head and front of the literary opposition to the papacy during the early part of the fourteenth century, was found in the university of Paris. Besides, as we have said, the idea of nationality, an idea fatal to the empire, was becoming well understood; and John Quidort, better known as John of Paris, a contemporary of du Bois, [i] dwells upon this as the proper basis of political organisation just as strongly as Thomas Aquinas from an opposite point of view had done before him.

[i] De potest. reg. et papal. iii, Goldast 2. 111 sq.

Thus while the imperialists were more or less obliged to answer any given pretension of the papacy by another theory, possibly no less distorted, of their own, the French writers were able to discuss matters in a more philosophical spirit. Nothing for instance can be more admirable than the criticism of John of Paris with reference to the worldly possessions of the clergy. [k] The Waldenses, he says, maintain that these possessions, originating in the Donation of Constantine, are the root of the demoralisation of the church; while others hold that they are intrinsically involved in the prerogative of the pope as the vicar of Jesus Christ. The former alternative was no doubt tempting to the opponents of papal claims, but John's sound sense was not deceived by the convenience of the argument. [l] The truth, he decided, lay in the middle between the two extremes: the church might unquestionably have worldly property; but as a matter of fact she did not hold it by virtue of any vicarship or apostolical succession, but simply by way of grant from princes or other persons, or by similar titles of possession. With equally clear judgement du Bois disposed of the common use of Biblical phrases to prove anything that

[k] prooem., p. 108.

[l] ibid., p. 109.

could be extracted from them by a violent adaptation of metaphor. It is no doubt usual, he says, [m] among professors of theology to take a double sense in the words of Scripture, the literal or historical, and the mystical or spiritual: but for purposes of argument none but the former can be valid.[7] He at once applies this axiom to demolish the favourite theory, [n] at least as old as Gregory the Seventh, which found in the relation of the sun to the moon an apt and conclusive evidence of the subordination of the secular to the spiritual power, and [o] suggested a variety of arithmetical puzzles as to the exact amount of their proportional magnitudes.[8]

[m] Quaest. de potest. pap., Dupuy 676; cf. Ockham, octo Quaest. ii. 12, Goldast 2. 344.

[n] cf. Bryce 267 n. 2.

[o] Du Bois, p. 677.

It was in fact in the purely critical work of controversy that the assailants of the hierarchy had almost uniformly the advantage: when they passed from criticism to the building up of a system of their own, their proposals are, in the view of a political philosopher, hardly less weak than those of their opponents. The French, as we have said, write with greater freedom than their imperial brethren; but in the latter too we find no lack of skill, no lack even of historical perception: and if their ablest recruits were drawn from the university of Paris, still the man who overtopped them all in the abstract splendour of his ideal was an independent Italian. Yet Dante's books *De Monarchia*, striking as they are, labour under the inevitable defect attaching to the attempt to exchange one impossible theory for another equally impossible. Supposing the human race to be entirely homogeneous, one might at once concede Dante's main proposition that the right and necessary form of government [p] is that of one universal state by a sole universal ruler. But in truth he has no practical arguments to adduce in favour of this, only the general *a priori* principle of the virtue

[p] De monarch. i. 7–18.

[7] The same statement occurs in the Supplication du peuple de France au roy contre le pape Boniface le VIII, Dupuy 216,—also nearly certainly the work of du Bois.

[8] According to one calculation the pope was thus 7744½ times greater than the emperor; another made the ratio as low as 47 : 1. See Friedberg 1. 6 n. 4.

CHAP. IX.

q lib. ii. 7.

r Verg. Aen. v. vi. 852 sqq.

s Bryce p. 264.

of unity, and the examples or precedents of ancient Rome. The resounding lines of the *Aeneïd* on which q he relies,

> r Tu regere imperio populos, Romane, memento;
> Hae tibi erunt artes; pacisque imponere morem,
> Parcere subiectis, et debellare superbos,

might come genuinely enough from a witness of the age of Augustus: in the fourteenth century, with the empire at its nadir and the Ghibellins of no small part of Italy, and Dante himself, suffering under a common proscription, they ring almost as an irony. Dante's scheme, as s has been finely said, was proved not a prophecy but an epitaph.

If an attempt thus to restore the glories of the empire failed of fruit because it looked backward instead of forward, those of some of Dante's contemporaries, the literary allies of the emperor Lewis the Fourth, were not less unsuccessful because they erred in the opposite direction, because they proceeded on the basis of a more advanced polity which it needed centuries for men to understand. Both alike were disappointed by reason of their neglect of the actual circumstances of their own day. Beyond question the most notable of the latter class of theories is that of the *Defensor Pacis*, a book which announces a clear constitutional system such as in the present day either exists not at all or exists only in name in the greater part of Europe. Its author, Marsiglio de Maynardino,[9] was one of those rare philosophers to whom fortune gave an opportunity of carrying their conceptions into practice; who discovered also that, however capable of constructing from the foundation, they were impotent to reconstruct in face of the old-established and irreconcilable facts of society with which they had to deal. The life of Marsiglio, of which we can only give a bare outline, is therefore of exceptional interest.

[9] So the name is given in a document of 1328, the Examen iudiciale Francisci Veneti asseclae Marsilii de Padua, Baluze, Miscell. 2. 280 a, ed. Mansi. Dr. Friedberg, pt. 2. 21, writes *Maynardina*. Albertino Mussato calls the author Marsilius de Raymundinis: see Riezler 30. But this seems to be an error.

t Born about the year 1270 of a plain burgher's family at Padua, he went no doubt through the customary course of studies in the university of his native town. He turned to medicine, perhaps to the active profession of arms; but we are ignorant of the particulars of his probably wandering, unsettled life [10] until he emerges in 1312 as rector of the university of Paris: this office a brief term of tenure opened to most of the distinguished masters in the faculty of arts who taught there. At that time the Invincible Doctor, William of Ockham, the second founder of nominalism, held undisputed supremacy over the minds of the Parisian scholars; and it is natural to claim the English schoolman [11] as one from whom Marsiglio derived more than the elements of his political, as of his metaphysical, ideas.[12] With Ockham Marsiglio went beyond the limits of speculation preserved by the liberal but prudent university to which they belonged. Both subsequently abandoned it in order to devote their intellects to the defence of Lewis the Bavarian, of whose political aims they were aware, and whose infirmity of purpose and want of resource only time could shew. Of the band of Franciscans who gathered round the German king, Marsiglio was the confessed leader; unlike his

t Riezler 30–34.

[10] Dr. Riezler, p. 33, is probably right in rejecting the story that Marsiglio studied in the interval at Orleans. But if exception be taken to his interpretation of the passage in the Defensor pacis ii. 18, Goldast 2. 252 sq., which has given rise to this supposition, it may be suggested that the passage is due to John of Jandun, who is expressly named as joint-author of the work. A few insertions of this kind would better satisfy the description than either Dr. Riezler's view, p. 195 n. 2, that John made a French version of the book, or Dr. Friedberg's suggestion, pt. 2. 25 n. 2, that he undertook merely its transcription.

[11] [See however Mr. James Sullivan's arguments to the contrary, in the American Historical Review, 2. 413 sqq., 1897.]

[12] Marsiglio may also have learned from John of Paris, whose death however is presumed to have taken place as early as 1306, Riezler 149. Dr. Friedberg, pt. 1. 18, in dating it in 1304 has apparently confounded John's deprivation with his death, which occurred later while he was at Rome prosecuting an appeal against that sentence. See the continuators of William of Nangy and Gerard de Frachet, Bouquet 20. 592 c, 21. 25 h. On the other hand, according to the Memoriale historiarum of John of Saint Victor, ibid., vol. 21. 645 e, f, John's deprivation seems to have been decreed in 1305.

CHAP. IX.

companions he was a secular clergyman, by occupation, as it seems, a physician.

Marsiglio must have already meditated a flight from Paris when in 1324 [13] he took a man of like spirit, John of Jandun, a village in Champagne, into his counsel and planned with his help the *Defensor Pacis*: [u] within, it is said, the space of two months the friends produced the most original political treatise of the middle ages. Soon afterwards they betook themselves to Nuremberg, the seat of Lewis's court. To them and to their Franciscan fellow-workers is due whatever of principle and of permanent historical significance belongs to that prince's scheme to rescue the empire from the unendurable pretensions of John the Twenty-Second, and to reässert for it a power and dignity such as even in the strongest days of the Franconian or Suabian Caesars had been proved totally incapable of lasting vindication. Lewis's career in Italy was short and inglorious.[14] He became for the moment master of Rome; an antipope was chosen, and [x] Marsiglio was named papal vicar in the city. But the opening of the year 1330 saw Lewis again in Germany: his Italian projects had failed utterly, his advisers were branded as heretics. In 1336 he was a suppliant to the power which he had defied. But Marsiglio remained firm in his opinions until his death, [y] which happened not long before April 1343. It is not necessary here to discuss how far the collapse of the undertaking was determined by the irresolution of Lewis, or by the hardy perseverance of his antagonist. The issue indeed lay in the nature of things. The real significance of Marsiglio is to be found less in the events in which he was of necessity precluded from exercising paramount control, even had he been able to exercise it with the desired success, than

[u] Examen Franc. Ven., Baluze 2. 280 b.

A.D. 1328.

[x] Raynald. ann. eccl. 5. 366 B, ed. Mansi, Lucca, 1750 folio.

[y] Friedberg 2. 28 sq., Riezler 122 sq. [Sullivan, ubi supra, p. 412 n. 4.]

[13] The date, which is given by Dr. Riezler, p. 196, as between the summer of 1324 and the autumn of 1326, is fixed precisely to 24th June, 1324 by the lines in the Vienna manuscript, 464 f. 117 A, which I have verified:

Anno trecenteno milleno quarto vigeno
Defensor est iste perfectus festo baptiste
Tibi laus et gloria Christe.

[14] See the narrative in Riezler, pp. 42–94.

in the book of which those events were so impotent illustrations. CHAP. IX.

[z]The *Defensor Pacis* starts from the same beginning as Dante and Peter du Bois had chosen for the first principle of their political treatises; namely, that [a]government is established for the purpose of maintaining peace. Marsiglio traces the origin of civil association in close conformity with the teaching of the *Politics* of Aristotle [15]: he adopts the definition that the state exists in order that men may live well; and *to live well* he finely [b]explains in the sense that men may have *leisure for liberal tasks, such as are those of the virtues of the soul as well of thought as of action.* Turning then to the various modes of government by which this end is sought to be attained,—these too [c]Marsiglio enumerates according to Aristotle's classification,—he decides that [d]*perhaps a kingly rule is the more perfect.* The qualified terms in which he expresses this preference at once distinguish our author from the common rank of imperialistic writers, especially when we remember that [e]his own book is dedicated to the emperor. His postulates of the character and attributes of the prince, his definitions of law and of the nature of the state itself, are indeed quite different from theirs. That which he insists upon as the very basis of the social organism is a principle which civilists were inclined altogether to ignore. The sovereignty of the state, he held, rested with the people; [f]by it properly are the laws made, and to it they owe their validity. From the nation itself proceeds all right and all power; [g]it is the authoritative lawgiver among

z cf. Friedberg 2. 32–48, Riezler 193–233.

a Def. pac. i. 1 Goldast 2. 154 sq.

b cap. 4 p. 157.

c cap. 8.

d cap. 9 p. 164.

e cap. 1 p. 155.

f cap. 12 pp. 169 sqq.

g lib. ii. 21 pp. 258 sq., &c.

[15] It is noticeable that in another connexion Marsiglio recurs to the old ecclesiastical notion, which was abandoned as we have seen, above, p. 214, even by Thomas Aquinas, that civil institutions are a consequence of the fall of man. Adam, Marsiglio says, was created in a state of innocence or original righteousness, 'in quo siquidem permansisset, nec sibi nec suae posteritati necessaria fuisset officiorum civilium institutio vel distinctio; eo quod opportuna quaeque ac voluptuosa sufficientiae huius vitae in paradiso terrestri seu voluptatis natura produxisset eidem, absque ipsius poena vel fatigatione quacunque:' cap. 6 p. 161, misprinted 171. On account of the frequent errors in the numeration of pages in Goldast's edition I have sometimes found it less confusing to refer simply to the chapters of the works cited without further specification.

CHAP. IX.

[h] lib. i. 13 pp. 172 sq.

men, *humanus legislator fidelis superiore carens.* [h] If the making of laws be entrusted to a few, we should not be secure against error or self-seeking: only the whole people can know what it needs and can give effect to it. The community therefore of all the citizens or their majority, expressing its will either by elected representatives or in their assembled mass, is the supreme power in the state.[16]

But it must have an officer to execute its behests, and for this purpose the people must choose itself a ruler.

[i] capp. 15, 16 pp. 175, 177–182.

[i] In Marsiglio's view election is the only satisfactory form of monarchy: to the hereditary principle he will make no concession whatever.

[k] cap. 17 pp. 182 sq.

[k] There must be, he says, a unity in the government; but a unity of office, not necessarily of number: so that the executive functions may be as effectively exercised by means of a committee as by a single prince; only no member of such a committee must venture to act by himself separately, its policy must be directed by the vote or by a majority of the entire body. If however, as is usually the wiser course, a king be chosen,

[l] cap. 14 pp. 174 sq.

[l] he must be supported by an armed force, large enough, according to the rule of Aristotle, to overpower the few but not large enough to overpower the mass of the nation. But this force is not to be entrusted to him until after his election, for a man must not secure the royal dignity by means of external resources, but by virtue of his own personal qualities.

[m] cap. 17 p. 184.

[m] The desirability of an universal monarchy Marsiglio

[16] Nos autem dicamus secundum veritatem atque consilium Aristotelis, 3 politicae, ca. 6, *legis latorem*, seu causam legis effectivam primam et propriam, *esse populum*, seu civium universitatem aut eius valentiorem partem, per suam electionem seu voluntatem in generali civium congregatione per sermonem expressam, praecipientem seu determinantem aliquid fieri seu omitti circa civiles actus humanos sub poena vel supplicio temporali: valentiorem, inquam, partem, considerata quantitate in communitate illa super quam lex fertur, sive id fecerit universitas praedicta civium aut eius pars valentior per se ipsam immediate, sive id alicui vel aliquibus commiserit faciendum . . . Et dico consequenter huic quod eadem auctoritate prima non alia debent leges et aliud quodlibet per electionem institutum approbationem necessariam suscipere, &c.: Defensor pacis i. 12 pp. 169 sq.

leaves altogether an open question. He is as little disposed to magnify the pretensions of the prince to whom he addressed his work, as he is to admit any theory of the indefeasible prerogative of kingship *per se;* prerogative indeed, strictly speaking, the king has none, for the authority which he receives by the act of election is purely official; the 'fountain of justice' remains with the law-giver, the people, whose instrument he is and to whom he is responsible.[17] [n] He has to interpret the law, not to make it. So too [o] the officers of the state derive their commission from the people, albeit the king, in conformity with law, decides the detail of their appointment, together with the other necessary arrangements of the executive government. Once establish the principle, and the consequences are easy to draw. The king's power is limited in every possible direction. He has the eye of the people or of its delegates on all his actions. [p] He may be restrained or even deposed if he overpass his prescribed bounds; and even though his conduct be not amenable to the letter of the law, he is still subject to the final judgement of the national will.[18] On no side is there any room for despotism; in no point is he absolute.

[n] lib. ii. 2 p. 193.
[o] lib. i. 15 p. 177.
[p] cap. 18 pp. 184 sq.

Such are the conditions which Marsiglio deemed proper for the main object of his speculations, the defence of peace in the civil state, and which occupy the first book of his treatise. But among the six necessary constituents of society which [q] he enumerates from Aristotle,—those who devote themselves to husbandry and handicraft, to provide its material support, those who defend it from

[q] cap. 5; cf. Arist. polit. vii. 8 p. 1328.

[17] We have, says Marsiglio, to explain the 'causam effectivam, instituentem et determinantem reliqua officiorum seu partium civitatis. Hanc autem primam dicimus legislatorem [the synonym with Marsiglio for 'civium universitas']; secundariam vero, quasi instrumentalem seu executivam, dicimus principantem, per autoritatem huius a legislatore sibi concessam, secundum formam sibi traditam ab eodem, legem videlicet, secundum quam semper agere ac disponere debet, quantum potest, actus civiles:' Lib. i. 15 pp. 175 sq.

[18] Siquidem [principantis excessus] lege determinatus, secundum legem corrigendus; si vero non, secundum legislatoris sententiam: et lege debet determinari quantum possibile fuerit: Cap. 18 p. 185.

CHAP. IX.

danger without or sedition within, those who amass wealth, and those who execute the office of religion and administer justice,—one, that of the priesthood (which, [r] Marsiglio admits, has not been universally considered necessary to the existence of the state), presents special difficulties. For whereas [s] the peculiar province of the clergy is to instruct the people according to the teaching of the Gospel with a view to their eternal welfare,—for which purpose it is well that they should arm themselves with all possible knowledge, as well in the departments of thought as of action,—[t] they have so far abandoned this exclusively spiritual function as to usurp all manner of temporal claims over secular as well as spiritual persons, and in particular over the Roman emperor: and these pretensions of the papacy, Marsiglio holds, are the chief causes of discord in the world. Accordingly in his second book our author addressed himself to the examination of the real nature of the spiritual office, and of its relation to the civil state.

[r] Def. pac. i. 5 p. 160.

[s] cap. 6.

[t] cap. 19 pp. 187 sqq.

[u] The name *church* Marsiglio would recall to its first and apostolical, its *truest and most proper* signification, as comprehending the entire body of Christian men: all, he says, are alike churchmen, *viri ecclesiastici*, be they laymen or clerks. It is intolerable that its prerogatives should be usurped by the sacerdotal order. Excommunication, for instance, cannot rightly be decreed by any single priest or any council of priests: they should doubtless be consulted as experts with reference to the charges alleged, but the actual decision belongs to the congregation in which the offender lives, or to its superior, or to a general council.[19] While moreover

[u] lib. ii. 2.

[19] I have translated the last two alternatives as they stand in Marsiglio's text, although they have rather the appearance of being saving clauses not very naturally connected with the argument. 'Its superior,' which Dr. Riezler, p. 211, renders by 'repräsentant,' would seem to be the emperor; 'exilium generale' in Goldast is a mere misprint for 'concilium.' The passage occurs in Goldast 2. 207 and belongs to the seventh chapter of book ii, which in the edition has been accidentally united with chapter 6.

the clergy have no right to engross the name of *churchman*, [x] they have also no right to extend the application of the word *spiritual* to all they do, as when they use it to cover their property and incomes in order to exempt them from legal burthens or conditions. The clergy have indeed a spiritual office in the church, but their dealings outside these definite functions, their tenure of land, their financial and other temporal engagements, are just as much secular as those of their lay brethren, and are just as much subject to the law of the state. Who would say that a clergyman's crimes, should he commit theft or murder, were to be regarded as spiritual acts? [y] These are evidently to be punished like other men's; only with greater strictness, because the culprits have not the same excuse of ignorance. The clergy are in these cases, and equally in all other civil relations, simply members of society, and as members of society they must be treated; they can claim no sort of exemption in virtue of their religious character. More than this, [z] since the business of government is to maintain peace, it is the duty of the ruler to limit the number of clergymen in any part of the kingdom, should their growth appear likely to disturb the order and tranquillity of the state.

[x] ibid., p. 192.

[y] cap. 8 p. 212.

[z] ibid., p.213.

The power of the clergy is thus not only restricted to spiritual affairs; [a] it can only be given effect to by spiritual means. Temporal pains and penalties do not belong to the law of the Gospel, which indeed is not, properly speaking, a law at all but rather an instruction, *doctrina;* for *it is not laid down that any man should be compelled to its observance,* and coercive force is part of the definition of law. The priest then may warn and threaten, but beyond this he has no competence. [b] If a heretic become obnoxious to the civil law—if, in other words, his doctrine is dangerous to society—by that law he is to be tried: but of heresy, as such, there is but one judge, Jesus Christ, and his sentence is in the world to come; errors of opinion lie beyond the cognisance of

[a] cap. 9 pp. 213–216.

[b] cap. 10 pp. 216–219.

CHAP. IX.

any human judicature.[20] Marsiglio has arrived at the fully matured principle of religious toleration, which modern writers are apt to vaunt as their own peculiar discovery.

c cap. 15 pp. 238–241.

d cap. 22 pp. 264 sq.

e cap. 16 pp. 241–244.

f ibid., pp. 245 sq.

g capp. 18, 22 pp. 252 sq., 268.

h capp. 20, 21 pp. 256–263.

It may be objected to Marsiglio's entire view of the spiritualty, that he seems to leave out of account the existing constitution of the church, that he seems to forget that custom had classified the priesthood in ascending orders of dignity and authority, each with its proper province of power and jurisdiction. [c] But in truth, he maintains, this arrangement is destitute of any scriptural warrant. In the New Testament *bishop* and *priest* are convertible designations of the same persons; and the popedom, however [d] convenient as symbolising the unity of the church, is none the less [e] a later development of which the historical growth is clearly traceable. Saint Peter had no superiority over the other apostles; but even supposing he had, it is hazardous to say that he communicated it to his successors in the Roman see, since [f] we cannot say for certain that he himself ever visited, far less was bishop of, Rome at all.[21] The [g] preëminence of the bishop of Rome proceeds in fact not from saint Peter's institution but from the connexion of the see with the capital of the Roman empire. [h] The supreme power in the church is the church itself, that is, a general council, formed of the clergy and laity alike, and convoked not by any pretended spiritual authority but by the source of all legislation and jurisdiction, the civil state. Thus constituted a general council may not only decide ecclesiastical questions but even proceed to excommunicate the temporal ruler and place his land under an interdict,

[20] Nemo quantumcunque peccans contra disciplinas speculativas aut operativas quascunque punitur vel arcetur in hoc seculo praecise in quantum huiusmodi, sed in quantum peccat contra praeceptum humanae legis: Cap. 10 p. 217.

[21] Dr. Riezler makes the singular remark, p. 215 n. 1, 'Marsiglio übersieht hier dass Petrus *nach* Paulus nach Rom gekommen sein kann.' This is exactly the conclusion that Marsiglio inclines to adopt: 'Romae vero non contradico, sed verisimiliter teneo ipsum [Petrum] in hoc non praevenisse Paulum, sed potius e converso,' Cap. 16 p. 246.

just because it represents the authority of the universal church and speaks the voice of the entire community both in its spiritual and temporal capacities. That it has power over the pope follows necessarily from the principles already laid down.

It is evident then that the pope in his quality of [i] Christian bishop can claim no right of supreme judgement in human things, even over the clergy. If he possess any such right it must have been conceded to him by human authority; as a spiritual person he has absolutely none, and therefore properly he ought to possess none. [k] The power bequeathed by Christ to the priesthood can only concern religious affairs: it is idle to suppose that in granting to it the keys of heaven and hell he gave any temporal jurisdiction. The keys open and close the door of forgiveness, but forgiveness is the act of God, determined by the penitence of the sinner. Without these conditions the priestly absolution is of no avail. [l] The turn-key, *claviger*, is not the judge. As for the special proof of the pope's superiority to the secular estate taken from his act in [m] the ceremony of crowning the emperor, a ceremony, it is plain, can confer no authority: it is but the symbol or public notification of a fact already existing. The same function as the pope has at the coronation of the emperor, belongs at that of the king of France to the archbishop of Rheims; but who would call this prelate the superior of his king? Marsiglio goes over the standard arguments in favour of the papal assumptions and rejects them one after another, partly by his resolute insistence on a literal interpretation of the text of Scripture, partly by his grand distinction between the sacred calling of the priesthood and their extrinsic or worldly connexions. With his ideal of a church in which these worldly ties have no existence, with his view of them as mere indications of the distance by which the actual church is removed from primitive purity, there is no room for any talk of ecclesiastical privileges or exemptions. The

[i] cap. 22 pp. 267 sq., cf. capp. 5, 8 pp. 204, 212.

[k] cap. 6 pp. 205 sq.

[l] p. 209.

[m] cap. 26 pp. 280 sqq.

CHAP. IX.

sole privilege of the clergy is their spiritual character. Temporal sovereignty or jurisdiction is an accident of their civil position; and all inferences from the Bible which have been imagined to authorise it, such as [n] the famous argument of the *two swords*, are incompatible not only with the conception of a church but also with the plain meaning of the texts from which they are deduced. [o] *My kingdom is not of this world.*

[n] cap. 28 pp. 299 sqq.

[o] John xviii. 36; Def. pac. ii. 4 pp. 195 sq.

[p] The two books of the *Defensor Pacis* thus comprise,—though we have been able to give but the briefest abstract of a work which fills more than a hundred and fifty folio pages in Goldast's edition of the original,—the whole essence of the political and religious theory which separates modern times from the middle ages. The significance of the reformation, putting theological details aside, lay in the substitution of a ministry serving the church, the congregation of Christian men, for a hierarchical class. The significance of the later political revolution, even now far from universally realised, lay in the recognition of the people as the source of government, as the sovereign power in the state. Both these ideas Marsiglio appropriated. He had not only a glimpse of them as from afar off: he thought them out, defined them, stated them with the clearest precision, so that the modern constitutional statesman, the modern protestant, has nothing to alter in their principle, has only to develop them and fill in their outline. Marsiglio may be stigmatised as a *doctrinaire*, but he belongs to that rarest class of *doctrinaires* whom future ages may rightly look back upon as prophets. It is this quality, this prescience of the new order for which the world was becoming ripe, that raises him above the whole body of antagonists to the hierarchical policy of the church in the middle ages. His great colleague Ockham, his successor Wycliffe, were immersed in the petty, or at best the transitory, interests of scholasticism. In theological doctrine Wycliffe may by some be considered to have done more signal service. But his thoughts and those of his fellows move

[p] cf. Friedberg 2. 48 sqq.; Riezler pp. 226–233.

within the confined limits of their own time. The political theory of Wycliffe, noble as it is, rests upon as wilful, as preposterous, a treatment of the Bible as that of any of his hierarchical adversaries. Carried into practice by those who were not able to appreciate his refinements, it resolved itself into a species of socialism which was immediately seen to be subversive of the very existence of society. Marsiglio of Padua on the contrary is almost entirely free from the trammels of tradition. Except when he urges the necessity of a return to evangelical poverty, and when he enlarges on the points at issue between the emperor Lewis and John the Twenty-Second, we are hardly recalled to the age in which he lived. But for these reminders we should be almost disposed to think his book a production of one of the most enlightened of the publicists, or of the advocates of civil and religious liberty, of the seventeenth century.

Yet if Marsiglio learned much from Ockham in the years when they worked together at Paris, the principles which he then adopted, he elaborated with far greater independence than his friend. Ockham remains through all his writings first and foremost a scholastic theologian; Marsiglio ventures freely into the open field of political philosophy. Nor on the other hand can it be questioned that Ockham in his turn fell strongly under the influence of the Italian speculator. All his known works on ecclesiastical politics were produced at a time posterior to the publication of the *Defensor Pacis*. The latter was written while Marsiglio was still at Paris; it was in all probability the thoughts brought into train by its composition that decided him to throw in his lot with the Bavarian emperor. Ockham's writings on the contrary are the effect of his association in active resistance to the pope; they are the defence and justification of his action. Thus though Marsiglio ran far ahead of him, though he shews us so marked an advance upon any previous theory of the relation of church and state, Ockham's

CHAP. IX.

books are the later in point of time. In fact, while the former quite overleaps the confines of the middle ages, Ockham preserves the orderly sequence and continuity of medieval thought : and more than this, while Marsiglio in the daring of his speculation stands absolutely alone and without a successor, Ockham, in virtue of his greater conformity to the spirit of his day, not to speak of his eminence as a philosopher, unequalled among contemporaries and hardly surpassed by Thomas Aquinas or John Duns Scotus, handed down a light which was never suffered to be extinguished, and which served as a beacon to pioneers of reform like Wycliffe and Huss. In politics, as well as in some points of doctrine, Ockham may be claimed as a precursor of the German reformers of the sixteenth century; but Marsiglio exercised little direct influence on the movement of thought.[22] The truths which he brought into view had to be rediscovered, without even the knowledge that he had found them out beforehand, by the political philosophers of modern times.

Ockham indeed, with a philosophy that directly tended towards rationalism, was by far the more practical speculator than his swifter and bolder fellow-worker. He was more sensible of the difficulty, of the almost hopeless intricacy, of the problems that called for solution.[23] As strenuous as any man in [q] contesting the 'plenitude of power' arrogated for the papacy, he was unwilling to transfer it to any other individual or to any body of human beings. The pope was no supreme autocrat; indeed [r] the emperor was within certain limitations his

[q] Dial. pt. iii. tr. i. lib. i. 9–16 Goldast 2. 780–786.

[r] pt. iii. tr. ii. lib. iii. 17, p. 948.

[22] [This statement requires to be modified. Mr. Sullivan, who underrates the influence of Ockham on later opinion, has shown, ubi supra, pp. 597-604, that there is a continuous strain of testimony to that of Marsiglio down to the period of the reformation and later.]

[23] The text of Ockham's Dialogus, of which a fragment (wanting the last six tractatus of the third part) fills five hundred and sixty of Goldast's closely printed pages, I do not pretend to have read consecutively through. Dr. Riezler, pp. 258–271, has however selected a sufficient number of passages to illustrate Ockham's general position; and I have sometimes contented myself with verifying his citations in the original.

CHAP. IX.

natural judge. But if [s] the pope was fallible, [t] so also was a general council. Even such an assembly, of the most perfect composition,—[u] strictly representative, according to Marsiglio's scheme, both of clergy and laity, both (this is his own addition) of men and women,[24]— he would not entrust with the absolute, final decision in matters of faith. [x] Any man, all men, may err; and Ockham is disposed in the last resort to find consolation in the scriptural paradox which speaks of the truth vouchsafed to little children. He is convinced that the faith must live, but cannot admit without qualification any of the suggested sureties for its maintenance. He is so embarrassed by the various alternatives that have been propounded, so persuaded of the elements of truth that each contains in different degrees, that he seems unable to form any fixed resolution on the whole subject. [y] Revelation of course cannot but be infallible, but he is not sure, or at least he does not tell us his opinion, of the limits to which the name is to be restricted. All that we can conclude with certainty is that Ockham does not extend its authority to the *Decretals* or to any part of the special Roman tradition.

[s] pt. i. lib. v. 1–5 pp. 467–476.
[t] pt. iii. tr. i. lib. iii. 5–13 pp. 822–831.
[u] pt. i. lib. vi. 85 pp. 603 sqq.
[x] pt. i. lib. v. 25–35 pp. 494–506.
[y] pt. iii. tr. i. lib. iii. 1–4 pp. 819–822.

One of the reasons why it is so difficult to affirm anything in detail about Ockham's views is that his principal works on the subject with which we are concerned are

[24] The principal points of difference between Marsiglio and Ockham in this respect appear to me to be two: first, what Marsiglio intended as a regular part of the constitution, the ordinary originator of legislation, Ockham thought of only as an instrument to be used in the last resort, in the case of the pope falling into heresy: the scheme of the one was political, that of the other was ecclesiastical. Secondly, unless Ockham was consciously committing himself to a paradox, he is distinguished from his colleague by the admission he makes of women to election to general councils, 'propter unitatem fidei virorum et mulierum, quae omnes tangit et in qua non masculus nec foemina. . . Et ideo ubi sapientia, bonitas, vel potentia mulierum esset tractatui fidei (de qua potissime est tractandum in concilio generali) necessaria, non est mulier a generali concilio excludenda:' p. 605. That Ockham was sensible of the ridicule with which the proposal would be received, appears plainly from the opening of the following chapter. For the rest, though it is possible that Marsiglio at an earlier time drew a good deal from Ockham; still the date of the Defensor Pacis furnishes a presumption of the former having the priority in his general conclusions.

CHAP. IX.

written in the form of a dialogue or of *quaestiones*.[25] The method allows him to throw out the most startling suggestions, but at the same time saves him from the necessity of formulating his own express answer. We are in most cases left to guess it from a balance of more or less conflicting passages. Thus we are hardly even able to arrive at a clear view of his conception of the empire and the papacy, in themselves and in their mutual relations. [z] He hints that in a certain state of society it might be better to have several popes and several sovereigns; and [a] although he recognises in some sort the claims of the theoretical universal empire, there is an [b] air of unreality about his assertions which lets us see that he had not forgotten his English birth and French training. No human institution is absolute or final, and neither pope nor [c] emperor can claim exemption from the general law of progress and adaptation. [d] If however at the present time, Ockham argues, the prerogative of the empire reaches over the entire world in its temporal relations, this must inevitably exclude the pope from all but spiritual functions. Ockham has travelled by a different road to the same point as Marsiglio. Neither is really in love with the imperial idea: all that is of importance to them is to erect the state into an organic, consolidated force independent of, and in its own province superior to, that of the spiritualty; and this done, they circumscribe even the spiritual part of the papal authority by making it in all respects subject to the general voice of Christendom. The pope remains the exponent of the church,

[z] pt. iii. tr. i. lib. ii. 25–30 pp. 812–819.

[a] ibid., tr. ii. lib. i. 1–13.

[b] cf. Riezler 252 sq.

[c] cf. Dial. pt. iii. tr. ii. lib. i. 5 p. 876.

[d] ibid., lib. ii. 6–9 pp. 906–910.

[25] It appears to me that the Dialogus was never written to form a single work. The second part admittedly stands by itself; and the third opens the whole subject of the first afresh, and comparatively seldom assumes conclusions which one might think had already been (from the author's point of view) proved many times over in the first part. It is also, unlike its predecessors, subdivided into tractatus as well as into books and chapters. How lax the composition of the Dialogus is, we may learn from the title of Ockham's Opus nonaginta dierum, Goldast 2. 993, which speaks of it as belonging to the sixth tractatus of the third part of the former work. [Compare Mr. A. G. Little's Grey Friars in Oxford, pp. 229–232, Oxford 1892, and my article on Ockham in the Dictionary of National Biography, 41. 359 sq., 1895.]

but appeal is always open to the church, to the whole society, itself. The only difference in the results of the two theorists is that Marsiglio is confident, while Ockham hesitates, about the unerring sagacity of this final arbiter.

But there is, as we have said, a fundamental distinction between the way in which they approach their subject. Marsiglio proceeds from purely philosophical reasoning; theology he proves that he knew well, but he is not primarily a theologian. He is in orders, but he is neither monk nor friar. Ockham on the other hand starts from the point of view of a theologian and of a Franciscan. Now it is well known that the fact which of late years had roused the great body of the Franciscans to opposition to John the Twenty-Second, was the latter's condemnation of their newly proclaimed doctrine of the necessity of 'evangelical poverty.' [e] From that day John became in their eyes a heretic; and although most of them had yielded to the papal threats in 1322–1324, yet the general of their order, Michael of Cesena, and a number of others, passed over to swell the ranks which supported Lewis the Bavarian. Among these was Ockham. It was thus a purely theological dispute, almost a mere matter of partisanship, from which he advanced to combat the general assumptions of the papacy. Once grant the doctrine that the clergy are bound to hold no property, and the whole territorial fabric of the Roman church falls to the ground. From this it is but a step, if it is not essentially involved in the same principle, to refuse to the clergy any temporal jurisdiction or in fact any temporal position whatsoever. With Marsiglio on the contrary the doctrine of 'evangelical poverty' is the consequence, not the premise, of his argument; it flows inevitably from the larger doctrine of the spiritual character of the clergy. Which of the two speculators had the stronger influence upon posterity has been variously estimated; but both in different ways left an unbroken line of successors until the enduring elements in their aims found a partial realisation in the religious revolution of the sixteenth century.

[e] cf. Ockham. Compend. error. papae, i, v. Goldast 2. 958, 964 sq.; Riezler 59–71.

CHAPTER X.

WYCLIFFE'S DOCTRINE OF DOMINION.

IN examining the various theories held in the middle ages concerning the relations of the civil and spiritual powers, two points in particular attract our notice. One is the marked disproportion between these theories and the facts which they were intended to support or overthrow. A prince might brave excommunication or interdict, might persuade himself and his adherents that such acts were invalid and of no effect unless duly, that is, divinely, authorised; he might ridicule the pretension of the spiritualty to exercise them. Yet when once the decree was pronounced, it was never long before the stoutest champion of national rights found himself isolated among a people to whom the interdict was a terrible reality, insensibly subsided into the same terror, and ended by meekly accepting the doctrine which he had but now repudiated. [a] The pope on his side might declare his indefeasible, absolute right to every sort of privilege in every land: over certain countries he might claim immediate sovereignty. But no pope ever thought of carrying the complete doctrine into practice. If Gregory the Seventh be considered an exception, the fact remains certain that he omitted to take any steps to enforce that [b] feudal superiority which he once claimed over England, and which William the Conqueror pointedly rejected. The phrase of the plenary jurisdiction and plenary lordship of the vicar of Christ served indeed well enough for manifestoes meant to animate men's loyalty; but when any specific demand had to be made and met, the high-sounding words were virtually exchanged for the more practical language of barter and the common chicane of the market. Neither party could afford to negotiate on their theoretical footing.

[a] cf. Milman, Hist. of Lat. Christ. 4. 32-36.

[b] Stubbs, Const. hist. of Engl. § 101.

The other peculiarity to which we have referred, is the medley of systems and maxims which had to do duty in the middle ages as the factors of a political philosophy. One theorist extracted from the Old Testament the model of a hierarchy; another read in Aristotle principles nearly approaching those of a modern constitutional polity. The civil law added something, added much to the imperialists' systems; the canon-law, with its wonderful adaptations of Biblical texts, was of no less value to the curialists. But the basis of all was either the Bible of the Christians or the Bible of the philosophers, the Scriptures or Aristotle. And what is perhaps the most curious fact of all is that none of the opponents of papal claims (the advocates were naturally contented with their own canon-law) make any attempt to adjust their schemes to the political or legal framework of their own country. The publicists not only of France but even of England and Germany, write as though the state were constructed on an Aristotelian basis or at most as though its only law was that of the Roman jurisconsults. To this rule however there is one exception, an exception perhaps more illustrative of it than any direct confirmation. For the most ideal scheme of polity conceived in the middle ages, and the furthest removed from practical possibility, was also one modelled closely on the organisation of feudalism. This is the Doctrine of Dominion suggested indeed by a previous English writer but so appropriated and matured by John of Wycliffe that he may be fairly considered its author.[1]

[1] The relation between Wycliffe's doctrine and that of Richard fitz-Ralph, archbishop of Armagh, was pointed out by William Woodford, a younger contemporary. See his treatise Adversus Johannem Wiclefum Anglum, xvi. in Edward Brown's edition of Orthuinus Gratius' Fasciculus rerum expetendarum et fugiendarum, 1. 237, 1690. Compare Mr. F. D. Mathew's introduction to the volume of English Works of Wyclif hitherto unpublished which he edited for the Early English Text Society in 1880, p. xxxiv. The fact is confirmed in many details by so much as I have read of fitzRalph's treatise De pauperie Salvatoris in the Bodleian manuscript, auct. F. infra, 1. 2. [In 1890 I printed the first four books of this work as an appendix to Wycliffe's books De dominio divino, pp. 257–476.]

In introducing the name of Wycliffe it is well to state at the outset that we have nothing here to do with his position as a precursor of protestant theology. The works in which he first treated the subject of dominion were the production of his years of teaching at Oxford; in these the doctrine is completely developed, and his later writings do but presuppose and resume their contents. At this time he was vigorous indeed in exposing the political abuses of the hierarchy, but in dogmatic theology he was without blemish.[2] His criticism was directed against the outer not the inner organisation of the church, and in such criticism he was the ally of many of the loyallest catholics. They saw as he did that the church was falling under the weight of an administration into which the vices of the world had entered almost too deeply to be eradicated. The necessity of reform was becoming gradually felt throughout Christendom; and except among those whose interests were identified with the existing state of affairs, the only question related to the means of carrying the reform into effect. It is important to bear this fact in mind, lest we should infer (as we are apt to infer, knowing Wycliffe's later history) that in resisting Roman encroachments he was therefore also resisting the current of catholic feeling. He was acting in truth as many catholic Englishmen had done before him. His Christianity did not efface his patriotism, and it was with honest reverence for the papacy that he sought to free it from those mundane temptations which

[2] The nineteen conclusions condemned by Gregory the Eleventh in his bulls of May 1377 relate exclusively to ecclesiastical politics, church-lands, the power of excommunication, and the like. Only one can be held to be of dogmatic significance; that, namely, which asserts that every priest has authority to dispense the sacraments and to absolve the penitent: nr xvi, in J. Lewis, History of the Life and Sufferings of John Wiclif 317, 2nd ed., Oxford 1820 (nr xv, in the Fasciculi zizaniorum 253, ed. W. W. Shirley, 1858). But this too when read with the context in Wycliffe's original, De civili dominio i. 38 cod. Vindob. 1341 f. 93 B, proves to be of political purport; since the explanation runs, 'Nam quantum ad potestatem ordinis omnes sacerdotes sunt pares, licet potestas inferioris racionabiliter sit ligata.' This has been already noticed by Dr. Lechler, Johann von Wiclif und die Vorgeschichte der Reformation 1. 573 n. 2.

had long proved an obstacle to its real work of guiding the spirits of men. CHAP. X.

Since almost every particular in Wycliffe's life has been made the subject of eager controversy, it is perhaps desirable that we should preface our account of his doctrine of dominion by a short sketch of his history as far as the time when he framed and published that doctrine. For the place of his birth we are dependent upon two notices of John Leland; one of which states that he [c] *drew his origin* from the house of Wycliffe, settled in the village of Wycliffe-upon-Tees, the other that he was born at Ipreswel, now known as Hipswell, in the immediate neighbourhood of Richmond in Yorkshire.[3] The date we can only conjecture; but as he died in 1384, it is natural to fix it somewhere about the year 1320.[4] [d] The well-ascertained connexion which subsisted between the family of Wycliffe and Balliol College, no doubt determined his enrolment at that foundation when he entered the university of Oxford; but considerable obscurity hangs over the details of his subsequent career. A confusion of dates has given rise to the common belief that he was at first a member of the Queen's College, and a confusion with a namesake has set him down as steward of Merton College.[5]

[c] Collectan. 2. 329.

[d] Shirley, intr., p. xi. n. 1.

[3] A long dispute about the place arose from a misprint in Hearne's edition of the Itinerary of Leland. It so happens that the original manuscript in the Bodleian library is defective exactly at the point where the name ought to occur, vol. v. fol. 114 b, and that of the various existing transcripts only one, John Stow's (cod. Tanner. 464), was made before the manuscript was mutilated. Stow therefore remains our sole authority for the name; but his handwriting is perfectly unambiguous, and the word is *Ipreswel*. This, as I pointed out in the Athenaeum newspaper, nr. 2960, p. 82 (July 19 1884), Hearne inexcusably read as *Spreswel*, mistaking the capital *I* for a long *s*; and from that day to this every single biographer of Wycliffe has perplexed himself (Dr. Robert Vaughan's exploits in the search are notorious) in endeavouring to discover a place which owed its existence purely to a scriptural error. [In Domesday Book f. 310 D the name is written *Hiplewelle*.]

[4] Dr. Lechler vol. 1. 268 sq., thinks 1320 the latest date possible. Shirley however was inclined to place it some years later: Fasciculi zizaniorum, intr., p. xii. The traditional date, since Lewis's conjecture, p. 1, has been 1324.

[5] The former supposition is refuted by Shirley, intr., pp. xii, xiii; the latter is to my mind decisively invalidated by the arguments of the same writer, pp. 513–516, as well as by those adduced by Peter Lorimer, in his notes to the English

CHAP. X.

But it may be taken as proved that Wycliffe began and continued at Balliol, where he must have been a fellow, until in or before the year 1360 he was elected master of the college. Very shortly however he withdrew for a time from the active work of the university to the seclusion of a college living. In the spring of 1361 he was instituted to the rectory of Fillingham in Lincolnshire, and not long afterwards gave up his office at Balliol.[6] He is supposed to have [e] occupied rooms at Queen's at various times between 1363 and 1380. It is natural to connect his return to Oxford with his procedure to degrees in divinity, in which he became doctor not long before December 1373;[7] and the renewed intercourse with the university, the attraction of schools and disputations, may have made it more difficult for him to feel at home in his country parsonage. At all events [f] in 1368 he obtained two years' leave of absence, *to the end that he might devote himself to the study of letters in the university.* [g] In November of that year he quitted the rectory in exchange for the living of Ludgarshall in Buckinghamshire, and nearly six years later (to pass on for a moment to the sequel of his preferments in the church) the crown presented him to the rectory of Lutterworth in Leicestershire. At Lutterworth he died on the 31st December 1384.

e ibid., p. 515.

f ibid., p. 527.

g ibid., intr., pp. xxxviii, xxxix.

From this bare summary of his official career one might think that there was little room for Wycliffe's remarkable influence as a teacher at Oxford. Yet although his principle of clerical duty did not apparently allow him to hold more than one living at a time, he seems not to have scrupled to spend a great part of the year in the university; and he has even been supposed on no contemptible authority to have filled the post of warden of Canterbury-hall, a

translation of Dr. Lechler's Wiclif, ed. 1881. It seems indeed clear that Balliol and Merton in Wycliffe's time formed the opposite poles of the academical world.

6 He first appears as master in 1360; see Lorimer, ubi supra, p. 133. The later dates are April and July 1361: Shirley, intr., p. xiv notes 4 and 5.

7 [Calendar of Entries in the papal Registers relating to Great Britain and Ireland, 4. 193; 1902. Shirley, intr., p. xvii erroneously fixed the date between 1361 and 1366.]

foundation of which the site is now occupied by a portion of Christ Church, between the years 1365 and 1367.[8] As to this matter it is only necessary to notice that a certain John Wycliffe was appointed to that office, and afterwards expelled in order to make room for a monk. The deprived warden appealed to Rome and lost his case. Now, this being known, when a religious agitator of the same name had made himself objectionable to the correct catholics of his day, and in particular to the religious orders, it was all but inevitable that the antecedent history of the one should attach itself to the other. There are indeed strong grounds for believing that the warden of Canterbury-hall was the same person with the steward of Merton whose name, as we have already seen, has caused a certain amount of confusion in the reformer's biography. But if on the whole we are inclined to reject the connexion of the latter with Canterbury-hall, it is right that we should explain that this decision is in

[8] The best argument in favour of this identification appeared in the Church quarterly Review 5. 119–141, October 1877. On the other hand Shirley's observations in the Fasciculi zizaniorum 513–528 remain of high critical value; although he erred in underestimating the authority of a contemporary chronicle, which he knew only from a translation of the sixteenth century, but of which the original has recently been discovered by Mr. [now sir] E. Maunde Thompson. See the latter's edition of the Chronicon Angliae 1328–1388 p. 115; 1874. In favour of our Wycliffe having been warden of Canterbury-hall it may be urged that Middleworth who had been at Merton and who was made fellow of Canterbury-hall at the same time with Wycliffe, was also at a later date resident, as Wycliffe was, at Queen's; but, as Shirley points out, pp. 519 sq., there was really not much choice, at a time when only six colleges existed and not all were open to all comers. [Nor is it at all certain that the Queen's resident was the same person as the reformer: see H. T. Riley's remarks in the Second Report of the Royal Commission on historical Manuscripts, pp. 141 *b* sq., 1871; and H. Rashdall, in the Dictionary of National Biography, 63. 203 *b*; 1900.] As for the extract printed by Dr. Lechler, vol. 2. 574 sq., and in part by Shirley, p. 526, from Wycliffe's treatise De ecclesia xvi [pp. 370 sq., ed. J. Loserth, 1886], it seems to me to decide nothing; Dr. Lechler's inference from the passage depends entirely on the force of a comparative, *in familiariori exemplo,* which need not be pressed to mean 'in the writer's personal case.' [Though most scholars accept the identification, one of the latest and most learned, Dr. Rashdall, now dean of Carlisle, inclines with me to reject it, ubi supra, p. 204 *b*.]

CHAP. X.

no degree owing to the scandal which Wycliffe's opponents have discovered in his ejection by the archbishop of Canterbury. So far as we can see, there was nothing discreditable to either party in the transaction, and nothing discreditable to the pope who dismissed Wycliffe's appeal, or to the English king who confirmed the papal sentence. It was simply a dispute, one of a kind that constantly arose, between the secular and the regular clergy. At the same time if the reformer be actually the person who was thus deprived we shall no doubt be right in looking upon this event in his personal history as one of the elements which produced his subsequent rancour against the monastic system.

At whatever decision we arrive with respect to this affair, it remains certain that Wycliffe continued active in the Oxford schools; and this is all that we are here concerned to know, since it was not until many years later that he became conspicuous as a leader of opposition to the established doctrine of the church. Yet even now he had made himself a name outside of Oxford. He was, it seems, a [h] chaplain to the king, and had already entered the lists of controversy as an advocate, though in guarded terms, of the rights of the English nation as against the papal claim to tribute from it. In the tract to which we refer [9] he puts in the mouth of seven lords in council the arguments which might be urged against this claim; and to one of these speakers he gives the announcement of his own special doctrine of dominion. This was in

[h] Determ., ap. Lewis 349.

[9] The Determinatio quedam magistri Johannis Wyclyff de dominio is printed by Lewis, pp. 349–356; not however, as Dr. Lechler, vol. 2. 322 n. 1, seems to suggest, as an excerpt: its fragmentary condition is due to the manuscript itself, which is in the Bodleian library, arch. Seld. B. 26 [olim 10] ff. 54 sqq. I agree with Mr. F. D. Matthew, intr., p. vi, as against Shirley, intr., p. xix, Lechler, vol. 1. 330, and apparently Milman, vol. 8. 163, that this does not contain a *report* in the strict sense of the word. Wycliffe was very likely present at the debate in parliament; but even though he may give what he supposes that the lords said, or ought to have said, still the language, the arrangement, and a good deal of the argument, are unmistakably Wycliffe's own. Wycliffe refers to the Responsio septem dominorum in his De civili dominio iii. 7 cod. Vindob. 1340 f. 41 B.

1366[10]: perhaps at this very time, [i]hardly in any case very long after, he was engaged in his treatise *Of the Divine Dominion*. About five years later he supplemented the work by a more extensive treatise *Of civil Dominion;* so that by 1371 or 1372 his views on this characteristic subject were fully formed and given to the world.[11]

CHAP. X.

[i] Shirley, intr. p. xvii.

Dominion and service, in Wycliffe's scheme, are the two ends of the chain which links humanity to God. Dominion is not indeed a part of the eternal order of things, since [k]it only comes into existence by the act of creation: *God* in the first chapter of Genesis becomes *Lord* in the second, because there are now creatures to be his servants; just as [l]the lower animals are put in the relation of servants by the creation of man. Dominion and service are thus necessarily correlative terms, including, but not identical with, other terms of human relation. [m]Dominion for instance presupposes right and power, and the exercise of either; but it is not the same with them: it cannot exist without the coexistence of an object to operate upon;[12] whereas a man may

[k] De dominio divino, i. 2 cod. Vindob. 1339 f. 3 C, D.

[l] cap. 1 f. 2 A.

[m] cap. 2 f. 3 B, C.

[10] [Dr. Loserth has brought forward convincing arguments to show that the tract cited was written at least eleven years later. See his papers in the English Historical Review, 11. 319–328, 1896; and in the Sitzungsberichte der kaiserlichen Akademie der Wissenschaften in Wien, philosophisch-historische Classe, 136. pt 1. 31–44, 1897.]

[11] These works I am now preparing for publication by the Wyclif society. I have not at present found reason to modify the view put forward by Shirley, intr., pp. xvii, xxi n. 2, with respect to their date. My citations are taken from transcripts in my possession of the original codices which are preserved in the palace library at Vienna: the De dominio divino from nr 1339 (which I sometimes correct from two other copies in the same library, numbered 1294 and 3935); and the De civili dominio from the only copy known to be in existence, books i, ii from nr 1341, and book iii from nr 1340. I should perhaps add that, as my work on these treatises is still incomplete, the following account of the doctrine they contain is only a tentative sketch. [My edition of the De civili dominio liber i was published in 1885. The second and third book was edited by Dr. J. Loserth in 1900–1903. It has not been necessary to insert references to the pages of my edition either of this book or of the De dominio divino, which I published in 1890, because the folios of the manuscripts are regularly entered in the margin of my editions.]

[12] Ius ergo, cum sit fundamentum dominii, licet sapiat relacionem respectu cuius dicitur *ius*, non tamen est formaliter ipsum dominium; sicut vis generativa patris non est formaliter ipsa paternitas, sed ad ipsum ut fundamentum pro aliquo tempore requisita. Et per

CHAP. X.

have right without actual possession, and power without the means of exercising it. *No catholic*, for instance, *will deny that the power of the keys is committed to the priest, albeit he have none subjected to his power.* Dominion then is neither a right nor a power; it is *a habit of the reasonable nature*,[13] essentially involved in the existence of that nature, and irrespective of any condition except that of being set above something inferior to it. Thus, in the case of the Creator, [n] *it seems probable that his dominion is immediate and of itself, by virtue of the act of creation, and not by virtue of his government or conservation of the universe.* [o] It surpasses all other dominion because God stands in no need of service, because it is sure and irremovable, and because it meets with universal service.

[n] ibid., f. 4 A.

[o] cap. 3 ff. 5 C–6 A.

As yet we are in the midst of scholastic definitions and distinctions; but Wycliffe soon finds occasion to state what may be called the fundamental principle of his theory. [p] *God*, he says, *rules not mediately through the rule of subject vassals, as other kings hold dominion, since immediately and of himself he makes, sustains, and governs all that which he possesses, and helps it to perform its work according to other uses which he requires.* There is a feudalism here, but a feudalism in which there are no mesne lords; all men hold directly of God, with [q] differences no doubt in accidentals, but in the main fact of their

[p] cap. 5 f. 11 A.

[q] cap. 4 ff. 7 D–8 B.

idem sequitur quod potestas non sit genus dominii: nam dominium dependet a possesso serviente vel suo principaliter [*cod.* 1294: *al.* principium] terminante; sed nulla potestas sic dependet, ergo nullum dominium est potestas: De dominio divino i. 2 f. 3 B; cf. cap. 1 f. 2 B.

[13] Dominium est habitudo nature racionalis secundum quam denominatur suo prefici servienti: cap. 1 f. 1 D; also in the De civili dominio i. 9 f. 20 D. Locke was very merry at sir Robert Filmer's expense for his having used the phrase 'in habit and not in act' of Adam's position as governor before there was any one to govern: 'A very pretty way,' he says, 'of being a governor, without government, a father, without children, and a king, without subjects. . . Adam, as soon as he was created, had a title only *in habit and not in act*, which, in plain English, is, he had actually no title at all.' See the first Treatise on Government iii. 18. Still Filmer's distinction is perfectly legitimate, and I only quote Locke's words in order to shew that we have to accept a certain logical terminology before we can pretend to criticise a scholastic position such as Filmer's or Wycliffe's.

tenure all alike. It is this principle of the dependence of the individual upon God and upon none else that distinguishes Wycliffe's views from any other system of the middle ages. He alone had the courage to strike at the root of priestly privilege and power by vindicating for each separate man an equal place in the eyes of God. By this formula all laymen became priests, and all priests laymen. They all 'held' of God, and on the same terms of service.

These are some of the elements of the doctrine of dominion which Wycliffe enunciates in the early chapters of his work *De Dominio Divino*. The rest of the treatise is principally occupied with the discussion of various questions of a strictly theological or of a metaphysical character, following upon his view of the relation of the Creator to the world, but only indirectly illustrative of that special portion of it with which we are here concerned. The practical application of the latter is found at large in the three books *Of civil Dominion* which fill more than a thousand pages of close and much-contracted handwriting in the only copy known to exist, a nearly contemporary manuscript now preserved in the palace library at Vienna. What is essential however for our present purpose will be found nearly complete in the first thirty-four chapters of the first book, which treat of dominion and government in themselves. This section, as the following sketch will show, indicates in its main outline Wycliffe's salient doctrine of the relation of the secular to the spiritual power; and we need not pursue its delineation further, when the author, with the exhaustive prolixity of a schoolman, defines its bearing in minute detail upon all the problems arising from this relation which called for criticism in his day.

Wycliffe begins his book by the proposition, of which the [r] latter part was already noted as dangerous by Gregory the Eleventh in 1377, that [s] no one in mortal sin has any right to any gift of God, while on the other hand every man standing in grace has not only a right to, but has

[r] Lewis 316 nr iv.
[s] De civili dominio i. 1 f. 1 A.

CHAP. X.

[t] ibid., f. 2 B; capp. 7, 12 ff. 16 A, 26 D.

[u] v. supra, p. 52 n. 15.

[x] De civ. dom. i. 1 f. 1 C.

[y] ibid., f. 2 C, D.

[z] cap. 5 f. 11 D.

[a] cap. 2 f. 3 D.

in fact, all the gifts of God. [t] He takes literally the aphorism which an ancient tradition inserted in the Book of Proverbs, *The faithful man hath the whole world of riches, but the unfaithful hath not even a farthing;*[14] and he supports it with much fulness and ingenuity of argumentation. The first part of his thesis is indeed a legitimate following out of the doctrine which saint Augustin had enforced, of the negative character of evil. [u] *Sin,* he said, *is nothing, and men, when they sin, become nothing:* [x] if then, argued Wycliffe, sinners, as such, are nothing, it is evident that they can possess nothing. Moreover [y] possession presupposes a right or title to possess, and this right or title can only be held ultimately to depend upon the good pleasure of God, who, it is evident, cannot be thought to approve the lordship of the wicked or the manner in which they abuse their power. Again, by the common law *it is not permitted to an inferior lord to alienate, in particular to mortmain, any real property without the license of his lord-in-chief,* and any grant in contravention of his will is unrighteous; accordingly, inasmuch as God is the lord-in-chief of all human beings, it should appear that any grant made to a sinner must be contrary to his will, and thus being unrighteous must be no possession in any strict or proper sense of the word. But even granting that the sinner have such possession, [z] *all human dominion, natural or civil, is conferred upon him by God, as the prime author, in consideration of his returning continually to God the service due unto him; but by the fact that a man by omission or commission becomes guilty of mortal sin, he defrauds his lord-in-chief of the said service, and by consequence incurs forfeiture: wherefore . . . he is rightfully to be deprived of all dominion whatsoever.* How then does the wicked man come to have property in earthly things? [a] Wycliffe's explanation turns upon the double meaning of the word *church,*

[14] It is found in the Septuagint version at the end of Prov. xvii. 6, in the Alexandrine manuscript after ver. 4: Τοῦ πιστοῦ ὅλος ὁ κόσμος των χρημάτων, τοῦ δὲ ἀπίστου οὐδὲ ὀβολός. Wycliffe knew the text from Augustin, Epist. cliii. 26, Opp, 2. 534 E, and Jerom, Epist. l., Opp. 4 (2) 575, in the Benedictine editions.

considered either as the holy spouse of Christ or as, in its transitory condition, the human society mixed of good and evil. To the church in its ideal signification God makes his grant; the wicked have their share only by virtue of their outward membership of it.[15] But since, as has been said, the sole sufficient title to any possession is the immediate grant of God, it results that such possession as the wicked have is not worthy the name of possession at all: and [b] *Whosoever hath not, from him shall be taken even that which he seemeth to have.*

[b] ibid., f. 4 A, cap. 3 f. 5 C; Matth. xxv. 29 Vulg.

By means of this and similar texts of Scripture the way is prepared for Wycliffe's second main principle; namely, that the righteous is lord of all things, or in precise terms [c] *every righteous man is lord over the whole sensible world.* If a man has anything he has everything: for, as Wycliffe says elsewhere, [d] *the grant of God is most appropriate, most ample, and most useful to the creature;* so ample indeed that [e] *God gives not any dominion to his servants except he first give himself* to them. Thus, [f] even when the righteous is afflicted in this life, he still has true possession of the whole universe, inasmuch as [g] *all things work together for good* to him, in assisting him towards eternal happiness. It would be impossible to indicate the spiritual nature of the dominion claimed by Wycliffe for the righteous, more distinctly than by this example: yet he proceeds to dwell upon its literal truth in a way that might almost persuade us that he is really developing a system of polity applicable to the existing conditions of life. He is not afraid to pursue his doctrine to the logical conclusion that, [h] as there are many righteous and each is lord of the universe, all goods must necessarily

[c] cap. 7 f. 15 D, 16 B, &c.

[d] De dom. div. iii. 2 f. 71 D.

[e] ibid.; de civ. dom. i. 7 fol. 16 D.

[f] ibid., f. 16 B.

[g] Rom. viii. 28.

[h] De civ. dom. i. 14 f. 31 C.

[15] Wycliffe makes a curious distinction between 'giving' and 'granting,' *dare* and *donare*; the former is a general term, the latter applies only to the righteous, or to the church. Donacio dicit gratuitam dacionem, et dacio est equivocum ad tradicionem solum ad bonum nature (aut esse primum) vel ad bonum gracie (vel perfeccionem secundam): primo modo dat Deus omni inanimato vel iniusto quidquid habet; sed secundo modo dacionis, que est donacio, non dat aliquid nisi iustis: Cap. 2 f. 3 D.

CHAP. X.

be held in common.[16] He expounds the rules of charity laid down by saint Paul (*charity* with Wycliffe is the correlative term to *grace*), and interprets the sentence, [i] *Charity seeketh not her own*—[k] *seeketh not to be a proprietor but to have all things in common.* Any objections to the doctrine he dismisses as [l] sophistical. [m] Those adduced by Aristotle hold, he says, only in regard to the community of wives proposed by Plato; but this application may be proved to be logically fallacious.

[i] 1 Cor. xiii. 5.
[k] De civ. dom. i. 15 f. 35 A, B.
[l] cap. 14 f. 31 C.
[m] ibid., ff. 32 B–33 A.

Such are in brief the fundamental principles of the treatise *Of civil Dominion*: the righteous has all things; the wicked has nothing, [n] only occupies for the time that which he has unrighteously usurped or stolen from the righteous. Dominion, in a word, is *founded in grace;* and grace, or, from another point of view, the law of the Gospel, being alone essential to it, it follows necessarily that [o] human ordinances are accidental or indifferent. These, Wycliffe maintains, are in fact [p] the mere consequence of the fall of man: they originate in sin, in *the lust of dominion;* and for the most part they betray their origin evidently enough by [q] the opportunities they offer for wrong-doing and tyranny. When therefore we require, in addition to the natural dominion which is that of the Gospel, [r] an inferior sort of dominion, civil dominion, the latter, it is clear, must not pretend to any absolute or essential character; it is transitory and liable to modification according to the changing conditions of human society; above all it is entirely subordinate to that natural dominion [s] from which it draws whatever claim it may have to righteousness.[17] Accordingly,

[n] cap. 5 ff. 10 D, 11 A.
[o] capp. 17, 34 ff. 38 C–40 C. 80 C, D.
[p] capp. 18, 21 ff. 41 B, 49 C.
[q] cap. 18 f. 42 B, C.
[r] ibid., ff. 41 B–42 A.
[s] capp. 5, 19 ff. 12 B, 43 A, B.

[16] Omnis homo debet esse in gracia, et si est in gracia est dominus mundi cum suis contentis; ergo omnis homo debet esse dominus universitatis: quod non staret cum multitudine hominum, nisi omnes illi deberent habere omnia in communi; ergo omnia debent esse communia.

[17] Wycliffe thus states the distinction between natural and civil lordship: Dominium quidem naturale est dominium divinitus institutum, in primo titulo iusticie fundatum, quotlibet divites ex equo compaciens, sed alienacionem dominantis, servata iusticia, non permittens: dominium autem civile est dominium occasione peccati humanitus institutum, incommunicabile singulis et ex equo multis dominis, sed abdicabile servata iusticia: Cap. 18 f. 40 D.

saving this one grand principle, Wycliffe does not care to lay down any fixed rules as to the best form of government. Like [t] Ockham, he feels too deeply the necessary infirmity of all human institutions to be able to dogmatise about their relative excellence. [u] Suppose, he says, the whole people desire a certain man to be their civil ruler, it does not follow on that account that he is rightly their ruler; nor can any human laws touching hereditary succession or the conveyance of property make such succession or transfer righteous or true, unless they are conformable to the law of nature.[18] The law of nature in Wycliffe's mouth is something far different from that of which other schoolmen found the exposition in the *Politics* of Aristotle. He adopts in fact the point of view of the strict hierarchical advocates, only with the all-important difference that his lawgiver is not the church but the Bible itself.

CHAP. X.

[t] cf. supra, pp. 277 sqq.

[u] De civ. dom. i. 18 f. 42 B.

There is therefore a lack of decision about Wycliffe's treatment of the different methods according to which a society may be governed. In the abstract [x] he thinks that an aristocracy, by which he understands the rule of *judges* in the Old Testament sense, must surpass any other constitution, because it is the least connected with civil ordinances. He applies the example of the Israelite history, according to which, he says, judges were first set by God over his people and monarchy was a sign of their defection from the divine rule; finally, he adds, they came under the worst sort of rule, that of priests, which was most of all vitiated by human tradition and indeed altogether corrupt. Balancing the two former modes of government, [y] Wycliffe appears to feel that, granted the sinful state of mankind, government by a single ruler is on the whole the most beneficial, since it is

[x] cap. 27 ff. 62 D–64 A.

[y] ibid., f. 65 A, B; cap. 28 f. 67 C.

[18] Nam non sequitur, 'Totus populus vult Petrum dominari civiliter; ergo iuste:' ymmo primus consensus populi ad aliquem civiliter dominandum, qui tamen fuit a peccato purior, non fuit iustus nisi presupposita racione, scilicet quod persona dominans sit a Deo accepta ad illud officium; et per idem nulla principia iuris civilis de successione hereditaria vel commutacione mutua terrenorum est iusta vel vera, nisi de quanto est legis nature particula: ibid., f. 42 B.

CHAP. X.

[z] cap. 29 ff. 67 C–69 D.

[a] cap. 29 f. 68 C, D.

[b] cap. 30 f. 70 B, C.

[c] ibid., f. 69 D; cf. cap. 29 sub fin.

[d] cap. 30 f. 71 C.

the strongest to restrain their excesses. [z] He goes on to enquire whether dominion should be transmitted by hereditary succession or whether a fresh choice should take place at every vacancy. On the one hand it may be urged that the security of tenure possessed by an hereditary monarch, and the certainty he has of handing down his dominion to his son, is an inducement to him to play the tyrant; on the other hand this very fact may increase his care for his dominion and cause him to make the best use of it. It is here assumed, as regularly in the middle ages, that a prince whom the community has elected, it may depose; while an hereditary monarch, according to the common belief, could not be legally deprived of his power. Again, in favour of the elective principle, [a] it may be said that an election in which all qualified persons take part must be right. But Wycliffe, as we have seen, has no opinion of the value of the popular vote: *since the fall of man*, he says, *it generally happens that the electing community is, altogether or in its greater part, infected by crime; and thus it happens that it is at fault in elections, even as in other acts alike concerning God and the commonwealth.*[19] Wycliffe argues at length on both sides; incidently he discloses a good deal of political acuteness, and [b] he leans towards a preference for the hereditary principle: but no experience or historical observation will induce him to forego the application here also of his first doctrine; and thus [c] he decides that neither heredity nor election furnishes any title sufficient for the foundation of human dominion, without the anterior condition of grace in the person so elected or so succeeding. [d] *Wherefore it appears to me that the discreet theologian will determine nothing rashly as touching these laws, but will affirm according to law that it were better that all things should be had in common.*

[19] The only concession he makes is as follows: Non est possibile communitatem in eleccione deficere, nisi peccatum pertinens sit in causa; Deus enim non potest deficere ab instinctu regitivo populi secundum sibi utilius, cum hoc quod populus utrobique Deo faciat quidquid debet: f. 69 c. But it will be seen that the qualification repeated in this sentence deprives it of most of its force.

But dominion, as was stated at the outset, has another aspect to it; [e] the theory of the community of dominion in itself involves its counterpart, the community of service. In this we find the only check recognised by Wycliffe, upon the action of kings: they have a responsibility, not—we may infer from the tenour of his argument—to the people over whom they rule, but to God from whom they derive their dominion. [f] They are his stewards, and lords only by virtue of service. God is the only lord whose dominion is unattended by this condition; all other lords are servants not only of God but also of all their fellow-men. [g] The superscription of papal letters, *servus servorum*, acknowledges this truth in the most exalted of ecclesiastical potentates: [h] it has the authority of the apostle who bade the Galatians, [i] *By love serve one another*. We have seen the corollary of this principle; since all are lords and all servants one of another, then, all things, all that we call property, must belong in common to all. But if we are startled by the premature socialism of the thesis, we have to bear in mind that Wycliffe had yet to learn its effects in practical life, as displayed in the excesses of the rebels of 1381. Such application indeed was never in his mind; nor did he ever pass a word which could be interpreted into approval of a violent assertion of those rights which notwithstanding he fully conceded. All things were all men's, but so long as the present state of polity subsisted it was unlawful to acquire them by force: for on the one hand the human constitution of society had the divine sanction, although it were imperfect by comparison with its eternal or evangelical ordering; and on the other hand force was incompatible with the primary dictates of the law of God.

[e] cap. 11 f. 24 C, D; cf. cap. 32 f. 76 A.
[f] cap. 19 f. 43 C, D.
[g] capp. 11, 14 ff. 24 D, 32 D.
[h] cap. 11 f. 26 A.
[i] Gal. v. 13.

Wycliffe's communism is thus expressly limited to a condition of the world not present, but to be looked for and worked for: nor only thus; it is also limited to a field of possession other than that of human or temporal acquirement. [k] Earthly loss is heavenly gain, and the care of earthly things is a barrier to our love of those

[k] cap. 9, 16 ff. 19 D, 20 A, 37 A, B, &c.

CHAP. X.

[1] cap. 12 f. 27 A-C.

which are our proper objects. [1] If we seek the shadow we shall fail of the substance, but if we press forward to the substance the shadow will follow and attend us too. The righteous therefore has all things, not necessarily, not principally, in this present life; but as his right now, and as his sure and indefeasible enjoyment hereafter. His dominion, being founded in grace, has the warrant of God's decree : the fruition of it may be delayed, so far as earthly goods are concerned, but possession of all things remains his inalienable right. The sinner on the contrary by the very fact of sinning loses all right to anything. His dominion is no longer founded in grace, it has no substantial existence; it may seem to stand for a time, but he reaps his good on this earth only to be one day terribly recompensed.

This opposition between the righteous who have all things and the unrighteous who have nothing, runs through all Wycliffe's argument on the question of dominion. In it he finds the secret of the differences of human lot; by its means he is able to reconcile the prosperity of the wicked with the troubles and disappointments of the good. He translates the Bible into the language of feudalism, and then he proceeds to explain his new-found polity on a strictly spiritual basis. But however ideal the principle on which Wycliffe goes, it has none the less a very plain meaning when applied to the circumstances of the religious organism in the writer's own time. For the essence of the whole conception lies in the stress which he laid upon inner elements, as opposed to outer, as those which determine a man's proper merit. To Wycliffe it was the personal relation, the immediate dependence of the individual upon God, that made him worthy or unworthy; it was his own character and not his office, however exalted in the eyes of men, that constituted him what he really was. The pope himself, if unworthy, if personally a bad man, lost *ipso facto* his entire right to dominion.

Here however, as so often in Wycliffe, an important

distinction has to be settled. Every good man, we have seen before, is lord of all things, but he is not on that account at liberty to assert his possession of them in contravention of civil right: so also [m] he cannot claim to disobey the civil ruler because that ruler is personally unworthy of his post; his rule is at least permitted by God. Thus Wycliffe expressly repudiates the inference which might naturally and logically be drawn from his premises. *God*, ran his famous paradox, *ought to obey the devil;* [20] that is, no one can escape from the duty of obedience to existing powers, be those powers never so depraved.[21] But there is logic also in Wycliffe's position. As things are, he felt, the spheres of spiritual and temporal sovereignty are kept asunder. The spiritual authority has no competence to interfere with the temporal, nor the temporal with the spiritual. Each is paramount within its own area of jurisdiction, so far as the present state of affairs is concerned; but in the eternal order of the universe right, power, dominion, and the practical exercise of authority, are dependent on the character, the righteousness, of the person to whom they belong.

[m] cf. Shirley, intr., pp. lxiii–lxv.

It is Wycliffe's veneration for the spiritual dignity of the church that led him to sever its sphere of action from that of the world. No pope or priest of the church, he held, could claim any temporal authority: [n] *he is a lord, yea even a king*, but only in things spiritual. So far as the pope, to take the salient instance, recedes from this position, so far as he holds any earthly power, so far is he unworthy of his office. [o] *For to rule temporal possessions after a civil*

[n] De civ. dom. l. II f. 24 A.

[o] cap. 17 f. 40 C.

[20] This appears first in the later list of Wycliffe's errors, 1382: Lewis 358 nr vii, Shirley 278, 494. But it is perfectly in keeping with his earlier doctrine.

[21] Wycliffe has a chapter in the De civili dominio, i. 28, in which he discusses, and decides in the affirmative sense, the duty of obedience to tyrants. 'Hic dicetur quod dupliciter contingit iuste obedire mundi potentibus; vel pure paciendo, servata caritate, quod non poterit esse malum; vel active ministrando in bonis fortune aut ministerio corporali, quod indubie, servata de possibili caritate, foret bonum.' Yet, he hints, a Christian, 'si esset verisimile homini per subtracciones temporalis iuvaminis destruere potentatus tyrannidem vel abusum, debet ea intencione subtrahere:' f. 66 A, B.

manner, to conquer kingdoms, and exact tributes, appertain to earthly dominion, not to the pope ; so that if he pass by and set aside the office of spiritual rule, and entangle himself in those other concerns, his work is not only superfluous but also contrary to holy Scripture. It would however be a mistake to regard Wycliffe's intention here as directed in any sense to the overthrow of the papacy. He has not only a clear perception of, a firm belief in, the supremacy of the spiritual chief of the church; he goes so far as to assert that [p] no one can have even the goodwill of his fellow-men, *amicitia*, except by grant of the pope, ratifying the grant of God. This dignity, he feels, is in truth incompatible with the business of the external world: he would free it from those impediments.

[p] cap. 13 f. 30 A.

In such an endeavour Wycliffe had forerunners in several of the controversial writers with whom we have been occupied in the preceding chapter. There was nothing new in his argument on this head, save only the way in which he fitted it into his framework of dominion. The pope, he explained, is indeed lord; all men are lords: but just by virtue of mutual service. If any one should seek to raise himself above service, to make himself lord absolute, he becomes by this very act all the more a servant, all the less a lord. This paradoxical position is protected by the altogether ideal character of the scheme. To resume for a moment his salient conception, Wycliffe tries to withdraw himself from the thought of any civil polity; he insists that [q] *the law of the gospel is sufficient by itself, without the civil law or that called canonical* (the qualification is noteworthy), *for the perfect rule of the church militant;* human laws and ordinances, he considers but the consequence of the fall of man. He looks forward to a state of things in which it will be possible to dispense with everything but the divine and eternal law: he has not, as [r] Thomas Aquinas had, the philosopher's insight which could recognise a human law as something inextricably involved in the existence of an human society.

[q] cap. 17 f. 39 B.

[r] v. supra, p. 214.

It was therefore when the powers of the spiritual and the temporal lord crossed one another that Wycliffe's strict principle came into play. [s] When the church exercised functions which justly belonged to the state, when it became involved in transactions about money and territorial possession, then, he held, it was time for the state to interfere and vindicate its right over its own affairs. The mis-used revenues of the church were to be won back and the spiritualty was to be limited to its proper spiritual office. Such at the date in Wycliffe's history to which alone our attention is directed, was the main result to which his theorising had led him.[22] But it is evident that the principle on which he built could not fail to bring with it other no less practical conclusions. By means of his doctrine of dominion he not only undermined the fabric of the hierarchy, since each individual is answerable to God alone; but also he was already moved to question, with Ockham, whether the pope be an indispensable element in the fabric;[23] he even speculates whether it be not possible that one day *the ship of Peter*, the church, may not consist exclusively of laymen.[24] Another step, such a step as was suggested by the schism of 1378, would lead Wycliffe into fixed opposition to the papacy. At present he is still animated by a loyal reverence towards the head of the church: he only disputes the pope's pretensions when they exceed the sphere of his true functions as such; he only discusses in a theoretical

CHAP. X.

[s] De civ. dom. i. 37 f. 87 c, d.

[22] Cf. de civ. dom. ii. 12 f. 198 A, B: Domini temporales possunt legittime ac meritorie auferre divicias a quocunque clerico habitualiter abutente; or in larger terms, f. 198 c: Domini temporales habent potestatem ad auferendas divicias legittime ac meritorie eciam a tota ecclesia possessionatorum in casu quo eis habitualiter abutatur.

[23] Caput Christus cum sua lege est per se sufficiens ad regulam sponse sue; ergo nullus alius homo requiritur tamquam sponsus. . . . Sufficit enim modo, sicut suffecit in primitiva ecclesia quod Christianus sit in gracia, credendo in Christum, licet nullum aliud caput ecclesie ipsum direxerit: Lib. i. 43 f. 123 c.

[24] Navicula quidem Petri est ecclesia militans . . . : nec video quin dicta navis Petri possit pure per tempus stare in laycis. Ideo nimis sophisticant qui triplicant templum Domini, et referunt navem Petri tamquam ad per se causam originalem, id est, ad istam Romanam ecclesiam vel quamcunque particularem citra Christum: ibid., f. 127 c.

CHAP. X.

way the abstract necessity rather than the expediency of the existing order of things.

The ultimate form which Wycliffe's teaching assumed is a commonplace of religious history. We have here restricted our consideration of it to a time when it might still be regarded as a genuine product of catholic thought. Like the ferment of questions which filled the deliberations of the councils of Constance and Basle half a century later, they are still charged with the spirit of the middle ages. Like those debates they point forward also to an age that is yet to come. The full solution of the political problems of the church was left for the more strenuous struggle of the sixteenth century; but if Wycliffe's later career made him in spirit the precursor of the protestant reformation, he had already found out for himself the great secret of modern belief, a principle far more important than any of the special doctrinal details which afterwards roused his antagonism. He has not indeed the credit of having discovered the peculiar formula of justification by faith, which to superficial readers appears to constitute the kernel of reformation-teaching, but he has dared to codify the laws which govern the moral world on the basis of the direct dependence of the individual man on God.[25] In using the word *individual* we are indeed departing from the strict meaning of Wycliffe's words, and introducing an apparent contradiction to that doctrine of community which lies at the root of his exposition. Such is however the purport of his language, as we should now understand it: to Wycliffe himself the individual Christian was nothing save by virtue of his membership of the Christian body; but since he divorced the idea of the church from

[25] Deus . . . dat sua carismata cuilibet Christiano, constituens cum eo, tamquam membro suo, unum corpus misticum; ad nullam talem influenciam requiritur persona hominis disparata; ergo nulla persona Romane ecclesie requiritur tamquam mediamen absolute necessarium ad regulandum ecclesiam: ibid., f. 123 B, C. Cf. f. 122 D: Quecunque ergo persona fidelis ecclesie, laycus vel clericus, Latinus vel Grecus, masculus vel femella, sufficit ad fidem instrumentaliter ac occasionaliter gignendam. The entire argument of the chapter is highly instructive.

any necessary connexion with its official establishment and left it purely spiritual, to say that a man's relation to God is determined by his union with the church, is the same as to say that he stands on his own private spiritual footing. Individualism is therefore only another aspect of Wycliffe's communism; and thus, however visionary and unpractical the scheme may be in which he framed it, however bizarre in many of its details, the fundamental principle of his Doctrine of Dominion justifies its author's title to be considered in no partial sense as the father of modern Christianity.

The uniqueness of Wycliffe's conception may justify the length at which we have dwelt upon it; but we must not claim for it more than its proper due. Wycliffe, it should seem, started from the point of view of an ecclesiastical politician. Leaving out of account some dialectical treatises, which were merely what was expected of a master in the university schools, his earliest productions were professed political pamphlets; and his maturer works on civil dominion have the appearance of giving the solution which he had discovered for the ecclesiastical problems which agitated his century, rather than the results of self-contained philosophical speculation. Wycliffe did not in fact possess the philosophical temper in its finer development. He was thoroughly grounded in what passed for philosophy in the scholastic world of his day; but it is impossible to deny that philosophy was by this time far gone in its decadence. The richer the materials in men's possession, the less they were concerned to apply to them the higher gifts of the intellect, the more they wearied themselves in fruitless ingenuity, in infinite refinements of infinitesimal distinctions. Even homely fallacies in logic they did not disdain to cloak by their expertness in its technical manipulation. Fashion demanded that a certain number of proofs should be adduced for every proposition; and the weight or even the relevance of the proof was, as often as not, immaterial. In the most laborious, or the most laboured, arguments we frequently find the elements of serious enquiry to be altogether wanting. In his formal exposition Wycliffe is as great a sinner as the rest. More than this, if we pardon the vices of his method, it is not, we must acknowledge, in deference to a commanding intellectual vigour. He had not, Ockham had only in part, that keen political insight which gives Marsiglio of Padua his enduring renown: but Ockham and Wycliffe were dominated by an overpowering religious principle; and it is the latter's instinctive, his prophetic, sympathy with the aims and ideals of the modern reformed churches that constitutes his real historical significance.

APPENDIX

APPENDIX.

I. Note on the origin of the legend respecting John Scotus's travels in Greece.

It has been constantly repeated, as an old story to which modern critics cannot be expected to give credence, that John Scotus made a journey into Greece, and derived thence a part of the materials of his extraordinary learning. The story, however, is itself of entirely recent origin, and rests exclusively upon the authority of bishop Bale. His words are: Append. I.

[a] Ioannes Erigena, Brytannus natione, in Menevia Demetarum urbe, seu ad fanum Davidis, ex patricio genitore natus, a quibusdam scriptoribus philosophus, ab aliis vero, sed extra lineam, Scotus cognominatur. Dum Anglos Daci crudeles bellis ac rapinis molestarent, et omnia illic essent tumultibus plena, longam ipse peregrinationem Athenas usque suscepit, annosque quam plures literis Graecis, Chaldaicis, et Arabicis insudavit. Omnia illic invisit philosophorum loca ac studia, imo et ipsum oraculum solis quod Aesculapius sibi olim construxerat. In quo, abstemio cuidam humilimus servivit ut sub illo abdita sciret philosophiae secreta. Inveniens tandem quod longo quaesierat labore, in Italiam et Galliam est reversus.

[a] Script. ill. Britann. catal. ii. 24 p. 124, Basle 1559 folio.

The source of this passage is manifestly the following chapter in the *Secretum Secretorum*, otherwise known as the *Liber Moralium de Regimine Principum*, and vulgarly ascribed to Aristotle. I quote from the manuscript in the library of Corpus Christi College, Oxford, cod. cxlix. f. 4, adding in the margin a collation of the small Paris edition of 1520, fol. v.

Various Readings.

[b] Iohannes qui transtulit [c] librum istum filius Patricii, linguarum interpretator peritissimus et fidelissimus, inquit, Non

[b] Ioannes.
[c] istum librum.

APPEND. I.

reliqui locum [d] nec templum, in quibus philosophi [e] consueverunt componere et [f] reponere sua opera [g] secreta [h] quod non [i] visitavi; nec aliquem peritissimum quem credidi [k] habere aliquam noticiam de scripturis [l] philosophicis quem non [m] exquisivi: quousque veni ad oraculum solis, quod [n] construxerat Esculapides [o] pro se. In quo inveni quemdam virum solitarium abstinentem, [p] studentem in philosophia peritissimum, [q] ingenio excellentissimum, cui me humiliavi in quantum potui, servivi [r] diligenter, et supplicavi devote ut mihi ostenderet secreta scripta illius oraculi: qui [s] mihi libenter tradidit. [t] Et inter [u] cetera [x] desideratum opus inveni, propter quod ad [y] illum locum iveram, et tempore longissimo [z] laboraveram. Quo habito [a] ad propria cum gaudio remeavi. Inde referens [b] gracias multis modis creatori, et ad peticionem regis illustrissimi laboravi: [c] studens [*inter lin.*, vel studiis] et transtuli primo ipsum de lingua Greca in [d] Caldeam, [e] et de hac in Arabicam. In primis [f] igitur, sicut inveni in isto codice, transtuli librum [g] peritissimum Aristotelis, in quo [h] libro respondetur ad [i] peticionem regis Alexandri sub hac forma.

[d] neque.
[e] consueverint.
[f] deponere.
[g] *praet.* et.
[h] que.
[i] visitaverim.
[k] aliquem habere.
[l] physicis.
[m] exquisiverim.
[n] construxit.
[o] perses.
[p] *deest.*
[q] ing. exc. *desunt.*
[r] *ins.* et.
[s] *deest.*
[t] *deest.*
[u] quod.
[x] opus desid.
[y] locum illum.
[z] laboravi.
[a] cum gaudio ad propria.
[b] grates multimodas.
[c] studui.
[d] romanam.
[e] *pro* et de hac. deinde.
[f] enim.
[g] peritissimi.
[h] *deest.*
[i] reg. Alex. pet.

I have been directed to this passage by a remark of [k] Anthony à Wood that 'the said John, whether Scotus, or Erigena, or Patricius (for by all those names he is written by authors), was one of great learning in his time, and much respected by kings for his parts. Roger Bacon, a great critic in authors, gives him by the name of Patricius, the character of *a most skilful and faithful interpretor of the tongues*, and to whose memory we are indebted for some true copies of certain works of Aristotle.' Wood then translates from the Corpus manuscript the passage, which I have given above in the original, and which he supposed to be by Roger Bacon because the glosses in the volume are ascribed to him. The extract however is taken not from the glosses, but from the text itself; a text which might as well have been quoted from one of the printed editions, so that Roger Bacon's name should not have been introduced into the matter at all. As it is, Bacon has been treated for centuries as the author of a fiction of which, so far as I can trace, the proper credit

[k] Hist. and antiqq. of the univ. of Oxf. i. 39, Oxford 1792 quarto.

belongs to Bale. [l] Fabricius in fact long ago found this out: 'Baleus hanc versionem libri de regimine principum male tribuit Ioanni Scoto Erigenae;' [1] the real John was a Spaniard.

APPEND. I, II.

[l] Biblioth. Graec. 3. 284, ed. G. C. Harles, Hamburg 1783 quarto.

II. Excursus on the Later History of John Scotus.

The statement that John Scotus retired into England after the death of Charles the Bald has been the subject of much discussion, and, as usually happens, the dispute has been complicated by a good deal of what is no real evidence, and by much confusion of the real and the false. The following extracts will put the reader in possession of the materials on which to form an opinion with respect to at least an important section of the enquiry.[2]

1. [m] Bishop Asser of Sherborne says that king Alfred

> legatos ultra mare ad Galliam magistros acquirere direxit, indeque [n] advocavit Grimbaldum sacerdotem et monachum, venerabilem videlicet virum, cantatorem optimum, et omni modo ecclesiasticis disciplinis et in divina scriptura eruditissimum, et omnibus bonis moribus ornatum; Iohannem quoque aeque presbyterum et monachum, acerrimi ingenii virum, et in omnibus disciplinis literatoriae artis eruditissimum, et in multis aliis artibus artificiosum; quorum doctrina regis ingenium multum dilatatum est et eos magna potestate ditavit et honoravit.

[m] De reb. gest. Aelfr., Mon. hist. Brit. 1. 487 B; 1848 folio.

[n] *ed.* advocarit.

This record stands between the years 884 and 886, but in a digression of a general character relating more or less to Alfred's whole reign.[3] Florence of Worcester, in quoting the passage, placed it as early as 872, and the only fact

[1] Gale also, in the Testimonia prefixed to his edition of the De divisione naturae, lays the mistake to Bale's charge, but without detecting its source.

[2] [Since this book was first published William of Malmesbury's Gesta regum has been reëdited by bishop Stubbs, 1889, and Asser's Life of King Alfred by Mr. W. H. Stevenson, Oxford, 1904.]

[3] [Bishop Stubbs, pref. to William of Malmesbury's Gesta regum, 2 p. xlv., gives evidence to show that Grimbald came to England from Flanders not earlier than 892; but Mr. Stevenson, Asser 308 sq., points out that Grimbald was not an uncommon name at his monastery of Saint Bertin, so that it is not certain that the two persons are the same.]

APPEND. II.

that we can presume as to its real date is that it probably refers to the state of peace subsequent to the treaty of Wedmore in 878. Afterwards, under the date of 886, occurs the famous passage describing the quarrel that arose at Oxford between Grimbald and his companions who had come there with him, and the old scholastics of the town. It was natural to suppose that these companions included that John already mentioned; and such is the inference drawn in the Hyde annals, a. 886, according to which, [o] *anno secundo adventus sancti Grimbaldi in Angliam, incepta est universitas Oxoniae, . . . legentibus . . . Grimbaldo* and others, the list ending with *in geometria et astronomia docente Ioanne monacho et collega sancti Grimbaldi.* Since, however, the passage in Asser relating to Oxford is known to be a modern interpolation, and since the Book of Hyde is a production not earlier than Edward the Third's reign, the evidence on this head may be wisely ignored. It is only necessary to add that one certain witness to the connexion shown by the passage first quoted from Asser, remains in king Alfred's preface to his translation of saint Gregory's *Pastoral Care,* which he says he learned [p] *of Plegmund my archbishop, and of Asser my bishop, and of Grimbold my mass-priest, and of John my mass-priest.*

[o] Lib. monast. de Hyda 41, ed. E. Edwards, 1866.

[p] T. Wright, Biogr. Brit. liter., A.-S. per., 400; 1842.

2. At a long interval from the mention of the arrival of the two scholars, and in what is [q] regarded as a quite distinct section of his book, Asser relates, a. 887, Alfred's foundation of the monastery of Athelney, and [r] describes its first abbat:

[q] Mon. hist. Brit. I., pref., pp. 78 sq.

[r] Pp. 493 C–494 E.

> Primitus Iohannem presbyterum monachum, scilicet Ealdsaxonem genere, abbatem constituit; deinde ultramarinos presbyteros quosdam et diaconos; ex quibus, cum nec adhuc tantum numerum quantum vellet haberet, comparavit etiam quamplurimos eiusdem gentis Gallicae, ex quibus quosdam infantes in eodem monasterio edoceri imperavit et subsequenti tempore ad monachicum habitum sublevari.

Asser proceeds to relate the attempted murder of abbat John by the servants of two Gaulish monks in the house.

They waylaid him in church, and fell upon him with swords so that he nearly died. In regard to this passage it may be argued from the specification *scilicet Ealdsaxonem genere*[4] that the author is introducing a new person whom he wishes to distinguish from the John already mentioned; at any rate Asser's words do not necessarily identify John the Saxon with John the comrade of Grimbald. It is, however, commonly held that [s] the latter inference has a predominant probability. The two stories we find repeated by [t] Florence of Worcester without any attempt at combining them.

APPEND. II.

[s] Gfrörer, Kirchengeschichte 3. 938.

[t] Chron., a. 872, 887, Mon. hist. Brit. 1. 557 E, 563 A.

3. Hitherto we have had no mention of John Scotus. It is evident that he may be the John whose name is associated with that of Grimbald; but it is impossible that he be John the Saxon. To combine the three was first attempted in the spurious compilation,—'undoubtedly a monkish forgery,' as it is described by [u] sir Thomas Duffus Hardy,—which goes under the name of abbat Ingulf of Croyland. Its author invents a mode of reconciling the different nationalities by making John not an Old Saxon, but simply summoned from Saxony.

[u] Descr. Catal. of materials, &c., 2. 61; 1865.

[x] Hinc sanctum Grimbaldum, artis musicae peritissimum et in divinis scripturis eruditissimum, evocatum e Francia, suo novo monasterio quod Wintoniae construxerat praefecit in abbatem. Similiter de veteri Saxonia Iohannem, cognomine Scotum, acerrimi ingenii philosophum, ad se alliciens, Adelingiae monasterii sui constituit praelatum. Ambo isti doctores literatissimi, sacerdotes gradu et professione monachi sanctissimi erant.

[x] Descr. comp., Rer. Anglic. script. post Bed. 870, ed. Savile, Frankfort 1601 folio.

The forger has merely confused Asser by importing into his narrative the name of John Scotus, which he knew, evidently, from the story long before made popular by William of Malmesbury.

[4] *Ealdsaxo* means a Saxon of continental Saxony as distinguished from a Saxon of England. Gregory the Second, when recommending saint Boniface to his future converts, addressed the letter 'universo populo provinciae Altsaxonum,' Jaffé, Biblioth. Rer. Germ. 3. 81; and Asser himself elsewhere mentions 'regionem antiquorum Saxonum quod Saxonice dicitur Ealdseaxum,' p. 484 A.

APPEND. II.

y lib. ii. 122 pp. 189 sq., ed. T. D. Hardy.
z lib. v. 240 pp. 392 sq., ed. Hamilton.

4. This story is told by William in three separate works, in the y *Gesta Regum*, the z *Gesta Pontificum*, and in a letter addressed to his friend Peter. The second of these accounts also rëappears, nearly word for word, in what is known as the *Second Chronicle* of Simeon of Durham; but this has no claim to be regarded as an independent authority.[5] Of William's three narratives, that contained in the epistle to Peter, which is entirely occupied with the subject of John Scotus, is the most complete, and I give it here as printed by Gale, *e cod. Thuaneo ms.*, among the Testimonia prefixed to his edition of the *De Divisione Naturae.*[6] From the point in the course of this letter, at which William's other works introduce the narrative about John Scotus and thenceforward run parallel with it, I give at the foot of the page a collation of them as well.

Petro suo Willelmus suus divinae philosophiae participium.

Fraternae dilectioni morem, frater amantisime, geris, quod me tam ardua consultatione dignaris. Est enim praesumtio caritatis, quod me tanto muneri non imparem arbitraris. Praecipis enim ut mittam in litteras, unde Ioannes Scottus oriundus, ubi defunctus fuerit, quem auctorem libri, qui περὶ φύσεων vocatur, communis opinio consentit: simulque, quia de libro illo sinister rumor aspersit, brevi scripto elucidem, quae potissimum fidei videantur adversari catholicae. Et primum quidem ut puto probe faciam si promte expediam, quia me talium rerum veritas non lateat: alterum vero, ut hominem orbi Latino merito scientiae notissimum, diuque vita et invidia defunctum, in ius vocem, altius est quam vires meae spirare audeant. Nam et ego sponte refugio summorum virorum

[5] The passage is not reprinted in the edition of Simeon in the Monumenta historica Britannica: see vol. i. 684 note b. It may be read in Twysden's Historiae Anglicanae Scriptores decem 148 sq., 1652 folio [and in T. Arnold's edition of Simeon's Works, 2. 115–117; 1885]. On the character of the Second Chronicle see the preface to the Monumenta, p. 88, and Hardy's Descriptive Catalogue, 2. 174 sqq.

[6] [It is also found in the Royal MS. append. 85 f. 25 b in the British Museum, which was written in the eleventh or twelfth century and is certainly not autograph, as is asserted in the index to Hamilton's edition of the Gesta pontificum, 531 b. In the first edition of this book I printed a collation of this manuscript, but the text has since been published from it by Stubbs in his preface to the Gesta regum, 1. pp. cxliii–cxlvi.]

laboribus insidiari, quia, ut quidam ait, *Improbe facit qui in alieno libro ingeniosus est.* Quapropter pene fuit ut iussis tam imperiosis essem contrarius, nisi iamdudum constitisset animo, quod vobis in omnibus deferrem, ut parenti gratissimo, in his etiam quae onerarent frontem, quae essent pudoris mei periculo. APPEND. II.

Ioannes igitur cognomento Scottus opinantes quod eius gentis fuerit indigena, erroris ipse arguit, qui se Heruligenam in titulo Hierarchiae inscribit. Fuit autem gens Herulorum quondam potentissima in Pannonia, quam a Longobardis pene deletam eorundem prodit historia. Hic,[7] relicta patria, Franciam ad Carolum Calvum venit, a quo magna dignatione susceptus, familiarium partium habebatur; transigebatque cum eo (ut alias dixi [8]) tam seria quam ioca, individuusque comes tam mensae quam [9] cubiculi erat : nec [10] unquam inter eos fuit dissidium, quia miraculo scientiae eius rex captus, adversus magistrum quamvis ira praeproperum, nec dicto insurgere vellet. Regis ergo rogatu Hierarchiam Dionysii de Graeco in Latinum de verbo verbum [11] transtulit : quo fit ut vix intelligatur Latina [12], quae volubilitate magis Graeca quam positione construitur nostra,[13] composuit et [14] librum quem περὶ φύσεων μερισμοῦ,[15] id est, de naturae divisione, titulavit propter quarundam perplexarum quaestionum solutionem [16] bene utilem si tamen ignoscatur ei in quibusdam,[17] quibus [18] a Latinorum tramite deviavit, dum in Graecos nimium [19]

[7] At this point the other narratives begin. The following is the text of the Gesta pontificum with which I collate that of the Gesta regum : Huius tempore venit Angliam [*G R* Hoc tempore creditur fuisse] Iohannes Scottus, vir perspicacis ingenii et multae facundiae, qui dudum relicta patria [*G R* dudum increpantibus undique bellorum fragoribus in] Frantiam ad Karolum Calvum transierat. A quo magna, &c. The Gesta regum proceeds at once to the sentence beginning in the text of the Epistle with the words *Regis ergo* [G R *cuius* ; G P *Caroli ergo*] *rogatu*.

[8] G P omit *ut alias dixi*.

[9] G P *et mensae et*.

[10] The rest of this sentence is wanting in the Gesta pontificum, which contain instead the famous stories about the Scot and the sot, and the little fishes and the fat clerks.

[11] G R and G P *Dionysii Areopagitae in Latinum de Graeco, verbum e verbo*.

[12] G P add *littera*.

[13] G R omit *quo fit* to *nostra*.

[14] G R and G P *etiam*.

[15] G P *Perifision merimnoi*.

[16] G R *propter perplexitatem necessariarum quaestionum solvendam* ; G P *propter perplexitatem quarundam quaestionum solvendam*.

[17] G R *aliquibus*.

[18] G R prefix *in*.

[19] G R and G P *acriter*.

APPEND. II.

oculos intendit.[20] Fuit multae lectionis et curiosae, acris sed inelegantis, ut dixi, ad interpretandum scientiae ; quod eum (ut verbis Anastasii Romanae ecclesiae bibliothecarii loquar) non egísse aliam ob causam existimo, nisi quia, cum esset humilis spiritu, non praesumsit verbi proprietatem deserere, ne aliquo modo a sensus veritate decideret. Doctus ad invidiam, ut Graecorum pedissequus, qui multa quae non recipiant aures Latinae, libris suis asperserit : quae non ignorans quam invidiosa lectoribus essent, vel sub persona collocutoris sui, vel sub pallio Graecorum occulebat. Quapropter [21] et haereticus putatus est, et scripsit [22] contra eum quidam Florus. Sunt enim [23] in libro περὶ φύσεων [24] perplurima quae multorum aestimatione,[25] a fide catholica [26] exorbitare [27] videantur. Huius opinionis [28] cognoscitur fuisse [29] Nicolaus papa, qui ait in epistola ad Carolum, *Relatum est apostolatui nostro quod opus beati Dionysii Areopagitae, quod de divinis nominibus vel coelestibus ordinibus, Graeco descripsit eloquio, quidam* [30] *vester Iohannes genere Scottus nuper in Latinum transtulerit ; quod iuxta morem nobis mitti, et nostro debuit iudicio* [31] *approbari, praesertim cum idem Ioannes, licet multae scientiae esse praedicetur, olim non sane sapere in quibusdam frequenti rumore diceretur.*[32] *Itaque* [33] *quod hactenus omissum est, vestra industria suppleat, et nobis praefatum opus sine ulla cunctatione mittat.* Propter hanc ergo infamiam, ut [34] credo, taeduit eum Franciae, venitque Angliam [35] ad regem Aelfredum, cuius munificentia illectus, et

[20] After *intendit* the Gesta regum go on directly with *Succedentibus annis munificentia Elfredi allectus, venit Angliam, et apud monasterium nostrum a pueris quos docebat graphiis, ut fertur, perforatus, etiam martyr aestimatus est : quod sub ambiguo ad iniuriam sanctae animae non dixerim, cum celebrem eius memoriam sepulchrum in sinistro latere altaris et epitaphii prodant versus, scabri quidem et moderni temporis lima carentes, sed ab antiquo non adeo deformes.* The verses follow. The Gesta pontificum omit the passage *Fuit multae* to *occulebat*, but from that point agree closely with the text of the Epistola.

[21] G P *quare.*

[22] For *et scripsit*, G P *scripsitque.*

[23] After *enim* G P insert *revera.*

[24] G P *perifision.*

[25] For *multorum aestimatione*, G P *nisi diligenter discutiantur.*

[26] G P *catholicorum.*

[27] G P *abhorrentia.*

[28] G P insert *particeps.*

[29] G P *fuisse cognoscitur.*

[30] So G P as quoted by Gale : Hamilton's edition by error has *quidem.*

[31] G P *iuditio debuit.*

[32] G P *dicatur.*

[33] G P omit this sentence.

[34] G P omit *ut.*

[35] G P omit *Angliam.*

magisterio eius, ut ex scriptis eius[36] intellexi, sublimis, Malmesburiae[37] resedit. Ubi post aliquot annos a pueris quos docebat, graphiis perfossus,[38] animam exuit tormento gravi et acerbo; ut dum iniquitas valida et manus infirma saepe frustraretur, et saepe impeteret, amaram mortem obiret. Iacuit aliquandiu[39] in ecclesia illa,[40] quae fuerat infandae caedis conscia; sed ubi divinus favor multis noctibus super eum lucem indulsit igneam, admoniti monachi in maiorem eum[41] transtulerunt ecclesiam, et ad sinistram altaris positum,[42] his praedicaverunt versibus martyrem:[43] APPEND. II.

Conditus hoc[44] tumulo, sanctus sophista Ioannes,
Qui ditatus erat vivens iam[45] dogmate miro,
Martyrio tandem meruit conscendere coelum,
Quo semper regnant cuncti per secula sancti.[46]

Sed et Anastasius de insigni sanctitate adhuc viventem collaudat his verbis ad Carolum.

[*Here follows an extract from Anastasius the librarian, to which William adds :*]

Alternant ergo de laudibus eius et infamia diversa scripta, quamvis iampridem laudes praeponderaverint. Tantum artifici valuit eloquentia ut magisterio eius manus dederit omnis Gallia. Verum si qui maiorem audaciam anhelant, ut synodus quae tempore Nicolai papae secundi Turonis congregata est, non in eum sed in scripta eius duriorem sententiam praecipitant. Sunt ergo haec fere quae controversiam pariunt.

5. This is the account of John Scotus's end which was received throughout the middle ages. The little that

36 G P *regis.*

37 G P *Melduni.*

38 G P *foratus.*

39 G P here insert *inhonora sepultura.*

40 G P *in beati Laurentii ecclesia.*

41 For *in maiorem eum*, G P *eum in maiorem.* [In the archetype of G P, preserved at Magdalen College, Oxford, cod. 172 p. 185, *eum* is inserted above the line.]

42 G P *ponentes* [in the Magdalen MS. corrected from *positum*].

43 For *his praedicaverunt versibus martyrem*, G P *his martirium eius versibus praedicaverunt.*

44 G P *Conditur hoc*; G R *Clauditur in.*

45 G R and G P *iam vivens.*

46 The last two lines are in the Gesta regum as follow:

Martyrio tandem Christi conscendere regnum
Quo, meruit, regnant sancti per secula cuncti.

In the Gesta pontificum:

Martyrio tandem Christi conscendere regnum
Quo, meruit, regnant cuncti per secula sancti.

Here the two narratives end, so far as the Scot is concerned.

APPEND. II.

[a] Spec. histor. xxv. 42.

[b] Chron. xlvi script. Cisterc. 114.

[a] Vincent of Beauvais, to take but a single instance, says about him, is all derived, including the epitaph, through the channel of [b] Helinand, from William of Malmesbury. William has, in common with Asser, just three points, (*a*) that John was a learned man, (*b*) that he was invited from Gaul by king Alfred, and (*c*) that he taught in England; in other words exactly what Asser relates about John the companion of Grimbald, with the exception of the notice that he was priest and monk: it has nothing corresponding to what he says of John the Saxon. Apart from the question of nationality, the latter was made abbat of Athelney, and his life was attempted by the servants of two Gaulish brethren of the monastery; whereas John the Scot, according to William of Malmesbury, went not to Athelney but to Malmesbury; he was not abbat, simply a teacher; was not wounded at the instigation of monks, but was actually killed by the boys whom he taught. The only point in common between the two is the name John.[47]

[c] Hist. univ. Paris. 2. 443.

6. With the epitaph quoted by William as commemorating this *sanctus sophista Ioannes*, we may connect a notice which is contained in a chronicle referred to by [c] du Boulay as the *Historia a Roberto Rege ad Mortem Philippi I*:—

In dialectica hi potentes extiterunt sophistae, Ioannes qui eandem artem sophisticam vocalem esse disseruit, Robertus Parisiacensis, Rocelinus Compendiensis, Arnulphus Laudunensis. Hi Ioannis fuerunt sectatores qui etiam quamplure habuerunt auditores.

[d] De la phil. scol. I. 174 sq.; Hist. de la phil. scol. I. 244–247.

[d] M. Hauréau rejects the comparison with the Malmesbury inscription, but he is in the meshes of the old snare about John the Saxon. His caution in refusing to apply the inscription as a help to explain the Paris chronicle will be respected; but when he urges on other grounds that

[47] [Mr. Stevenson observes, intr. to Asser, p. cxii. n. 2, that bishop Stubbs 'has, by one of his rare lapses, confounded Malmesbury's account of John the Scot with that of John the Old Saxon in the Life' by Asser; but he has not detected the source of this confusion in Ingulf.]

the Johannes 'sophista' of the latter is identical with John Scotus, we are entitled to use this conversely as evidence for the credibility of William of Malmesbury's account. M. Hauréau's identification has since received powerful support from the arguments of [e] Dr. von Prantl;[48] and if their conclusion be accepted, it is surely reasonable to claim this John Scotus 'the Sophist' as the same person with his contemporary John the Sophist, whose epitaph William records; especially when the latter, no doubt repeating an old tradition of the monastery, expressly identifies *this* sophist with the Scot.[49] The extract in du Boulay is therefore a piece of evidence that converges with those in the preceding paragraphs to one centre. We may or may not believe all that William says, but this we may affirm, that his narrative is self-consistent and intelligible, and that it is incompatible with, and contradictory to, the whole concoction with which the false Ingulf has entrapped our modern critics.[50]

[e] Gesch. der Logik im Abendl. 2. 20–31 [22–33].

7. Mabillon and others have objected that John Scotus could hardly have visited England so late as after the year 880. But there is no reason, because he is known to have gone to France before 847, to conclude that he must have been born before 815. We may fairly presume that the young Scot came to the Frankish court when he was between twenty and thirty: he can hardly have been born much later than 825, but he may have been born as early as 815. But even should we accept an earlier date for John's birth, it does not follow as a matter of course that [f] 'since, according to Asser's account, he must have

[f] Huber 117.

[48] I have since read the objections of Dr. Deutsch, Peter Abälard 100 n. 3, which, though undoubtedly of weight, appear to me to depend too much upon considerations as to the character and contents of a chronicle which we know in fact only through du Boulay.

[49] [See however Mr. Stevenson's note to Asser, 335, where the sophist is identified with 'Johannes se wisa,' whose burial at Malmesbury seems to be recorded later than 1020.]

[50] [Most of the foreign scholars who have discussed this subject have ignorantly treated Ingulf as a genuine authority: so Gfrörer 3. 938, and the biographers of John Scotus, Staudenmaier i. 120, 137, 140, Huber 115 sq., Christlieb 51. In the first edition of this book I dealt at some length with their various criticisms.]

APPEND. II.

gone to England as late as 884, he must have been called by Alfred at an age when one can look forward to little or no future activity as a teacher,' and when he could hardly have had much inclination to change his country and enter upon new surroundings. Setting aside the fact that Asser's notice, if indeed it refers to John Scotus, is not placed under any particular date, it is evident that one cannot assert the impossibility of a man's working power lasting until or beyond his seventieth year. At the same time there is no positive ground for excluding the alternative date for John Scotus's birth, which would make him fifty-three in 878 or fifty-nine in 884.

[g] Christlieb 43, 45; Huber 111, 118.

8. Another question arises about John's ecclesiastical position. Here we must note that William of Malmesbury makes no mention of him as anything but a plain teacher. It is true that Staudenmaier, whose conclusion on this head is repeated by the [g] later biographers, insists that William's John was abbat; but the only reason he can give is that the historian relates the destruction of John's tomb in connexion with Warin de Liro's sacrilegious treatment of past abbats of Malmesbury. The passage is as follows:

Gest. pontif. v. 265 p. 421.

[h] Huic [Turoldo] substitutus est Warinus de Lira monachus. . . . Is, cum primum ad abbatiam venit, antecessorum facta parvipendens, tipo quodam et nausia sanctorum corporum ferebatur. Ossa denique sanctae memoriae Meildulfi et ceterorum qui, olim ibi abbates posteaque in pluribus locis antistites, ob reverentiam patroni sui Aldhelmi se in loco tumulatum iri iussissent, quos antiquitas veneranda in duobus lapideis crateris ex utraque parte altaris, dispositis inter cuiusque ossa ligneis intervallis, reverenter statuerat; haec, inquam, omnia pariter conglobata, velut acervum ruderum, velut reliquias vilium mancipiorum, ecclesiae foribus alienavit. Et ne quid impudentiae deesset, etiam sanctum Iohannem Scottum, quem pene pari quo sanctum Aldhelmum veneratione monachi colebant, extulit. Hos igitur omnes in extremo angulo basilicae sancti Michahelis, quam ipse dilatari et exaltari iusserat, inconsiderate occuli lapidibusque praecludi praecepit.

Reading this extract carefully, it should appear that we

have just as much right to infer that William is carefully distinguishing between John and the abbats, as that he intends to identify them. It was Ingulf who first made John Scotus an abbat.

Returning then to the John, the companion of Grimbald, in the narrative of Asser, we find him described as 'priest and monk.' Now all we know about John Scotus's clerical position from contemporary evidence is negative. Prudentius of Troyes, indeed, ridicules him for setting himself up as a disputant in a grave controversy, being [i] *barbarum et nullis ecclesiasticae dignitatis gradibus insignitum.* But it is plain that his not holding any rank in the church, which is all the words need mean, does not involve the consequence that John was not ordained. [k] Abailard, for instance, had, in all probability, only minor orders until he was in middle life; yet he afterwards was appointed abbat. It is no doubt the fact that John is never styled 'priest' or 'monk' by any of his opponents: nor does he ever describe himself as such, after the prevailing fashion, in his writings. But the latter circumstance, at least, has a very natural explanation: he desired to rank as a philosopher, not as a priest. This is indeed, as [l] Dr. Reuter observes, a salient characteristic of his position in the history of Christian thought; and it would be readily accepted by his enemies as a confirmation of their judgement that he was a heretic. We are not to expect that they would signalise, if they were aware of, his priestly calling.

[i] De praedest. ii. Migne 115. 1043 A.

[k] v. supra, p. 126.

[l] Gesch. der relig. Aufklärung im Mittelalter 1. 51.

9. On the other hand, it is a mistake to infer from the title of *martyr*, as to which even William of Malmesbury, [m] in one of his accounts, expressed a doubt, an identification with another John Scotus, who held a place in the martyrologies, at least in England and France, until 1586, when I presume it was discovered that the philosopher was unqualified for the dignity.[51] It is strange that [n] Staudenmaier and others who repeat the statement

[m] supra, p. 278 n. 20.

[n] Pp. 147 sqq.

[51] Thus in André du Saussay's Martyrologium Gallicanum, the name (which is given as *tempore Caroli Calvi*) is relegated to the appendix, vol. 2. 1226, Paris 1637, folio.

APPEND. II.

o Actt. SS. O.s. Bened. 4 (2) 513.

p Adam. Brem. gest. Hammaburg eccl. pontif. iii. 20, 50, Pertz 7. 343, 355.

q Hist. of Lat. Christ. 4. 333.

have not observed o Mabillon's refutation of it. There is no doubt that the martyr who was commemorated on the 14th of November was p John Scotus, bishop of Mecklenburg, who was killed on that day in 1066.[52]

10. Milman attempts to select from the various opinions with regard to John Scotus's retirement into England. q He thinks (*a*) that John fled into England 'under the general denunciation of the church and the pope,' apparently following William of Malmesbury, here disregarding the long interval between John's participation in the Gottschalk controversy and the earliest possible date for his withdrawal from France; (*b*) 'he is said to have taken refuge in Alfred's new university of Oxford.' In a note we read that 'the account of his death is borrowed by Matthew of Westminster from that of a later John the Saxon, who was stabbed by some monks in a quarrel,' which statement is evidently taken directly from Guizot's Cour d'Histoire moderne, 3. 174 sq. (1829). 'The flight to England,' adds Milman, 'does not depend on the truth of that story.' The writer known as Matthew of Westminster however did not borrow his story about John Scotus's death from an account of 'a later John the Saxon,' but took his matter directly from William of Malmesbury.[53] Besides, we have already seen the entire dissimilarity of the stories about John Scotus and John the Saxon.

11. In conclusion, if Asser intends to distinguish John the Old Saxon, the abbat of Athelney, from John the companion of Grimbald, it is possible that the latter is John Scotus. William of Malmesbury may have drawn a

[52] It is curious to notice that Trittenheim dichotomises the Scot. According to him, De Scriptoribus ecclesiasticis, 119 sq., ed. Cologne 1546, quarto, 'Iohannes dictus Erigena' translated the 'Hierarchiam et libros Dionysii' with commentaries, 'et quaedam alia.' 'Johannes Scotus,' on the other hand, p. 115, was a pupil of Bede and a comrade of Alcuin; to him is due the exposition of saint Matthew, 'one book' [*sic*] De divisione naturae, and another book, De officiis humanis; 'alia quoque multa composuit,' adds Trittenheim, 'quae ad notitiam meam non venerunt.'

[53] Why do Milman and Hauréau, Histoire de la Philosophie scolastique 1. 151, and so many others, refer to the so-called Matthew for facts which he only states at second or third hand?

fact or two from what is said about the latter, but his account is altogether irreconcileable with the notice of the Old Saxon. It is the combination of the two persons mentioned by Asser, derived from the spurious authority of Ingulf, that has misled the modern critics, and induced most of them to discredit the narrative of William of Malmesbury, as though it depended upon that late forgery. William's account may therefore be judged by itself, and accepted or rejected just as we may rate the historian's general credibility: there is no reason for excluding these particular passages from that respect which [r] those scholars who know William best are ready to pay to his honest, conscientious labours.[54]

APP. II, III.

[r] cf. Hardy 2. 156, 164.

III. Note on a supposed Theological Exposition by Gerbert.

In Bernard's [s] *Catalogi librorum manuscriptorum Angliae et Hiberniae*, the Bodleian manuscript 2406, now known as Bodl. 343, is described as containing at f. 170 *b* an *Expositio in Canticum Gereberti Papae in Spiritum sanctum.* [t] Oudin by mistake quotes the title as *in Canticum Canticorum.* The [u] *Histoire littéraire de la France* says that Gerbert 'composa un Cantique sur le saint Esprit, qui avec son commentaire faisoit autrefois partie des manuscrits de Thomas Bodlei, sous le nombre 1406. [*sic*] 10,' and the writer speculates as to its date and contents. The manuscript itself, however, at the place indicated, contains, at the end of a volume of Anglo-Saxon homilies, a page filled up in a thirteenth-century hand with glosses upon a sequence for the feast of saint Michael the Archangel, which is known from the Sarum Missal, and of which the authorship is apparently claimed by the glossator for Gerbert.[55] Whether

[s] P. 124, Oxford 1697 folio.

[t] Comment. de script. eccl. 2. 512.

[u] Vol 6. 589; 1742

[54] 'A steady attempt,' says Stubbs in his preface to the Gesta regum, 1 p. x, 'to realise the position of the man and the book has had, in the case of the present Editor, the result of greatly enhancing his appreciation of both.'

[55] [My friend the late Dr. H. M. Bannister informs me that this prose appears in a service-book of Saint Martial's of Limoges written between 988 and 996 in the Bibliothèque nationale at Paris, MS. 1118, and in an Autun troper written between 996 and 1024 in the Bibliothèque de l'Arsenal, MS. 1169. It was widely current before 1050.]

APPEND. III.

also a portion of the glosses themselves is to be regarded as Gerbert's composition, I must leave undecided : certainly the introductory passage proclaims itself to be the work of a commentator. Hitherto the text of the glosses has only been published in M. Olleris's edition of [x] Gerbert's works. The editor gives the following account of it— 'On attribue à Gerbert un cantique sur le saint-Esprit, cantica de s. Spiritu, conservé dans la bibliothèque Bodléienne, et une prose ajoutée au canon de la messe en honneur des anges. . . M. H. O. Coxe n'a pas trouvé le cantique, et il a eu la complaisance de copier lui-même le commentaire suivant.' Since, however, M. Olleris could not identify the *canticum* nor print the glosses without a multitude of grammatical and other mistakes, I have transcribed the text afresh; and I have prefixed the sequence to which it refers, and with the punctuation unaltered, from the edition of the [y] Sarum Missal published at Paris in 1555, folio :—

[x] Pp. 568–572.

[y] Sanctorale, cl. lix.

Ad celebres rex celice laudes cuncta.
Pangat nunc canora caterva symphonia.
Odas atque solvat concio tibi nostra.
Cum iam renovatur Michaelis inclyta valde festa.
Per quem letabunda perornatur machina mundi tota.
Novies distincta : pneumatum sunt agmina per te facta.
Sed cum vis facis hec flammea ceu rutilantia sydera.
Inter primeva sunt hec nam creata tua, cum simus nos ultima factura : sed imago tua.
Theologa categorizent symbola nobis hec ter tripartita : per privata officia.
Plebs angelica, phalanx et archangelica principans turma, virtus uranica, ac potestas almiphonia
Dominantia numina, divinaque subsellia cherubin etherea ac seraphim ignicoma.
Vos o Michael celi satrapa, Gabrielque vera dans verbi nuncia.
Atque Raphael vite vernula : conferte nos inter paradisicolas.
Per quos patris cuncta complentur mandata que dat.
Eiusdem sophia : compar quoque pneuma : una permanens in usia.
Cui estis administrancia deo milia milium sacra.
Vices per bis quinas bis atque quingenta dena.

Centena millena assistunt in aula ad quam rex ovem centesimam. APPEND. III.
Verbigena drachmamque decimam vestra duxit super algamatha.
Vos per ethera nos per rura devia.
Pars electa armonie vota demus hyperlyrica cithara.
Ut post bella Michaelis inclyta.
Nostra deo sint accepta auream circa aram thymiamata.
Quo in celesti iam gloria.
Condecantemus alleluia.

[z] AD [56] CELEBRES, REX CELICE. In primo notandum quod hoc nomen *canticum* plures habet acceptiones. Dicitur enim canticum applausus qui fit ad laudem alicuius divitis, dicitur etiam canticum leticia de terrenis habita. Dicitur etiam canticum cantus quem fecerunt filii Israel quando rediere de servitute, id est, cantica canticorum. Dicitur etiam canticum omne tale gaudium quod fit de supercelestibus; et secundum hoc hic accipitur hoc nomen *canticum*. Sed querendum est, quis sit autor huius opusculi quod pre manibus habemus, que materia, que utilitas, que intencio, cui parti philosophie pertineat; ita dico si alicui pertineat. Autor huius operis fuit papa Girebertus, qui, cum mirabilis esset in omnibus actibus suis, precipue verborum et sententiarum erat perturbator. Materia est spiritus increatus et spiritus creatus. Spiritus increatus est ipse deus. Spiritus creati sunt, ut angeli et archangeli. Intentio est excitare animos auditorum ad laudes supercelestium. Utilitas est celestes laudes exercere. Sed videtur quod nulli parti filosophie pertineat, sed potius teologie. *Theos* idem est quod *deus; logos, sermo*. Theologia in duas dividitur species: in ypoteticam et apoteticam. Ypotetica est sermo trinitatis ad unitatem; et econtra apotetica est sermo de supercelestibus, ut de angelis et archangelis. Autor iste primo utitur apologo, quasi proemio tocius operis sequentis, captando benivolentiam ipsius creatoris, antequam incipiat opusculum suum; dicens, O REX. Sed quia hoc nomen convenit regibus nostris, adjunxit CELICE: et est composita diccio ab hoc nomine *celum* et hoc nomine *cunctos*, quasi *cunctos celi*. CUNCTA CATERVA NOSTRA, tam homines quam angeli. CLANGAT, id est

[z] Cod. Bodl. 343 f. 170 *b*.

[56] The initial is not filled in.

APPEND. III.

quodam clamore clamet; vel PANGAT, id est *cantet.* CUM NOSTRA SIMPHONIA, id est *cum clara simphonia;* vel CANORA SIMPHONIA, id est *sonora simphonia. Simphonia* dicitur a *sin.* quod est *con,* et *phonos,* quod est *sonus.* Sic *triumphus* dicitur quasi *trium phonos,* quasi *vox trium sonorum;* et potest dici illa concordantia que est mentis et oris, vel illa que est inter ipsos sonos plurium personarum. AD CELEBRES LAUDES, id est *ad festivas laudes;* ATQUE NOSTRA CONTIO, idem est quod *nostra caterva.* SOLVAT, id est quasi *debitum reddat.* ODAS, id est *laudes;* unde dicitur in alio loco *palinodas,* id est *duplices laudes,* a *palin,* quod est *duplex,* et *odas,* quod est *laudes.* Deinde redit ad propositum. Sed notandum quod hec festivitas non fit de pugna que fuit inter Michaelem et draconem, sed de miraculo quod contigit in Gargano monte. CUM IAM FESTA MICHAELIS VALDE INCLITA. *Cleos* idem est quod *gloria;* inde *inclita,* id est *valde gloriosa,* quia *in* ponitur ibi augmentative et non privative. *Renovantur,* id est *annuatim quadam renovatione celebrantur.* PER QUEM, id est *Michaelem,* PERORNANTUR, id est *bene ornantur,* LETABUNDA; id est *illa festa sunt quadam leticia habundanter celebranda.* TOTA MACHINA, id est *cum omni illo quod continetur sub firmamento.* MUNDI: Mundus dicitur *microcosmos,* a *micros* [57] quod est *longus,* et *cosmus* quod est *mundus;* id est *celestis mundus qui semper durat:* vel *microcosmus* dicitur a *micros,* quod est *brevis,* et *cosmus, mundus,* id est *minor mundus,* id est *ipse homo.* Quia sicut mundus constat ex quatuor elementis, sic homo ex quatuor humoribus qui concordant quatuor elementis. Sanguis enim concordat aeri, quia calidus est et humidus sicut aer. Colera concordat igni, quia calida est et sieca sicut ignis. Flegma concordat aque, quia frigidus et humidus sicut aqua. Melancolia concordat tèrre, quia frigida et sicca sicut terra. Vel mundus dicitur a *mundiori* parte mundane machine, id est a firmamento. AGMINA, id est *consortia.* NEUPMATUM: hoc nomen *neupma* duplicem habet acceptionem et potest cognosci in scripcione. Quando sic scribitur, *pneuma,*[58] per *p* et *n,* tunc portendit *iubilum,* qui fit post antiphonam; qui iubilus non potest exprimi corde et ore, sed sono tantum: et fit ad designandum celeste gaudium, quod non potest corde nec ore, pre

[57] Originally written *mecrocosmus a mecro;* but dotted for correction, and with an *i* in each case above the *e.* [58] Cod. *pnema.*

eius magnitudine, sed sono et intellectu tantum, demonstrari. Quando vero scribitur sic, *mneuma*, per *m* et *n*, vel sic per *n* tantum, *neuma*, tunc significat *spiritum*, secundum quod hic accipitur. *Mneumatum*, id est *spirituum*. *Per te*, id est deum. *Facta:* improprie utitur hic nomine *facta*, quia aliud est *fieri* et aliud est *creari*. *Fieri* enim est facere aliquid ex traduce,[59] id est ex preiacenti materia; *creari* est aliquid facere sine preiacenti materia, quia deus creavit angelos sine preiacenti materia et cotidie potest creare sic cotidie novas animas. DISTINCTA, id est *divisa*. NOVIES, id est *per novem*, id quia novem sunt ordines angelorum. NAM CUM VIS, id est *quando vis*. FACIS HEC FLAMMEA, id est *accipere igneam formam* quando nunciant hominibus: vel aliter, *flammea*, propter ardorem caritatis quem predicant hominibus. INTER PRIMEVA SUNT HEC: hic ostendit quod quodammodo antiquiores sunt angeli quam homines; ut dicitur, *In principio creavit deus celum et terram*. Per *celum* intellege *celestia*, per *terram*, *terrestria*; et sic quemdam primatum habent angeli ante homines. CUM NOS SIMUS CREATA, id est *procreata:* et notandum quod aliud est *creari* et aliud *procreari* et aliud *fieri*: *creari*, ut superius dictum est, facere aliquid sine traduce; ut cum materiali fit et forma, et cum forma fit et materia: *procreari*, id est *procul creari*, ut ex nuce lignum: et *fieri* pertinet ad ipsum hominem et proprie.[60] Unde dicitur homo *facitor*. ULTIMA CREATA, id est *procreata*. SED YMAGO TUA: aliud est imago et aliud similitudo. *Ymago*, quia nos imitamur deum in iusticia et sapientia et prudentia, quia ipse iustus est et iusticia; sic et nos iusti per iusticiam, etc.: *similitudo* est in lineamentis corporis. CATHEGORIZENT, id est *predicent*. THEOLOGA: quid sint theologa, superius dictum est. SIMBOLA: *symbolum* est communis proporcio vel comproporcio, ut in convivio; et dicitur a *sin*, quod est *con*, et *bolos*, quid est *proporcio*. Et dicitur simbolum dominica oratio, scilicet *Credo* et *Quicunque vult*, ubi est colleccio plurium articulorum Christiane fidei; vel simbolum dicitur ministeria[61] angelorum, quia sepe ea que ministrant et alia significant. TER TRIPARTITA, id APPEND. II.

[59] Apparently the original reading was *ratione*, which has been corrected into *traduce*. M. Olleris has *divisione*, but this the manuscript will not allow.

[60] This word is miswritten in the MS.

[61] Cod. *mist'ia*.

APPEND. III.

est *per novenarium disposita.* PER PRIVATA OFICIA, id est *per propria oficia.* Notandum quod hoc nomen *officium*, quando scribitur per unum *f*, tunc idem est quod *servire;* et quando scribitur per duo *f*, tunc idem est quod *nocere*, unde officit ei. PLEBS ANGELICA PHALANX ET ARCHANGELICA. Sed quia autor in sequentibus facit mentionem de *gerarchia*, ideo videndum est, quid sit gerarchia, et unde dicatur, et in quot species dividatur. *Gerarchia* est legitimum nature rationalis dominium; et videndum est quid quodlibet membrum in hac descriptione positivum [62] operetur. *Dominium* dicitur, quia in nullo loco est gerarchia nisi ubi sit dominium nature. *Rationalis* dicitur, quia bruta animalia habent dominium super alia, que non dicitur gerarchia, quia ibi non contingit, nec eis convenit. *Legitimum* dicitur, quia reges et huiusmodi habent potestatem super alios, et hic forsitan non habent secundum legem legitime. *Gerarchia* dicitur a *gere*, quod est *sacer*, et *archos*, quod est *principatus* sive *dominium.* Gerarchia in tres dividitur species; in supercelestem, celestem, et subcelestem. Supercelestis est summe trinitatis ypostasica monarchia : *ypostasion* vel *ypostasis* idem est quod *substancia.* Celestis gerarchia est ordo angelicus, qui dividitur in novem ordines. Subcelestis gerarchia, id est apostolatus et archiepiscopatus et episcopatus, et huiusmodi. De supercelesti gerarchia fecit autor inferius mentionem quando dixit, PER VOS PATRIS CUNCTA COMPLENTUR MANDATA QUE DAT. De celesti gerarchia fecit mencionem quando dixit, VOS PER ETHRA. De subcelesti gerarchia fecit mentionem quando dixit, VOS PER RURA. Sed quia dixi superius quod celestis gerarchia dividitur in novem ordines, ideo videndum est, quid sit *ordo*, et qualiter dicatur ordo, et in quot species habeat dividi. Ordo angelicus, ut ait magister Johannes Scotus, est *caractere theophanie simplicis et non imaginarie et reciproce uniformis spirituum insignita multitudo. Multitudo* aponitur quia ordo angelicus non potest esse nisi ubi sit multitudo. *Spirituum* apponitur ad differenciam hominum, quia sepe homines contemplantur ipsum creatorem per ipsas creaturas. *Insignita caractere*, id est quodammodo sigillata signo. *Caracter* idem est quod *signum:* et ideo caractere apponitur [63] theophanie. *Theophania* dicitur a *theos*, quod est *deus*, et *phanos*, quod est

[62] Cod. p^{9}*ītū*.
[63] This word is repeated also after *theophanie.*

visio sive *contemplacio:* unde *theophania,* id est *visio dei.* *Simplicis* apponitur ad differenciam composite contemplationis; quia quedam contemplacio est simplex, quedam composita. Composita contemplacio etiam in duas dividitur species, in contemplacionem secundum sensum, et contemplacionem secundum racionem. Secundum sensum fit contemplacio, quando contemplamur deum creatorem per ipsas creaturas; scilicet per solem et per lunam et per stellas, et huiusmodi. Secundum racionem fit contemplacio, quando nos contemplamur coherenciam inter materiam et formam; unde scimus quod abunivit materiam et formam: et hec etiam contemplacio est composita, quia quedam compositio est materiei ad formam et forme ad materiam. Simplex contemplacio est que fit inter angelos, quia contemplantur deum prout est in maiestate sua, et non per aliquas creaturas. *Non imaginarie* apponitur, quia quedam contemplacio est imaginaria, quedam non. Imaginaria est illa contemplacio. APPEND. IV.

. . [*The rest is wanting.*]

IV. NOTE ON THE PRECURSORS OF NOMINALISM.

DR. VON PRANTL was the first to [a] explain how John Scotus could be reckoned as the founder of nominalism, and to define the limits within which this ascription could be justly claimed. M. Hauréau had indeed previously interpreted the reference in du Boulay's chronicle [b] already quoted, in the same sense as Dr. von Prantl; but he was led to this conclusion by the help of a passage in the [c] *De Divisione Naturae* which he misread in an inexplicable manner. John Scotus omits *grammar* and *rhetoric* from the class of strict sciences, because *non de rerum natura tractare videntur, sed vel de regulis humanae vocis,* &c. [d] M. Hauréau understood this of *dialectic* and *rhetoric,* and thus actually inverted the real significance of John's position in respect of the function of logic.

[a] Gesch. der Logik im Abendlande 2. 24–37 [26–39]; cf. pp. 76 sq. [78].

[b] supra, p. 280.

[c] lib. v. 4 p. 229, ed. Gale.

[d] De la phil. scol. I. 174 sq.; cf. pp. 118 sq.: Hist. de la phil. scol. I. 246 sq.; cf. pp. 44 sq.

Some commentaries attributed to Rabanus Maurus discover so close an affinity to John Scotus's logical theory

APPEND. IV.

[e] l. c., p. 38.

[f] Ouvr. inéd. d'Abél., intr., pp. lxxxii–lxxxv notes; append., pp. 619. sq.
[g] De la phil. scol. I. 136–142; hist. I. 188–196.
[h] Abélard I. 314 n.
[i] l. c., pp. 42 [41] sq.

[k] Pp. 59 [60] sq.

[l] Append., pp. 647, 657–669.

as to suggest that they are immediately derived from him.[64] [e] Dr. von Prantl, therefore, maintains that if genuine they can only be placed among Rabanus's latest productions, and thinks that they have been wrongly attributed to him. Dr. von Prantl's reasoning does not appear quite decisive, and the conflict asserted to exist between the views contained in these glosses and in Rabanus's other works is not perhaps so substantial as to be fatal to their common authorship. Nor is it impossible that the former are independent of John Scotus's influence.

The next symptom of a nominalistic tendency appears in certain glosses in a Paris manuscript (now numbered Fonds Latin 12,949), of which specimens are given by [f] Cousin and [g] M. Hauréau. The latter, and before him [h] Charles de Rémusat, claimed their authorship for Heric of Auxerre. Dr. von Prantl, on the contrary, [i] considers the major part to be by another, though contemporary, writer. But he is in error in saying that the codex itself gives a different author to one section of the glosses in dispute (those on the *Isagoge*). It is true that the line,

Iepa hunc scripsi glossans utcunque libellum,

stands in f. 52 *b*, but *Iepa*, which Cousin had noted with a query, is a later insertion, written over an erasure with room for about seven letters. This point was ascertained for me by the kindness of M. G. Saige.[65]

The logical summary found in a metrical version in another Paris manuscript, to which [k] Dr. von Prantl refers, can hardly be admitted as material for the history of the time before Roscelin, until we are better informed about its date. Cousin, who prints these hexameters, [l] describes them as of the tenth or eleventh century, and hints the possibility that they were dedicated to a man who died

[64] Extracts are printed by Victor Cousin, Ouvrages inédits d'Abélard, intr., pp. xvii, lxxviii, lxxix, and app., pp. 613 sqq.

[65] [Subsequent examination has shown that the word is not *Iepa* but *Icpa*, and it has been suggested that the letters are the beginning of a Greek name, possibly ICPAHΛ. See L. Traube, in Neues Archiv, 18 (1892) 105, and E. K. Rand, Johannes Scottus, p. 84; 1906.]

in 1107. We cannot, then, be sure that they are anterior to Berengar of Tours, or even to Roscelin.[66] APPEND. V.

V. Excursus on a supposed Anticipation of Saint Anselm.

1. SAINT ANSELM has been generally regarded as the first writer in the course of the middle ages who put forth a formal argument in favour of the existence of a God. Dr. von Prantl, however, claims the priority for William abbat of Hirschau, and infers from the fact that William is known to have been in correspondence with Anselm, at a date anterior to the publication of his *Monologium*, that the latter derived from William the idea of framing the argument in question. Dr. von Prantl's hypothesis is contained in a paper printed in the first part of the *Sitzungsberichte der königlich Bayerischen Akademie der Wissenschaften zu München* for 1861; and his results on the particular point which I have stated are given in full in his m *Geschichte der Logik im Abendlande*. The two arguments, however, are quite different, William's resting upon the design and orderly government of the universe, while Anselm's proceeds from the existence of relative good to that of an absolute Good; a reasoning which he subsequently exchanged for the simple proof that the being of God is implied in our thought of him. Besides, it is clear that the link sought to be established is at best a plausible conjecture: we have no evidence that the two men corresponded on the subject. Still it would be a sufficiently interesting coïncidence if we could show that the first attempt among Christians during the middle ages to prove the existence of a God suggested itself to these two contemporaries.

m vol. 2. 83 sqq.

2. Dr. von Prantl thinks that the argument was derived from Constantine the Carthaginian, afterwards a monk of

[66] [Further evidence of a nominalistic tendency is found in an anonymous commentary on the Categories attributed to saint Augustin, which is preserved in a tenth-century manuscript at Vienna. See Prantl, 2. 44 sq., in the second edition.]

APPEND. V. Monte Cassino, who died before the year 1072, and who had acquired it, together with the physical learning for which he was famous, during a scholar's life of near forty years in the Mohammadan east. It is certain that the 'argument from design' appears in Arabian philosophy a century earlier,[67] but there is no hint that it occurs in Constantine's writings. William, it is added, was in Rome in 1075, a few years after Constantine's death, and may then have made the acquaintance with the latter's books, which his own productions show him to have turned to good account. We have, however, no information as to the date at which William himself wrote the treatise; and an examination of the book will soon show us that it is really later by a couple of generations than its supposed date, and has only by a blunder been attributed to William of Hirschau.

3. The little volume of *Philosophicarum et astronomicarum Institutionum Guilielmi Hirsaugiensis olim Abbatis Libri tres*, which was printed at Basle in 1531, quarto, is textually the same book with the *Περὶ Διδάξεων sive Elementorum Philosophiae Libri IV*, printed among the works of [n] Bede in the Basle edition of 1563, folio. This *Περὶ Διδάξεων*, however, although it is actually quoted as Bede's, and as a possible source of an opinion of Abailard, by so accomplished a scholar as [o] Charles de Rémusat, has been generally recognised as the work of William of Conches, certainly since the publication of [p] Oudin's *Commentarius de Scriptoribus Ecclesiasticis*, and of the [q] twelfth volume of the *Histoire littéraire de la France*. As long ago too as 1838 Charles Jourdain pointed out that the work in question existed also in the twentieth volume of the Lyons *Maxima Bibliotheca Patrum* the title *De Philosophia Mundi*, and under the name of Honorius of Autun;[68] and neither

[n] Opp. 2. 311-343.

[o] Abélard 2. 223 n., 307 n.

[p] vol. 2. 1230.

[q] pp. 457-462.

[67] See the passage cited in the Sitzungsberichte, ubi supra, p. 20, n. 55, from Dieterici, Die Naturanschauung und Naturphilosophie der Araber im zehnten Jahrhundert, p. 162; Berlin 1861.

[68] Jourdain claims the discovery in the Notices et Extraits des Manuscrits, 20 (2) 43, n. 1. The Histoire littéraire impartially describes the same work under the head both of Honorius (vol. 12. 178 sq.) and of William of Conches. M. Hauréau, Singularités his-

Jourdain nor any other writer (previous to Dr. von Prantl) who had mastered the facts, with reference either to the *Περὶ Διδάξεων* or to the *De Philosophia Mundi*, had any doubt that their, or rather its, authorship belonged to William of Conches. Nor is manuscript authority wanting: it is found with his name, to take a single example, in a manuscript of [r] University college, Oxford, nr vi p. 389, under the title *Philosophiae Compendium*. The fact, however, that the contrary hypothesis is supported by a scholar so distinguished as Dr. von Prantl, even though he has failed to observe the identity to which I draw attention, seems to justify a renewed examination of the question, in order to ascertain whether the book already thrice obscured under the names of William of Hirschau, Bede, and Honorius of Autun, could by any possibility be by the first of the three. I shall cite the three recensions as 'Hirschau,' 'Bede,' and 'Honorius,' premising that when I speak of identity I do not exclude divergences, often wide divergences, extending not only to the interchange of unimportant words, inflexions, &c., but also to the order of words in a sentence, and even further; such, in fact, as one is prepared to find in works so carelessly reproduced as those of a medieval writer, not of the first rank, would naturally be.

APPEND. V.

[r] Coxe, Catal. I. 3 a.

4. In each edition the work bears a different title, and in 'Hirschau' it is divided into three books, while the others have four. The manner in which quotations are introduced throws a curious light on the processes by which writings were adapted to different authors. The writer of the manuscript from which 'Bede' is printed, intentionally effaced what occurred to him as incompatible with the age of the presumed author.[69] He

toriques et littéraires 243, supposes that the original ascription of the work to Honorius by the editors of the Maxima Bibliotheca Patrum was a mere guess: this is improbable.

[69] M. Haureau, Singularités 238, has not noticed this peculiarity, and charges the editors with inadvertence in admitting a work as Bede's which contained references to later writers. As a matter of fact M. Hauréau takes his quotations from Honorius.

APPEND. V.

[s] Hon. i. 21. [t] Bede 2. 314. [u] Hon. iv. 20; Bede 2. 340. [v] v. Prantl, Sitzungsberichte, ubi supra, p. 14 n. 35.

has, however, gone carelessly enough to work. After, for instance, changing [s] *Constantini*, which refers to the eleventh-century Carthaginian, into the plural [t] *philosophorum*, he has left *secundum eum* immediately after: and he suppresses the name [u] Johannitius, which indicates Honain ben-Isaac, a Jewish physician of the ninth century, while he leaves untouched the reference to this writer's [v] medical treatise known as the *Isagoge*, possibly through an ignorant confusion with the work of Porphyry which exercised so signal an influence on the learning of the middle ages. Yet the citations of classical and subclassical authors, some perhaps more obscure than Constantine, are as a rule correctly given. In one instance a reference has been obscured in 'Hirschau,' apparently in the interest of his authorship; it is suggested in 'Bede' and is given fully in 'Honorius':

[w] Lib. i. 15.

HONORIUS p. 999 A.	BEDE 313.	HIRSCHAU 8.
[w] Cuius expositionem si quis quaerat, in glossulis nostris super Platonem inveniat.	Cuius exponere, si quis quaerat in aliis nostris scriptis inveniet.	Cuics expositio alias est.

[x] p. 77 (lib. iv. 30, Hon. p. 1019 c). [y] ib. iv. 29–34. [z] capp. 35, 36.

5. Of the three recensions of the treatise, 'Bede' is by far the worst;[70] as a rule it is inferior to 'Hirschau,' while the latter is perhaps slightly inferior to 'Honorius.' None of the three editions, however, is complete. 'Hirschau' breaks off first, just [x] after having introduced the subject of the soul, whereas 'Bede' proceeds from that point for a page and a-half further and 'Honorius' a few sentences further still, the additional matter consisting of nearly twelve chapters in 'Honorius.' This continuation is partly occupied with [y] the soul, which, however, is only cursorily treated. The author then passes on to [z] the ages of man and their characteristics, and thus arrives at the subject

[70] In a few cases it contains good readings, as in p. 316, where *commixtio* and *coniunctio* stand in an inverted order from that in Hirschau 18, thus rendering Dr. von Prantl's emendation, p. 15 n. 39, superfluous.

of [a] education. These last four chapters occur also in 'Hirschau,' but at the beginning of the book, under the title of *Aliquot philosophicae Sententiae*. In the closing sentence of 'Bede,' which also concludes the section prefixed to 'Hirschau,' we read the following scheme of the order in which learning should proceed:

APPEND. V.

[a] capp. 37–41.

[b] Ordo vero discendi talis est ut quia per eloquentiam omnis fit doctrina, prius instruamur [71] in eloquentia cuius sunt tres partes. . . . Initiandi ergo sumus in grammatica, deinde in dialectica, postea in rhetorica. Quibus instructi et ut armis muniti, ad studium philosophiae debemus accedere, cuius hic est ordo, ut prius in quadrivio, . . deinde in divina pagina, quippe ut per cognitionem creaturae ad cognitionem creatoris perveniamus.

[b] Bede 343; Honorius 1020 E, F.

This in reality opens a new division of the author's whole subject; for, as 'Honorius' continues, *quoniam in omni doctrina grammatica praecedit*, it is his design to treat of grammar and, we may presume, of the other studies in their order. [c] *Sed quoniam*, he concludes, *de propositis supra . . sectantes compendia diximus, ut animus lectoris alacrior ad caetera accedat, hic quartae partis longitudinem terminemus*.

[c] p. 1020 G.

6. Hitherto I have assumed nothing with respect to the authorship of the work in question, although at the outset its absence from the list of William of Hirschau's works given by [d] Trittenheim, who had peculiar qualifications for knowing about the monastery of Hirschau, may seem to raise a presumption against its accuracy; not to speak of the surprise with which we find that most orthodox abbat credited with a theology betraying only too evidently the influence of Abailard. I have limited myself to showing the identity of the three works, which had previously, as I thought, escaped detection. In this I have since learned that I was mistaken. The fact was pointed out by Dr. Valentin Rose in the *Literarische Centralblatt* so long ago as [e] June 16, 1861. The sequel was interesting. [f] Dr. von Prantl in a reply professed with remarkable courage his

[d] De script. eccl. 148.

[e] nr xxiv. col. 396.

[f] ibid., nr xxvii. col. 444, July 6.

[71] I correct from Hirschau.

APPEND. VI.

familiarity with the phenomenon of which Dr. Rose charitably supposed him to be ignorant. It was difficult to believe that a man could describe at length a treatise which he knew to be textually identical with another work printed under a different name, and purporting to belong to a different century, without a word of allusion to the latter.[72] Dr. von Prantl added that he proposed to prove from further evidence that William of Conches had *used* the work of William of Hirschau. [In his second edition Dr. von Prantl suppressed the pages about William of Hirschau, and transplanted something from them into his account of William of Conches, pp. 127 sq.]

The blunder, however, has survived, and Dr. von Prantl's theory was treated seriously by professor Wagenmann in the [g] *Goettingischen gelehren Anzeigen* for 1865 and by [h] Dr. Reuter.

[g] p. 1371 sqq.
[h] Gesch. der relig. Aufklärung im Mittelalter 1. 285 n. 4.

VI. EXCURSUS ON THE WRITINGS OF WILLIAM OF CONCHES.

1. THE number and attribution of the works of William of Conches have always been a standing puzzle in medieval bibliography. It has already been stated that the book which forms the subject of the preceding excursus, and which has been confused among the editions of the venerable Bede, William of Hirschau, and Honorius of Autun, is now generally ascribed to William of Conches. But it will be best to assume nothing about it until we have gathered sufficient evidence to warrant a certain conclusion. All William's productions hang so closely together that the proof that one of them is his involves all the rest: and if the following investigation goes over a good deal of ground which has already been covered by previous bibliographers, it does not in all points arrive at the same results as they have done.

2. The book that may serve as a foundation for our inquiry is the *Dialogus de Substantiis physicis ante annos ducentos confectus a Wilhelmo aneponymo philosopho*, pub-

[72] The work is described under William of Hirschau, Gesch. der Logik 2. 83–85; and under William of Conches, 2. 127 sq.

lished in octavo at Strasburg in 1567.[73] The editor, G. Gratarolo, a Basle physician, who discovered the book in Italy, apparently at Padua, took it (as appears from the title-page) to be a composition of the fourteenth century: the internal evidence, however, is decisive on this head. The dialogue is held between the author and a certain *dux Normannorum et comes Andegavensium*, a style by which only two persons could possibly be designated. One is Geoffrey the Fair, the husband of the empress Matilda, from the year 1143 or 1144, until his resignation of the duchy in 1150[74]; the other is his son, our king Henry the Second, from the latter date until his accession to the English throne. Henry, however, is excluded[75] by the [i] mention of the education of the duke's sons, since he only married in 1152. It may be observed that the belief that Henry was intended, combined with the mistaken inference from [k] John of Salisbury that William was about the year 1138 a teacher at Paris, plainly originated the fable which we read in [l] Oudin, that Henry the Second *olim in curia regis Franciae enutritus et litteris in Parisiensi academia initiatus sub Guillelmo fuerat.* The same passage which shows that Henry was not the interlocutor in the dialogue helps to fix the composition of the work within narrower limits. *In te tamen*, says William, *et in filiis tuis aliquid spei consistit; quos non, ut alii, ludo alearum sed studio literarum, tenera aetate imbuisti: cuius odorem diu servabunt.* The dialogue was written therefore some time, probably some years, before Henry was of an age to be knighted, in 1149; and we shall not be far wrong if we place it about the year 1145.

APPEND. VI.

[i] praef., pp. 3 sq.

[k] Metalog. ii. 10 p. 804.

[l] Comm. de script. eccl. 2. 1231.

[73] This at least is the date that appears in the two copies of this very rare work that I have used, one in the Stadtbibliothek at Zurich and the other in the Bodleian library. It has been repeatedly given as 1566; see the Histoire littéraire de la France 12. 464, and Hauréau, Singularités historiques et littéraires 246.

[74] [See C. H. Haskins, Norman institutions 130; 1918.]

[75] This, I see, is observed by M. Hauréau, Singularités, 232 sq., who also notices the source of the statement that Henry was William's pupil at Paris; although I do not find that he disputes the story that John of Salisbury heard the latter there. Compare, however, above, p. 181 n. 6.

APPEND. VI.

3. The author describes himself at the opening of the sixth book:

m pp. 210 sq.

[m] Ea autem quae a magistris, dux serenissime, multotiens audivi, atque omnia quae recordatione usque ad meditationem memoriae commendavi, et ut firmius verba retinerem (quae irrevocabilia volant) stili officio designavi, et iam quae per viginti annos et eo amplius alios docui, adhuc vix plene et perfecte intelligo, vixque intellecta propriis et apertis verbis explicare valeo: et unde mihi tam hebes ingenium, tam modica memoria, tam imperfecta eloquentia? an quia in patria vervecum [76] crassoque sub äere Nordmanniae sum natus? alios affirmare audio non solum minima, sed etiam maxima, quae nunquam a magistris audierunt, per se intellexisse, nihilque esse tam inusitatum, tam difficile, quod si sibi ostensum fuerit, statim non intelligant atque expedite alios doceant.

The passage therefore tells us what William's native country was,—and we have only to add the concordant testimony of [n] all the known manuscripts of the work, which bear any title, to identify the place as a matter of certainty with Conches;—it tells us also the author's age, as having been a teacher since about 1120–1125, besides some other particulars about him to which we shall return hereafter.

n cf. Hauréau, Sing. hist. et litt. 246.

4. Walter of Saint Victor in his polemic against the opinions of Abailard, Gilbert of La Porrée, Peter Lombard, and Peter of Poitiers, written about the year 1180, expressly mentions, in his fourth book, William of Conches as having adopted the Epicurean doctrine of atoms: *Quae forte Democritus cum Epicuro suo atomos vocat. Inde Willielmus de Conchis ex atomorum, id est, minutissimorum corporum, concretione fieri omnia* The passage occurs among the

[76] The edition reads *Vernecum* for *vervecum*, as though it were a proper name: the reference, however, to Juvenal, Sat. x. 49, 50, is obvious,

Summos posse viros et magna exempta daturos
Vervecum in patria crassoque sub äere nasci.

M. Hauréau had the right reading in his manuscript, and translates 'la patrie des béliers,' p. 231. [It is found also in the Arundel MS. 377 f. 131 in the British Museum.]

copious extracts from Walter given by [o] du Boulay, and the reference is to the dialogue i. pp. 25 sqq.: APPEND. VI. [o] Hist. univ. Paris 2. 659; cf. p. 743.

Sunt igitur in unoquoque corpore minima, quae simul iuncta unum magnum constituunt. Haec a nobis dicuntur elementa.

The interlocutor here objects, *Ut mihi videtur, in sententiam Epicureorum furtim relaberis, qui dixerunt mundum constare ex atomis:* to which the author replies,

Nulla est tam falsa secta quae non habeat aliquid veri admixtum; sed tamen illud admixtione cuiusdam falsi obfuscatur. In hoc vero quod dixerunt Epicurei, mundum constare ex atomis, vere dixerunt: sed in hoc quod dixerunt, illas atomos sine principio fuisse, et diversas, permagnum et magne volitasse, deinde in quatuor magna corpora coactas fuisse, fabula est.[77]

5. In most manuscripts the work is called the *Dragmaticon Philosophiae*, 'dragmaticon' being a synonym of 'dialogus.' [p] Ducange quotes a sentence describing it as 'a work conducted by means of question and answer,' and [q] Dr. Schaarschmidt, who does not profess to have seen the dialogue with which we are concerned, rightly corrects the title into *Dramaticon*. William, as it happens, himself explains the source of the title: [p] Gloss. s. v. [q] Joh. Saresb. 77 n. 1.

[r] Sed quia, similitudo orationis mater est satietatis, satietas fastidii, nostram orationem dragmatice distinguemus. Tu igitur, dux serenissime, interroga: philosophus sine nomine ad interrogata respondeat. [r] Praef., pp. 7 sq.

The published book was edited from a comparison of two manuscripts, one of which bore yet another title. The preface is headed 'Authoris Wilhelmi in suam *Secundariam* praefatio: nam hoc eius nomen fuit et haec libri

[77] Dr. Reuter verifies Walter's citation in that work which is the subject of the foregoing excursus, and which, for reasons that will appear immediately, I shall cite simply as the *Philosophia*. He says, Geschichte der religiösen Aufklärung in Mittelalter 2. 309 n. 28, that it occurs there in book i. ch. 21 (Honorius, pp. 999 G—1001 C); but in that passage there appears neither the reference to Epicurus nor the word 'atoms,' while both are found in the dialogue. The authors of the Histoire littéraire de la France were unable to find the reference in *any* of William's writings, vol. 12. 456.

APPEND. VI.

inscriptio, ut ex antiquo exemplari constat.' Possibly therefore the printed title *De Substantiis physicis* is an insertion of the editor. From the *Secundaria* we pass to a fourth title, namely, *Secunda Philosophia*, which appears in two manuscripts of the Staats- und Hof-Bibliothek at Munich. A fifth designation is found in a manuscript, nr xcv, of Corpus Christi college, Oxford, dating, according to Coxe's Catalogue, from the thirteenth century: 'Gulielmi de Conchis, alias Shelley, *Universalis Philosophiae Libri III.* per modum dialogi,' &c. Sixthly, in one of the Digby manuscripts in the Bodleian library, nr cvii, the work is entitled *Summa Magistri Willelmi de Conchis super naturalibus Quaestionibus et Responsionibus*, &c. In the following pages I shall cite the book as the *Dragmaticon*.

6. We have now to inquire in what way it bears upon the other works of its author. Here its testimony is precise and unambiguous. It is a new edition of a former work entitled *Philosophia*, modified in concession, as would appear, to certain complaints on the score of heresy; and the passages thus altered or expunged are to be found in that work which in the preceding excursus was recognised under the different names of Bede, William of Hirschau, and Honorius of Autun. It is also known that [s] objections were raised to a work of William of Conches, entitled the *Philosophia*, which objections are substantially the same with those enumerated in the following paragraph of the *Dragmaticon*. I have inserted in the margin the corresponding places in the *Philosophia*.

[s] v. supra, p. 110.

After announcing the subject of his treatise William proceeds:

[t] Est tamen de eadem materia libellus noster qui *Philosophia* inscribitur, quem in iuventute nostra imperfectum, utpote imperfecti, composuimus; in quo veris falsa admiscuimus, multaque necessaria praetermisimus. Est igitur nostrum consilium, quae in eo vera sunt hic apponere, falsa damnare, praetermissa supplere. Falsa vero illa quae contra fidem catholicam nobis in eo videntur esse, ante auspicium dictionis, nominatim dam-

[t] Praef., pp. 5 sq.

nare dignum duximus. Unde omnes qui illum habent libellum rogamus quatenus ea nobiscum damnent et exterminent. Verba enim non faciunt haereticum sed defensio. APPEND. VI.

[u] In illo diximus, in divinitate esse tria, potentiam, sapientiam, voluntatem: potentiam esse patrem, sapientiam esse filium, voluntatem spiritum sanctum. Sed quod dictum est de potentia quod sit pater, de voluntate quod sit spiritus sanctus, etsi possit quoquo modo defendi, tamen quia nec in evangelio nec in scripturis sanctorum patrum illud invenimus, propter illud apostoli damnamus, *Prophanas novitates verborum devita.* De sapientia quod sit filius, non damnamus, cum apostolus dicat Christum dei virtutem et dei sapientiam.

[u] cf. Philos. i. 6 (Bed. opp. 2. 312; Honorius, Max. bibl. patr. 20. 998 A).

[v] In eodem conati sumus ostendere quomodo pater genuit filium, illudque quod dictum est, *Generationem eius quis ennarabit?* ideo esse dictum quod sit difficile, non quia impossibile: hoc iterum damnamus, et aliis damnandum esse pronunciamus.

[v] cf. ibid., cap. 8 (Bed. 312 sq.; Hon. 998 B, C).

[w] Cum in eodem de creatione primi hominis loqueremur, diximus deum non ex Adam vel ex costa foeminam fecisse, sed ex limo qui coniunctus illi fuerat, ex quo viri corpus plasmaverat; ideoque translatitie esse dictum quod ex costa Adae facta sit foemina: hoc iterum damnamus damnandumque iudicamus, sanctae et divinae scripturae consentientes quae ait quod immisso sopore in Adam tulit deus unam costam de costis eius, ex qua materialiter corpus mulieris plasmavit.

[w] cf. ibid., cap. 23 (Bed. p. 318; Hon. p. 1002 D).

Haec sunt igitur quae in illo libro damnamus.

7. There is therefore no doubt that the early work of William of Conches to which reference is here made, is that same production which forms the subject of the preceding excursus and which, according to [x] Dr. Wagenmann, actually bears the specific title of *Philosophia Willihelmi Magistri* in a Stuttgart manuscript.[78] Of this the *Dragmaticon* is in fact a new edition, rewritten and cast in the form of a dialogue. The substantial agreement of the two has been already pointed out by professor Karl Werner in the [y] *Sitzungsberichte der philosophisch-historischen Classe*

[x] Goetting. gel. Anz, 1865, p. 1371.

[y] vol. 75. 309 sqq.; 1873.

[78] The work also, according to M. Hauréau, Singularités, 237 sq., bears the name of William of Conches in two Paris manuscripts; the titles added to the name, *Tractatus Philosophiae* and *Philosophia* are modern. M. Hauréau, pp. 240 sq., takes the same argument as I have done from the Dragmaticon.

APPEND. VI.

der kaiserlichen Akademie der Wissenschaften at Vienna. This point being established it remains to apply the evidence thus obtained to clear up the other disputed facts in William's bibliography. One of these may be cursorily mentioned before we attack more serious difficulties.

[z] Append. v. § 4.

In the *Philosophia* i. 15, quoted [z] above, there is a reference to *glossulis nostris super Platonem*, a reference which [a] Cousin easily discovered in a Paris manuscript of which he gives extracts. Knowing however only the 'Honorius' recension of the *Philosophia*, which is in its turn referred to as 'nostra *Philosophia*,' in the glosses in question, Cousin supposed that the latter were by Honorius of Autun, because he failed to observe the identity of the presumed Honorius with that printed as Bede; which latter [b] he rightly attributed to William of Conches.[79] The glosses themselves are on the *Timaeus*, and abound in silent allusions to William's other works. Some of the definitions, those, for instance, of [c] *philosophia* and *ingenium*, occur verbally in the [d] *Philosophia* or the [e] *Dragmaticon*;[80] but I am inclined to think that the quotation from the *Dragmaticon* is only apparent, and really comes from the *Philosophia* which [f] we have seen to be a fragment as we now have it. If this be so the *Philosophia* and the *Timaeus* glosses may have been written about the same time and naturally contain cross-references.

[a] Ouvr. inéd. d'Abélard. app., 646 sq.

[b] p. 669.

[c] ibid., pp. 649, 651.

[d] lib. i. 1 Bed. 312.

[e] lib. vi. p. 307.

[f] Append. v. § 5.

To this same early date are evidently also assignable a set of annotations on Boëthius's *Consolation of Philosophy*,[81] of which extracts have been printed by [g] Jourdain, and which [h] the editor claims to be the first real Commentary, as distinguished from formal glosses, with the partial exception of that of Bovo of Corvey, devoted to the favourite author of the middle ages.[82]

[g] Not. et extr. des manuscr. 20 (2).

[h] p. 57.

[79] In his later edition, entitled Fragments philosophiques 2. 355, Cousin still only goes so far as to say that the glosses on the Timaeus 'pourraient bien être de Guillaume de Conches.'

[80] See other examples in Hauréau, Singularités, 244.

[81] At least they contain a precise declaration of a doctrine which William may be presumed to have withdrawn with his other impeached errors. See the quotation, above, p. 151, n. 11.

[82] The manuscript which contains the glosses on the Timaeus includes a fragmentary commentary on Pr. cian, which M. Hauréau,

8. Two other works of William of Conches, the *Secunda Philosophia* and the *Tertia Philosophia,* are described in the twelfth volume of the *Histoire littéraire de la France.* They remain in manuscript at Paris; but specimens, some chapters at length, and tables of contents, are printed by [i] Cousin. The first, [k] we are told, is a dialogue on anthropology between a master and a disciple; the second, also a dialogue, is an abridgement of the author's system of cosmography, derived from the *Philosophia.* Had however Cousin been acquainted with the *Dragmaticon* he would probably have suspected that this was the immediate source, and would have found that *D.* stands not for *discipulus* but for *dux,* the duke of Normandy to whom the work is dedicated. Moreover these works are not abridgements at all. The one is a literal transcript of part of the *Dragmaticon,* the other is a set of disconnected extracts from it. The latter is taken from different parts of books ii.—vi., and leaves off just before the point from which the former is transcribed. Of course it is impossible to speak with absolute certainty from Cousin's specimens, but the following details of collation suggest a sufficiently plain inference.[83]

[i] Ouvr. inéd. d'Abélard 670–677; Fragm. phil. 2. 391–400.
[k] Hist. litt. 12. 465.

The *Secunda Philosophia* begins with the words *Dicendum est,* &c., which introduce the section on animals occupying the major part of the sixth book of the [l] *Dragmaticon.* The

[l] pp. 235–312.

pp. 244 sq., conjectures is also by William.

[83] M. Hauréau in his Singularités still clings to the idea of these works being independent productions. I may, however, take leave to doubt whether this distinguished scholar had always the Dragmaticon itself before him. At least it is certain that every reference he makes to the Secunda Philosophia occurs, just as Cousin's do, in the Dragmaticon [e. g. ch. xviii. (Hauréau, p. 252) = Dragm. p. 281; ch. xxx. (Hauréau, p. 252 n. 2) = Dragm. p. 306]: and not in the fourth book of the Philosophia, as M. Hauréau says (p. 241), nor anywhere else in that work. The substance may be there very possibly, though Cousin's excerpts contain much that is definitely not there; but the form is that of a dialogue, and this fact alone decides the point. M. Hauréau speaks (p. 247) of the Dragmaticon as borrowing from the Secunda Philosophia; but when the smaller work is contained *verbatim* (within the limits of scriptural aberration) in the greater, we need not be long in deciding which is the original and which the extract. With regard to the Tertia Philosophia M. Hauréau says little (p. 248), and does not seem to suspect that it is in fact derived from the Dragmaticon.

APPEND. VI.

extracts which Cousin gives represent with trivial variants the identical text of the corresponding passages in the *Dragmaticon*, and the order of the thirty-five chapters is exactly the same. The two copies end with the same words.

The *Tertia Philosophia* contains ten chapters of which Cousin has printed the first. This is simply a set of extracts from the *Dragmaticon*. I take the sentences as they follow. *Mundum . . . extra quem nihil est* will be found in the *Dragmaticon*, ii. p. 41; *Nota quod tempore Martii . . . moritur*, in lib. iv. pp. 123 sq.; *Nota: dicit Constantinus . . . pessima*, in lib. iv. pp. 127 sq.; *Verbi gratia . . . iudica*, in lib. iv. p. 128; *Nota: in autumno . . . periclitantur homines*, on the same page. Chapters ii.—ix. from their headings correspond to passages in the fourth and fifth books of the *Dragmaticon*; chapter x. to something near the beginning of the sixth. The extracts speak for themselves: the *Tertia Philosophia* is nothing more than a note-book of selections from the *Dragmaticon*.

m Prantl. Gesch. der Logik im Abendlande 2. 127 n. 94 (1st ed.); cf. Werner, ubi supra, p. 311.

Such are the [m] 'valuable fragments' from which later scholars have drawn. Beyond insignificant various readings they add nothing to what was already printed in a complete form in 1567.[84] William's original works therefore (excluding his glosses) are now reduced to two: the early *Philosophia* and the corrected edition of the same, the *Dragmaticon*. Is there a third to be added?

9. The literary historians speak of a *Magna de Naturis Philosophia* by William of Conches as having been printed

[84] I have already stated, above § 5, that the title Secunda Philosophia is also borne by the complete Dragmaticon itself. The manuscripts thus entitled Dr. Reuter described as containing an entirely different work from Cousin's Secunda Philosophia, Geschichte der religiösen Aufklärung 2. 309 n. 30. What he quotes however certainly exists in the printed Dragmaticon, and I make no doubt that had Dr. Reuter read the manuscripts further he would have found all Cousin's extracts there, as I have found them in the printed text. Moreover he misread Cousin, Ouvrages inédits d'Abélard, 669, and applied what the latter said of the Tertia Philosophia to the Secunda. Here he was no doubt misled by M. Hauréau, who speaks, p. 241, of part of the Secunda Philosophia being borrowed directly from the Philosophia, book iv. The immediate source is incontestably the Dragmaticon, though the substance may often agree with that of the Philosophia. See preceding note.

in folio, without place or date, about the year 1474. * This is a statement which has grown up by several stages. Josias Simler in his Epitome of Gesner's Bibliotheca, published at Zurich in 1574, says on p. 254 [a] that William

scripsit philosophiam universalem lib. i. De naturis inferiorum, seu philosophiam primam lib. i. De superiorum naturis, seu philosophiam secundam lib. i. Sunt autem duo magna volumina, ante multos annos impressa.

Then [n] Possevinus spoke of a work by William *super Opere sex Dierum*, of which he had seen only the volume beginning with book xix. His description leaves no doubt that the work he mentions is the second volume of Vincent of Beauvais's *Speculum naturale* in the edition, *s. l. aut a.*, presumed to have been printed at Strasburg in 1468 [85] or 1473 (not in that of Nuremberg, assigned to the year 1483, and also in folio). The first page of this volume begins book xix. (after the table of contents) with an extract from William of Conches, headed conspicuously: *De opere sexte diei. Et primo de animalibus. Guillerinus de conchis.* This is the very title which has been constantly repeated as William's by the [o] bibliographers, and which even M. Hauréau [p] once sought to restore to the catalogue of William's writings.[86] In 1722 [q] Casimir Oudin connected the description given by Possevinus with the statement in the Epitome of Gesner.

n Appar. sacer. 1. 701, Cologne 1608, folio.

o cf. Denis, Ann. typogr. supplem. 2. 544 nr 4716, Vienna 1789 quarto; Hain, Repert. bibliograph. 5605, vol. 1 (2) 186 b, Stuttgart 1837.

p De la phil. scol. 1. 285.

q Comm. de script. eccl. antiq. 2. 1229 sq., Leipzig folio.

Scripsit igitur Guillelmus de Conchis *Magnam de naturis Philosophiam*, desumptam ferme verbotenus ex Operibus veterum Ecclesiæ Patrum.

* The remainder of this excursus has been recast in the present edition.

85 It is attributed to Mentelin's press under this date by Robert Proctor, Index to early printed Books, No. 255; 1898 quarto. Both volumes are in the Bodleian library, Auct. Q sub fen. 4, 5.

86 In correcting this mistake (which is repeated by cardinal Pitra, Spicileg. Solesm. 2. 188, Paris 1855 quarto), M. Hauréau has fallen into a new one, in speaking, Singularités 236 sq., of the original as the Speculum historiale, in which what little is said about the sixth day of creation occurs in bk. ii. (misnumbered i.) ch. 38, and bk. xix. (opening with the history of Honorius) does not begin a volume.

APPEND. VI.

It was a book of extracts systematically arranged. But Oudin, too, had only seen the second volume printed without date or place about 1474. The same work manifestly is intended by J. A. Fabricius, when he says of William of Conches:

[r] Biblioth. Lat. med. et inf. aet., i. 1145, Hamburg, 1734.

[r]Prodiit etiam sub tempus nascentis typographiae Philosophia eius maior de naturis creaturarum superiorum, sive super opere sex dierum libri. xxxiii. duobus maioribus in folio voluminibus rarissime obviis, excusisque sine anni nota locive.

[s] vol. 12. 457; cf. vol. 18. 492 (1835).

The authors of the [s] *Histoire littéraire de la France* complicated the matter by erroneously asserting that Fabricius spoke of the book as in three volumes and confused it with the work of Vincent of Beauvais. Fabricius said two volumes, of which the second is beyond doubt the second volume of the *Speculum naturale*. The probable inference is that the first volume of which Possevinus, Fabricius, and the authors of the *Histoire littéraire* were unable to find a copy, was likewise the first volume of the *Speculum*.

[t] Ouvr. inéd. d'Abél., app. 669.

[u] l. c.

[x] Schaarschmidt 76.

10. These last writers state, with Oudin, that the book contained little original matter, being mainly compiled by means of extracts from the fathers. Nevertheless they regard it as the source from which (*a*) the *Philosophia*, (*b*) the *Secunda Philosophia*, and (*c*) the *Tertia Philosophia*, were successively abridged; a statement which has been repeated by [t] Cousin and others. Even the accurate Hauréau, who had the *Dragmaticon* before him, said in the first edition of his [u] *Philosophie scolastique*, that the *Secunda* and *Tertia Philosophia* 'paraissent avoir été faits pour venir à la suite de celui que nous venons de nommer,' the *Magna de Naturis Philosophia*; 'si, toutefois,' he adds, 'ils n'en forment pas une partie.' [x] It has further been asserted that the great work was largely used by Vincent of Beauvais in his *Speculum naturale;* but all the extracts from William which I have met with in it are taken either from the *Philosophia* or the *Dragmaticon*.[87]

[87] For instance in book xxxii. 77, Vincent cites the latter as 'Guilhermus de Conchis' without further specification, and then adds a quotation from the Philosophia as 'Ex libro de natura rerum.'

11. The character of the supposed *Magna de Naturis Philosophia*, as described, is in itself such as to arouse suspicion. For in William's known writings we do not find very many patristic quotations. His authorities are Hippocrates, Plato and Aristotle, Cicero, Pliny, Ptolemy, Galen, Solinus, Macrobius, Boëthius, Constantine, etc.; he draws illustrations from Lucretius, Virgil, Horace, Ovid, Seneca, Juvenal. But engaged as he was in the pursuit of natural philosophy and natural history, he had small occasion to quote the fathers, and his references to them seem to be limited to Augustin, Ambrose, Gregory, and Bede. In fact he expressly declares his independence, as a philosopher, of the fathers. *In eis*, he says, *quae ad fidem catholicam vel ad morum institutionem pertinent, non est fas Bedae vel alicui alii sanctorum patrum* (*citra scripturae sacrae authoritatem*) *contradicere: in eis tamen quae ad philosophiam pertinent, si in aliquo errant, licet diversum affirmare.* This statement occurs in the [y] *Dragmaticon*, a work which we have seen to be scrupulously modified in deference to orthodox objections. It is therefore the less likely that, even before his plain-spoken *Philosophia*, William should have written a great philosophical work chiefly constructed of select passages from the fathers. Besides, if such be the nature of this *Magna Philosophia*, how can it contain the material which he subsequently, *ex hypothesi*, 'abridged,' so as to form the *Philosophia* as we know it? The latter, as I believe on account of this assumed chronological arrangement, the authors of the *Histoire littéraire* designate the *Philosophia minor*, a title, however, which they do not assert to be found in any manuscript or edition of it.[88] I believe further that the entire basis of their theory rests on a misunderstanding of a passage in John of Salisbury, on which I shall comment in the ensuing excursus.

APPEND. VI.

[y] lib. iii. pp. 65 sq.

12. I have spoken of the *Magna de Naturis Philosophia* on the authority of those who profess to have seen the

[88] William excuses the imperfections of this book by the plea that, 'studiis docendi occupati, parum spacii ad scribendum habeamus,' lib. iii. praef. (Bed. 2. 330; Hon., p. 1010 B). This is scarcely the way in which an author would speak of abridgement.

APPEND. VII.

z Hist. litt. 12. 457.

book and who declare that it bears this title [z] 'in most of the manuscripts.' But since writing this and the foregoing excursus I have had the advantage of reading M. Hauréau's admirable criticism contained in the eighth chapter of his *Singularités historiques et littéraires*.[89] He there states positively that no such manuscript exists in France, nor to his knowledge elsewhere. Accordingly he conjectures that the bibliographers mistook some other book, published about the same time, for William of Conches's; and he suggests that the book in question is the *De Universo* of William of Auvergne. The precise identification will not serve, but there can be little doubt—as I think, a confusion with the *Speculum naturale*—that some blunder of this kind originated the whole theory which, it has already appeared, is so difficult to reconcile with the known facts about William of Conches.

VII. Excursus on the interpretation of a place in John of Salisbury's Metalogicus, i. 24 pp. 784 sq.

a vol. 12. 457.

1. William of Conches has been generally regarded as a teacher who abandoned the thorough and honest system of the school of Chartres in order to compete with the shallower and more pretentious masters of his day. The [a] *Histoire littéraire de la France* illustrates this defection by the instance of his work, the *Philosophia*, which it supposes to be an abridgement of a previous book, the very existence of which the preceding excursus has shown to be more than doubtful. 'Ce qui l'engagea,' we are told, 'de composer cet abrégé, ce fut vraisemblement l'envie de se conformer, ou plutôt la nécessité où il se trouva de céder au torrent des philosophes de son temps, qui décrioient la prolixité de leurs prédécesseurs, et se piquoient de donner toute la philosophie en deux ans. Car il est certain par la témoignage de Jean de Sarisbéri, qu'après avoir longtemps résisté à ces

[89] M. Hauréau's essay, I have lately found, is in the main an enlargement of his article on William of Conches in the twenty-second volume of the Nouvelle Biographie générale, pp. 667–673; 1858.

sophistes, il se laissa entraîner par leur exemple, pour ne pas voir déserter son école.' The same statement involves also the character of William's colleague, Richard l'Évêque, and is accordingly repeated under his article in the [b] fourteenth volume of the *Histoire*. It has become the accepted view in regard to William, and is adopted, to give a single instance, in [c] Ritter's *Geschichte der Christlichen Philosophie*. It is therefore the more necessary to subject the hypothesis to a close examination.[90] The part of it, however, concerning the sequence of William's works needs no refutation, since it is directly contradicted by his own [d] statement that he wrote the *Philosophia* in his youth, many years before John of Salisbury came in contact with him.

APPEND. VII.

[b] p. 216.

[c] vol. 3. 395 n. 3.

[d] supra, append. vi. § 6.

2. John of Salisbury's words are as follows :

Ad huius magistri [Bernardi Carnotensis] formam praeceptores mei in grammatica, Gulielmus de Conchis et Richardus cognomento episcopus, officio nunc archidiaconus Constantiensis, vita et conversatione vir bonus, suos discipulos aliquandiu informaverunt. Sed postmodum, ex quo opinio veritati praeiudicium fecit et homines videri quam esse philosophi maluerunt, professoresque artium se totam philosophiam brevius quam triennio aut biennio transfusuros auditoribus pollicebantur, impetu multitudinis imperitae victi, cesserunt. Exinde autem minus temporis et diligentiae in grammaticae studio impensum est, etc.

The language is no doubt ambiguous, and everything hangs on the sense we give to *cesserunt*. We may understand the passage, 'Once they taught well, but after a while they *yielded* to the rush of incompetent rivals *and followed their example* ;' or equally legitimately, 'Once these worthy successors of Bernard handed on his tradition, but after a while, disgusted with the prevalent method of teaching, they *withdrew from the field*.' The words will bear either rendering; but John of Salisbury's other evidence about

[90] The only writer I have found who interprets the passage of John of Salisbury as I do, is M. Léon Maitre, Écoles épiscopales et monastiques 209; but he does not seem to be aware of the difference of opinion that has arisen on the point.

APPEND. VII.

his masters, as well as the incontrovertible language of William of Conches' own writings, can only be reconciled with the second alternative : the first is altogether excluded by the known facts about William and Richard.

3. Taking first the testimony to be drawn from John of Salisbury's writings, we find that Richard l'Évêque remained through life a valued correspondent of his, and [e] was consulted by him on exactly those points of scholarship on which, if Richard's career were as is commonly supposed, John would be the least likely to trust him. William of Conches died before John had become conspicuous in the learned world, but John's recollections of his master are uniformly honourable. [f] He couples William's name with those of Gilbert of La Porrée, Abailard, and others of his most respected teachers, just by virtue of William's steady hostility to the empty-headed 'crammers' of his day. John also speaks of the jealousy which William and his friends excited in the latter; but of their yielding in consequence of it there is not a word.

[e] Schaarschmidt 77, 121.

[f] Metalog. i. 5 p. 745.

4. It is precisely to these envious detractors that William constantly alludes in the prefaces to that *Philosophia* which, according to the *Histoire littéraire*, he condensed in deference to their opinion. The evidence of the prefaces to books i., ii., and iii. bears directly on the point; that of the two former, which I quote, is especially pertinent :

[g] Multos tamen nomen magistri sibi usurpantes, non solum hoc agere sed etiam aliis sic esse agendum iurantes, cognoscimus, nihil quippe de philosophia scientes, aliquid se nescire confiteri erubescentes, sive imperitiae solatium quaerentes, ea quae nesciunt nullius utilitatis minus cautis praedicant.

[g] Philos. i. praef. (Hon. p. 995 F, G).

[h] Quamvis multos ornatum verborum quaerere, paucos veritatem scire [*al.* scientiae] cognoscamus, nihil tamen de multitudine sed de paucorum probitate gloriantes, soli veritati insudamus.

[h] lib. ii. praef. (Hon. p. 1002 H Bed. 319).

Another passage answers the allegation of the *Histoire littéraire* in a curiously exact manner. Speaking of the duties of a teacher, William says :

APPEND. VII.

[i] Sed si amore scientiae ad docendum accesserit, nec propter invidiam doctrinam subtrahet; nec ut aliquid extorqueat, veritatem cognitam fugiet; nec si deficiet multitudo sociorum, desinet; sed ad instructionem sui et aliorum vigil et diligens erit.

[i] lib. iv. 37 (Hon. p. 1020 c, Bed. 342).

These quotations, I repeat, are taken from a work which, we are asked to believe, was shortened in concession to the rage for short and easy methods.

5. At a considerably later date William wrote the *Dragmaticon*, and in this the protests against the fashionable tendency are if possible stronger than in the *Philosophia*. One ironical reference to the author's constitutional dulness and incapacity to understand things after long thought, which his pretentious rivals professed to grasp in a moment, has been [k] already quoted. [l] In another he complains of the way in which the teachers of his time have lost credit among their scholars. Both he says are in fault; for to establish confidence one needs two things, knowledge and uprightness:

[k] supra, append. vi. § 3.

[l] Dragm. praef., pp. 1 sqq.

Quia igitur omnes fere contemporanei nostri sine his duobus officium docendi aggrediuntur, causa sunt quare sibi minus credatur. Discipuli enim culpa non carent, qui relicta Pythagoricae doctrinae forma (qua constitutum erat discipulum septem annis audire et credere, octavo demum anno interrogare), ex quo scholas intrant, antequam sedeant, et interrogant, imo (quod deterius est) iudicant; unius vero anni spacio negligenter studentes, totam sapientiam sibi cessisse putantes, arreptis ab ea panniculis, vento garrulitatis et superbiae pleni, pondere rei vacui abeunt: et cum a suis parentibus vel ab aliis audiuntur, in verbis eorum parum aut nihil utilitatis perpenditur; statimque quod hoc solum a magistris acceperint, creditur unde magistri authoritas minuitur.

6. The words of John of Salisbury, as I construe them, read precisely as an echo of what we now find to have been the consistent attitude towards learning and teaching maintained by William alike in his earliest and in his latest works. It is right to add that I was led to my

interpretation of the passage in dispute, by a comparison of John of Salisbury's different references to William of Conches and Richard l'Évêque, and before I had entered upon the examination of William's own writings. It may be doubted whether the common view which I combat would ever have been suggested, far less accepted, had the historians of medieval literature taken the trouble to acquaint themselves personally with the books they describe.

VIII. Note on Abailard's Masters.

The manuscript of Saint Emmeram's, Ratisbon (now at Munich), from which Pez printed Abailard's *Scito te ipsum* and Rheinwald more recently the same writer's [m] *Sententiae* contains a notice of his biography which, it seems to me, is worthy of attention. The character of the works in the volume is such as to mark it as proceeding from the inner circle of Abailard's disciples; for the *Scito teipsum* had the reputation at least of being peculiarly esoteric, in fact, like the *Sic et non*, of shunning the light.[91] The presumption therefore is that the biographical record which accompanies these pieces is based upon special sources of information. Unfortunately a part of it is so evidently apocryphal that it has discredited the remainder. It runs as follows:

[m] supra, p. 147 n. 12.

[n] Petrus, qui *Abelardus*, a plerisque *Baiolardus*, dicitur, natione Anglicus, primum grammaticae et dialecticae, hinc divinitati operam dedit. Sed cum esset inaestimandae subtilitatis, inauditae memoriae, capacitatis supra humanum modum, auditor aliquando magistri Roscii, coepit eum cum exfestucatione quadam sensuum illius audire. Attamen im-

[n] Thes. anecd. noviss. 3. dissert. isagog. p. xxii.; 1721.

[91] Sunt autem, ut audio, adhuc alia eius opuscula quorum nomina sunt, *Sic et non*, *Scito te ipsum*, et alia quaedam, de quibus timeo ne, sicut monstruosi sunt nominis, sic etiam sint monstruosi dogmatis: sed, sicut dicunt, oderunt lucem nec etiam quaesita inveniuntur: Epist. Guill. de S. Theod. ad Gaufr. et Bern., (Bern. Opp. 1. 303 B, ep. cccxxvi. 4, ed. Mabillon). The *Sententiae* are coupled with the *Scito te ipsum* by Bernard, Ep. clxxxviii. 2, p. 181 E.

peravit sibi ut per annum lectionibus ipsius interesset. Mox ergo socios habere, et Parisius palam dialecticae atque divinitatis lectiones dare coepit; et facile omnes Franciae magistros in brevi supervenit. Qui cum de Quadruvio nihil audisset, clam magistro Tirrico in quasdam mathematicas lectiones aures dabat, in quibus supra quam aestimaret obtentu difficultatis intellectus resiliebat audientis. Cui semel afflicto et indignanti per iocum magister Tirricus ait, *Quid canis plenus nisi lardum baiare consuevit? Baiare* autem *lingere* est. Exinde *Baiolardus* appellari coepit. Quod nomen tanquam ex defectu quodam sibi impositum cum abdicaret, sub litteratura non dissimili *Habelardum* se nominari fecit, quasi qui haberet artium apud se summam et adipem.

Taking these statements in order, we remark—

1. That the *natione Anglicus, Britannus* having been obviously changed into an apparent synonym, gives the impression of the writer being but remotely acquainted with Abailard's history.

2. On the other hand, the order of his studies is correctly given. We have, it is true, no information about the time when Abailard learned grammar and it must be presumed that the writer merely conjectured that Abailard followed what was after all the natural and customary curriculum.

3. But the mention of Roscius (though the corrupt form in which the name is given may be considered to tell both ways) is of distinct importance. For a long time this passage was the only one, besides the notice of [o] Otto of Freising, that spoke of Abailard's personal relations with Roscelin; and Otto's testimony was [p] commonly discredited, especially because Abailard in his *Historia Calamitatum* altogether ignored the fact. So soon however as Abailard's *Dialectic* was printed, it was found that he was in all probability the person referred to under the abbreviated style of [q] *magistri nostri Ros.* The discovery in a Munich manuscript of a [r] letter unquestionably addressed by Roscelin to his former pupil (though here the names are indicated only by initials), has finally decided the matter, and to this

[o] Gest. Frider. i. 47, Pertz 20. 376.

[p] Hist. litt. de la France 9. 359 (1750), 12. 87.

[q] Cousin, ouvr inéd. d'Abél. 471.

[r] Abael. opp. 2. 792–803, ed. Cousin.

APPEND. VIII.

extent confirmed the evidence of the record here under consideration.

4. The next point, namely, that Abailard was unversed in the arts of the quadrivium is also of importance, since it is incidentally corroborated by Abailard's own statement that he was ignorant of mathematics: after quoting a geometrical argument from Boëthius, he adds,

s Dialect. p. 182.

[s] Cuius quidem solutionis, etsi multas ab arithmeticis solutiones audierim, nullam tamen a me praeferendam iudico, quia eius artis ignarum omnino me cognosco.

t supra, pp. 115 sq.

u Hist. de la phil. scol. I. 397 n. 1, 402 n. 1.

5. Then follows the story of his attendance upon the lectures of master Tirric. After what [t] we have said about Theodoric or Terric of Chartres, it is natural that we should be disposed to identify him with this teacher of mathematics, especially since Tirric is found among the audience at Abailard's trial at Soissons. But what raises this conjecture to a higher degree of probability is the circumstance that the extracts which [u] M. Hauréau has recently printed from an unpublished treatise by Theodoric, show an evident partiality for mathematical illustrations. The account then of Abailard's connexion with Tirric suits exactly with what we know from other sources of these scholars' attitude towards mathematics.

x Rob. de Monte a. 1129, Pertz 6. 489.

6. The concluding story about the origin of the name Abailard is of course a figment. Apart from its grotesqueness and intrinsic improbability (especially when we remember that, on the narrator's showing, Abailard must have adopted a new name after he had acquired his remarkable reputation as a teacher), there is sufficient evidence that the name is not unique. A little before Peter Abailard's birth, a son of Humphrey the Norman and nephew of Robert Wiscard received the name of [x] *Abaielardus*.

7. Dismissing this legend then, we find that our document names two of Abailard's teachers, one of whom (though the name is corrupted) points to an established fact, and the other to one inherently probable. The chronology however presents serious difficulties. There is no

interval after Abailard entered upon the study of theology in which we can plausibly insert the lessons he had from Tirric; so that I incline to believe that Abailard made a short stay at Chartres during his first years of student life, after he left Roscelin and before he reached—possibly on his road to—Paris; or at the latest [y] during the period for which, suffering from ill-health or the hostility of William of Champeaux, he retired from the neighbourhood of Paris. However this may be, I see no reason for doubting the truth of the bare fact that Abailard did enter upon a course of learning under Tirric.

[y] supra, p. 139.

IX. Note on the second preface to Gilbert of La Porrée's Commentary on Boëthius.

1. [z] John of Salisbury states that after the events of the council at Rheims Gilbert continued to suffer from the injury then done to him by those who sought to convict him of heresy, and took means to vindicate his position. *Scripsit ergo postea contra illos alterum prologum in expositionem Boëthii sui, in quo quosdam, videlicet emulos suos, asserit sic hereticorum vitare nomina, ut tamen errores eorum sequantur et doceant.* The date of this new preface appears not only from the words of John just quoted, but also from the fact that according to John's account it was addressed to the *capitula* or articles of faith which were only produced by saint Bernard at Rheims. It therefore forms a sort of summing-up of the case from Gilbert's side, and was written for his own satisfaction at some time after the controversy had come to an end.

[z] Hist. pontif. xiii. Pertz 20. 527.

2. This preface seems to have disappeared, but an important fragment of it has been brought to light by professor Usener of Bonn, in the fifth volume of the [a] *Jahrbücher für protestantische Theologie* for 1879. [b] Dr. Usener says, 'Each of the four commentaries has its introduction, and although that to the first treatise *De Trinitate* is more extensive than the following ones, it is not more general in its character but is concerned with discussions raised

[a] vol. 5. 183–192.

[b] p. 185.

APPEND. IX.

c Boëth. 1125. by Boëthius' text:' this is the preface beginning, [c] *Omnium quae rebus percipiendis suppeditant rationum.* But, says Dr. Usener, in a Vatican manuscript (Lat. 560) of the thirteenth century we find further *Item alius prologus*, and this also appears in a manuscript of Saint Victor. It was written, [d] he thinks, for a second edition of Gilbert's Commentary, after the council of Paris and thus presumably in preparation for that of Rheims. The hypothesis is no doubt possible, but it is curious that Dr. Usener should be unacquainted with John of Salisbury's account, with which it is natural to connect this 'new preface.' It is more curious that the editor should not have observed that this very preface, only in a briefer form, is to be found in the very edition of Boëthius which Dr. Usener had in his hands (that of Basle 1570), prefixed not to the Commentary but to the [e] treatise of Boëthius itself. The preface is therefore not a discovery; it is only an enlarged edition of that identical 'general preface,' the supposed absence of which puzzled Dr. Usener.

d Jahrb. p. 186.

e p. 1119.

3. The new part is however of sufficient interest to be transcribed here, especially because when printed in the midst of a mass of old matter its importance does not immediately attract attention. It is inserted, after the words *scriptoribus recedamus*, before the concluding sentence, exactly where we should expect such an addition to be made; and it runs as follows:

f Jahrb. pp. 187 sq.

[f] Quamvis nos ab eis dissentire garriant quidam fennii atque preconii, qui cum nichil didicerint, opinione sua nesciunt nihil, homines sine ratione philosophi, sine visione prophete, preceptores impossibilium, indices occultorum, quorum mores plurimis notos describere nil nostra interest. Ipsi vero tanquam excussi propriis aliena negotia curant et obliti suorum satiras satirorum [*sic*] de ceteris animi ingenio et vite honestate preclaris multarum personarum fingunt comedias. Qui etiam in Deum blasphemi illos de ipso profitentur errores quorum nomina diffitentur. Nam, ut ita dicatur, hereticorum catholici in Sabellii, Donati, Pelagii, et aliorum huiusmodi pestilencium verba iurati, horum nomina (eo quod edictis publicis dampnata

noscuntur) cum catholicis detestantur, ut cum blasphemiarum caussis sint iuste dampnabiles, blasphemorum detestatione putentur indempnes : sed quia non tam res nominibus quam nomina rebus accommodat impositio, quibuscunque res conveniunt, nomina non convenire non possunt. Quoniam vere sunt, recte vocantur, Sabelliani, Donatiste, Pelagiani, et huiusmodi. Et bene quod novi heretici nil afferunt novi, ut ad improbandum adinventiones novas novis sit laborandum inventis. Antiqua sunt dogmata, olim per preclari et exercitati ingenii viros evidentissimis atque necessariis rationibus improbata, quibus eadem novissimis his rediviva temporibus possunt refellere, quicunque recte intelligentes virorum illorum scriptis lectitandis invigilant. Sed qui neque legunt neque lecturiunt, ideoque scientiarum elementa, si qua prioribus annis attendere consueverant, post longa desuetudine desciverunt aut etiam corruptis artibus a via veritatis exorbitaverunt, has omnino rationes ignoraverunt. Quorum si forte aliqui humano errore aut potestate aliqua presunt aut preminent dignitate, precipiunt ut verum falsum et falsum verum, iterumque bonum malum et malum bonum esse credatur : et quod impudentissimum est, ad sui magnificenciam quoslibet infames magnificant et magnificos infamant. Sed quia non tam cognitores quam cogniti resident, sepe contingit ut rerum consequentibus cancellatis cuiuspiam boni fame aliquid illorum favor detrahat et vituperatio addat. Quod nimirum attendentes, illorum maledicta de nostris moribus et precepta de rebus contempnimus. Nam neque mores nostros convictu neque rerum proprietates disciplina noverunt.

Then follows the concluding sentence of the printed edition, whose text I retain, appending the two variants that occur in Dr. Usener's copy :

Quae [g] autem a nobis scripta sunt bene exercitatis lectoribus non modo rationibus firma, verum etiam scripturis autenticis adeo consona esse videntur ut nostra non tam inventa quam [h] furta esse credantur.

[g] vero, *Usener.*

[h] firma ? *U.*

4. The personal reference of the added passage is exactly in the same spirit as that answer which [i] John of Salisbury reports Gilbert to have given when Bernard suggested an

[i] v. supra, p. 193.

APPEND. X.

interview. It is also a valuable specimen of the language which could be used about the saint by neither an insignificant nor an irreligious section of his contemporaries. But the addition to the preface, although partly agreeing closely with what John of Salisbury says about the 'new preface,' does not cover the whole ground which he describes. Either therefore the new preface itself is lost, or rather has been curtailed to its present dimensions, or else possibly John has mixed up with his account of it reminiscences of his conversations with Gilbert on the subject, reminiscences perhaps of his master's former lectures, or even his own independent vindication of Gilbert derived from a study of the Commentary on Boëthius.

X. NOTE ON CLARENBALD OF ARRAS.

k Henr. Gandav. de script. eccl., app., cap. 10; Mirae. Bibl. eccl. 174.

l vol. 3. 355 A, ed. Piolin, 1876.

m vol. 12. 445.

CLAREBALDUS, archdeacon of Arras, is named in the continuation of k Henry of Ghent, just after Peter Lombard, as having written a commentary on the books of Boëthius *On the Trinity*, in which he argued against certain opinions of Gilbert of La Porrée, condemned Abailard, and favoured saint Bernard. In the l *Gallia Christiana* he appears as holding the office of provost of the church of Arras in 1152 and 1153; and since his successor emerges in the year 1160, it is presumed that he died before that date. His commentary should therefore offer valuable contemporary evidence in regard to the controversies spoken of in my sixth chapter; but the m *Histoire littéraire de la France* says it is 'non imprimé et peut-être perdu.' It exists,[92] however, among the manuscripts of Balliol college, Oxford, in the very same volume, cod. ccxcvi, which contains some of Abailard's most treasured writings.[93]

92 [R. Peiper mentions another manuscript, at Valenciennes, theol. 185: pref. to Boet. Philos. Cons., 1871, p. l.]

93 Among them the Commentary on the Epistle to the Romans which Cousin stated to be found in no known manuscript, although he had a portion of this very volume transcribed for him for his edition of another work of Abailard. [There is also a manuscript in the Vatican, Reg. Lat. 242: see Denifle, Luther und Luthertum i. 2. Quellenbelege p. 49 (1905).]

The Commentary was written after August 1153, since it speaks of [n] *iocunde recordacionis abbas Bernardus.* We learn also from it that the author—his name is here spelled *Clarenbaldus*—was a disciple of Hugh of Saint Victor, and of Theodoric the Breton, [o] no doubt the famous chancellor of Chartres.

APPEND. X.

n f. 198.

o supra, p. 115

[p] Has causas mihi aliquantulum pertinaciter investiganti doctores mei venerabiles, Hugo videlicet de Sancto Victore et Theodericus Brito reddidere. Magister vero Gillebertus Pictavensis episcopus verbis perplexis hanc causam reddit. Que tametsi dispendiosa videri possunt, tamen in medium proferam, ne tam clarum doctorem cum famosis doctoribus ascribere videar invidere.

p f. 190 *b*.

He therefore writes his criticism on Gilbert with the object, in part, of showing that his judgement of him is not influenced by any grudge *against including the illustrious doctor in the same class with the famous doctors* first named; so I understand the concluding words of the quotation. He charges Gilbert, as [q] so many others did, with an excessive obscurity of style:

q cf. supra, pp. 182, 186 sq.

[r] Exemplum huius lucidissime planitiei magister Gillebertus Pictavensis episcopus multo verborum circuitu tenebrosam obscuritatem inducit, liberatque verbis rem frivolam involventibus, ut credatur, etc.

r f. 204.

Clarenbald even finds fault with Gilbert's logic, speaking of him as [s] *falsum sibi in logica fingens, aut certe male intelligens principium, quod est hoc,* etc. In one place he describes some views of his as expressly heretical and as having been condemned at the council of Rheims:

s ibid.

[t] Ex hoc loco episcopi Pictavensis error ortus esse videtur, ut tres personas numero differentes esse assereret. . . . Ergo nec numero tres persone inter se differunt. Quum vero in concilio Remensi sub Eugenio papa super aliis rebus liber eius reprehensus dampnatusque tam scolarium lectionibus quam claustralium ademptus est, et hic error, utpote heresibus eius aliis nullo modo preferendus, ibi commemoratus non est,

t f. 208 *b*.

APPEND. X. commodum mihi visum est verba quibus hunc ipsum locum pertransire voluit, in medium revocare.

With respect to Abailard Clarenbald's language is still more hostile; he accuses him of virtually resuscitating the opinions of Arius:

u f. 197 b. [u] Eandem pene heresim Petrus Abailardus nostris diebus, longo sopore antiquatam, renovavit; cum spiritu iactancie et impietatis plenus, divinitati ignominiam inferre, sibi gloriam conatus est parare.

INDEX